The Limits of Party

Chicago Studies in American Politics

A SERIES EDITED BY SUSAN HERBST, LAWRENCE R. JACOBS, ADAM J. BERINSKY, AND FRANCES LEE; BENJAMIN I. PAGE, EDITOR EMERITUS

Also in the series:

The Limits of Party

Congress and Lawmaking in a Polarized Era

JAMES M. CURRY AND
FRANCES E. LEE

The University of Chicago Press
Chicago and London

The University of Chicago Press, Chicago 60637
The University of Chicago Press, Ltd., London
© 2020 by The University of Chicago
Published 2020

29 28 27 26 25 24 23 22 21 20   1 2 3 4 5

ISBN-13: 978-0-226-71621-3 (cloth)
ISBN-13: 978-0-226-71635-0 (paper)
ISBN-13: 978-0-226-71649-7 (e-book)
DOI: https://doi.org/10.7208/chicago/9780226716497.001.0001

Library of Congress Cataloging-in-Publication Data

Names: Curry, James M., author. | Lee, Frances E., author.
Title: The limits of party : Congress and lawmaking in a polarized era /
    James M. Curry and Frances E. Lee.
Other titles: Chicago studies in American politics.
Description: Chicago : University of Chicago Press, 2020. | Series: Chicago
    studies in American politics | Includes bibliographical references and index.
Identifiers: LCCN 2020008838 | ISBN 9780226716213 (cloth) |
    ISBN 9780226716350 (paperback) | ISBN 9780226716497 (ebook)
Subjects: LCSH: United States. Congress. | Legislative power—United States. |
    Political parties—United States.
Classification: LCC JK1021 .C86 2020 | DDC 328.73/0769—dc23
LC record available at https://lccn.loc.gov/2020008838

CONTENTS

ONE

Majority Party Capacity in a Polarized Era

The impulse of the parties . . . to clothe themselves in a dogmatic and argumentative garment of high public purpose is so strong that a wholly misleading picture
of the process is likely to be conveyed by the mere words of party propagandists.
Party pronouncements exaggerate the unanimity, enthusiasm, and consistency of
the parties, but . . . conceal the truth about the internal structures and interior processes of these organizations.

—E. E. Schattschneider (1942, 129–30)

"This is our plan," said Speaker of the House Paul Ryan, holding a copy
of Republicans' "Better Way" policy agenda.[1] Rolled out in the summer of
2016, the agenda encompassed a far-reaching platform and policy blueprint. Republicans then went on to sweep the November elections, winning
House and Senate majorities and control of the presidency. As he gaveled
in the new Congress in January 2017, Ryan told his fellow Republicans that
they had been given a "once-in-a-lifetime opportunity." "This is the kind of
thing that most of us only dream about," he said. "I know—because I used
to dream about it. The people have given us unified government."[2]

In committing the party to a policy agenda before the elections, Speaker
Ryan was implicitly operating from a "responsible parties" model of democratic politics. According to such a model, political parties should clearly lay
out their agenda priorities and policy solutions in advance of elections. Voters can then assess the alternatives on offer and make an informed choice.
Following the elections, a party that wins power should then carry out its
policy mandate. With its straightforward logic of democratic choice and
majority rule, the responsible parties model has long commanded support from normative theorists, empirical political scientists, and practical

politicians from Woodrow Wilson to Newt Gingrich to Paul Ryan (American Political Science Association 1950; Bolling 1965, 1968; Gingrich 1994; Rosenblum 2008; Rosenbluth and Shapiro 2018; Rosenfeld 2017; Schattschneider 1942; Stid 1994; Wickham-Jones 2018; Wilson 1885).

Despite its intellectual appeal, however, the model has long stood at odds with the American political system. Rather than appearing before voters as party teams as is done in other democracies, aspirants for Congress compete as individuals before separate and diverse constituencies, crafting their own campaign messages and priorities without binding themselves to a national platform. Obviously, such a method of election tends not to foster strong party discipline (Mayhew 1974). Furthermore, in a presidential system like that in the United States, both presidents and legislative party leaders assert leadership over congressional parties, often pulling members in contradictory directions even in unified government (Burns 1963; Samuels and Shugart 2010; Shugart and Carey 1992). Moreover, when and if congressional parties are able to coalesce around a policy agenda, they must operate within a complex political system of checks and balances where the minority party may well control veto points that can block action. In these circumstances American parties have never lived up to the expectations of the party government model.

Nevertheless, compared with the political parties of earlier eras, contemporary American parties seem much more capable of developing and delivering on a policy agenda. Today's parties are far more ideologically coherent than the parties of the twentieth century, which encompassed deep internal factions (Brady and Bullock 1980; Polsby 2004; Sundquist 1968). By a long process of sectional and coalitional realignment, the two parties sorted along ideological lines, with a Republican Party today that is more homogeneously conservative and a Democratic Party that is more homogeneously liberal (McCarty 2019; McCarty, Poole, and Rosenthal 2006; Theriault 2008). Moreover, Congress now organizes itself in a way that more fully empowers parties. Power is centralized in top party leaders. Committees and committee chairs are accountable to their parties. Members coordinate on strategy and policy by meeting in party caucus at least once a week while Congress is in session. Party leaders manage major legislative drives in both House and Senate so as avoid party splits and hold party ranks intact. It stands to reason that contemporary parties would be better positioned than those of the twentieth century to arrive at policy agendas and carry them out, notwithstanding the constraints imposed by the American constitutional system.

In this book we examine whether today's stronger, more cohesive parties in Congress are indeed more capable as policymakers. Are today's parties better able to deliver on their campaign promises? Does the centralizing of power in Congress permit majority parties to steamroll the opposition and enact their programmatic agendas? In short, we want to know whether the more ideologically cohesive, institutionally empowered parties of the twenty-first-century Congress are better able to steer the ship of state in American politics.

These questions have seen surprisingly little attention. There has been a great deal of research on the factors affecting Congress's ability to pass important legislation (Adler and Wilkerson 2012; Binder 2003, 2014; Mayhew 2005) or presidential success with Congress (Bond and Fleisher 1990; Canes-Wrone and De Marchi 2002; Edwards 1990; Mayhew 2011), but scholars have not taken stock of *majority party capacity* in contemporary American politics. We want to know not whether Congress is more or less legislatively productive overall or whether it successfully addresses pressing policy problems on the national agenda. Instead, majority party capacity refers to a party's ability to bend legislative outcomes toward its policy preferences when given control of institutional power in Washington, DC. Voters today perceive the parties as offering distinct policy alternatives (Hetherington 2001). But are parties in government capable of following through on their vision for public policy? Can they leverage their enhanced cohesion and procedural power to enact their partisan programs? Do we have something more akin to responsible party government today than we did in the past?

Taking Stock of Congressional Transformation

Most people perceive Congress as much more partisan than it used to be. Certainly, roll-call votes are now far more likely to break down on party lines. Figure 1.1 displays a measure of partisan conflict in Congress: the percentage of roll-call votes that divided at least 90 percent of Republicans against at least 90 percent of Democrats. This is a higher bar than is traditionally used to gauge party conflict in Congress, which often looks only to the share of votes that pit a majority of one party against a majority of the other. As is evident here, more than half of House roll-call votes in recent Congresses result in party blocs arrayed in nearly perfect opposition to one another, as do 30–40 percent of Senate roll-call votes. Today's Congress often exhibits an almost parliamentary level of partisanship.

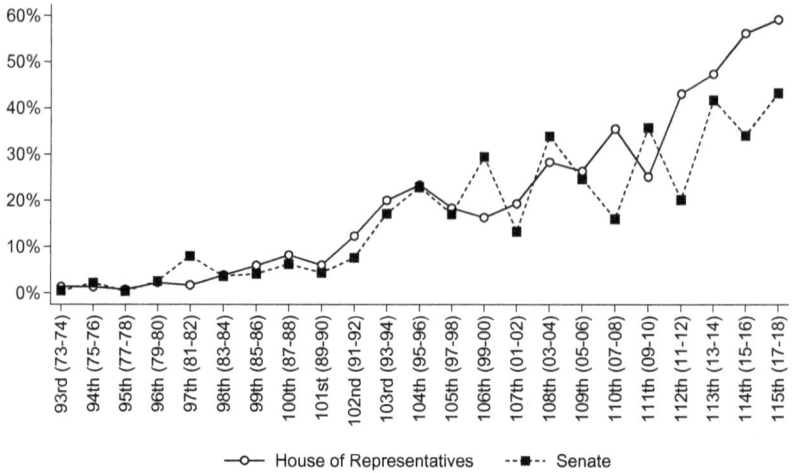

Figure 1.1. Percentage of roll-call votes with 90 percent of each party opposed to the other

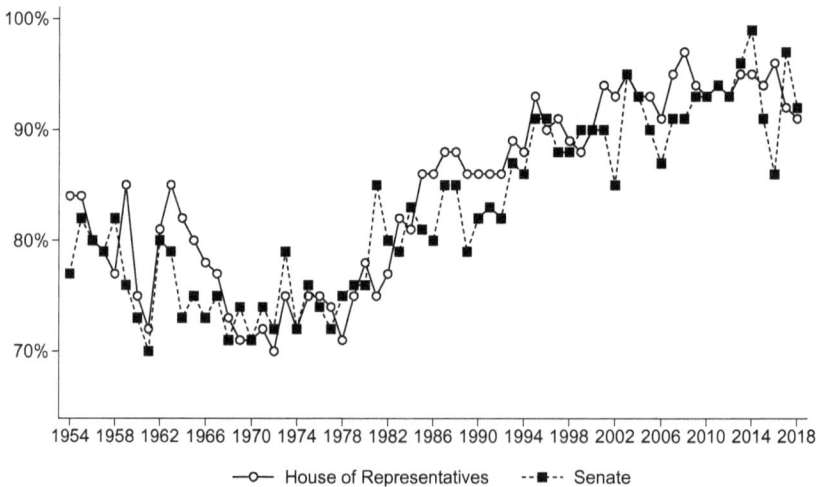

Figure 1.2. Congressional majority party cohesion on roll-call votes, 1954–2018
Source: Brookings Institution (2019); CQ Vote Studies: Party Unity (2018, 2019).

Likewise, trends in party cohesion also suggest more efficacious major-ity parties. Figure 1.2 displays majority party loyalty on roll-call votes in both House and Senate from 1954 to 2018. In the 1950s, 1960s, and 1970s, majority party senators voted with their party on controversial issues just over 60 percent of the time.[3] In the 1980s, they voted with their party just over 70 percent of the time. In the 1990s, they voted with their party just over

80 percent of the time. Since the turn of the twenty-first century, majority party senators have voted with their party on average more than 87 percent of the time. Similar increases in party cohesion occurred in the House. In both chambers, party cohesion has increased dramatically over the past few decades.

The question, then, is whether this increased party cohesion makes the majority party in Congress more legislatively efficacious. To ascertain a majority party's lawmaking capability, one cannot just compare party cohesion statistics over time, because the level of cohesion a majority party *needs* to legislate varies according to the number of seats it holds. A majority party with only a narrow margin of control must marshal extremely high cohesion to carry legislation over unified minority party opposition. A party with a larger majority can tolerate higher levels of internal dissent while still passing its program (Patty 2008; Smith 2007). Since 1994, margins of control have been thin in both House and Senate.

Figure 1.3 displays (as a solid black line) the level of cohesion that would be necessary for the majority party to muster a chamber majority from within its own ranks each year since the mid-1950s. In other words, it tracks the share of the majority party capable of yielding a simple majority in the House or Senate for each Congress. By comparing average party cohesion levels in each year with those necessary for chamber majorities, we can ascertain whether majority parties over time have been cohesive enough to legislate without cross-party help.

By this measure, recent majority parties should be capable of passing legislation on their own, even over total minority party opposition. Indeed, in this regard the contemporary Congress stands out from this long time series. As displayed in figure 1.3a, House majority parties before the late 1980s usually lacked sufficient cohesion to muster chamber majorities in the absence of support from the minority party. The Democrats of the late 1960s and 1970s almost never reached the bar despite their large majorities. Democrats under Speakers Jim Wright and Tom Foley began to achieve the necessary cohesion before they lost the House majority in 1994. Although the Republican House majorities during the presidencies of Bill Clinton and George W. Bush were highly cohesive, their margins of control were so narrow that they still usually had to secure at least some cross-party votes to reach a House majority. Since 2007, however, every House majority party has routinely been capable of mustering chamber majorities without any minority party support.

Figure 1.3b displays the same data series for the Senate. Of course, the Senate does not operate by majority rule, so on many measures even a

A

House of Representatives

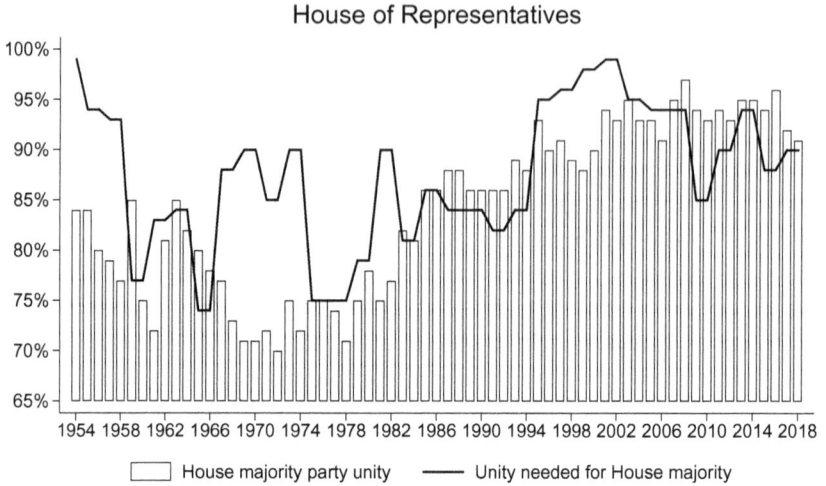

Figure A — House of Representatives chart, 1954–2018, y-axis 65% to 100%.

House majority party unity   Unity needed for House majority

B

Senate

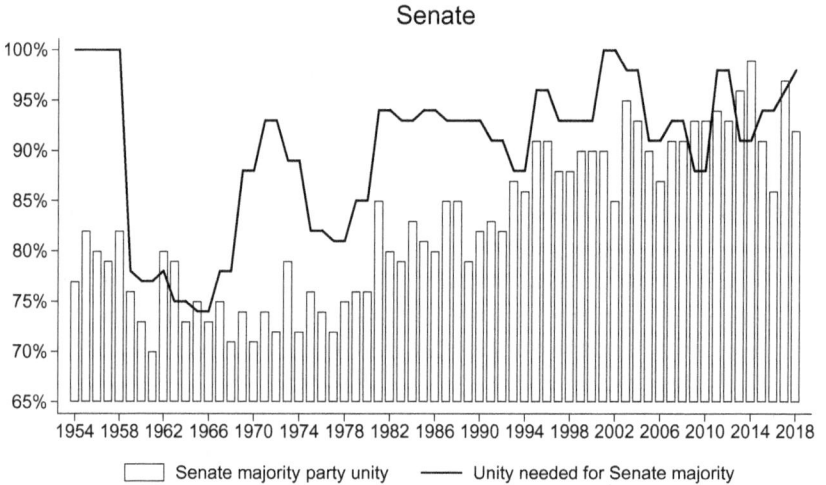

Figure B — Senate chart, 1954–2018, y-axis 65% to 100%.

Senate majority party unity   Unity needed for Senate majority

Figure 1.3. Majority party cohesion necessary for chamber majorities, 1954–2018
Source: Brookings Institution (2019); CQ Vote Studies: Party Unity (2018, 2019).

100 percent unified majority party cannot carry the day. But for those votes on which a simple majority can decide the outcome (Reynolds 2017), recent Senate majorities have often possessed the necessary cohesion to assemble a Senate majority without cross-party help. The Republican Senate majorities since 2014, as well as the Democratic majorities of 2009–10 and 2013–14, could consistently produce chamber majorities from within their own ranks. Set in the context of this time series dating back to the middle

of the twentieth century, recent levels of Senate majority party unity look remarkable. The large Democratic majorities from the mid-1960s through the mid-1970s were rarely cohesive enough to yield a chamber majority without minority party assistance. But recent Senate parties have done so regularly, even with narrow margins of control. On divisive issues, the 2014 Democrats averaged a stunning 99 percent cohesion rate, and the 2017 Republicans averaged 97 percent.

Not only is Congress more partisan, the entire legislative process operates differently than it did in the twentieth century (Sinclair 2016; Smith 2014). Concurrent with dramatic increases in partisanship, members instituted more centralized procedures, driven by party leadership, that are thought to promote partisan lawmaking (Evans 2018; Meinke 2016; Pearson 2015). Rather than relying on committees to develop legislation, made final by open amending on the floor, today's Congress frequently operates by what Sinclair (2016) terms "unorthodox" processes. Leaders now take a much more central role, bypassing committees (Bendix 2016a; Howard and Owens 2019), directly negotiating policy (Curry 2015; Wallner 2013), setting the agenda (Harbridge 2015), and limiting floor debate (Tiefer 2016).

Major policy development is now centralized in the offices of party leaders. This is evident in the share of bills passed that go through "regular order" in committees, shown in figure 1.4. In the 1970s and 1980s, virtually all bills were reported from a committee before further action was taken on

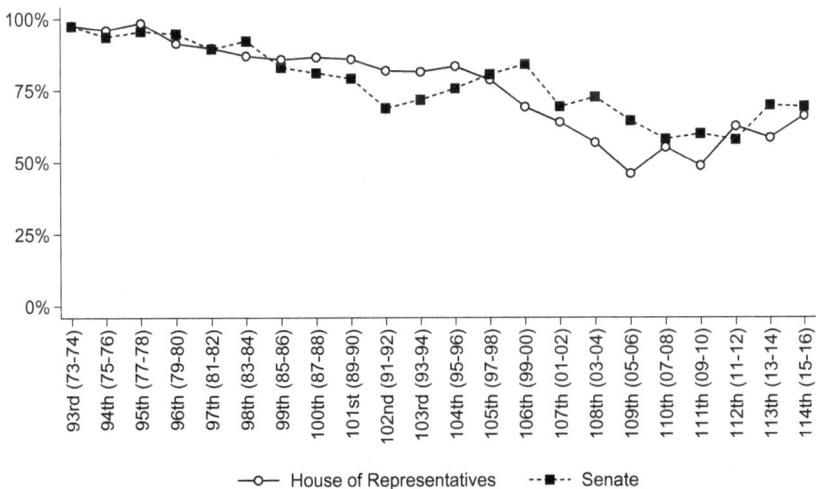

Figure 1.4. Share of bills that passed the House and Senate with a committee report

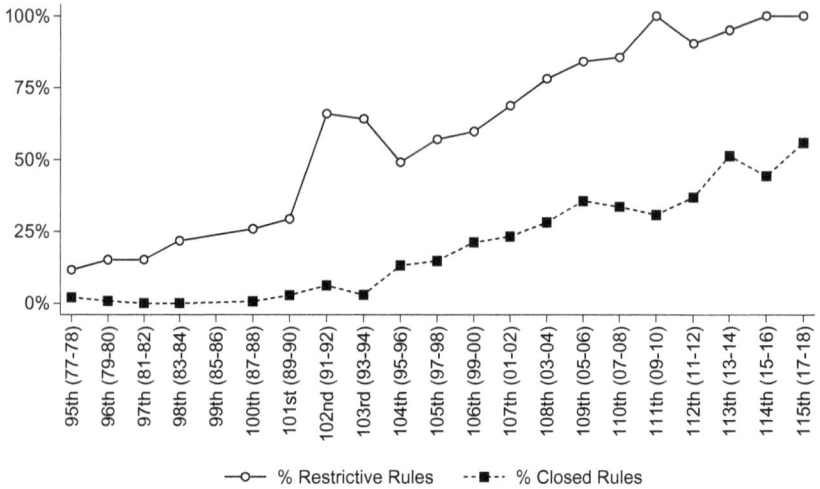

Figure 1.5. Restrictive and closed rules in the House of Representatives

the floor. In recent Congresses, just over half went through a regular committee process before being passed in the House and Senate.

Contemporary party leaders dominate the final stage of the policy process as well. In both chambers they manage the floor more assertively, limiting opportunities for rank-and-file members to amend pending legislation. In the House this takes the form of restrictive and closed rules.[4] Figure 1.5 tracks the rise in restrictive floor procedures. In the 1970s and 1980s almost all rules permitted at least some amendments, and fewer than 30 percent imposed any restrictions. Since 2010 nearly all rules were restrictive, and almost half were closed to all amendments. The 115th Congress set a new record for restrictions on amending, with a full majority of rules (56 percent) permitting no amendments at all (Thorning 2019). Likewise, Senate leaders make much heavier use of their prerogative to limit amendments (Davis 2017; Smith 2014). As is evident in figure 1.6, Senate floor amending has been significantly curbed. The 115th Congress was second only to the 113th Congress (2013–14) for the fewest amendments considered on the Senate floor (Thorning 2019).

In sum, there should be no doubt that the contemporary Congress operates very differently from the Congress of the 1970s and 1980s. There is much more party conflict on the floor of both House and Senate. When conflict occurs, members vote much more reliably with their parties. Party leaders take a central role in negotiating policy, as is evident in the decline

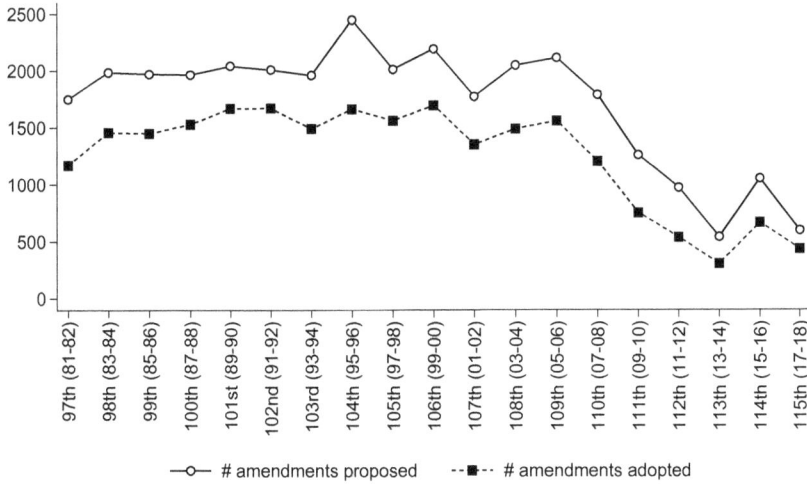

Figure 1.6. Amending activity on the Senate floor

of committees as the central gatekeepers and arenas for policy development. Floor processes are much more tightly managed, with amending in both House and Senate brought under leaders' control. All these changes seemingly empower congressional majority parties to shape and drive policy outcomes.

Theories and Perceptions of Party Power

Given these wide-ranging changes in congressional party politics and internal procedure, it seems reasonable to expect that majority parties would be better able to enact their policy agendas. An array of scholarship on Congress certainly suggests so. Likewise, news portraits of Congress give the impression of an institution where important policy is either enacted on party-line votes or mired in gridlock.

Prominent scholarly theories view cohesive parties and centralized processes as preconditions for party power. Rohde (1991, 34), for example, coined the term *conditional party government* to describe how intraparty agreement and empowered leaders can permit "strong partisan action" on policies that command consensus within the majority party. In other words, congressional parties can approximate the responsible party government model, at least under some conditions. In a later formulation of the concept, Aldrich and Rohde (2000a, 38) argue that, as the parties polarize, members delegate more authority to their partisan leaders and encourage them to use those powers to "enact as much of the party's program as possible." Den Hartog and Monroe (2011) apply a similar logic to the Senate.

Other theories of party power, including Cox and McCubbins's (2005) *procedural cartel theory* and Koger and Lebo's (2017) *strategic party government*, contend that the majority party in Congress structures the institution to enable it to amass a record of accomplishments that will aid the party in future elections. Cox and McCubbins (2005) argue that the majority party provides its leaders, or "senior partners," with substantial power both to block legislation that divides the party internally and to facilitate the passage of laws that its members can tout in subsequent election campaigns. These prerogatives are expected to grow along with party organizational strength, since "the better the majority party's control of such powers is, the more able will it be to fashion a favorable record" (Cox and McCubbins 2005, 7).[5]

These theories of party power in Congress differ in their causal logic and in specific predictions. Nevertheless, taken together they imply that strong and unified majority parties with centralized power and decision-making authority should be better positioned to deliver on their campaign promises than the weaker and less cohesive majority parties of earlier eras.

News coverage of Congress also tends to portray an institution where policy is either decided on a party-line vote or bogged down in partisan bickering. "Just as White House Counsel John Dean famously proclaimed the Watergate cover-up of the 1970s a 'cancer on the presidency,' there is now a growing cancer on Congress. The rapid and pervasive rise of party-line voting is a cancer," writes one representative of the journalistic conventional wisdom.[6] "What little is accomplished in Washington is done through party-line votes and executive orders."[7] Journalists proclaim the death of bipartisanship in Congress with some frequency. "Bipartisanship wheezed its death rattle," at the end of 2017 when Congress passed the Republican tax bill.[8] "The death of [Senator] John McCain," intoned National Public Radio, "symbolizes the near extinction of lawmakers who believe in seeking bipartisanship to tackle big problems."[9] "Someone please tell Joe Biden that bipartisanship is dead," exhorted the *New Republic*.[10]

Journalists reinforce this narrative even when writing about legislation that garners bipartisan support. When Congress works in a bipartisan fashion, journalists tend to deem it "rare." "Something rare and wondrous is happening. It is a momentary, precise alignment of the stars and the planets, a sort of legislative solar eclipse," writes *Washington Post* reporter Karen Tumulty of a bipartisan reform bill.[11] "In a rare show of bipartisanship," begins an account of the 2018 two-year budget deal.[12] Ironically, headlines describing a "rare" bipartisan bill, agreement, or success are not at all rare.[13] Journalists routinely describe bipartisan legislation as exceptional, a break from the contemporary norm.

Taken together, a great deal of scholarship and news reporting combines to create the impression that majority parties in the contemporary Congress commonly enact policies over the opposition of the minority party. Legislative scholars see the contemporary Congress as meeting the conditions for strong majority party policy leadership. Journalists describe partisan legislating as the norm and bipartisanship as exceptional. Both scholars and reporters portray congressional majority parties as positioned to drive national policy.

Enduring Obstacles to Party Success

Congressional majority parties, nevertheless, still have to confront harsh realities that stand in the way of partisan achievement in the US political system. These constraints stem both from the constitutional system's barriers to majority rule and from the political incentives of members elected to serve in such a system. In other words, majority parties struggle to legislate not just because they can be blocked by veto players among the system's many checks and balances, but because party members often lack the political incentives to coalesce on a party agenda in the first place.

Constitutional Barriers

Regardless of how the House and Senate might organize themselves internally, the constitutional system's bicameralism and separation of powers persistently frustrate efforts at partisan lawmaking (Krehbiel 1998; Mayhew 2005, 2011). Reflecting on such constraints, Schattschneider (1942, 8) described American political history as "the story of the unhappy marriage of the parties and the Constitution, a remarkable variation of the case of the irresistible force and the immovable object." Hofstadter (1948, 11) termed the Constitution a "harmonious system of mutual frustration." Even vast institutional change inside Congress may avail little against such constraints.

The separation of powers between Congress and the president regularly stands in the way of a congressional majority party's passing a partisan agenda. Not surprisingly, vetoes and veto threats are more common under divided government (Cameron 2000). Furthermore, as in presidential systems generally, midterm (or nonconcurrent) elections tend to reduce legislative support for the president and increase the likelihood of divided party control (Shugart and Carey 1992, 242–72). Indeed, divided government has been the typical state of affairs since the middle of the twentieth century: 67 percent of the time since 1954 and 75 percent of the time since 1980. For some observers, the infrequency with which one party has unified control of the government "invalidates the entire theory of party government" (Sundquist 1988, 626).

Congress's bicameral structure can also stymie a majority party's efforts. The two chambers' different methods of apportionment, election, and internal procedure often frustrate bicameral agreement even when the same party has a majority in both chambers. The staggered election of senators can put the Senate and House out of sync, especially after electoral waves. The Senate's supermajoritarian cloture requirements frequently prevent the majority from advancing legislation on party lines (Binder and Smith 2001; Koger 2010; Smith 2014; Wawro and Schickler 2006). Binder (2003, 81) finds that "bicameralism is perhaps the most critical structural factor shaping the politics of gridlock."

Veto points become an even bigger obstacle when the minority party operates as a more cohesive bloc. Like the majority party, minority parties have delegated more authority to their leaders, as well as empowered them to aggressively and creatively check the majority (Green 2015; Smith 2014). When the majority party cannot legislate with votes from its own ranks alone, an organized, unified minority party can either bargain for concessions or block the legislation altogether. More cohesive, coordinated minority parties combine with the other difficulties present in the constitutional system to further limit single-party lawmaking. As President Barack Obama said in the midst of tough budget negotiations in 2011, "We have a system of government in which everybody has to give a little bit."[14]

Political Incentives

Competing incentives grounded in US electoral and constitutional systems also make it difficult for majority parties to achieve internal consensus and coordinate on policy priorities. First, the individual election of legislators from geographically diverse single-member, plurality-winner constituencies undermines intraparty agreement on legislation. Generally speaking, members benefit electorally from maintaining some distance between themselves and their party (Canes-Wrone, Brady, and Cogan 2002; Carson et al. 2010). As former representative Clem Miller (1962, 117) joked, "Few campaigns are directed at the general idea of 'My party on a National basis stands for this, and this, and this. Do not consider me or my opponent as men, consider us only as members of a party. Vote for the party not for the man.'" Although decades have elapsed since Miller made that observation, it remains true. Members still seek to build personal followings and reputations that can serve as alternative bases of electoral support rather than casting their lot wholly upon the electoral fortunes of their party (Donnelly 2019).

Second, members of Congress operate in a political system that fractures parties across separate branches of government. The political strategies needed for a party to win control of executive and legislative offices differ, creating divergent incentives and internal conflict within a party that seeks to control both branches. "The separation of powers does not merely split one branch from the other; it splits parties internally," write Samuels and Shugart (2010, 251). Along the same lines, Burns (1963, 7) famously characterized the American system as a "four-party system" in which there is both a majority and a minority party in Congress as well as a party in and out of presidential power. In contrast to a "two-party system that allows the winning party to govern and the losers to oppose," he observed, such an arrangement "compels government by consensus and coalition."

Within a separation of powers regime, presidents and legislative party leaders can pull in contrary directions even when they share a party label. As both presidents and legislative party leaders attempt to lead their parties, each has control of resources that rank-and-file legislators value, such as pork, patronage, campaign resources, and agenda access (Carey 2007; Chaisty, Cheeseman, and Power 2014; Raile, Pereira, and Power 2011). The upshot of these competing pressures is that legislators in a presidential system operate somewhat independently of both party leaders and presidents (Mainwaring and Shugart 1997, 463). Accordingly, comparative scholars have found that separation of powers systems simply do not engender the strong party loyalty characteristic of parliamentary systems and long admired by party government theorists (Carey 2007; Samuels and Shugart 2010; Shugart and Carey 1992).

In these respects, members of today's party-polarized Congress still operate in an electoral and constitutional system that undermines parties' common purpose. Even though contemporary congressional parties are more cohesive in their roll-call voting than those in the twentieth century, party leaders still struggle to wrangle support for specific legislative proposals they can bring to the floor for a vote. Joking about the challenges of negotiating intraparty consensus, Rep. Barney Frank (D-MA) once said, "Our goal is to find something that's 60 percent acceptable to 52 percent of the members, and I think we have a 75 percent chance of doing that."[15]

In short, parties must overcome contradictory political incentives in a system that both undercuts parties' common purpose and constrains them with constitutional checks and balances. Although increases in party polarization and party organization might be expected to promote more partisan lawmaking, institutional and political obstacles still stand in parties' way.

Assessing Party Influence on Lawmaking

So the question is, What have the changes of the past half-century meant for lawmaking and policy outcomes? Are parties better able to shape public policy than in the past? Despite a burgeoning literature on party polarization in Congress,[16] scholars have not investigated the effect of increased partisanship and empowered leadership on *lawmaking*.

Many of the empirical findings that make a case for majority party power in Congress analyze legislative action in just one chamber and do not consider whether the majority party's efforts resulted in new, partisan-favorable *laws*. For instance, Monroe and Robinson (2008) and Young and Wilkins (2007) show how the majority party successfully achieves partisan outcomes in the House-passed version of bills. Cox and McCubbins (2005) document the ability of majority parties to prevent the consideration of bills they oppose and to pass bills over the minority's opposition, but they do not examine whether these chamber successes translate into new laws. Aldrich and Rohde (2000a, 2000b) also detail many cases of the majority leadership's using its powers to advance partisan policies in the House, but most of these successes did not result in enacting legislation.[17]

In this book we take stock of congressional majority parties' capacity to pass partisan *laws* since the 1970s. We want to know whether majority parties are better able to enact their preferred outcomes as national policy. We focus on the following six questions:

1. Is lawmaking in the contemporary Congress less bipartisan than in the past? Are more laws enacted via party-line votes?
2. Are majority parties in Congress better able to enact their legislative agendas?
3. When majority parties fail to enact their priorities, when and why do they do so?
4. When majority parties succeed in passing their priorities, how do they do so? Do they win by steamrolling or co-opting the minority party?
5. Do more centralized legislative procedures and departures from "regular order" promote the passage of more partisan laws?

6. When Congress succeeds in passing legislation, how do members discuss their achievements in public? Are contemporary majority party members more pleased with legislative outcomes than their counterparts in the less partisan Congresses of the 1970s? Are contemporary minority party members less pleased?

To answer these questions, we assemble a large amount of data. To gauge levels of bipartisanship on lawmaking, we analyze the size and composition of the enacting coalitions for all laws since 1973, as well as all the major laws Mayhew (2005) designates as "landmark."[18] To measure majority party agenda success, we build a unique dataset of 265 majority party agenda priorities from 1985 to 2018 (99th–115th Congresses) that allows us to benchmark each Congress's legislative enactments against the agenda items majority party leaders designated as priorities. To better understand the etiology of majority party success and failure, we delve into the legislative histories of these 265 priorities. To ascertain whether leaders use today's more centralized legislative procedures to ram through more partisan laws, we track the procedural histories of important laws passed since the mid-1980s. And to discern patterns in lawmakers' reactions to legislative enactments over time, we build a dataset of statements members give to the press commenting on legislation that passes, allowing us to analyze them for tone and content.

In addition to these quantitative datasets, we also sought out first-person perspectives from Washington insiders with long experience working in Congress. We wanted to know more about the strategies leaders pursue to pass legislation, the obstacles they encounter in these efforts, and the mind-sets and motivations of key congressional policymakers as they have engaged in lawmaking in the contemporary partisan era. All together, we conducted thirty interviews with current and former high-level staffers and members of Congress. These in-depth and generally unstructured interviews typically lasted forty-five minutes or longer. The interviews were conducted with the understanding that sources would be kept anonymous. Interviewees were obtained using a snowball selection technique (Esterberg 2002, 93–94). In the end, the group of interviewees included considerable partisan and cameral diversity: 50 percent were Republicans, 50 percent were Democrats, 83 percent had House experience, and 27 percent had Senate experience. Further details on the interviews and interview technique are found in appendix C.

Across our questions and all our analyses, we find remarkable continuities in congressional lawmaking over time and clear limits to party influence.

Although legislative *processes* in this highly partisan, centralized contemporary Congress differ markedly from the past, legislative *outcomes* have changed little. Most important, we find no evidence at all that majority parties' lawmaking capacities have improved. Lawmaking in recent Congresses is about as bipartisan as it was in the 1970s, and congressional majority parties are simply no better at enacting their legislative priorities today than they were in the 1980s. Contemporary majority parties frequently fail in legislating on their priority items. When they succeed, they rarely enact laws by party-line votes or over the opposition of a majority of the minority party. Rather, they usually win on policy by co-opting the minority party, and frequently with the support of one or more of the minority party's top leaders. Across our analyses, we find that patterns of party influence in congressional lawmaking have remained largely unchanged over recent decades.

Congressional majority parties also fail to enact their agenda priorities for the same reasons as in the past. Majority parties today regularly cannot overcome veto points controlled by the opposing party, especially the Senate filibuster (see Krehbiel 1998). But this cause of majority party failure is no more prevalent than it was during the 1980s and 1990s. Rather, opposing party veto players remain a constant source of frustration for majority parties over the past thirty-five years. Not surprisingly, the presence of divided government has an effect on the ability of majority parties to carry out their agenda priorities, though that effect has not grown in importance. Today's majority parties frequently fail on their agenda items because they cannot coalesce around specific legislation. The rise of party cohesion in roll-call voting does not mean that majority parties have an easy time organizing themselves around legislative initiatives at earlier stages in the process. Neither intraparty disagreement nor minority party obstruction has become more or less common as a cause of majority party failure over the period we examine.

Congressional majority parties also succeed on their agenda priorities in the same ways as in the past. Largely, they either seek broadly supported, bipartisan proposals or work across the aisle to come to bipartisan compromises. Cases of the majority party's steamrolling the minority party and passing laws over persistent minority party opposition remain rare, even in Congresses with unified party control. Although majorities often start out attempting to steamroll, they typically have to back off their most contentious proposals in order to pass legislation. Our interviews show that, even today, party leaders and key negotiators typically plan for and negotiate toward a bipartisan outcome behind the scenes. Despite all the partisan change in Congress, the predominant strategy for achieving legislative success—including success on the majority party's agenda priorities—is to secure bipartisan support.

While the contemporary Congress tends to use more centralized legislative processes to develop and pass laws, these new procedures yield outcomes that are no less bipartisan than the traditional processes of the past. In analyzing the procedural pathways by which laws are enacted over time, we find little evidence that the use of more centralized legislative processes is a leading indicator of partisan lawmaking. Congressional leaders often depart from "regular order" not to pass partisan programs, but to resolve legislative impasses. The flexibility and secrecy that these more streamlined processes permit frequently help lawmakers to negotiate broadly supported agreements and are often employed to pass highly bipartisan legislation. The procedural path a bill takes to enactment correlates little with the extent of partisan conflict when the legislation passes the chamber. Rather than tools of party power used to enact partisan laws, unorthodox processes are just different means to achieving similar legislative ends.

Finally, we find that members of Congress talk about their legislative achievements much as they did in the past. Analyzing the public reactions of lawmakers to successful congressional action quoted in the news media, we find that members today frequently are negative and dissatisfied about legislative outcomes, but that this was just as true in the 1970s. Majority party members do not express satisfaction or happiness with legislative outcomes more frequently than they did in the past. In fact, they frequently give disparaging assessments of their legislative achievements! Nor do minority party members complain about or criticize legislative outcomes more often today than in the past. Nothing about how members discuss legislative outcomes would lead one to conclude that policy outcomes in contemporary American politics please the majority party or displease the minority party more than the policy outcomes of the much less partisan Congress of the 1970s and 1980s.

At the broadest level, this research reveals that Congress has not changed nearly as much as is often assumed. Put differently, Congress has changed less in its policy outcomes and impacts than in its internal processes. Much about congressional lawmaking remains the same, despite the tremendous rise of partisan conflict and the empowering of party leadership.

Even though they are much more cohesive in roll-call voting, today's congressional parties still struggle with internal divisions on their legislative priorities. In fact, they contend with much more intraparty conflict than one might expect based on their cohesion in roll-call voting. Today's parties do not feature the same deep ideological and regional divisions that characterized the parties of the mid-twentieth century. But as Speaker John Boehner testified, it still remains difficult for a party leader to "keep 218 frogs in a wheelbarrow at one time."[19] Parties may not contend with internal divisions along the rigid ideological fault lines of the twentieth century, but the United States is a big country in which any majority party encompasses significant diversity of interest and perspective. Congressional parties in a separation of powers system made up of lawmakers elected individually in single-member districts still have a hard time reaching consensus.

This chapter began with Speaker Ryan's enthusiasm for Republicans' "once-in-a-lifetime opportunity" to transform national policy in 2017. Given Republicans' sizable majorities and their record of party unity on controversial roll-call votes, optimism about reorienting public policy might have seemed justified. Yet by the time the 115th Congress (2017–18) closed in December 2018, few of the policies outlined in Republicans' Better Way agenda had been enacted. High-profile attempts at one-party lawmaking had failed, most prominently the effort to repeal and replace the Affordable Care Act that consumed nine months of 2017. Republicans did not reorient much domestic policy in 2017–18. They were unable to cut domestic discretionary spending, repeal financial regulations, limit health coverage for abortion, or impose work requirements on food stamp recipients, all agenda priorities laid out when the Congress convened. Most of what they did pass cleared with strong bipartisan support, including each of the omnibus budget and spending measures.[20] Only one major partisan law stands out from the 115th Congress, the Tax Cuts and Jobs Act of 2017 (Pub. L. 115-97), enacted via budget reconciliation. As will be evident from the analyses that follow, the outcomes of the 115th Congress are not out of the ordinary for majority parties across the whole period we analyze, including those in control of unified government. For all the increases in party cohesion and strengthening of leadership, majority parties continue to suffer frustration in American politics at roughly the same rates as in the 1970s and 1980s.

The bottom line is that parties may be more influential in the contemporary Congress, but lawmaking has not become more partisan. In fact, at its core, lawmaking looks very much the same today as it did a half-century ago. Enacted laws continue to rest on the same broad bipartisan assent that has traditionally characterized congressional lawmaking. When it comes to policymaking, the responsible parties vision of government remains well out of reach.

TWO

The Persistence of Bipartisan Lawmaking

Every bill that I authored that became law had Republican support of one sort or another except for one, and that was the Affordable Care Act.

—Rep. Henry Waxman (D-CA, 1975–2015)[1]

You cannot legislate without the ability to compromise.

—Sen. Alan Simpson (R-WY, 1979–97)[2]

In this chapter our goal is to offer a "top line" answer to two questions about the majority party's lawmaking capacity in the contemporary Congress. We want to know, Do majority parties in today's party-polarized Congress pass laws on a partisan basis more often than majority parties in less polarized eras? and Are today's stronger congressional parties more effective at enacting their agenda priorities?

We find that the answer to both questions is generally no. First, we do not find that contemporary Congresses enact a larger share of laws on party-line votes. Instead, minority party support for enacted legislation remains as high as it was in the 1970s. Just as in the less partisan decades of the twentieth century, most laws still garner the support of a majority of the minority party. Bipartisanship not only characterizes the enactment of low-profile, routine bills, it also remains the norm on major legislation. There is no trend toward an increasing share of laws' being enacted in the manner of the Affordable Care Act (2010)[3] or the Tax Cuts and Jobs Act (2017).[4]

Second, we find that recent congressional majority parties are no more effective in accomplishing their legislative goals than the majority parties of the 1980s. Across all the Congresses we analyze, majority parties struggle to a similar degree to enact their partisan priorities and rarely get most of what they want on their agenda items. When they do succeed or partially succeed, they usually need bipartisan support to get it done.

After presenting these data, we turn to our interviews with members and staff to shed light on the persistence of bipartisanship in contemporary lawmaking. We wanted to know more about how and why the majority party reaches out to the minority party for support, and under what conditions minority party members are willing to engage in bipartisan negotiations. Our interviewees testify to the extreme difficulty of one-party legislating in the US system. In particular, they repeatedly emphasize the importance of winning bipartisan support to clear the supermajority threshold for Senate cloture. In a self-reinforcing dynamic, the quest for the bipartisan support necessary for sixty votes in the Senate can cause a falloff in support among the majority party's hard-liners, thus requiring even more bipartisan outreach.

Most remarkably, our interviewees suggest that party polarization may, paradoxically, result in *more* bipartisanship on successful legislation. With the decline in the size of centrist blocs in both House and Senate, majority parties do not have a substantial group of swing voters in the opposing party to draw on for support of their legislative efforts. It is generally not possible for a contemporary majority party to pick off just a few minority party members to win enactment of legislation. When minority party votes are needed, majority party leaders find that they must often enter into direct negotiations with minority party leaders. When such negotiations are successful, legislation tends to pass overwhelmingly.

Data Sources

We take stock of majority party lawmaking capacity using two sources of data: roll-call votes on the enactment of laws passed by Congress and signed by presidents from 1973 to 2018, and a unique dataset identifying the major partisan legislative priorities of each congressional majority party from 1985 to 2018.

For our analyses, we define a congressional majority party as a party with majority control of the House or the Senate during each Congress. If a party controls both chambers during a Congress, we treat that as a single majority rather than two separate majorities. While we recognize that there can be a disconnect between House and Senate majorities of the same party, we combined the chambers in these circumstances for simplicity's sake and because the agendas of House and Senate majorities of the same party typically overlap greatly. When there is split party control of the House and Senate, we analyze two separate majority parties for that Congress. For example, for the 112th and 113th Congresses, we assessed the successes and failures of both the Senate Democratic majority and the House Republican majority.

The congressional majority party's agenda is never identical to the president's agenda, even in unified government. Congressional majority parties and a copartisan president typically share many priorities, but their agendas by no means fully overlap. Some major presidential initiatives (such as President Donald Trump's immigration reform or border wall proposals during the 115th Congress) were not part of the congressional majority party's agenda. Meanwhile, other major presidential initiatives (such as President Obama's push for health care reform during the 111th Congress) were also a central part of the congressional majority party's agenda. Scholars have devoted a great deal of study to the determinants of presidential success with Congress (e.g., Bond and Fleisher 1990; Canes-Wrone 2006; Edwards 1990; Mayhew 2011), work we do not attempt to duplicate here. Instead, our focus is the legislative capacity of congressional majority parties, a subject that has seen much less scholarly attention.

Passage Votes

We compiled passage votes in the House and Senate on bills becoming law from 1973 to 2018 (the 93rd–115th Congresses). We analyze all House bills (H.R.) receiving passage roll-call votes in the House that went on to become law[5] and all bills and joint resolutions receiving passage roll-call votes in the Senate that went on to become law.[6]

We focus on the *initial* passage roll-call votes and not votes on bicameral reconciliations (e.g., conference reports) that typically broaden support. Focusing on initial passage votes biases our analyses toward finding higher levels of partisanship on legislation, since bills often clear Congress on final passage by wider margins than they pass at first (see Ryan 2018).[7] Examining initial passage votes also allows us to ascertain if bipartisanship results only when the House must accommodate the Senate's supermajoritarian processes in reaching bicameral agreement or whether the House typically legislates in a bipartisan manner from the outset.

We also analyze separately the enactments on Mayhew's list of landmark laws from 1973 to 2018, examining the final roll call taken in each chamber on each measure.[8] Looking at this subset of laws allows us to gauge whether there is more partisan division on significant legislation than on the typical bill. We can also track trends to ascertain whether lawmaking has become more partisan on major legislation, if not across all bills generally.

Party Agenda Priorities

An even more important test of a majority party's capacity is its ability to enact its highest legislative priorities. Even if legislation generally has not become more partisan, we want to know whether today's more cohesive, more centralized parties are better at accomplishing the legislative goals they care about most. We take stock of whether majority parties were able to enact their priority legislative items in each Congress from 1985 to 2018 (99th–115th Congresses). This analysis required us to establish lists of the priority items for each congressional majority party and then track the legislative outcomes on each item.

We used a multipronged approach to identify majority party priorities during each Congress. First we read the opening speeches the leader of the majority party in each chamber made at the start of each Congress.[9] In each speech, we identified any policy items or issues the leaders said they hoped or planned to address in the coming two years and recorded those items as priorities. Second, we looked at the bills inserted into the slots reserved for the Speaker of the House and the Senate majority leader.[10] The policy proposals introduced in these slots were also recorded as majority party agenda priorities in each Congress. Third, we read articles in *CQ Magazine* during the weeks before and after the start of each Congress that discussed policy items expected to be on the congressional agenda. Items addressed in leaders' speeches or introduced into leadership bill slots were often discussed in some detail in *CQ Magazine*, allowing us to sharpen our understanding of each item.

Most agenda items were identified in more than one source. For instance, some agenda items were mentioned in one or both speeches, introduced in reserved bill slots in one or both chambers, and discussed by *CQ Magazine*. Most items (58 percent) were identified in at least two sources, and the average agenda item was found in 2.2 sources. Items that were mentioned in *CQ Magazine* but did not appear in a leader's speech or in a leadership-reserved bill were not included on our list of party priorities.

This approach yielded a list of 265 priority agenda items. Majority party agendas ranged from 11 to 24 items, with the average number of priority agenda items about 16.[11] In the few Congresses with split partisan control of the House and Senate (the 99th, 107th, 112th, and 113th), we identified each majority party's agenda items. The full list of agenda items and additional descriptive information is found in appendix A.

This approach for identifying majority party priorities performs well for the post-1984 era. Before 1985, the utility of leaders' speeches is spotty, since Senate majority leaders did not regularly give these speeches before that time. In the House, although the Speaker and minority leader have long given speeches at the start of each Congress, those given by Speaker Tip O'Neill (D-MA) and Minority Leader Bob Michel (R-IL) in the early 1980s were particularly devoid of policy content. The "leadership bills" indicator also performs inconsistently before 1985, particularly in the Senate. The GOP Senate leaders in the 97th (1981–82) and 98th (1983–84) Congresses, newly returned to the majority after nearly three decades out of power, did not appear to use their reserved bill slots, often allowing Democrats to introduce bills with those designations. Extending our data series on party agenda priorities before 1985 would require a different approach.[12]

The agendas of Democratic and Republican majorities were similar in size and scope during 1985–2018. In our data, there are 132 Republican priorities and 133 Democratic priorities. Republicans average 12 priorities per congressional majority, and Democrats average 13. The longest list of priorities for any majority was from a Republican majority (104th Congress, 1995–96). Even in recent years, there are few differences between the parties in legislative ambition. Since 2011, Republicans had 9 agenda items per congressional majority and Democrats had 11. The parties clearly want different things out of federal policy. Republicans often prioritize shrinking the welfare state, reducing federal regulations, and implementing conservative social policies. Democrats, in contrast, seek to expand the safety net, beef up federal regulatory action, and liberalize social policy. Nevertheless, both parties generally advance wide-ranging platforms that require legislative action.

For each item identified during the period, we coded the outcome obtained by the majority party into one of three categories.

1. the majority got *most* of what it wanted with a new law or laws enacted achieving most of what the majority set out to achieve.
2. The majority got *some* of what it wanted, passing a new law or laws falling short of the party's goals or requiring substantial compromise.
3. The majority got *none* of what it wanted, failing to enact any new law on its policy priority.

We relied on journalistic coverage of each item to do this coding, drawing primarily on *CQ Magazine* and on articles providing an overview of the accomplishments of each Congress in various editions of the *CQ Almanac*. Occasionally we also drew on other periodicals such as *Roll Call*, *The Hill*, and the *Washington Post*. It was not difficult to differentiate between laws widely regarded as a "win" for the majority party and laws where the majority party had to drop key priorities or make concessions. After coding each item for its outcome, we also recorded the partisan split on the relevant final passage votes (if any).[13] In addition, we noted the support or opposition from the top leaders of each party in each chamber.[14]

The list of agenda items obtained using this method overlaps significantly but not overwhelming with Mayhew's landmark legislation. Overall, about 39 percent of Mayhew's landmark laws (76/193) during this period were majority party agenda successes.[15] Of course, our list of agenda items also contains many priorities on which the majority party failed to legislate successfully. When majority parties succeed in legislating on their agenda priorities, their efforts result in landmark enactments more than half the time.[16]

Enacting Coalitions

If majority parties have gotten better at legislating their partisan preferences, and if lawmaking has become more partisan, then we should find that more laws are passed on party-line votes. But we do not find that more laws are enacted over the opposition of a majority of the minority party than in past eras when parties were less cohesive and majority leaders exercised less power.

Figure 2.1 shows the average percentage of minority party lawmakers voting in favor of all new laws and of Mayhew's landmark laws during each Congress from 1973 to 2018. The most striking pattern in these data is the lack of any clear trend toward decreased minority party support for legislative enactments. Instead, robust minority party support characterizes lawmaking in the contemporary Congress at roughly the same level as in the 1970s and 1980s. In every Congress since the early 1970s, the average share of minority party members supporting new laws on the initial House passage vote was higher than 62 percent. In most Congresses, the average share exceeds 80 percent.

Figure 2.1 displays a reference line at 50 percent to designate lawmaking that garnered support from a majority of the minority party. The five Congresses with the highest average levels of minority party support all took place after 2000: the 107th (2001–2), the 108th (2003–4), the 109th (2005–6), the 113th (2013–14), and the 115th (2017–18). Because the data displayed are from *initial* House passage votes, these high levels of minority support mean that bipartisanship in the House does not emerge only late in the legislative process when it becomes necessary for the House to work out disagreements with the supermajority-rule Senate. Although legislation will often eventually clear Congress on final passage with even broader consensus, House bills that result in new laws typically command broad bipartisan support even on initial passage.

A

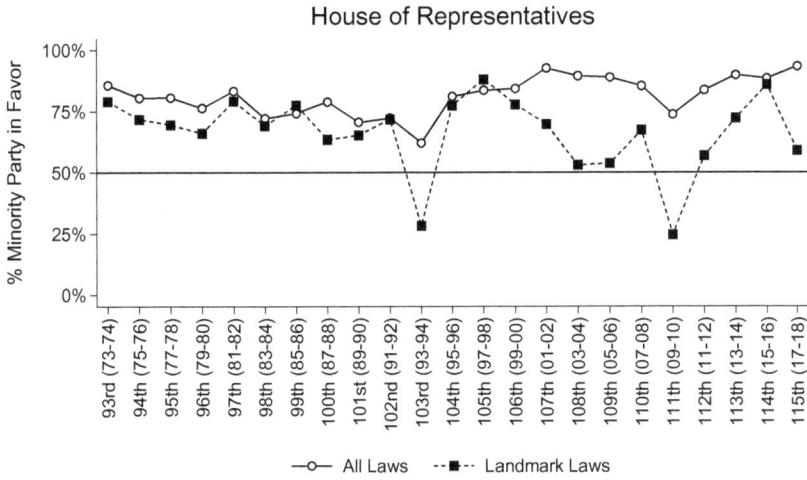

B

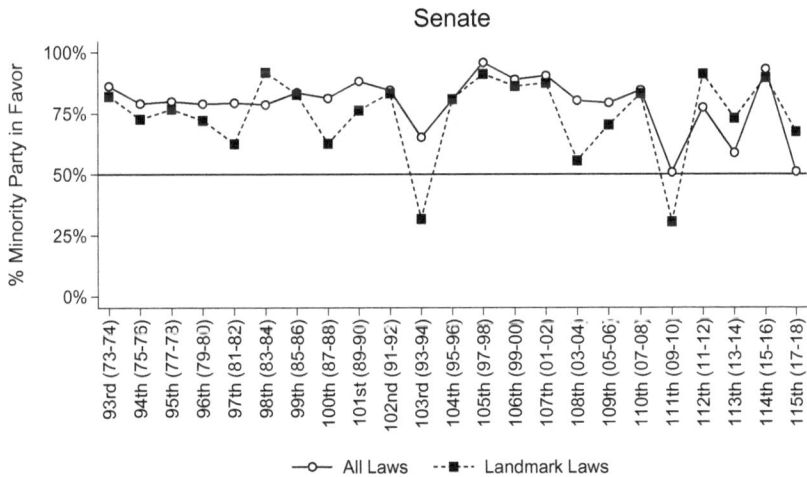

Figure 2.1. Average percentage minority party support on passage
of bills becoming law, 1973–2018

The data also do not show that minority party support for enacted legislation is meaningfully lower in unified government.[17] Note that although
minority party support for enacted legislation was relatively low in the
103rd (1993–94) and 111th (2009–10) Congresses under unified government, other recent Congresses with unified government—including the
108th (2003–4) and the 109th (2005–6)—do not stand out from the overall

time series. Minority party support is very high under both unified and divided government.

High levels of minority party support on laws are not simply an artifact of broad bipartisan support for low-profile or inconsequential legislation. The minority party also votes at high rates in favor of landmark laws. Minority party support for landmark laws is 66 percent on average and dips below 50 percent only twice (in the 103rd and 111th Congresses, both with unified government under Democratic control). Compared with all laws, there is more Congress-to-Congress variation in minority party support for landmark laws but little evidence of an overall decrease in recent years as majority party strength and party polarization increased.[18]

Similar patterns are found in the Senate. Since the early 1970s, the average share of minority party senators supporting new laws is 80 percent, with few Congresses registering average levels of minority party support lower than 75 percent. Since the start of the George W. Bush administration, only three Congresses have seen levels of Senate minority party support dip below 70 percent for all new laws: the 111th (2009–10), 113th (2013–14), and 115th (2017–18). These Congresses do not mark the emergence of a trend; instead, they stand out from the time series as anomalous. The 114th Congress (2015–16) had one of the highest rates of minority party support recorded, and other recent Congresses were entirely average.

Among landmark laws, the pattern is similar: minority party senators back the passage of landmark laws at high rates, with most Congresses registering average minority party support at 70 percent or better and with no appreciable trend in the data. In both the House and the Senate, these data indicate that most new laws, including landmark laws, attract substantial minority party support, and they do so at rates similar to those found in less partisan periods.

Figure 2.2 assesses partisan lawmaking by another metric—the minority party *roll*. A party is rolled when a measure is passed even though a majority of that party votes in opposition. Rolls have frequently been used to assess partisan legislating and partisan strength in legislatures (Cox and Mc-Cubbins 2005; Finocchiaro and Rohde 2008; Gailmard and Jenkins 2007; Jenkins and Monroe 2016). Scholars focus on how often the majority rolls the minority because a majority party seeking to claim partisan credit for lawmaking needs to pass laws over the opposition of the minority party.[19] If most of the minority also supports the legislation, the majority will gain less relative advantage in party reputation. Rather, both parties can claim a win.

Figure 2.2 exhibits little upward trend in minority party rolls in House lawmaking overall despite the increased centralization of power in the

A

House of Representatives

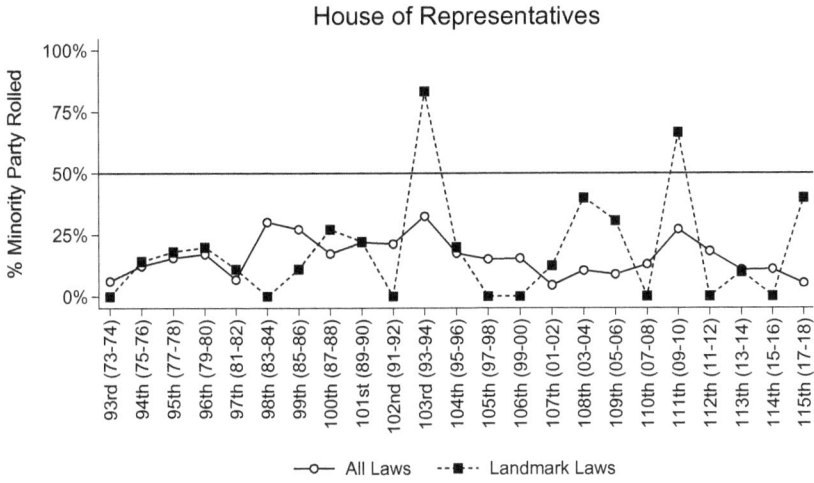

B

Senate

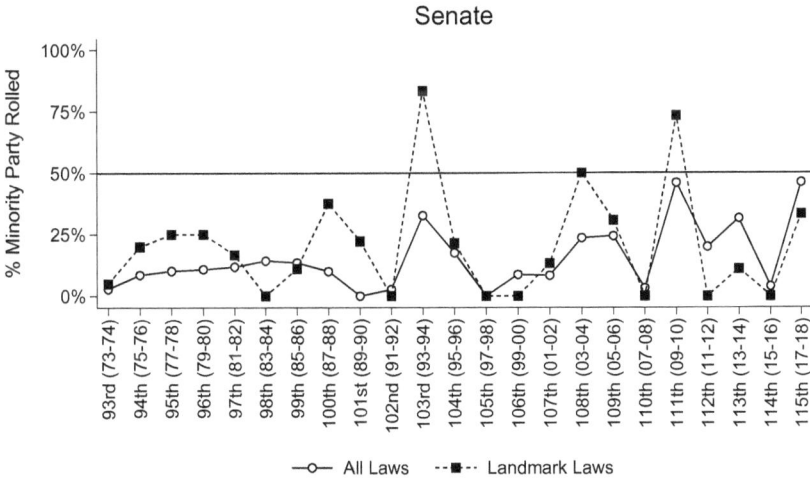

Figure 2.2. Minority party roll rates on passage of bills becoming law, 1973–2018

majority party leadership.[20] In all but four Congresses, the minority party was rolled on less than 25 percent of new laws, and minority party roll rates typically fell below 15 percent. House minority party roll rates are higher on landmark laws, but they still occurred in only 20 percent of cases. And for both all laws and landmark laws, the trend in minority party rolls over time is not statistically significant.[21] The only notable features in the data are spikes in minority party rolls on landmark laws during the 103rd (1993–94) and 111th (2009–10), the two recent Congresses with unified Democratic Party control. Equivalent spikes in minority party rolls are not evident for the 108th, 109th (2003–6), and 115th (2017–18) Congresses, each featuring unified Republican Party control.[22]

In the Senate, the majority party rarely rolls the minority party on the passage of new laws. Minority party rolls are generally uncommon, happening on just 13 percent of all new laws and rarely exceeding 25 percent of new laws in any Congress. Some recent Congresses had higher than average percentages of minority party rolls, but others, including the 110th (2007–8) and 114th (2015–16), saw very few. Overall, the slight uptick in Senate minority party rolls on all new laws is statistically significant[23] but small, with an increase of less than one percentage point in rolls, on average, per Congress over the period. On landmark legislation, the Senate minority was rolled only 22 percent of the time. Several recent Congresses never saw the Senate minority party rolled on the passage of a landmark law, including the 110th (2007–8), 112th (2011–12), and 114th (2015–16) Congresses.[24]

Figure 2.3 looks for evidence of partisan (or bipartisan) lawmaking in one additional way: assessing how often the majority party in each chamber *needed* minority party votes to pass new laws. For each law, we simply calculate whether or not the majority party supplied a chamber majority for passage with its own members, thereby making any minority party votes superfluous. These figures show the percentage of enacted laws on which the majority party did *not* muster enough votes to pass the bill from among its own ranks alone. For those roll-call votes in which the Senate imposed a sixty-vote threshold, we consider whether members of the majority party alone provided the necessary sixty votes.[25] Figure 2.3 thus gauges those pieces of legislation where the issues were sufficiently controversial and the majority party insufficiently cohesive to have passed the law without assistance from at least some members of the minority. In this way, it points to a critical form of bipartisanship. Even where a majority of the minority party opposes a bill, individual members of the minority may provide the votes decisive for a successful outcome.

If majority parties had become more efficacious over time, we would find a negative trend for this indicator, but figure 2.3 shows that recent House majority parties are no more self-sufficient in lawmaking than the majority parties of the 1970s and 1980s. For laws generally, the House majority party usually, but not always (86 percent of the time on average), musters the votes necessary for passage of laws without requiring any votes from the minority party. However, despite increases in majority party strength, the need for minority party votes has not decreased.[26] On landmark laws, the House

A

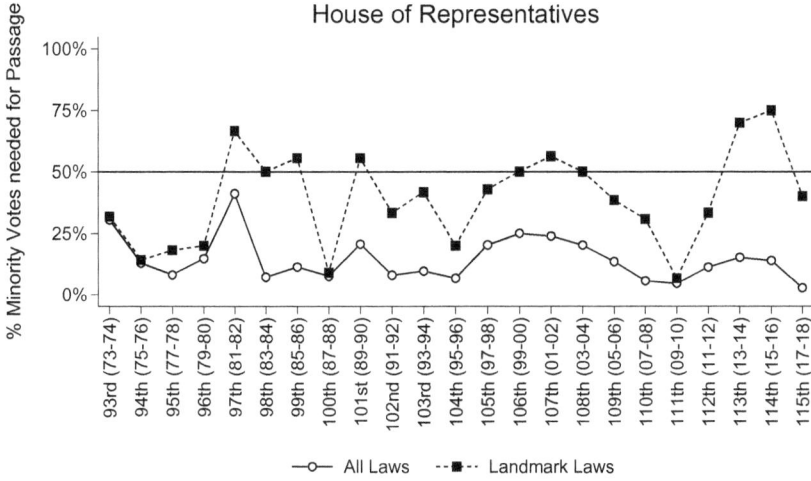

B

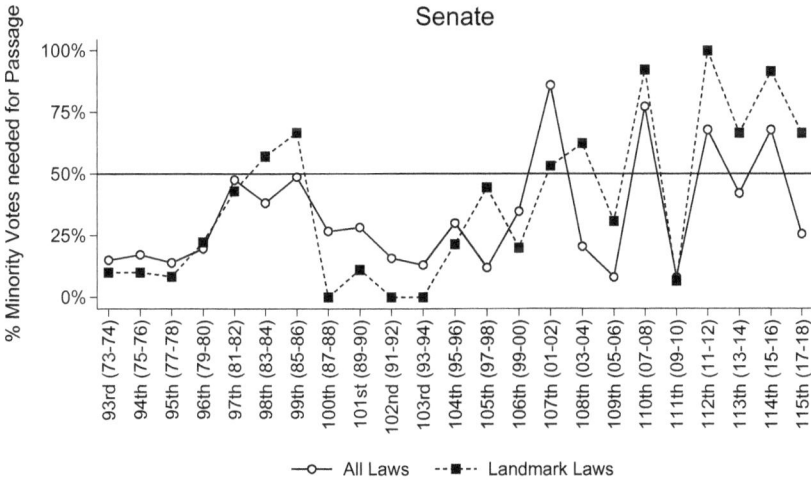

Figure 2.3. Minority party votes needed for passage on bills becoming law, 1973–2018

majority party musters sufficient support from among its own ranks less frequently—about 63 percent of the time. Put differently, the majority party tends more often to need minority party help to pass the most important laws. But again, no significant trends are evident in the data.[27]

Compared with the House, Senate majorities more frequently need minority party support to enact laws. On average, the Senate majority party provided the necessary votes about 71 percent of the time for all laws and

64 percent of the time for landmark legislation. A greater need for minority party support in the Senate is not surprising given how the minority party exploits the chamber's cloture rules under polarized conditions (Binder and Smith 2001; Koger 2010; Smith 2014; Wawro and Schickler 2006). As a result, the Senate majority has needed minority votes *more* frequently over time, and this increase is statistically significant for landmark laws.[28]

All together, across figures 2.1 to 2.3, we find little evidence that partisan lawmaking has increased along with increases in party polarization and majority party strength. There is some evidence that majority parties in the Senate have increased their capacity to roll the minority, but Senate majorities also need minority party votes more often to enact landmark laws—a trend that runs counter to the expectation that today's more cohesive majorities would be more legislatively effective. In the House, there are hardly any trends in the data.

To assess the robustness of these bivariate findings, we also conducted multivariate analyses, reported in tables 2.1 and 2.2. The analyses are of each of the variables assessed above (percentage of minority party support, minority party rolled, and minority party support needed) for each of the passage votes on each law. Several independent variables are included. The most important are, first, a measure for party polarization—*party median distance*—which is measured as the absolute difference between the parties' first-dimension DW-NOMINATE medians in each chamber and, second, a measure for majority party strength—*majority party unity*—which is measured as the inverse of the standard deviation of first-dimension DW-NOMINATE scores among members of the majority party. As *party median distance* and *majority party unity* increase, party government theories expect that we should see lower levels of minority party support, higher likelihood of minority party rolls, and lower likelihood of minority party votes needed, all else being equal.

We include in the analyses several other variables that might affect levels of partisanship on lawmaking votes. These are the number of seats held by the majority party in each chamber, a dichotomous indicator of *divided government* for each Congress, whether the sponsor of each law was a member of the majority party, and the law sponsor's first-dimension DW-NOMINATE distance from the chamber median. We also included fixed effects for each bill's issue topic,[29] and in each analysis robust standard errors are calculated to correct for clustering by Congress. We employ OLS regression to analyze variation in *percentage minority party support* and logistic regression to analyze variation in the incidence of *minority party rolls* and *minority votes needed*.

The results show a limited, and often only conditional, relation between measures of party distance and majority party unity and predicted levels

Table 2.1 Party voting on initial passage roll calls in the House of Representatives, 1973–2018

	% Minority party support		Minority party rolls		Minority votes needed	
	(1)	(2)	(3)	(4)	(5)	(6)
Party median distance	0.167 (0.171)	0.281 (0.217)	0.641 (2.020)	−0.058 (2.212)	−4.168* (1.984)	−3.958 (2.067)
Majority party unity	−1.729 (1.216)	32.90** (10.210)	20.94 (15.380)	−218.8* (86.530)	−18.94 (11.520)	91.19 (60.600)
Majority party seats	−0.002* (0.001)	0.117** (0.035)	0.020* (0.008)	−0.792** (0.286)	−0.037** (0.008)	0.345 (0.201)
Majority party seats × majority party unity		−0.143** (0.042)		0.976** (0.341)		−0.461 (0.240)
Divided government	−0.006 (0.032)	0.005 (0.024)	0.079 (0.258)	0.016 (0.198)	0.112 (0.225)	0.169 (0.230)
Majority party sponsor	−0.093* (0.041)	−0.066 (0.048)	3.88 (2.344)	3.503 (2.214)	−0.099 (0.535)	−0.053 (0.560)
Sponsor distance from median	0.0891 (0.065)	0.114 (0.080)	1.736 (2.949)	1.256 (2.733)	−1.211 (1.112)	−1.201 (1.163)
Majority party sponsor × sponsor distance from median	−0.146 (0.081)	−0.204* (0.095)	−1.325 (2.952)	−0.608 (2.794)	1.268 (1.085)	1.168 (1.143)
Policy issue fixed effects	yes	yes	yes	yes	yes	yes
Constant	2.459* (1.054)	−26.47** (8.634)	−27.13* (11.890)	173.4* (73.240)	26.92** (9.494)	−64.73 (50.670)
N	2,215	2,215	2,215	2,215	2,215	2,215

Note: Columns 1 and 2 are OLS regressions; columns 3–6 are logistic regressions. Each analysis includes robust standard errors correcting for clustering by Congress. Since the unit of analysis for the key independent variables in these analyses is by Congress, the effective N for these analyses is $n = 23$ rather than $n = 2,215$. *$p < .05$; **$p < .01$.

of partisanship in House passage votes (table 2.1). The coefficients for the polarization measure (*party median distance*) are not significant except in one test, and the level of *majority party unity* never has an independent effect. The unity of majority party members is relevant only when the majority also controls a large share of the chamber's seats (as demonstrated by the inter-action term between *majority party seats* and *majority party unity*), a condition rarely found except for the large, unified Democratic chamber majorities of the 111th Congress (2009–10).

In the Senate (table 2.2) there is slightly more evidence that partisan change in Congress has affected levels of partisanship on passage votes, but the results are still mixed. A bigger distance between party medians consistently predicts higher likelihood of minority party rolls (columns 3 and 4), but minority

Table 2.2 Party voting on initial passage roll calls in the Senate, 1973–2018

	% Minority party support		Minority party rolls		Minority votes needed	
	(1)	(2)	(3)	(4)	(5)	(6)
Party median distance	−0.815 (0.416)	−0.958* (0.436)	8.210** (2.308)	8.567** (2.254)	7.791* (3.058)	7.404* (3.354)
Majority party unity	−0.086 (0.504)	26.93** (7.561)	0.366 (5.761)	−237.5** (59.810)	−3.112 (4.334)	117.4 (106.600)
Majority party seats	−0.008 (0.005)	0.410** (0.116)	0.008 (0.048)	−3.663** (0.935)	−0.148** (0.057)	1.745 (1.656)
Majority party seats × majority party unity		−0.492** (0.136)		4.298** (1.084)		−2.214 (1.953)
Divided government	0.084* (0.035)	0.059 (0.033)	−1.139** (0.293)	−0.941** (0.282)	0.527 (0.410)	0.423 (0.429)
Majority party sponsor	0.013 (0.070)	0.036 (0.063)	a	a	0.02 (0.925)	0.085 (0.938)
Sponsor distance from median	0.288 (0.159)	0.293 (0.155)	0.916 (0.682)	1.247* (0.625)	−0.900 (2.444)	−0.928 (2.389)
Majority party sponsor × sponsor distance from median	−0.387* (0.169)	−0.423* (0.159)	a	a	1.480 (2.369)	1.418 (2.324)
Policy issue fixed effects	yes	yes	yes	yes	yes	yes
Constant	1.594* (0.569)	−21.31** (6.347)	−6.115 (5.522)	196.6** (52.060)	5.077 (5.231)	−97.71 (90.340)
N	1,179	1,179	1,179	1,179	1,179	1,179

Note: Columns 1 and 2 are OLS regressions. Columns 3–6 are logistic regressions. Each analysis includes robust standard errors correcting for clustering by Congress. Since the unit of analysis for the key independent variables in these analyses is by Congress, the effective N for these analyses is $n = 23$, rather than $n = 1,179$. *$p < .05$; **$p < .01$.
[a] Majority party sponsor had to be dropped from these analyses because it perfectly related to the dependent variable. In other words, all minority party rolls happened on bills sponsored by a majority party lawmaker.

rolls remain unlikely in any case. The model (column 4) predicts that at one standard deviation below the mean of party distance there is an 8 percent likelihood of a minority party's being rolled, and at one standard deviation above the mean that likelihood increases to 16 percent. This is an increase, but it underscores that minority party rolls are uncommon even at high levels of party distance in the Senate. In fact, even at the highest level of party difference, minority rolls are predicted to *not* occur 70 percent of the time.

As in the House, the unity of the majority party has little effect on law-making votes in the Senate, and in fact it does not have an independent effect in any analysis. Again, the number of seats held by the majority party appears to have the most significant effect, as well as a conditioning effect on majority party unity. Large *and* unified Senate majority parties obtain lower rates of minority party support, higher likelihood of minority party rolls, and lower likelihood that minority party votes are needed for passage. This makes sense, since large, unified Senate majorities can more easily work around the Senate's filibuster rules. However, again, this combined condition is extremely rare. Across our time frame, only one Senate majority met these criteria—and only for part of the 111th Congress (2009–10).

A few other results from the analyses are worth discussing. Across the analyses, the effect of divided government is very modest. The coefficients never have a significant effect on passage votes in the House. In the Senate, minority party rolls are predicted to occur significantly less often under divided government (on an estimated 9 percent of votes), but they are still uncommon under unified government (18 percent). Otherwise, divided government appears to have little relevance for how partisan or bipartisan lawmaking is in Congress.

We conducted analyses similar to those in tables 2.1 and 2.2 for Mayhew's landmark laws, but without any bill-level measures such as the party or extremity of each law's sponsor (information not included in Mayhew's data). Limited inferences can be drawn among solely Congress-level covariates, since the effective Ns are too small. Nonetheless, these results largely reinforce the findings in tables 2.1 and 2.2.[30]

Little in the data presented here suggests that contemporary congressional majorities are better able than those of the 1970s and 1980s to pass partisan laws. Increases in party polarization and majority party unity have had minimal effect on levels of partisanship on passage votes. Although minority party rolls have become slightly more common in the Senate as partisan change has occurred, they remain uncommon overall. Only under conditions of large *and* unified majorities does partisanship on lawmaking appear to noticeably increase, but Congresses meeting these conditions are rare—the 111th Congress (2009–10) appears to be only example in the years we analyze.

It is not the case that bipartisanship has persisted only as Congress has accomplished less. In other words, some might expect that Congress is less productive than it used to be, in terms of lawmaking, so that while it is still bipartisan it hardly does anything at all. Figure 2.4 suggests otherwise. While the figure shows that the number of laws enacted by each Congress has clearly declined over time, the number of *pages* of law enacted has substantially increased since the 1950s and remained steady since the 1980s. In other words, the contemporary Congress passes fewer individual laws, but the laws it enacts tend to be much longer and more omnibus in character than in the 1950s

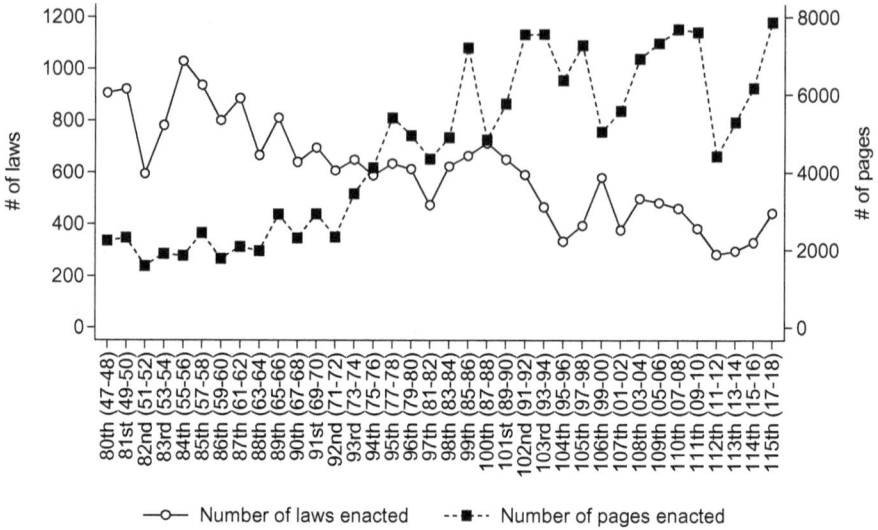

Figure 2.4. Number of bills and pages of statutes enacted, 1947–2018
Source: Brookings Institution (2019).

and 1960s. As gauged by the sheer volume of legislative output, Congress today is no less productive than it was in the 1970s and 1980s.

Despite decades of partisan and procedural change in Congress, lawmaking remains an overwhelmingly bipartisan exercise. Contemporary majority parties do not enact laws on party-line votes more frequently than those of earlier eras, and party polarization has had little effect on levels of partisanship found on enactments.

Contemporary Efforts to Enact Partisan Agendas

The acid test for congressional party government is a majority party's ability to enact its programmatic agenda priorities. Congressional parties do not have partisan goals on all issues, and many items taken up and passed into law do not relate to party goals, including some landmark laws. Theories of party power indicate that we are most likely to find significant party influence on party priority items (Aldrich and Rohde 2000a, 2000b; Koger and Lebo 2017). A party's agenda reflects its central goals, the campaign promises its members made, and the issues on which its members would like to establish a record of accomplishment.

Taking stock of the outcomes of majority parties' legislative priorities also allows us to assess more directly if party polarization and increased party organizational strength in recent years have enabled congressional majority parties to succeed better in enacting their programmatic agendas. These data allow us to gauge overall party effectiveness at turning partisan priorities into laws, as well as to assess the means by which they succeed in passing laws related to these priorities. In other words, when the majority succeeds on agenda items, does it do so on a partisan or bipartisan basis?

Figure 2.5 first provides an overview of the outcomes of each majority's agenda items for the 99th–115th Congresses (1985–2018). The full tallies for each congressional majority are found in appendix table A.1. For each Congress, the panels in the figure show the percentage of the majority's priority items falling into each of the three outcomes—the majority party achieving most, some, or none of what it wanted to achieve. During most Congresses one party controlled the House and Senate, but in the four Congresses with split control (the 99th, 107th, 112th, and 113th) we assessed both parties' agenda priorities. In the interest of simplicity, we merge House and Senate majority party priorities to display these averages over time.

The overall results show that contemporary congressional majorities are rarely able to enact partisan agendas. Typically, a majority party successfully acts in any form on only half of its agenda priorities. The modal outcome is failure. On 48 percent (127/265) of policy priorities, congressional majorities achieved none of what they wanted to achieve. Congressional majority parties thus fare somewhat worse in enacting their agendas than presidents do. Mayhew (2011) finds that presidents since Truman have succeeded in getting Congress to enact about 60 percent of their proposals. Meanwhile, majority parties succeed (either fully or in part) on only about half of their proposals.[31]

As is evident in figure 2.5, majority party success varies quite a bit from Congress to Congress. Some congressional majorities avoided racking up failures, including the Republican majorities during the first six years of the George W. Bush administration (2001–6) and the Republican Revolution majority of the 104th Congress (1995–96). Nonetheless, in eight of the seventeen Congresses, majority parties failed on their agendas half the time or more. Some majorities, including Democrats in the 112th (2011–12) and Republicans in the 106th (1999–2000), 113th (2013–14), and 114th (2015–16) Congresses, got none of what they wanted on the vast majority of their agenda priorities.

Rather than achieving better rates of success, the highly cohesive majority parties of recent years have in many cases fared worse in terms of legislative outcomes. Majorities from 2011 to 2016 (112th–114th Congresses) racked up the highest failure rates and the lowest success rates over the

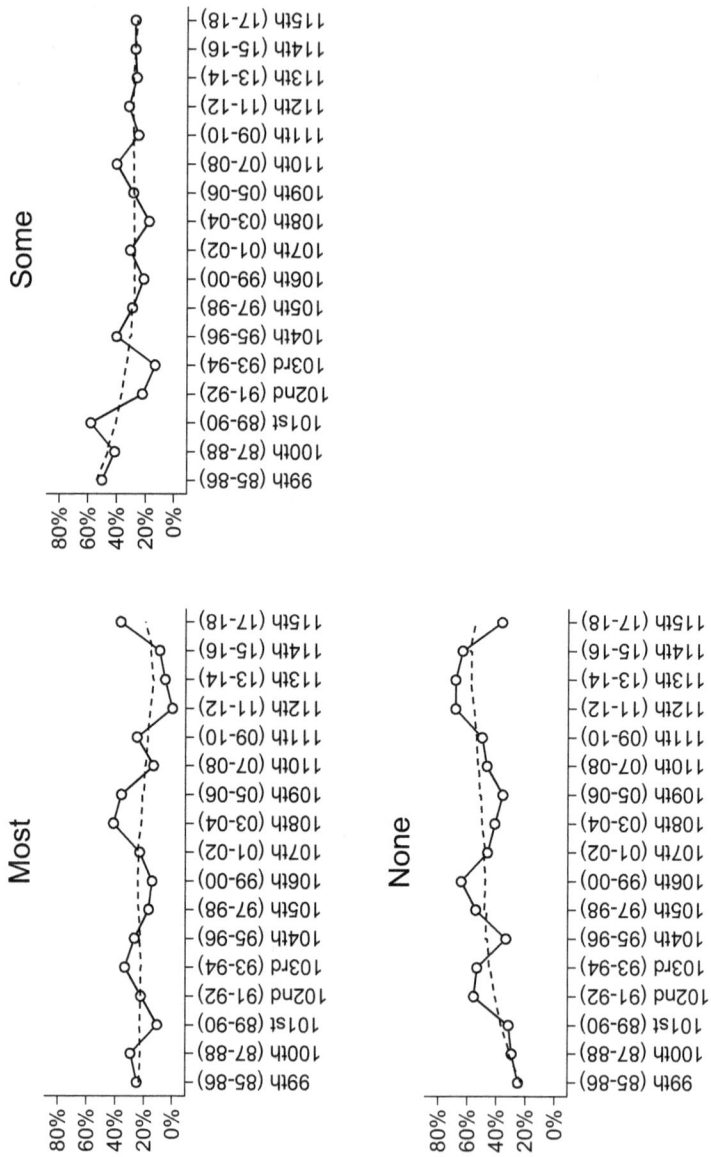

Figure 2.5. Legislative outcomes of majority party agenda items

Note: The 99th, 107th, 112th, and 113th Congresses featured split party control of the House and Senate. The combined agenda items of both parties are included in these tallies.

whole period since 1985.[32] This happened even though the majority parties of these Congresses did not advance lengthier or more ambitious agendas than the agendas of the 1980s or 1990s. With a 36 percent failure rate, the unified Republican government of the 115th Congress (2017–18) achieved better results than other post-2010 Congresses, returning to a majority party failure rate comparable to those under President George W. Bush from 2001 to 2008 (107th–110th Congresses).

If failure is common, overwhelming success is exceedingly rare. On just 21 percent of agenda items (fifty-five items in total over the period) did a congressional majority achieve *most* of what it set out to achieve. During some Congresses such successes were nonexistent. Neither party got most of what it wanted on any agenda item during the 112th Congress (2011–12). Senate Democrats had only one such success during the 113th (2013–14), when they ushered through a reauthorization of the Violence against Women Act (Pub. L. 113-4). Republican majorities in the 113th (2013–14) and 114th (2015–16) Congresses got most of what they wanted on just one item as well (passage of the Hire More Heroes Act—part of Pub. L. 114-41—which exempted veteran-employees from being counted toward the number of employees required by the employer mandate under the Affordable Care Act).

Across the data, majority parties were somewhat more successful at getting *some* of what they wanted. In fact, in most cases majority party success appears to be achieved more easily through compromise. In ten of the seventeen Congresses, majority parties achieved some of what they wanted more frequently than they achieved most. There is no trend in the data. While the majorities of the late 1980s were relatively adept at achieving some of what they wanted, majorities have achieved these kinds of successes at a steady rate since 1991.

Not surprisingly, agenda failure rates are higher in divided government than in unified government, but the difference is hardly stark. On average in divided government, the majority party achieved none of its goals on 49 percent of its agenda priorities, compared with 43 percent of majority party agenda priorities resulting in legislative failure on average in unified government. There is so much variability in failure rates across both unified and divided government that this difference in mean failure rates falls short of statistical significance.[33]

Although majority parties "strike out" at roughly similar rates in divided and unified government, they are more than twice as likely to achieve most of what they want on their agenda priorities in unified government as in divided government. On average, majority parties get most of what they want on 35 percent of their agenda priorities in unified government, as opposed to only 15 percent on average in divided government, a statistically significant difference.[34] But majority parties are actually more likely to win a partial success on their agenda priorities in divided government than in unified government. On average, the majority party realized some of what it wanted on 35 percent of its agenda priorities in divided government, compared with only 22 percent in unified government, also a statistically significant difference.[35]

To summarize: when majority parties succeed in enacting their legislative priorities in unified government, they are much more likely to get "most of what they want" than they are in divided government. But even in unified government, majority parties are far more likely to fail outright on their legislative priorities than to get most of what they want, and they are only slightly better at avoiding legislative failure in unified government than in divided government.

Beyond just looking at successes and failures, we also need to assess *how* bills addressing agenda items were passed. For those agenda priorities on which majority parties achieved either some or most of their policy goals ($n = 138$), figure 2.6 displays the percentage of the time they did so (1) over the opposition of a majority of the opposing party in both chambers, (2) with the support of a majority of the opposing party in at least one chamber, and (3) with the support of one or more of the opposing party's top leaders in at least one chamber. Items can fit into more than one category, but only the first of these categories captures successes in *partisan* lawmaking.

Just as majority parties rarely achieve most of what they set out to achieve, they rarely enact new laws addressing agenda items over the opposition of the minority party. On just 21 percent (29/138) of successfully legislated agenda priorities did a congressional majority party enact legislation over the opposition of a majority of the opposing party in both chambers. More than one-fifth of this total (six cases) occurred during the 111th Congress (2009–10) alone. In five Congresses this outcome never occurred. Instead, the vast majority of party agenda items passed with the support of a majority of the opposing party in at least one chamber (79 percent, 109/138), or with the endorsement of at least one of the opposing party's top elected leaders (84 percent, 115/138). In fact, in eight of seventeen Congresses, opposing party leaders in at least one chamber voted in favor of fully 100 percent of the majority party agenda items that passed into law. In sum, even when majority parties succeed in getting most of what they want on their agenda priorities, they usually do so with substantial buy-in from the opposing party.

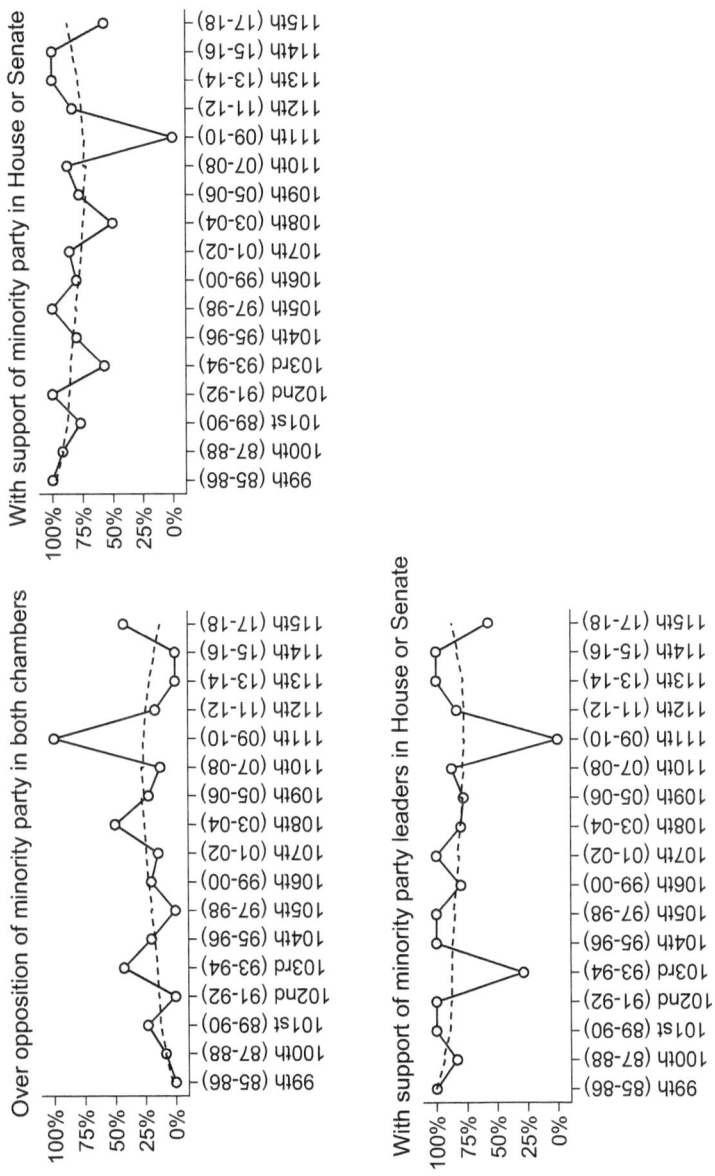

Figure 2.6. How majority parties succeed on their agendas

Note: The 99th, 107th, 112th, and 113th Congresses featured split party control of the House and Senate. The combined agenda items of both parties are included in these tallies.

Contemporary congressional majorities almost never enact laws achieving most of what they set out to achieve by rolling their party opponents. Among the 265 agenda items we identified, on just 12 items (4.5 percent) did a congressional majority get most of what it wanted *and* enact a new law over the objections of most of the opposing party in both chambers and without the endorsement of at least one elected party leader of the opposing party in either chamber. Despite their increased party cohesion and centralization of power, congressional majorities have not become significantly better at enacting their priorities over party opposition.

These twelve purest of party victories are listed in the left column of table 2.3. Not surprisingly, all but one was passed in unified government. The one case occurring in divided government, Pay-as-You-Go (PAYGO) budgeting, was adopted in 2007 as a rule of the House of Representatives and thus did not require a presidential signature. As one might also expect, the list includes a set of signature policy achievements valuable for partisan credit claiming: the Tax Cuts and Jobs Act (2017), the Affordable Care Act (2010), the Dodd-Frank financial regulatory reforms (2010),[36] the second round of the Bush tax cuts (2003),[37] the Class Action Fairness Act (2005),[38] and the Family and Medical Leave Act (1993).[39]

But even this short list of party victories is a mixed bag. In addition to

Table 2.3 Major partisan and bipartisan agenda successes, 1985–2018

Partisan successes	Bipartisan successes
1. Family and Medical Leave Act (103rd)	1. Tax Reform Act of 1986 (99th)
2. National Voter Registration Act (Motor Voter) (103rd)	2. Clean Air Act amendments (101st)
3. Violent Crime Control and Law Enforcement Act of 1994 (103rd)	3. Civil Rights Act of 1991 (102nd)
4. Medicare Modernization Act (108th)	4. Personal Responsibility and Work Opportunity Act (104th)
5. Jobs and Growth Tax Relief Reconciliation Act of 2003 (108th)	5. Balanced Budget Act of 1997 (105th)
6. Class Action Fairness Act (109th)	6. Gramm-Leach-Bliley Act (106th)
7. Pay-as-You-Go Budget Rule (110th)	7. No Child Left Behind (107th)
8. Patient Protection and Affordable Care Act (111th)	8. Economic Growth and Tax Relief Reconciliation Act (tax cuts, 107th)
9. Dodd-Frank Wall Street Reform and Consumer Protection Act (111th)	9. 2008 FISA amendments (110th)
10. State Children's Health Insurance Program reauthorization (111th)	10. American Taxpayer Relief Act ("fiscal cliff") (112th)
11. Tax Cuts and Jobs Act (115th)	11. Medicare Access and CHIP reauthorization (doc fix, 114th)
12. Disapproval of Obama administration agency rules (115th)	12. 21st Century Cures Act (114th)

some sweeping partisan victories, the list includes legislation of compara-
tively modest significance. Despite the partisan battle royal it engendered,
the "Motor Voter" law (1993)[40] has obtained only weak compliance from
local officials (Hess, Hanmer, and Nickerson 2016) and has had little effect
on voter turnout (Fitzgerald 2005). The 2009 reauthorization of the State
Children's Health Insurance Program (SCHIP)[41] entailed incremental policy
change compared with the far more important enactment on this issue, the
creation of SCHIP itself, which occurred on an overwhelmingly bipartisan
basis as part of the 1997 Balanced Budget Act during divided government
under President Bill Clinton.[42] The 2007 PAYGO House rule did not survive
a change of party control, with Republicans abandoning it in favor of a different budget rule (Cut-as-You-Go) when they regained the majority in 2011.

Remarkably, the list of purely partisan victories also includes two enactments that proved to be ideologically embarrassing for the enacting party:
the Violent Crime Control and Law Enforcement Act of 1994,[43] passed in
unified Democratic government under President Clinton, and the Medicare
Modernization Act (MMA) of 2003[44] creating a prescription drug benefit for
seniors (Medicare Part D), passed in unified Republican government under
President George W. Bush.

With its "three strikes and you're out" sentencing enhancements, the 1994
crime bill did not provide enduring credit-claiming opportunities for the
Democratic Party. The legislation contributed significantly to the rise in federal mass incarceration. In fact, the law later emerged as a major line of criticism against presidential candidate Hillary Clinton[45] and was even disavowed
by the former president himself. "I signed a bill that made the [mass incarcer-
ation] problem worse, and I want to admit it," he told an NAACP gathering.[46]

Similarly, the MMA was viewed by conservative activists as ideological
apostasy.[47] Before the MMA, Medicare offered no insurance coverage for
outpatient prescription drugs. The MMA created a new federal entitlement
benefit for seniors, largely funded out of general revenue, which by 2018
covered more than 70 percent of Medicare beneficiaries[48] and represented
fully 15 percent of all Medicare spending.[49] For the post-2009 Tea Party activists and other conservatives, "the Medicare prescription drug benefit—an
expensive, unfunded entitlement sponsored by Republicans—came to em-
body the idea that the GOP had lost its way and needed to return to core
conservative values of limited government, balanced budgets, and welfare
state retrenchment" (Oberlander 2012, 170).

In sum, out of this list of twelve majority party priorities enacted over
strong and sustained minority party opposition from 1985 to 2018, three are
of rather modest policy importance and two were ideologically problematic

for the enacting party. As gauged by a majority party's capacity to legislate its priorities by steamrolling its opposition, the unified governments in our time series yielded a surprisingly meager harvest.

While the list in table 2.3 shows that unified party control of government can facilitate the purest of partisan victories, these same Congresses also saw some of the most disastrous majority party defeats in our data. The 103rd Congress (1993–94) enacted the long-sought Democratic Party priority of (unpaid) family and medical leave, but it also presided over the total defeat of comprehensive health care reform. In fact, the headline story of the 103rd Congress at the time was one of failure, with pundits and commentators churning out lengthy analyses of the astonishing collapse of the Clinton health care plan (see, e.g., Johnson and Broder 1996; Skocpol 1996). Four years of Republican unified control of government during the 108th and 109th Congresses (2003–6) enabled enactment of the MMA and the second round of the Bush tax cuts, both major achievements. But Republicans also saw their objective of Social Security reform fail to launch even though House and Senate leaders designated the legislation as S. 1 and H.R. 1 and the newly reelected President Bush and Vice President Dick Cheney campaigned around the country promoting it. The 111th Congress (2009–10), which saw Democrats rack up several policymaking victories, including the Affordable Care Act (ACA) and Dodd-Frank, nonetheless saw the Democrats fail to leverage their large majorities to enact legislation addressing climate change. Finally, although the 115th Congress (2017–18) saw Republicans realize their goal of tax cuts and corporate tax reform, that victory was to a great extent overshadowed by the very public defeat of their effort to repeal and replace the ACA.

Of course, the twelve pure victories of these years include some of the most notable laws enacted in Washington during the past few decades. Even so, an equally impressive list of *bipartisan* enactments related to majority party agenda priorities occurred during this same period. The right column in table 2.3 lists twelve of these enactments. Each is a landmark law, per Mayhew's data. Each also affected American public law as consequentially as many of the laws in the left column, if not more so. These include the historic 1986 tax reform effort,[50] the Clean Air Act amendments (1991) that successfully addressed the problem of acid rain,[51] the welfare reform effort (1996) that abolished Aid to Families with Dependent Children (AFDC) and created Temporary Assistance for Needy Families (TANF),[52] the Balanced Budget Act of 1997 that also created the State Children's Health Insurance Program,[53] the Gramm-Leach-Bliley major deregulation of the financial industry (1999),[54] No Child Left Behind's (2001) expansion of the federal role in elementary and secondary education,[55] the American Taxpayer Relief Act ending the fiscal cliff standoff and raising tax rates on the highest-income taxpayers (2012),[56] and the 21st Century Cures Act (2016),[57] which broadly transformed Food and Drug Administration drug approval processes and significantly boosted federal funding for medical research.

A further comparison of partisan and bipartisan successes shows that bipartisan successes were not confined to a narrow range of noncontroversial policy areas. In fact, the majority party agenda successes enacted with bipartisan support during the period studied actually covered a broader array of policy issues than majority party agenda successes passed on party-line votes. Using the Policy Agendas Project coding of policy issues into twenty distinct areas, our data show that the 29 cases coded as "partisan successes" in figure 2.6 addressed nine policy areas, while the 109 cases coded as "bipartisan successes" addressed seventeen. Even just since 2001, majority parties won priority enactments with bipartisan support across a broader range of issues than those priorities enacted with only partisan support. In our study post-2001, there were forty-four bipartisan successes addressing thirteen policy issue areas, compared with nineteen partisan successes addressing eight issue areas. Even as Congress has become more partisan, majority parties are still able to achieve legislative success more often and on a broader array of issues by cultivating bipartisan support.

We analyzed our data on majority party agenda priorities in a few additional ways to ensure that our findings here are robust. Recognizing that not every agenda priority is likely to have been equally important to each majority party, we reconstructed the analyses in figures 2.5 and 2.6 including only the subset of agenda items that were identified in more than one of our indicators of agenda priorities. In other words, this subset of 157 agenda items—59 percent of the full dataset—excludes agenda items that were identified in only one leadership speech or in one set of leadership bills and thus might have been less important goals for the majority. The results, found in figures B.1 and B.2 in appendix B, show patterns similar to those discussed in this chapter. Even on this subset of enactments, the most common outcome for majority parties on their priority items is failure (44 percent), with successes on which the majority got only some of what it wanted (38 percent) outpacing those on which it got most of what it set out to achieve (18 percent). The data also show that bipartisan enactments (73 percent) are still more common than partisan enactments (27 percent). There is slight evidence of an uptick in partisan enactments over time among this subset of priorities, but the trend is not statistically significant.[58]

The limited number of uncompromising partisan victories across our analyses underscores our most salient finding: despite rising party polarization and increased party strength in both the House and the Senate, congressional majorities still rarely succeed in legislating partisan policy change over sustained opposition. In fact, they rarely do so even when they have unified party control. Instead, when parties succeed in enacting their agenda priorities, they usually have the support of a majority of the opposing party in at least one chamber of Congress and the endorsement of at least one of the opposing party's top leaders. The most likely outcome for majority parties across both unified and divided government is failure, with no improvement in outcomes over time. Consequently, congressional majority parties have few partisan lawmaking accomplishments to tout on the campaign trail and can rarely claim to have decisively moved public policy is a partisan direction.

First-Person Perspectives on Persistent Bipartisanship

The data are clear that most legislation, including the vast bulk of majority party agenda priorities, continues to be enacted with bipartisan support, even in the party-polarized contemporary Congress. Our interviews with members of Congress and staff offer some perspective on the reasons majority parties still reach out for bipartisan support, as well as on when and why minority parties cooperate with the majority party to obtain legislative results.

Bipartisanship as a Condition for Success

Most important, majority parties seek minority party support for legislation because doing so makes legislative success much more likely. A staffer explained: "A bill still has a lot greater chance to make it into law if it's bipartisan. . . . So that gives you an incentive to find bipartisanship if you are actually trying to do something."[59] "You want to overcome friction if you can," said a former committee chair. When he wanted to advance a bill, he continued, "My first thought is what the other side might possibly think" of the proposal.[60] Likewise, "if someone comes to me with a legislative idea, I'll ask them if there's any interest on the other side. If they don't know, then I'll say, 'Go ask them.'"[61]

Not only does reducing "friction" make it easier to pass legislation in one chamber, bills with bipartisan support are more attractive to the other chamber: "Generally speaking, it's well understood that if you get a big vote on a bill coming out of the House, you make it hard for the Senate to ignore you. A bill that comes out of the House on a party-line vote is one that's likely to be dead on arrival in the Senate."[62] "DC is such a place of no," summed up another staffer. "Getting anything done is hard, but it's even harder on a partisan basis."[63]

Interviewees repeatedly cited supermajority procedures in the Senate as a powerful constraint on partisan lawmaking. "Unless you have sixty-votes in the Senate, or you can use reconciliation, you can't get 100 percent [of what you want]," said one House staffer. "That's true under unified government and divided government. If you don't have sixty votes, you need bipartisanship."[64] The sixty-vote Senate "makes you shoot for compromise," said another.[65] "We *have* to look ahead," explained a House staffer. "If it is a big picture piece—a major item—then you have to think about where the Senate is going to be, where the White House is going to be. . . . You can't ever think about those big picture items in a vacuum of just the House, because it's not just the House."[66] Looking toward the challenges of getting a bill through the whole legislative process, another staffer said, "[Leaders] try to broker agreement and work the arbitrage between what you want to do and what you can do. The math is . . . usually sixty votes in the Senate."[67]

For many we spoke with, bipartisanship is simply what it takes to make a law, even today. A longtime House committee staffer explained:

> I see bills falling into three buckets: (1) ideas that have bipartisan support worked out between individual members that would be good candidates for the suspension calendar; (2) larger items that will need to be worked out at the leadership level, still on a bipartisan basis, to get through the Senate; and (3) must-pass bills that will be negotiated by the "four corners," meaning top party leaders in both chambers where any one of these players has a veto.[68]

Asked about bills that the majority party intends to pass on party-line votes, he replied, "It's not a large enough category to constitute a bucket."[69] Describing his work in lobbying, a former staffer said, "I tell my clients all the time—you have to design everything for unanimous consent if you want to actually pass it."[70] Although our data show that majority parties sometimes do succeed in enacting legislation by steamrolling the minority party, Hill insiders know that even in the party-polarized Congress and even under conditions of unified party control, party-line legislative enactments are far from routine.

Our interview subjects offered divergent perspectives on whether the House majority party should stake out a hard-line bargaining position in advance of dealing with the Senate by passing partisan bills initially. Several argued that although this tactic might sound like a good idea, it could endanger a bill's prospects:

The view is, particularly in the House, that you should start everything with just the majority and compromise with the Senate later to bring about bipartisanship. [But] my observation is that that rarely works unless you absolutely *have* to do the thing you are working on—debt ceiling or something. Usually what happens as a result of that tactic is a bare-minimum, status quo extension.[71]

If a majority party is going to need bipartisan support for legislation eventually, our interviewees noted, it can be risky to wait too late. "If you need to go across the aisle, you can't just drop in on them only when you need them," said a veteran member. "They'll say, 'Where were you when I wanted to talk with you? But now you need me?' These are human relationships."[72] Along similar lines, a longtime staffer remarked, "You can't choose bipartisanship halfway through the process, just like you can't choose sobriety after five martinis!"[73]

On the other hand, House committee and party leaders do not necessarily find it easy to induce rank-and-file members to go along with a bipartisan approach in anticipation of needing minority party support later in the legislative process. A leadership staffer explained:

I seem to notice that the House leadership is most responsive to their rank-and-file members. They are not as interested in the Senate, and they aren't as interested in the White House. They are responsive to their core constituency: rank-and-file members of the Republican conference. And this is going to sound bad, like they are a bunch of guys running around in overalls with pitchforks, but [rank-and-file House members'] level of sophistication compared with Republican senators' is not exactly an apples-to-apples comparison. . . . So the House designs perfect and the Senate has to design doable.[74]

In other words, House leaders often find that they cannot easily get rank-and-file members to come to terms with the compromise that will be necessary for legislative enactment.

As is evident from the comments above, rank-and-file members' "level of sophistication" in that regard can be a source of frustration for leaders, who may have to do a lot of coaxing and member management to bring about acceptance of the doable. Along similar lines, another staffer described the process: "Generally, the House's position with the Senate was to pass the toughest bill possible, and we'll talk to you later. . . . We were generally very reluctant to shortchange ourselves when you know the Senate is probably going to cut down whatever we passed anyway."[75]

Passing a partisan bill initially can also serve as a way to get majority party members to accept a compromise at the end. As a leadership staffer explained,

> There's different ways to help members save face so they can eat the compromise at the end. One way is to pass the craziest thing possible and send it to the Senate. Then you go to your counterparts in the Senate . . . and you ask them to please put the bill on the floor so it can get destroyed, so they can have a failed cloture vote and declare it dead. Then you can go back to your members and try to convince them to do something else.[76]

Another House staffer argued for an intermediate approach: "You just get the basics of the package somewhere in the middle so it can get through the Senate and pass. But you also want to have things to trade off with them, because they are always going to come back and say, 'Well, this is all we can do.'"[77] Clearly, leaders must weigh many strategic considerations as they seek to marshal support for a legislative enactment. But in the end they understand that success will almost always require bipartisanship.

Minority Party Responses to Bipartisan Outreach

Our interviewees were clear that a majority party's bipartisan outreach offers no guarantee that the minority party will be eager to negotiate. As is clear from the preceding, minority party members may not jump at the chance to participate if they felt excluded from discussions earlier in the legislative process. "I thought that the other side being willing to play ball was the real driver of whether or not we could build bipartisanship," said one longtime committee staffer. "The minority can either engage with you or simply choose not to."[78]

The minority party's willingness to engage depends on both policy and political considerations. Obviously, bipartisanship may not be possible if the two parties share no agreement on the nature of the problem being addressed. Describing the lack of bipartisan cooperation on climate change legislation, a former staffer recalled, "Joe Barton [R-TX] said to [Henry] Waxman [D-CA], 'Why would I work with you on something that I don't believe is real?'"[79] There's simply "not a ton of overlap between what the parties want" in policy terms.[80] When there is no genuine agreement on what a piece of legislation should accomplish, bipartisanship can just result in bad policy. Legislation "is always bipartisan, but sometimes that means you get an incomprehensible bill that doesn't accomplish anything," said a veteran staffer. "Knowing when it's worthwhile to move forward and cut a deal is a mark of skill."[81]

Our interviewees also pointed to electoral considerations as affecting minority party members' willingness to negotiate. Asked when bipartisanship is possible, a former leadership staffer explained, "An important factor is the need to maintain the party's electoral position. . . . That's the precondition for reaching across the aisle or taking any action on these kinds of items today."[82] On policy issues that do not define the parties, such as No Child Left Behind or the highway bill, "acting on bipartisanship works and is doable if it doesn't undercut the party's electoral position."[83] But on more salient, party-defining issues, bipartisanship will primarily happen in crisis situations: "With issues like the debt ceiling or the fiscal cliff, the crisis supersedes partisanship. . . . [In such circumstances] it reflects bad on everyone, on both parties, not to act."[84]

Our qualitative and quantitative data reinforce the point that lawmaking rarely happens without significant minority party buy-in. But minority party participation and engagement cannot be taken for granted, even if the majority party initiates a quest for bipartisan agreement. Successful bipartisanship depends on human relationships, some level of policy agreement, and compatible political incentives.

Majority Party Disunity as a Driver of Bipartisanship

Our interviewees also pointed to factionalism in the majority party as yet another factor that drives bipartisan outreach. Asked about looping in the minority party at the outset of a legislative drive rather than later on, a staffer explained: "It depends a lot on the circumstances. If you don't have your majority together to start with then it [becomes] a bipartisan approach by necessity."[85] "Dysfunction in the majority makes the minority relevant," said another.[86] "If you can't get votes from across the aisle, you're paralyzed if your caucus is divided."[87]

For their part, minority party members recognize that majority party disunity gives them leverage. "At this point—today—we're relevant because they are such a fractured party," explained a minority party staffer. "We absolutely *should not* have any power. We should be wallowing in self-pity after the last election. But on these big items they need our votes."[88] By the same logic, a minority party can extract concessions from a divided majority party by holding its ranks intact in negotiations: "Right now we can prevent things from happening if we're unified. If we can get all 184 of our people together on something we have a lot of leverage because they cannot do it alone."[89]

Just as majority party factionalism can make bipartisan outreach necessary, bipartisan outreach can further endanger majority party unity. In engaging in negotiations with the opposing party, "leaders have to spend a lot of time worrying about keeping their members together."[90] Hard-liners within the majority party may reach a breaking point where they simply refuse to go along with their leaders' efforts to put together a bipartisan coalition. Consequently, party negotiators accept that "You're just going to lose some of those people. We'd just factor that in. You aren't going to cut a deal that [Sen.] Ted Cruz [R-TX] supports that also has Democrats on it."[91]

Because bipartisan outreach can cause majority party members of a legislative coalition to peel off, legislation may need to be highly bipartisan to pass at all. Coalition leaders find it challenging to identify a legislative proposal that will simultaneously please partisan extremists and find support across the aisle:

> When you're trying to get to sixty votes in the Senate you have to worry about losing the right flank. . . . In the Senate we need Democrats, but as soon as you get something the Democrats will vote for you lose some Republicans. Ultimately, you go into the process knowing it's going to have to be an 80–20 vote or something close to that to pass.[92]

Through these dynamics, heterogeneity within the majority party can induce bipartisanship. In other words, majority parties need bipartisanship not only to navigate a bicameral legislature with veto points controlled by the opposing party. They also need bipartisanship because their own hard-line rank-and-file members may decide that the necessary concessions are a bridge too far.

Party Polarization as a Driver of Bipartisanship

Finally, our interviewees point to party polarization itself as driving bipartisanship on legislation. Paradoxically, increased unity within the party caucuses may make it necessary to seek even *broader* bipartisanship. Today a majority party may find it cannot just pick off individual moderates in the minority party to get enough votes to pass a bill. With a unified minority party holding its ranks together in opposition to majority party proposals, negotiations can feature a most-or-nothing prospect for bringing along minority party lawmakers. "It's hard to calibrate the difference between what will get you eight Democrats or thirty Democrats," one staffer told us. "It's hard to figure out. Members tend to go in groups."[93]

Given the marked decline in the size of centrist blocs in both parties, majority party leaders may not be able to identify minority party moderates willing to buck their party leaders. Instead, they may have to go directly to minority party leaders for votes. "It's really hard to pick off individual members on any bill that has a partisan cast," explained a longtime staffer. "If the bill is seen as having a partisan inflection, you're likely to need to work with minority party leaders or ranking members in order to broaden support."[94] Rather than coalition leaders' reaching out to individual members of the minority party, "more party-to-party negotiations are being done at the leadership level."[95] The upshot is that party polarization itself may result in big, bipartisan coalitions on successful legislation. If bipartisanship is necessary, a majority party seeking minority party votes may need to win over the bulk of the whole minority party to get any of them.

Lawmaking as a Process of Bipartisan Accommodation

Even amid today's party polarization, Congress continues to pass laws with broad bipartisan support. Despite increased party organizational strength inside Congress, the findings presented here are unambiguous: contemporary majority parties do not succeed in enacting partisan laws or their programmatic agendas at rates any higher than the less party-polarized Congresses of the 1970s and 1980s.

Our interviews show that these basic empirical facts are well understood on Capitol Hill. Majority party leaders understand that bipartisanship will almost always be necessary to overcome veto players, especially the high hurdle of the Senate cloture requirement. Majority party leaders also see bipartisanship as necessary owing to heterogeneity within their own party's ranks on important issues. Holdouts in their own party can force them into bipartisan negotiations. Ironically, party polarization itself may induce high levels of bipartisanship on successful legislation, as majority parties confront cohesive minority parties where the accommodation necessary to bring along a few minority party votes will bring along most of them.

These findings have important implications for our understanding of majority party capacity in Congress. Despite many changes in the legislative process that have strengthened parties and leaders, there is simply not appreciably more partisan *lawmaking*. When Congress gets down to the brass tacks of enacting laws, it still typically needs to cultivate bipartisan support. House majority parties may pass bills on party-line votes, but these bills are unlikely to pass both chambers or earn a presidential signature. Many more laws look like the 21st Century Cures Act[96] than the Affordable Care Act.

The persistence of bipartisanship in lawmaking calls into question the majority party's ability to campaign on its record of partisan achievement. Scholars argue that wavering legislators may be induced to support their parties because the outcome—a partisan policymaking success—will give the party as a whole something to run on in the next election (Cox and Mc-Cubbins 2005; Koger and Lebo 2017). Parties simply do not have many such successes to claim. Legislative votes that distinguish the parties abound, but these votes are rarely the enactment of laws. Instead, they are often messaging efforts that have no effect on public policy (Lee 2016).

On the occasions when majority parties do succeed in lawmaking, they rarely do so over the opposition of the minority party. Most lawmaking accomplishments are *bipartisan*, allowing both parties to claim credit (and shoulder blame). Clear partisan successes enacted over strong minority party opposition are exceedingly rare—occurring on just 4.5 percent of the agenda items we analyzed. Even in periods of strong parties, legislative enactments continue to draw strong bipartisan support and rarely skew public policy toward the majority party's preferences.

In policy terms, these bipartisan enactments of recent decades are neither unimportant nor merely routine. As shown here, majority agenda items that passed with bipartisan support encompass a broader range of separate policy topics than those enacted by party-line votes. Comparing the specific policies passed by partisan and bipartisan coalitions, it is hard to contend that partisan laws are more consequential in policy terms than bipartisan laws. Rather, both bipartisan and partisan enactments include both landmark and relatively unimportant legislation.

The pervasive extent of bipartisanship in lawmaking raises questions about party accountability more broadly within the American system of separated powers and checks and balances. As we discussed in chapter 1, congressional party strength today is arguably at its highest point in over a century, leaders have been empowered, and committees have been eclipsed. Party reformers of the past would have welcomed these developments, hoping that more programmatic and cohesive parties would improve democratic accountability and responsiveness in our otherwise fractured political system.

However, our results indicate that even when legislative parties are at their strongest, programmatic partisan lawmaking is still rare in American politics. Even today, congressional majority parties struggle to steer the ship of state and move public policy decidedly in one direction or the other. Laws still typically reflect bipartisan compromises, muddling party responsibility for public policy outcomes and making it difficult for voters to accurately determine who deserves the credit (or blame). Increases in party polarization and party organization have not solved or even appreciably mitigated the problems that concerned advocates of party reform seventy years ago. Where lawmaking is concerned, strong parties have not vanquished the compromise-inducing structure of the US political system.

THREE

Why Do Majority Parties Fail?

It will be a difficult task but failure is not an option.

—Sen. Lindsey Graham (R-SC, 2003–) on the Republican drive to repeal and replace Obamacare[1]

Legislative failure not only is an option for majority parties in Congress, it is exceedingly common. As shown in chapter 2, majority parties failed to enact legislation on nearly half their stated agenda priorities from 1985 to 2018. In this chapter we ask two questions: Where and how do majority parties fall short in their legislative ambitions? and Have patterns in majority party failure shifted over time?

Historically, scholars saw congressional parties' lack of internal discipline—rather than constitutional and procedural constraints on majority rule—as the primary obstacle to executing a party program (Fiorina 1980; Schattschneider 1942). Twentieth-century majority parties often struggled to enact their legislative priorities not because the minority blocked their efforts, but because of their own deep internal divisions (Polsby 2004; Sundquist 1968). In contrast, a prominent diagnosis of contemporary American political dysfunction describes "parliamentary-style parties" embedded in a "governing system that, unlike a parliamentary democracy, makes it extremely difficult for majorities to act" (Mann and Ornstein 2012, xxiii). Indeed, both parties have become far more ideologically coherent (McCarty, Poole, and Rosenthal 2016; McCarty 2019), and data on roll-call voting behavior certainly suggest that contemporary legislative parties are far less factionalized than those of the mid-twentieth century (see Barber and McCarty 2015; Brady, Cooper, and Hurley 1979; Lee 2015; Mayhew 1974).

In a Congress where parties maintain much more cohesive ranks, the political system's numerous obstacles to majority rule should instead emerge as the primary source of majority party frustration. Majority parties in the twenty-first-century Congress have faced more veto points controlled by the opposing party than most majority parties of the twentieth century. Divided government has become much more prevalent over the most recent four decades (75 percent of the time from 1980 to 2020) than in the preceding four decades (40 percent of the time from 1940 to 1980). The filibuster almost always serves as an opposition-party-controlled veto point,[2] and the filibuster has become much more pervasive in Senate procedure (Smith 2014; Sinclair 2016), so that observers now regularly refer to the "sixty-vote Senate" (Koger 2010; Wawro 2011). Likewise, split party control of the House and Senate characterized seven Congresses from 1980 to 2020, whereas this configuration did not appear in the four decades before 1980.

We thus seek to get a better understanding of whether contemporary congressional majority parties fail to pass their agendas because they are blocked by the opposing party or because of insufficient intraparty agreement. Scholars have not generally tried to sort out the relative importance of intraparty dissent and opposition-party-controlled veto points as sources of frustration for congressional majority parties. There is a large body of work on whether presidents succeed in getting Congress to pass their agendas (see, e.g., Bond and Fleisher 1990; Canes-Wrone and De Marchi 2002; Edwards 1990; Mayhew 2011). There is also a substantial literature on the determinants of overall congressional productivity (Adler and Wilkerson 2012; Binder 2003; Mayhew 2005). But scholars have given little attention to when and how congressional majorities fail to execute their policy agendas or whether the etiology of majority party failure has changed over time.

Surprisingly, we find little evidence that veto points controlled by the opposing party have become a greater problem for congressional majority parties. Of course, today's majority parties do regularly fail when they cannot overcome the opposing party's use of veto points such as the Senate filibuster or a president of the opposing party. But opposing party veto players are not a more pervasive cause of majority party failure in the contemporary Congress than they were during the 1980s and 1990s. Despite extraordinary levels of party polarization in roll-call voting, we do not find evidence that opposition party veto players block a larger share of the majority party's initiatives over time. Opposition party veto points have been a roughly constant source of frustration for majority parties over the past thirty-five years.

Instead, we find that today's majority parties continue to struggle with intraparty coalition building. No doubt contemporary congressional majority parties put up impressive statistics in terms of overall roll-call voting cohesion (see figs. 1.2 and 1.3). Nevertheless, it is evident from our analyses that majority parties often fall short of internal consensus when it really counts for policymaking. Although majority parties do not frequently lose in public on the chamber floor, they regularly fail to enact agenda items because they do not coalesce around specific legislation early in the legislative process. In particular, we find that majority parties often lack sufficient intraparty agreement to get their agenda priorities reported from committee. It is also not unusual for the majority party to decline to schedule agenda items for floor consideration owing to internal dissent. Our interviews offer insight into the sources of intraparty conflict that stand in the way of majority party agenda success.

Taken together, we find more continuity than change in the etiology of majority party failure over the period 1985–2018. Majority parties struggle with both intraparty disagreement and opposing party veto points, in roughly equal measure both overall and across time.

Data and Coding

To gauge the incidence of majority party legislative failure, we draw on our dataset of the legislative priorities that congressional majority parties sought to enact in each Congress, 1985–2018 (the 99th–115th Congresses). We then identify all the agenda priorities on which the majority party failed to enact *any* legislation ($n = 127$; see appendix table A.2). Such items are classed as majority party agenda failures. This is a conservative coding scheme in that we do not classify majority parties as failing on an agenda item if they succeed in passing any legislation at all, even if it falls far short of their ambitions.

Figure 3.1 shows the overall descriptive data on the number of majority party agenda items as well as the overall failure rate for each Congress in the study. As is evident, recent congressional majority parties have failed to legislate on a high percentage of their agenda priorities.[3] This is so even though their agendas are not longer or in any obvious way more ambitious in policy scope than those advanced in earlier Congresses. Across the whole period, Republicans failed on a slightly higher share of their agenda items (50 percent) than Democrats (46 percent), though this difference is not statistically significant.[4]

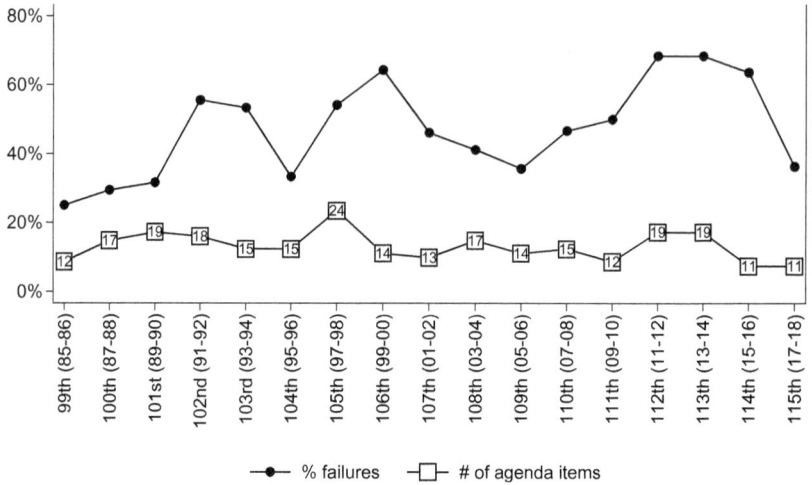

Figure 3.1. Majority party agenda size and failure rate, 99th–115th Congresses

For each case of majority party agenda failure, we then researched the legislative history of the initiative to ascertain when and where the legislative drive came to a halt.[5] Each failure was coded into one of the following six categories:

1. Senate's sixty-vote threshold. The bill is actively filibustered or the majority party cannot bring it up for consideration because they do not have sixty votes to break a filibuster.
2. Presidential veto. Either the bill is vetoed or the president's veto threat appeared to stop action.
3. One chamber passes a bill but the other does not (for reasons other than a filibuster).
4. No formal action occurs. A bill might be unveiled or introduced, but it is not reported by a committee in either chamber.
5. Committees in one or both chambers report a bill, but no floor action occurs.
6. The House and Senate pass different bills but cannot reconcile the differences.

We then group the cases of majority party agenda failure under two broad headings: problems with opposition-party-controlled *veto players* and *intraparty disagreement*. For most cases this is a straightforward exercise as laid out in table 3.1. Bills that die because of a presidential veto or threatened veto (#2) in conditions of divided government are coded as failing

Table 3.1 Classification of majority party agenda failures

Veto player problems	Intraparty disagreement
Senate's sixty-vote threshold (if the minority party opposition kept the Senate from sixty votes) (#1)	Senate's sixty-vote threshold (if majority party disunity kept the Senate from sixty votes) (#1)
Presidential veto (#2)	No formal action (with exceptions) (#4)
Only one chamber passes (divided chambers) (#3)	Committee action, but no floor (with exceptions) (#5)
House and Senate cannot reconcile bills (divided chambers) (#6)	Only one chamber passes (unified chambers) (#3)
	House and Senate cannot reconcile differences (unified chambers) (#6)

because of an opposition party veto player.[6] When bills fail because the second chamber does not act for reasons other than the Senate's sixty-vote threshold (#3), the failure is generally classified as a veto player problem if the two chambers are controlled by different parties but as a matter of intraparty disagreement if the same party controls both chambers. In other words, our expectation is that congressional majority parties should be able to put forward chamber majorities on their priority legislation. When majority parties fail not because of a Senate filibuster but because they cannot get to a House or Senate majority, our coding classifies this as a problem of intraparty disagreement.

When committees do not report a bill on an agenda priority (#4) or when reported priority bills are not scheduled for floor action (#5), we code these as failures stemming from intraparty disagreement unless it is clear from the reporting that party or committee leaders halted action on the bill because they anticipated problems with an opposing party veto player (e.g., filibuster; majority party in the other chamber will not take up the bill). News coverage finds a number of such cases in our data.[7] When the House and Senate cannot reconcile differences on their separate chamber-passed bills (#6), we code this as a veto player problem when different parties control the two chambers but as stemming from intraparty disagreement when the same party controls both House and Senate.

Cases where bills failed because of the Senate sixty-vote threshold (#1) required some extra attention. This classification includes both bills that were actively filibustered and those for which it is clear from news reporting that the majority abandoned an agenda item because it anticipated difficulties securing sixty votes for cloture. We carefully evaluated the evidence in these cases, because majority parties have an incentive to blame their failures on the minority party and the filibuster even when the majority party itself was not unified on a legislative proposal. We sought to distinguish between cases in which the Senate failed to reach a sixty-vote threshold because of minority party opposition (the majority party put up a chamber majority of votes, but the minority lined up in opposition), and those cases in which the Senate majority party was not even able to muster a chamber majority because of internal disagreement. The former cases are coded here as due to veto player problems, and the latter as instances of failure due to intraparty disagreement.

Note that these codes should not be read as designating the ultimate *causes* of legislative failure. We are coding where legislative drives came to a halt in the congressional process—as in the point at which the initiative ended. In many cases it is quite possible that had bills proceeded further they would have been killed at some later point. For example, the Senate minority party often uses the filibuster to stop bills that would otherwise result in a presidential veto. Agenda items that do not get reported from committee might never have been scheduled for floor action even had the committee reported a bill. Likewise, a bill that was never taken up on the House floor might have later provoked a filibuster in the Senate if it had passed the House. If it is clear from the reporting on a bill that the majority party declined to move forward because it anticipated problems with veto players later in the process, our coding scheme notes that. But we do not attempt to gauge whether a bill would have succeeded "but for" any particular legislative obstacle. In short, our coding scheme *reflects only the proximate locations of legislative demise*.

Where Do Majority Parties Fall Short?

Figure 3.2 displays the frequency of each outcome in our coding scheme. As shown here, the Senate's sixty-vote threshold is one of the most common sources of majority party frustration. This obstacle halted 27 percent ($n = 34$) of all the cases of majority party agenda failure in our dataset. Among these failures were the efforts of Republicans to restrict abortion in the 114th (2015–16) and the 109th (2005–6) Congresses; of Democrats to raise the minimum wage in the 113th Congress (2013–14); of Democrats to pass a stimulus package in the 112th Congress (2011–12); of Democrats to pass immigration reform in the 110th Congress (2007–8); of Republicans to limit medical malpractice liability in the 108th Congress (2003–4); of

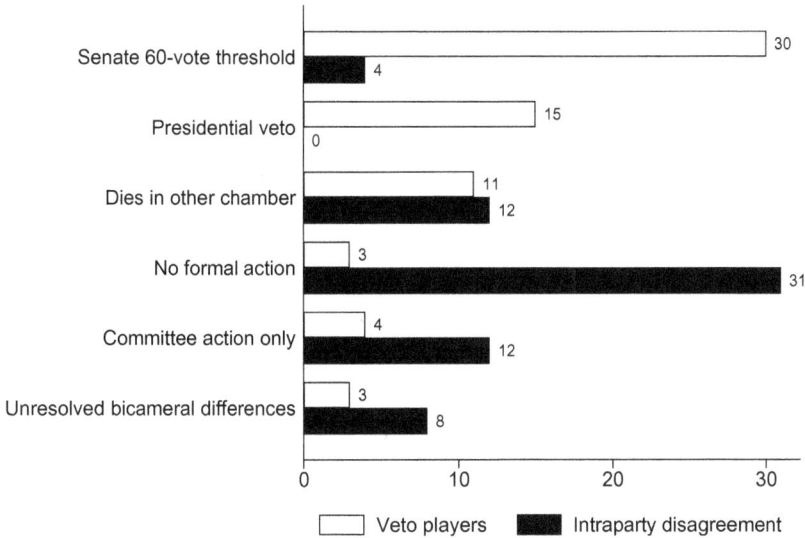

Figure 3.2. Where congressional majority party agenda items
fail in the legislative process, 1985–2018 (n = 127)
Note: The figure displays the frequency with which majority party agenda items failed at each
point in the legislative process. These categories are then grouped by whether the failures largely
entailed opposition-party-controlled veto points or disagreement within the majority party.

Republicans to pass a prescription drug bill in the 107th Congress (2001–2); and of Republicans to limit the allowable amount of publicly held debt in the 106th Congress (1999–2000). The list could be extended, since every Congress in the study except two (the 99th [1985–86], and the 115th [2017–18]) featured at least one majority party agenda item blocked by Senate filibuster.

Another 27 percent of cases (n = 34) failed when the majority party simply took no formal action on an agenda priority. The legislation died in committee, meaning that the majority party did not secure even a favorable committee report on the issue. The Republican effort at tax reform in the 113th Congress (2013–14), for example, takes this form. Party leaders flagged tax reform as a top priority. Ways and Means chair Rep. Dave Camp (R-MI) then worked throughout the Congress and eventually unveiled a 979-page bill that was never reported from committee because it lacked the support of rank-and-file Republicans and party leaders worried about opening up a contentious issue involving complex trade-offs in the lead-up to the 2014 midterms.[8] Other majority party agenda failures in this category include Democrats' never developing measures to encourage renewable energy in the 112th Congress (2011–12) or making an effort to roll back Bush-era regulations in the 111th Congress (2009–10). For their part, Republicans never developed proposals to reduce the costs of entitlements in the 112th Congress (2011–12) and could not coalesce on a Social Security overhaul in the 109th (2005–6) or 108th (2003–4) Congress or move forward on a Medicare reform proposal in the 106th Congress (1999–2000), despite having identified each as a party priority.

These cases of majority party failure do not bear much resemblance to the "death by committee" that liberal Democrats complained about when so many committees in Congress were chaired by conservative southern Democrats (Burns 1963; Polsby 2004; Zelizer 2004). Such cases in the post-1985 era do not involve committee chairs' deliberately blocking their party's priorities on the historical model of Rules Committee chair Howard W. Smith (D-VA, 1955–67). Instead, they generally reflect circumstances in which committee leaders were unable to write or identify a specific bill that could rally sufficient intraparty support, even though party leaders had designated the issue as a priority at the start of the Congress.

The second chamber's refusal or inability to act on a bill for reasons other than a filibuster is the third most common location of majority party agenda failure (18 percent of failures, $n = 23$). About half of these cases ($n = 11$) occurred in Congresses where different parties controlled the House and Senate and, not surprisingly, differed on priority legislation. However, in the other half of these cases ($n = 12$) the same party controlled both House and Senate yet did not successfully coordinate on companion legislation. Most prominently, Senate Republicans in the 115th Congress (2017–18) were unable to pass a bill to repeal and replace Obamacare after House Republicans had finally mustered their majority to do so, even though Senate Republicans needed to garner only a simple majority to pass their budget reconciliation vehicle. Likewise, two Senate Republicans killed a Republican Party priority in 2018 by voting against a House-passed bill (H.R. 3) cutting previously approved domestic spending by $15 billion.[9] The 115th Senate also declined to move forward in committee on House-passed priority bills to reform the agency rule-making process (H.R. 5) and to end coverage of abortion in insurance policies sold on Obamacare exchanges (H.R. 7). In the 104th Congress (1995–96), House Republicans could not get broad enough support among Senate Republicans to advance a bill to compensate landowners for regulations reducing property values.[10] In the 108th Congress (2003–4), Senate Republicans opted not to proceed with the House's estate tax repeal (H.R. 8) because of intraparty disagreement about whether to hold down the cost of the repeal by retaining some taxes on the very highest-value estates.[11]

Failure to advance committee-reported bills to the floor is the fourth most prevalent site of majority party legislative defeat (13 percent of failures, $n = 16$). This was the fate of patent reform efforts in the 114th Congress (2015–16) as Republicans disagreed among themselves about how proposed legislation would affect some patent holders.[12] Similarly, House Republicans in the 112th Congress (2011–12) declined to advance committee-reported legislation replacing No Child Left Behind (H.R. 3990), in part owing to disagreements between Republicans who wanted to use standardized tests to hold teachers accountable for student learning outcomes and conservatives who saw no role for the federal government in local education.[13] Generally, leaders decline to schedule committee-passed agenda priorities for floor consideration when they anticipate problems with passage. When we find evidence that the concern is an anticipated filibuster or other veto player problem, we code the case as such. But many of these bills are proposals that remained controversial within the majority party, despite the progress on the issue made in committee.

Threatened or actual presidential vetoes constitute the fifth most common source of frustration for majority parties (12 percent of failures, $n = 15$). Vetoes doomed the Republican repeal of the Affordable Care Act and the Keystone XL pipeline approval in the 114th Congress (2015–16); the Democrats' efforts to expand the State Children's Health Insurance Program and to fund stem cell research in the 110th Congress (2007–8); Republicans' bankruptcy reform bill in the 106th Congress (1999–2000); Democrats' enterprise zones legislation in the 102nd Congress (1991–92); and others.

There are no cases in our dataset where a majority party agenda item failed in unified government because of a presidential veto (or veto threat). We thus code all the cases in this category as majority parties' failing because they encounter veto points controlled by the opposing party. This is a conservative coding, inasmuch as parties may sometimes deliberately design veto bait to embarrass opposing party presidents (Groseclose and McCarty 2001). It is likely easier for a party to agree on a messaging vehicle that is sure to be vetoed than to hammer out legislation that stands a real chance of enactment, as illustrated by the ease with which Republicans passed legislation repealing the Affordable Care Act under President Obama in 2015 (H.R. 3762) and the difficulty they faced in doing so in 2017 when President Trump would have signed the repeal into law (Lee 2018).

Given the sequential nature of the legislative process, these data probably understate the importance of the presidential veto as an obstacle to congressional majority parties. After all, divided party control of govern-ment is the normal state of affairs during the period. Yet vetoes and veto threats account for only 12 percent of majority party agenda failures. These data must be interpreted in light of the winnowing involved in the legisla-tive process, inasmuch as many bills that fail at earlier points in the legisla-tive process would have been vetoed had they progressed further. In divided government, the president's party will often filibuster to protect presidents of their party from having to use the veto to stop legislation. As a result, many agenda priorities defeated at the Senate's sixty-vote threshold would have drawn a veto had they cleared the Senate.[14] Even so, it is clear from these data that presidential vetoes have only rarely been the proximate cause of legislative death for majority party agendas in the post-1985 era.

Unresolved bicameral differences were the least common location of majority party agenda failure. Consistent with Sinclair (2016, 261), we find that it is relatively unusual for a measure to pass both House and Senate yet fail because the two chambers could not reconcile their differences ($n = 11$; 9 percent of failures). Most of these cases (8/11) occurred when the same party controlled both House and Senate.[15] In the 101st Congress, for exam-ple, House and Senate Democrats were unable to work out their disagree-ments on different campaign finance bills.[16] In the 114th Congress, House conferees were unwilling to make the concessions necessary to produce a conference report on energy infrastructure security that could pass the Sen-ate.[17] The only cases in which chambers controlled by different parties could not achieve bicameral resolution on their different chamber-passed bills were in the 107th Congress, when the House and Senate passed very dif-ferent partisan patients' bill of rights proposals and the Democratic Party–controlled Senate did not act on a Republican energy bill.

Figure 3.2 groups these different categories of majority party agenda fail-ure by whether they primarily involved problems associated with intraparty disagreement or with veto points controlled by the opposing party. In the aggregate, the two sources of difficulty contribute equally to majority party agenda failure during the period. Obstacles associated with opposition-party-controlled veto points constituted 47 percent ($n = 60$) of the failed agenda items, while challenges associated with intraparty disagreement characterized 53 percent ($n = 67$). It is not surprising in this partisan era that majority parties regularly fail to enact their agendas because the opposing party blocks their efforts. However, these findings show that majority parties in the contemporary Congress also regularly fail on their agenda priorities when they cannot reach the necessary consensus within their own ranks.

Failure under Different Configurations of Party Control

As we discussed in chapter 2, congressional majority parties fail on their agendas overall at surprisingly similar rates across unified and divided government. The failure rate differs only modestly between divided (49 percent) and unified (43 percent) government.[18] Even so, majority parties tend to fail in different *ways* depending on their control of national government.

The veto players that majority parties encounter differ depending on the configuration of party control. Figure 3.3 displays the frequencies of different categories of legislative failures under different configurations of party control. As is evident here, the Senate's sixty-vote threshold is a much bigger impediment to majority parties in unified government than in divided government. Fully 33 percent of failed agenda items in unified government were blocked when the majority party could not overcome the Senate's sixty-vote requirement for cloture. Meanwhile, the Senate filibuster accounts for only about a quarter of majority party failures under conditions of divided government.[19] Not surprisingly, the presidential veto is a much greater obstacle when there is divided party control. Presidential vetoes and veto threats accounted for 15 percent of agenda failures under divided government but for none under unified government.[20]

Divided party control of the House and Senate also affects patterns in majority party failure. Generally, a second chamber controlled by the opposing party will often decline to act on agenda items. In the four Congresses with divided party control of the House and Senate, second chamber inaction (not stemming from the Senate's sixty-vote threshold) accounts for 31 percent of majority party agenda failures, compared with only 13 percent of failures in Congresses where the same party controlled both House and Senate.[21] Likewise, in Congresses with divided control of House and Senate, it was rare for majority parties to fail on an agenda item by not scheduling a committee-reported bill for floor consideration, whereas not advancing committee reports to the floor was fairly common in other Congresses.[22]

The incidence of majority parties' failing to advance a bill in committee—the type of majority party failure most likely to stem from intraparty divisions—does not vary in any notable way across different configurations of party control. Committee inaction is one of the most common ways majority parties fail on their agenda items in every Congress we studied. It is the most frequent location of agenda failure under divided government and the second most frequent location under unified government, with almost no difference between unified and divided government.[23] In short, majority

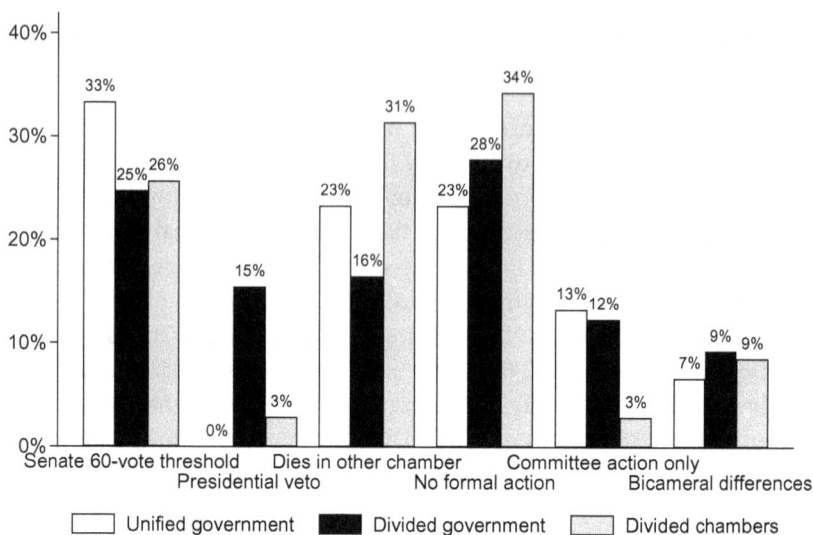

Figure 3.3. Where majority party agenda items fail in the legislative
process, by party control, 1985–2018 ($n = 127$)

parties regularly struggle to coalesce around a specific bill and advance it to
the floor. Intraparty consensus building in the early stages of the legislative
process remains a challenge, even in the contemporary Congress where parties are more ideologically homogeneous and committee chairs are far more
accountable to their parties than during the conservative coalition era when
chairs served based solely on seniority.

Figure 3.4 groups the categories of majority party failure under summary
headings denoting whether the obstacle was primarily a matter of being
blocked by veto players or a lack of intraparty consensus. Viewed in summary, the data show that, as expected, majority parties struggle more with
veto players when power is divided between the parties. Nevertheless, veto
points present challenges for majority parties in unified government as well.
Under conditions of divided government or divided chambers, opposition-
party-controlled veto players account for 52 percent and 57 percent of majority party failures, compared with 33 percent of failures under unified
government. The difference between unified and divided government is
statistically significant,[24] but the difference between divided chambers and
unified control of the chambers is not.[25]

At the same time, intraparty disagreement remains a significant challenge
for majority parties regardless of party control, even though it accounts for a

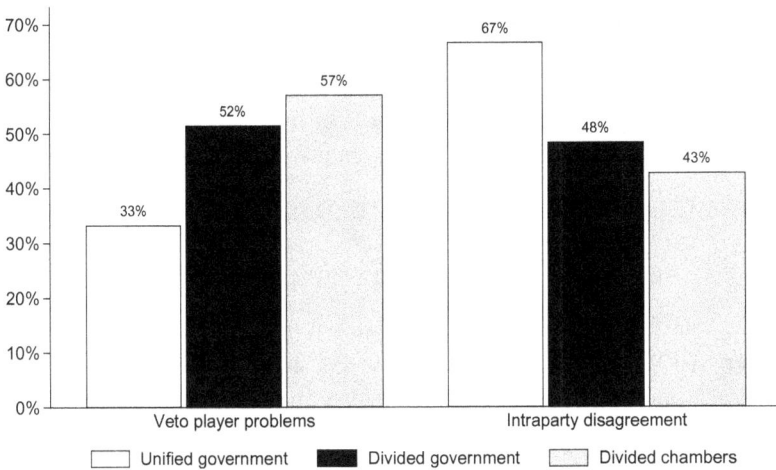

Figure 3.4. Veto players and intraparty dissent in majority party agenda failure, by party control

larger share of majority party failures under unified government. Specifically, intraparty disagreement accounts for 67 percent of majority party failures under unified government and 48 percent and 43 percent, respectively, under divided government and divided chambers. Again the difference between unified and divided government is statistically significant,[26] while the difference between divided chambers and same-party control of the chambers is not.[27] Given the fragmentation of congressional majority party power in these split-control Congresses, it is remarkable that opposing party veto players were not an even greater obstacle.

We do not find any notable difference in how frequently Republican and Democratic majority parties fail owing to either intraparty dissent or opposing party veto players. Republican priorities fail owing to veto players 48 percent of the time, compared with 46 percent for Democrats.[28] Republican priorities fail owing to intraparty dissent 52 percent of the time, compared with 54 percent for Democrats.[29]

Taken together, it is clear that both veto players and intraparty consensus remain challenges for majority parties regardless of unified and divided party control. The incidence of specific veto players differs across different institutional configurations (as shown in fig. 3.3), but congressional majority parties struggle with both categories of problems in nearly every Congress studied. The American political system almost never grants a majority party freedom from opposing party vetoes. In fact, unified and divided party

control differ only modestly in the overall frequency with which majority parties have to confront opposition party veto players: such Congresses
mainly differ in which specific veto players are most predominant. At the
same time, parties also fall short in executing their agendas when they cannot agree internally—and this is a constant feature of congressional politics
as well.

The Challenges of Reaching Intraparty Agreement

Closer examination of cases of congressional majority party failure underscores that majority parties, even in an era of strong and homogeneous
parties, frequently struggle to come together around specific legislative language. Intraparty disagreement presented a serious challenge for majority
parties under every configuration of party control throughout the period
analyzed here. These difficulties were pervasive in circumstances of unified
government, when party members might seem to have most to gain from
successful cooperation.

High-Profile Failures Due to Intraparty Dissent

Remarkably, every majority party possessing unified control of government
in our dataset (the 103rd, 108th, 109th, 111th, and 115th) was unable to
reach sufficient internal consensus on at least one of its top agenda priorities.[30] On each of these agenda items, the majority party failed when it could
not advance a bill past points in the legislative process where a unified majority party could have succeeded alone. This is not to claim that these majority parties would have successfully enacted their favored legislation "but
for" their internal disagreements, since the Senate's sixty-vote threshold is
a high hurdle. However, in each of these Congresses, majority parties could
not find enough intraparty agreement to move forward on some of their
own top legislative priorities.

Democrats controlling unified government under President Bill Clinton
in the 103rd Congress (1993–94) collapsed on comprehensive health care
reform, easily the party's highest legislative priority during that Congress.
While Republicans opposed the effort across the board, liberal and moderate Democrats could not reach internal agreement on fundamental policy
questions such as whether employers should be required to pay employees' health care costs or whether the cost of premiums should be capped.[31]
House Democrats were unable to get a bill reported from the Energy and
Commerce Committee, one of the three House committees with jurisdiction

over the issue.[32] The Senate Finance Committee reported a bipartisan bill, and the Senate Committee on Labor and Human Resources reported a partisan bill. Despite heroic efforts, Senate Majority Leader George Mitchell (D-ME)—who had declined President Clinton's offer to nominate him to the Supreme Court in order to push health care reform[33]—could not break the intraparty deadlock between liberals and conservatives. After more than a year of effort, Mitchell declared defeat just before the 1994 midterms.[34] Comprehensive health care reform never received a floor vote in either House or Senate in the 103rd Congress. Even though Democrats almost certainly would have failed to overcome a Republican filibuster of health care reform, they never reached intraparty consensus on what their reform should include.

Making the Bush tax cuts permanent was a leading priority of Republican unified government in the 108th Congress (2003–4). But with the economy slowing, the party struggled with a "dispute in their own ranks about how and when to push for additional tax cuts at a time of growing deficits."[35] Moderate Senate Republicans floated less-expensive proposals for making some of the Bush tax cuts permanent, while conservative Republicans in House and Senate insisted the tax cuts would pay for themselves. The House passed a bill on party lines (H.R. 8), but the Senate Finance Committee did not seek to advance new legislation on individual taxes, preferring to move forward on a bipartisan corporate tax reform instead.[36] Given the intraparty dispute over whether or where to find offsets, Senate Finance Committee chair Charles E. Grassley (R-IA) declared that renewing the Bush tax cuts would not happen in that Congress: "I expect it to be an issue in the [presidential] campaign."[37]

Republicans' foremost legislative priority for unified party government in the 109th Congress (2005–6) was to restructure Social Security by adding individual investment accounts to the government pension program. Newly reelected President George W. Bush and Vice President Dick Cheney launched a campaign-style national tour to promote comprehensive Social Security reform. Republican leaders set aside H.R. 1 and S. 1 as placeholders for the legislation they planned to develop on the issue. House Ways and Means chair Bill Thomas (R-CA) initially suggested a June 2005 deadline for his committee to vote on an overhaul bill, but the committee never reported legislation on the issue. Senate Finance Committee chair Grassley did not evince enthusiasm for the effort, letting conservative hard-liners Sen. Jim DeMint (R-SC) and Sen. Rick Santorum (R-PA) take the lead through an informal strategy group.[38] The policy complexity and political sensitivity of the issue dampened support among usually reliable rank-and-file

Republicans.[39] Neither House nor Senate Republicans were able to come together around a plan, and no Social Security reform bill advanced beyond introduction in the 109th Congress.[40] Launched with great fanfare, the Republican Party's top legislative initiative in the 109th Congress was tacitly shelved.[41]

Democrats' most notable agenda failure during their control of unified government in the 111th Congress (2009–10) was their inability to pass legislation combating climate change. Early on, coastal Democrats and those from the interior of the country clashed over the right approach to the legislation. Even otherwise reliably liberal Democrats like Sen. Sherrod Brown (D-OH) warned, "There's a bias in our Congress and government against manufacturing, or at least indifference to us, especially on the coasts. . . . If we pass a climate bill the wrong way, it will hurt American jobs and the American economy, as more and more production jobs go to places like China, where it's cheaper."[42] Although House Democrats were eventually able to pass a bill, forty-four Democrats opposed it, and they needed several Republican votes to pass the measure.[43] In the Senate, these intraparty divisions proved even more difficult. A fully cohesive Senate Democratic caucus could have advanced a climate change bill, given that the party controlled sixty Senate seats for just over five months in the 111th Congress. But with Democratic senators from oil-drilling and coal-mining states expected to vote no, proponents needed support from at least three and as many as five Republican senators in order to get to sixty votes in the Senate.[44] Although the Senate Energy and Natural Resources Committee reported a bill, the compromises struck in committee alienated some conservation-minded Democrats, and the issues would have to be resolved on the Senate floor.[45] Ultimately, with Democrats divided on the issue, no bill was advanced even for a failed cloture vote in the Senate.

Democrats in the 111th Congress were also unable to unify around a "new direction" in the wars in Iraq and Afghanistan. Democratic leaders had called for a new plan for the wars in their opening speeches to Congress in 2007 (at the start of the 110th Congress), and the issue was again designated a priority in the 111th Congress. Democrats, however, were not able to get anywhere near a House majority to redirect military strategy.[46] Democrats' sole accomplishment on this agenda item was the adoption of an amendment to the war funding supplemental bill substantially boosting funding for domestic spending priorities.[47] A bipartisan majority in the Senate, however, rejected the House's amendment by unanimous consent, forcing the House to recede. In the end, the 111th Congress's supplemental war appropriations bill simply continued operations in Iraq and Afghanistan and passed both chambers with stronger support from Republicans than from Democrats.[48] Pelosi described the war supplemental bill as the single hardest issue of her speakership up through October 2009. "You thought energy was a heavy lift, health care, the budget, the recovery package. Nothing was as hard as funding the war."[49]

With unified party control in the 115th Congress (2017–18), Republicans' top agenda priority was to repeal and replace the Affordable Care Act ("Obamacare"). The morning after the 2016 elections, Speaker Paul Ryan and Majority Leader Mitch McConnell indicated at a press conference that Republicans intended to immediately move forward on Obamacare repeal.[50] During the first week of the new Congress Republicans passed a budget resolution authorizing the use of budget reconciliation to enact health care legislation without any bipartisan support in the Senate.[51]

Despite devoting the first nine months of the 115th Congress to the effort, Republicans were never able to muster sufficient intraparty support to repeal and replace Obamacare. The House leadership's first bill, the American Health Care Act, had to be pulled from the floor, with conservatives denouncing the proposed replacement as "Obamacare Lite" and Heritage Action whipping members to vote no.[52] In a second effort two months later, House Republicans regrouped to narrowly pass a revised bill[53] (217–213)—modified to accommodate conservative demands that states be permitted to opt out of some of the Affordable Care Act's insurance regulations—with twenty Republicans voting in opposition.[54] With Senate Republicans balking at the House bill, Senate leaders worked for two more months but failed to produce a compromise that could win the support of both moderates and conservatives. As a last-ditch effort, Senate leaders proposed a scaled-down "skinny repeal" in late summer that would have dismantled none of Obamacare's major provisions, leaving untouched its Medicaid expansion, insurance regulations, levies on high-income taxpayers, and subsidies to purchase health insurance. Even this exceedingly modest effort failed on the Senate floor (49–51) when Sen. John McCain (R-AZ), back from cancer treatment, dramatically signaled thumbs-down.[55] Despite the earlier failures, Sen. Lindsey Graham (R-SC) and Sen. Bill Cassidy (R-LA) spearheaded one final push to repeal Obamacare by converting the program into a block grant to states, but they could not win over the three Republican holdouts who had voted down the "skinny repeal." At the end of September 2017, Republicans finally abandoned the effort and moved on to their next agenda items, tax cuts and tax reform.

Our data on majority party agenda failures include numerous cases beyond the examples discussed here. These cases simply illustrate that intraparty disagreement resulted in the failure of a top agenda priority for every majority party with unified control in the period studied. Of course, it is also worth noting that some majority party failures precede future success. Occasionally a party fails on an agenda item in one Congress before succeeding in the next. For instance, congressional Republicans failed to pass a Medicare overhaul during the 106th and 107th Congresses but succeeded with the Medicare Modernization Act in the 108th. A generous accounting identifies twenty-one cases of failure in our data that found at least partial success in a future Congress (16 percent of all failures).[56] However, in many cases, success came only after a substantial watering down of the party's ambitions. This was certainly the case with the Medicare overhaul, on which Republicans evolved from envisioning broad-based reform to a narrow proposal that added a prescription drug program and allowed for some additional health savings accounts. The next chapter delves more into the pathways of majority party success and the ways majority parties often have to moderate their aspirations in order to find legislative success.

Painting with a broad brush, there are some clear patterns to the parties' respective failures during 1985–2018. Republican majorities often aspire to reform major entitlement programs but rarely get as far as advancing particular legislation to do so. Republicans indicated an intention to move forward with reform of Social Security in the 107th, 109th, and 112th Congresses, to reform Medicare in the 106th and 113th Congresses, and to repeal the Affordable Care Act in the 115th Congress. In each of these cases the party failed to coalesce in support of specific bills. The list of Democratic failures is more diverse in policy terms, but Democrats clearly struggle with internal divisions on environmental issues (e.g., the 110th–112th Congresses) and trade (e.g., the 101st and 103rd Congresses).

Most important, agenda failure is a common experience for congressional majority parties. Not every majority party achieves a stunning success. They all experience utter failure.

First-Person Perspectives on Intraparty Dissent

Our interviews shed some light on the sources of intraparty disagreement that get in the way of majority party agenda success. Three challenges emerged with some frequency in our interviews with Hill insiders of both parties: the high bar for agreement necessary with narrow majorities; the difficulty of reconciling party base demands with the broad support necessary to legislate; and the struggle to get members to see the big picture on what bills can navigate the whole legislative process. Beyond these three challenges, Republican and Democratic interviewees also flagged more party-specific difficulties.

Our interviewees frequently pointed to the challenges of governing with narrow majorities. Party polarization often means that majority parties must try to assemble chamber majorities entirely on their own. If the minority party is simply not interested in discussing a priority issue, a majority party must either give up on the goal or assemble a chamber majority with votes only from within its own ranks. Comparing negotiations that had occurred over the Clean Air Act in 1990 with the politics of climate change and health care in 2009–10, one longtime Democratic staffer explained, "The GOP wasn't negotiating [in 2009–10]. This wasn't because industry was uniformly opposed to action. . . . To the contrary, business wanted reform."[57] But if the minority party for either political or policy reasons has no interest in engaging on an issue, the majority has no choice but to try to go it alone.

Going it alone presents its own difficulties. Given the narrow margins of control characteristic of the contemporary Congress, the majority party typically has few votes to spare. Under such conditions, majority parties need to muster extremely high cohesion (usually 90 percent or more) in order to put up a chamber majority without cross-party assistance (see figs. 1.2 and 1.3). Parties struggle to reach this level of internal agreement. "If you have 240 votes in the majority, or even 220 votes or whatever they had in the Hastert years," said one staffer, "if you have these small margins it is hard to get the party together."[58] As a Democratic leadership aide explained, "The goal on our side (when we were in the majority) was to get to a point where you could get the Blue Dogs, the New Democrats, and the progressives on board."[59] Recognizing that any group can potentially hold the party hostage, the question is, What will get enough of each on board?[60]

Party leaders find it challenging to negotiate nearly perfect intraparty consensus. When a majority party can expect no help from across the aisle, every intraparty faction knows it has leverage to try to extract concessions. Former House Speaker Tom Foley (D-WA) explained this dynamic in his memoir:

> Even a few minority party votes can be helpful. When you do it all within the Democratic Caucus you have a lot of potential vetoes. Every group thinks. "Hell, they don't have a majority without us. They can't pass this without our support. Therefore we ought to accept nothing less than this, that, or the other thing." (Biggs and Foley 1999, 214)

Echoing Foley's point, a Democratic staffer we interviewed explained, "Your ability to get votes from across the aisle is very limited. This entails a heightened power within the party caucus. Everyone within the majority party is empowered to some extent, because they can threaten to withhold support."[61] Discussing frustration along these lines, a Republican staffer exclaimed, "We're so fractured right now and it's impossible to appease everyone. The Democrats just have to stick together and they have us by the balls."[62]

Party leaders may discover that only a very narrow range of issues can command the necessary level of intraparty unanimity. "[Senate Majority Leader] McConnell turned to working on judges because that's all they have consensus on," said a Senate Republican aide about the 115th Congress (2017–18). "The House passes all this stuff, but the Senate doesn't even have a hearing on it, and the members just let it die."[63] Consensus issues may well differ across House members and senators of the same party. "Because it is so difficult to move legislation in your own chamber, you don't really coordinate with the Senate," explained an aide:

Republicans actually tried to do a joint [House-Senate] retreat this year. Usually House and Senate Republicans do their own separate retreats. They had hopes of coming up with a common agenda, but apparently it was a disaster. You also see that in the "Better Deal" plan Schumer and Pelosi both released this year . . . in an effort to show that Democrats had a jobs message. But Schumer and Pelosi couldn't agree on what the message was, so the Senate approach on "Better Deal" is different from the House approach.[64]

When tasked with marshaling nearly perfect intraparty consensus, leaders are likely to discover that only a narrow range of issues can simultaneously traverse the gauntlets of their party's House and Senate caucuses.

A second challenge discussed by our interviewees of both parties is the difficulty of reconciling the demands of party base constituencies with the concessions necessary to build the broad support needed to enact legislation. "What I worried about the most was our own guys—intraparty issues," said one veteran aide. "Ultimately you can't craft a deal where the majority of your party feels they got screwed."[65] As leaders try to work out disagreements within their caucus, they have to anticipate how issues will play in public with the party's base. "The intensity of organized constituent interests has a big effect on getting the party together," said one staffer. "Our members have to worry about primaries."[66] Another said that party base groups "stop people from agreeing to deals they otherwise want to support. . . .

Partisanship is happening out in the public, and elected officials have to respond to it."[67]

Base constituencies also affect the capacity of a majority party to recruit cross-party support. "These days, we might be working with a Democrat or a couple of Democrats on some small thing—a nothing burger," said one Republican staffer. "And [Sen.] Elizabeth Warren [D-MA] will find out about it and blow it up. She'll talk about it or tweet about it, and the Democrats just drop it. Even though it's something we could get done, they'll say, 'We can't do this when Warren will light us up with her base.'"[68] He concluded, "This happens on both sides, obviously. We have the same problem on our side."[69]

Holding on to party base support grows even more difficult when a majority party needs to secure opposing party votes for Senate cloture. As we discussed in chapter 2, majority parties seeking bipartisan support in the party-polarized Congress often find they cannot pick off a few votes from among moderate members of the minority party. There simply are very few such members willing to buck their own party in the contemporary Congress. As a result, majority party coalition leaders seeking some minority party votes will need to go directly to the minority party's leaders:

> Look at the coalition that was put together for Reagan's fiscal package [in 1981]. You had Republicans working with this set of conservatives or Blue Dogs or Boll Weevils or whatever you want to call them. Republicans could work with those folks and try to build support. Now if you want to cut a deal you have to work with the leadership of the other party.[70]

Majority leaders who need to go to the minority party leadership to cut a deal obviously risk substantial blowback from their own hard-line or even mainstream members. In such circumstances, leaders may well discover that they cannot produce an agreement that will please their own members and win sufficient support for enactment.

A third, related problem parties face in delivering on agenda priorities is getting members and leaders to see the larger picture of what is necessary to legislate in a system of separated powers. Leaders must be able to get their own committee leaders and rank-and-file members to both anticipate and accept the likely endgame. Enacting legislation thus requires players to think beyond the narrow task of passing a bill out of committee or a single chamber to envisioning a package that can survive the whole legislative process: House, Senate, and presidential signature.

Party leaders often find themselves under pressure from their own rank and file to advance partisan bills rather than anticipate the compromises that will be necessary later. House Republicans "always want to go all Republican if they can," said one longtime staffer, meaning that they do not want to consider what is needed to win the cross-party support required to clear the Senate or garner a presidential signature.[71] Reflecting back on the challenges of delivering on the Clinton health care package, one veteran aide said, "The president's interest is almost always to do it in a bipartisan way. The congressional leaders don't give a shit about that. It's, 'Let's see if I can get it with my Democrats first and then we will see about the Republicans.' That's the same today as it was then."[72]

In addition, party leaders may struggle to get even key players to look beyond their own personal priorities. On the Clinton health care drive, "Dingell paralyzed himself. Either he was going to get everything he wanted or nothing. He wouldn't compromise with anyone. Moynihan wanted to do welfare first, and he didn't give a shit. And we let the clock tick."[73] Assembling a package that can accommodate all these divergent perspectives can present insoluble puzzles. Such challenges can often explain why agenda priorities flagged by party leaders at the start of a Congress never make it out of committee. As one former member said, "You don't move to do the reauthorization if there's no semblance of a coalition about how to improve it."[74]

Finally, our interviews suggest that Republicans and Democrats face unique challenges in building intraparty agreement. Republicans frequently discussed the rank and file's mistrust of their own leaders as an obstacle to party coordination. "It's absolutely harder when the rank and file won't follow the leadership—can't follow the leadership," said one Republican staffer. "When you get elected by opposing the leadership, it makes it very difficult."[75] He went on to describe how Speaker Boehner, despite his misgivings, had to allow a government shutdown because he could not persuade his rank and file to support his negotiating strategy:

> I said [to Boehner], "You just can't let the government shut down after what happened that time [in 1995]!" And he said, "You know, it's like with your kids . . . you can warn them over and over not to touch the stovetop, the burner. You can tell them it's going to hurt. But sometimes you have to let them put their finger on the flame and let them find out about the pain." . . . Stuff like that absolutely makes it harder to cut deals. It's absolutely harder when the rank and file won't follow the leadership.[76]

Republican interviewees complained about their own leaders' lack of leverage in dealing with recalcitrant backbenchers. Party leaders were described as lacking control over resources, especially access to media and campaign funds, to induce rank-and-file members to toe the party line. "One of the key things is the lack of authority leaders have in the House because they no longer control the spoils," explained a leadership staffer:

> The only way to get money in the past was through the leadership. You needed them to get access to party donors or for help with fund-raisers. Members today aren't as dependent on leadership for access to the media. There are so many new ways to build a media profile that aren't dependent on leadership.[77]

"New communication platforms help members create their own networks of support," explained another longtime aide. He continued, "This makes managing party unity with some members difficult [i.e., Freedom Caucus]. Members never had the opportunity to become celebrities unless they did something like drive into the Tidal Basin with a stripper. Now they all have Twitter to lead their followers into the pond."[78]

It stands to reason that such challenges arising from evolution in media and campaign fund-raising should affect both parties. But such complaints arose more often in our Republican interviews. Although we cannot claim to have interviewed a representative sample, we did not encounter Democrats who focused heavily on contentiousness between leaders and rank-and-file members. Although it is entirely possible that Democratic leaders have confronted such problems in the past or will confront them in the future, the rank and file's distrust of Democratic Party leaders did not emerge as a prominent theme as we probed for sources of intraparty dissent.

Democrats, however, were more likely to flag regional divisions within the party as a difficulty. One staffer discussed the challenges of reconciling competing regional interests on environmental and trade issues, which are often a party priority:

> There were a lot of regional divisions that made for a free-wheeling process. . . . Waxman-Markey was hard to negotiate. There was Rick Boucher from southwestern Virginia and the coal interests. There was Gene Green of Texas and the oil and gas interests. There was Mike Doyle of Pennsylvania concerned about trade-affected areas. There were many regional interests that had to be worked out.[79]

Along similar lines, a former member of Congress discussed how Energy and Commerce chairman John Dingell (D-MI) ran into problems putting together a health care reform bill because he had assembled a committee that reflected regional divides over clean air issues:

> He had selected people who were conservative on clean air issues. As it turns out, people who are pro-industry on clean air tend to be pro-industry with respect to health insurers, providers, and other issues. The result was that Dingell couldn't get a bill out of committee.[80]

No doubt Republicans must work out regional divisions on their priorities as well. But Republican interview subjects did not often flag region as a source of intraparty tension on party priorities.

Taken together, it is clear from these first-person perspectives that intraparty disagreements and frictions remain a challenge for party leaders. The high levels of party cohesion on roll-call voting characteristic of recent Congresses simply do not indicate that contemporary leaders find it easy to unify party members around achievable policy objectives. Leaders in the polarized Congress still struggle to organize their rank and file in support even of their party's top agenda priorities.

Trends and Continuities

The rise in party cohesion in congressional roll-call voting (shown in figs. 1.2 and 1.3) suggests that majority parties have grown more internally homogeneous since 1985. Given the closely balanced competition between the two parties for control of national institutions in the post-1980 context (Fiorina 2017; Lee 2016), recent majority parties might seem more likely to confront problems with veto players, in the form of an opposing party that controls the presidency, the other chamber of Congress, or both. In addition, minority party obstruction ties the contemporary Senate in procedural knots (Smith 2014). Given these trends, we examine whether opposition-party-controlled veto players have indeed become a bigger obstacle for majority parties, and whether contemporary majority parties are less hindered by intraparty disagreement.

The time frame examined in the study is not long, but it offers a window into whether patterns in majority party failure have changed since the mid-1980s. For every Congress from 1985 to 2018, figure 3.5 displays the percentage of majority party agenda items that failed at the Senate's sixty-vote threshold, by presidential veto, in committee, and by not being scheduled for floor action.[81] The frequency with which majority parties fail at the most important veto points—the Senate's sixty-vote threshold and

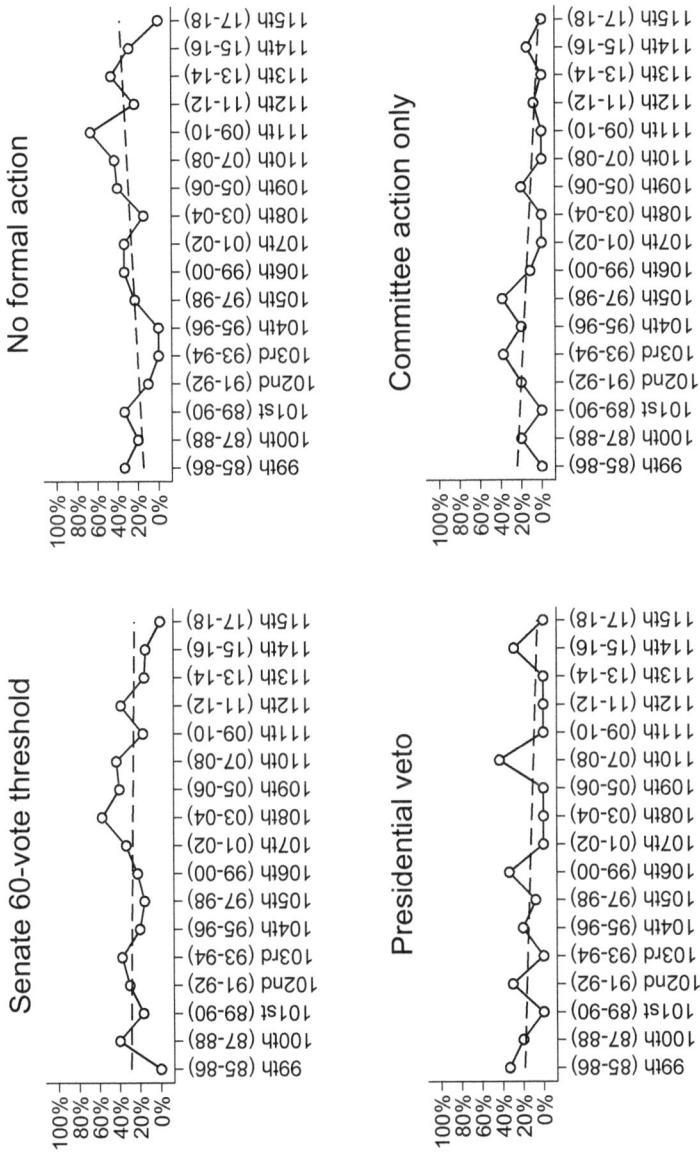

Figure 3.5. Trends in where majority parties fail, 1985–2018

the presidential veto—did not increase over the period. Compared with the 1980s–1990s, the Senate's sixty-vote threshold was a more important obstacle in the Congresses of the early 2000s. From 2001 to 2012 (107th–112th Congresses), the Senate's sixty-vote threshold blocked 39 percent of the majority party's failed agenda items compared with 24 percent of majority party failures in the 1980s–1990s (99th–106th Congresses).[82] But in the most recent Congresses (2013–18), the sixty-vote threshold declined in prominence, returning to earlier patterns and accounting for just 13 percent of majority party agenda failures on average.

At the same time, the presidential veto and veto threats contributed less frequently to majority party failure in recent Congresses. On average, in the Congresses of the 1980s and 1990s presidential vetoes accounted for 17 percent of majority party agenda failures, but that was true for only 7 percent of majority party failures in the Congresses from 2001 through 2018. Of course, most of the lowest points in the failure-by-veto time series shown in figure 3.5 are the Congresses with unified government (the 103rd, 108th, 109th, 111th, and 115th). After accounting for Congresses with unified government, there is still a slight downward trend, albeit not statistically significant, in how frequently majority party agenda items die by veto.[83]

Taken together, the data do not bolster a generalization that opposition-party-controlled veto players have become a more serious problem for majority parties since the 1980s. Given the weak and contradictory trends, one would fail to reject a null hypothesis of no change over time.

The categories of majority party agenda failure most likely to entail intraparty disagreement exhibit a contrary trend. Although parties have grown more cohesive in roll-call voting, majority parties may have gotten slightly worse at reporting bills dealing with their agenda items from committee. Figure 3.5 shows that a higher percentage of majority party agenda failures in recent Congresses occurred on items that did not advance beyond initial introduction or committee consideration. On average from 2001 through 2018, 34 percent of majority party failures were on agenda priorities that did not get reported from committee in either chamber of Congress, compared with 19 percent of majority party failures in the 1980s and 1990s.[84]

Not advancing a committee-reported bill to the floor is a somewhat less common way for majority parties to fail in recent Congresses. On average across the Congresses of the 1980s and 1990s, 22 percent of agenda item failures were on bills that got reported from committee but did not get scheduled for floor action. In the Congresses from 2001 through 2018, such cases account for 4 percent of majority party failures. This decline may reflect closer coordination between committee and party leaders in recent

Congresses so that committees advance only bills that leaders are prepared to green-light for floor consideration. But as with the other categories of majority party failure, difference over time in scheduling committee-reported bills for floor consideration also falls short of statistical significance.[85] Again, one could not reject a null hypothesis of no change over time.

Figure 3.6 offers a broad summary perspective on the relative importance of veto players and intraparty disagreement as contributing to majority party agenda failure across recent Congresses. Taken together, the data point to continuity rather than change. On average in the Congresses from 2001 through 2018, 49 percent of majority party agenda failures occurred at veto points controlled by the opposing party, almost precisely the same as the 46 percent of agenda failures attributable to veto points in the Congresses of the 1980s and 1990s.[86] By the same token, intraparty dissent remains as important a contributor to majority party agenda failure in recent Congresses as in those of the 1980s and 1990s. Intraparty disagreement appears to account for 54 percent of majority party failures across the Congresses in the 1980s and 1990s and 51 percent in the Congresses from 2001 through 2018.

In understanding how majority parties fail on their agenda items, there simply are no notable trends over time. Throughout the period we studied, majority parties struggle to overcome veto players controlled by the opposing party as well as to achieve intraparty agreement. The two sources of difficulty are similar in importance for understanding majority party agenda failure across all the Congresses since the 1980s.

Parliamentary-Style Party Discipline?

I can't get anything done without getting 50 of you sumbitches to agree with me and then I have to worry about the other side of the aisle.

—Sen. Birch Bayh (D-IN, 1963–81) recalling something he'd heard from Sen. Gaylord Nelson (D-WI, 1963–81)[87]

The data presented here simply do not provide much support for an interpretation of contemporary American government as characterized by majority parties routinely capable of parliamentary-style discipline. Intraparty disagreement remains a persistent obstacle to majority parties' advancing their agenda priorities in the legislative process. Today's majority parties in Congress routinely fail to enact their agenda items—and not simply because of the complex division of power in the American constitutional system. Majority parties regularly fall short when they cannot agree among

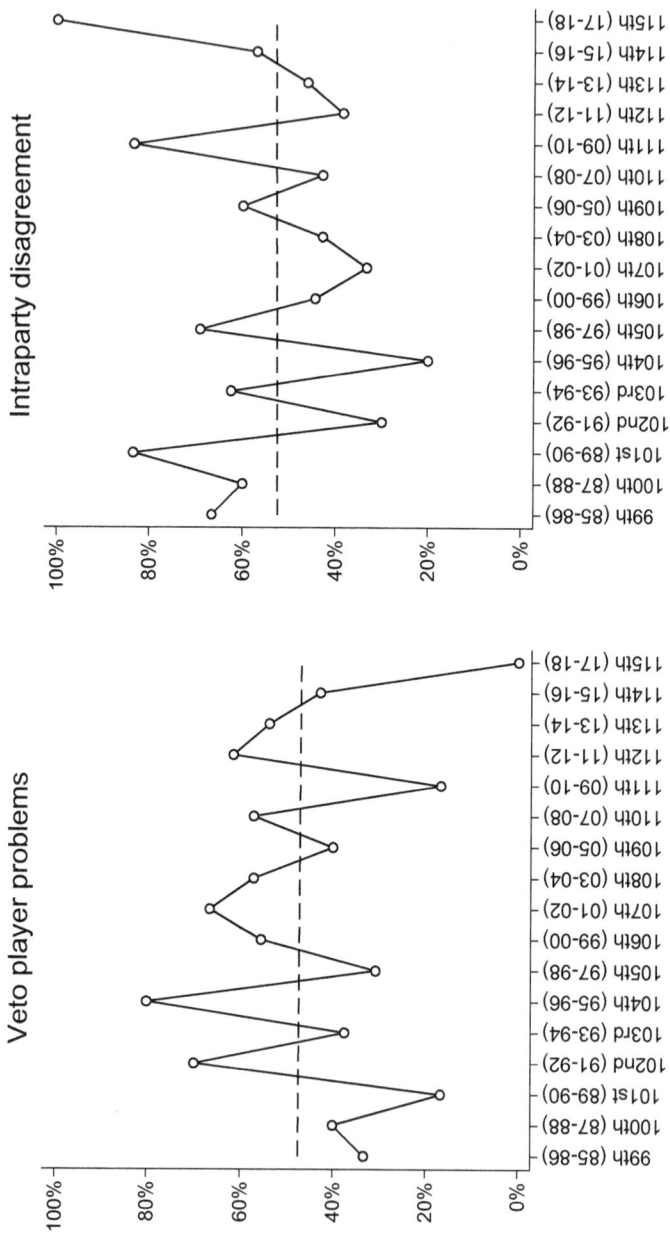

Figure 3.6. Veto points and intraparty dissent as a share of majority party agenda failures

themselves. Now as in past eras, congressional majority parties struggle not just because of a political system that obstructs their ambitions but also because they cannot obtain internal consensus on controversial national issues.

The roll-call voting cohesion of contemporary majority parties is unquestionably impressive, particularly compared with majority parties of the mid-twentieth-century "textbook" Congress. But vote-based indicators of party unity track members' behavior only on measures that make it to the floor for a vote. What roll-call measures fail to gauge are the many occasions when majority parties cannot coalesce behind a specific bill in committee or marshal sufficient intraparty support to justify scheduling a bill for floor consideration. The roll-call record is censored (Carrubba and Gabel 2008; Clinton and Lapinski 2008): when majority parties cannot get their act together to advance a bill, the party's lack of unity on that issue may well never be reflected in any floor votes. Many of the majority party failures analyzed here occurred without leaving a trace in the roll-call record.

Rather than looking to roll-call voting data, here we have benchmarked majority parties' performance against their stated agenda priorities. When majority parties fail, we ask where and how those failures occurred. Reviewing these cases highlights the continued persistence of intraparty disagreement as a challenge for congressional majority parties, even in today's party-polarized era. Indeed, we find little evidence of improvement over time in majority parties' ability to agree internally on their agenda priorities. Clearly, congressional parties remain sufficiently heterogeneous that leaders cannot assume their committee leaders and rank-and-file members will be able to reach intraparty agreement on even the party's top legislative priorities. The story we tell here is primarily one of continuity rather than change.

Factional divisions within contemporary majority parties are less clearly defined than those of the conservative coalition era. But even if contemporary congressional parties are more homogeneous in ideology, they are not capable of marching in lockstep on the complex policy issues they confront when they attempt to enact major legislation. The cases analyzed here point to many occasions when committee chairs and majority party leaders could not marshal majorities to move forward on the party's highest legislative priorities. A congressional party may well have broad consensus as a matter of abstract ideology but still fall short of agreement on specific legislation. The Democratic Party of 2009–10 likely had universal agreement that climate change is an important issue deserving of federal government action, and virtually all members of the Republican Party of 2017–18 disapproved of the Affordable Care Act as an exercise of federal power. But in these and other cases, intraparty agreement on abstract principle did not entail agreement on actual public policy. The devil is in the details.

As a result, we do not find that opposing party veto players account for a larger share of majority party agenda failures today than in the 1980s or 1990s. As a cause, veto players may well be more prominent in media coverage. Normally, when majority parties fail on agenda items because they cannot agree internally, they do not do so in public on the chamber floor. These failures usually happen early in the legislative process and without formal roll-call votes. Failure that is due to intraparty disagreement usually occurs not with a bang but with a whimper. Such differences in visibility may contribute to an inaccurate impression that today's majority parties are relatively unconstrained by intraparty disagreement and unusually hemmed in by opposition party veto players. But our data benchmarking majority party agenda performance against stated intentions over time undercut the conventional wisdom that veto players have increased in importance.

Examining the patterns in their failures, majority parties appear to have particular difficulty pushing through agenda items that would impose substantial costs on identifiable constituencies. In particular, Republicans often designate major entitlement reform as a party priority but regularly fail to coalesce around and advance specific proposals to deliver on this ambition. One Republican staffer we interviewed expressed particular frustration on this point: "I am personally surprised that, after decades of saying that we want to do entitlement reform, when we get together to discuss it we can't get traction. [On a recent proposal to change indexing of Medicare growth] we got so much pushback from within the party."[88] Speaker Paul Ryan also flagged this party agenda failure in his farewell speech as he retired from Congress: "I acknowledge plainly that my ambitions for entitlement reform have outpaced the political reality and I consider this our greatest unfinished business."[89]

For their part, Democrats have repeatedly had trouble advancing priority legislation in the areas of environmental regulation and trade policy. Taking stock of Democrats' internal debates on how to respond to climate change as the party assumed the House majority for the 116th Congress (2019–20), a 2017 reporter wrote:

> The Democratic Party does not have a plan to address climate change. This is true at almost every level of the policy-making process: It does not have a consensus bill on the issue waiting in the wings; it does not have a shared vision for what that bill could look like; and it does not have a guiding slogan—like "Medicare for all"—to express how it wants to stop global warming.[90]

Even though addressing climate change has long been a Democratic Party priority, internal frictions between labor and environmentalists—both key constituencies in their party coalition—make it hard for Democrats to move beyond rhetoric to actual policy proposals that can command broad intraparty support.

For both parties, enacting partisan priorities in each of these issue areas would necessarily involve some identifiable losers, such as entitlement beneficiaries, regulated industries, and firms subjected to import competition. It is hard for majority parties to maintain cohesion on policies with clear trade-offs and obvious downsides for particular constituencies. Senate Majority Leader Mitch McConnell (R-KY) conceded as much in 2018 when he stated that entitlement reform would not be forthcoming under President Trump, despite unified Republican control. "I think it's pretty safe to say that entitlement changes, which is the real driver of the debt by any objective standard, may well be difficult if not impossible to achieve when you have unified government."[91] As is evident from the data analyzed here, McConnell's point generalizes beyond entitlement reform. Despite the parties' increased ideological cohesion, leaders struggle to organize and maintain their ranks to deliver on agenda priorities that saddle their parties, and their members individually, with political responsibility for imposing costs.

This chapter began with a tweet from Sen. Lindsey Graham deeming failure in repealing and replacing Obamacare "not an option." Nevertheless, the 115th Congress (2017–18) went on to fail spectacularly, despite Republicans' otherwise extraordinary party cohesion.[92] It is certainly unusual for a majority party to collapse on an agenda priority in such a public way. However, the data assembled here reveal that it is not at all unusual for congressional majority parties to fail on their top agenda priorities, owing to the high hurdle of reaching intraparty agreement. Indeed, every recent example of unified party control has featured a similarly high-profile agenda failure. When it comes to public policy, congressional majority parties' reach still regularly exceeds their grasp.

FOUR

How Do Majority Parties Succeed?

Compromise is the name of the game in the legislative process. Very few bills . . . become laws and still retain more than 50 to 75 percent of what their authors originally envisioned as necessary in the public interest.

—Rep. Richard Bolling (D-MO, 1949–83) (1968, 24)

It's a paradox of sorts. . . . People come here with ideals, and this place reinforces their idealism. But Congress is an institution of compromises, and that's the antithesis of idealism.

—Sen. Howard H. Baker Jr. (R-TN, 1967–85)[1]

[T]he fact is that most, if not all, of the accomplishments in the history of this country that have been achieved by the United States Congress have been achieved through compromise.

—Rep. Jim Himes (D-CT, 2009–)[2]

Although congressional majority parties often fail, they succeeded in enacting legislation achieving some or most of their policy goals on about half of their agenda items across the period we analyzed (1985–2018). So majority parties do indeed steer public policy to some degree. This chapter investigates *how* they achieve their successes.

As we discussed in earlier chapters, theories of congressional party government expect today's cohesive majority parties to achieve policy victories by uniting behind party proposals to address core agenda priorities and then employing their organizational and procedural powers to muscle those proposals through the House and Senate in spite of, and over the objections of, the minority. Although chapter 3 demonstrates that internal disunity remains a leading cause of majority party *failure*, we might still expect that when contemporary majorities *succeed* they do so by coalescing behind partisan proposals and pushing them through the chamber using partisan tactics. In the House, a determined majority is expected to impose its will, and in today's partisan context "the House minority can forget about participating in anything significant" (Jacobson 2017, 132). In the Senate and beyond, compromises extended to the minority party should be minimal—just enough to achieve cloture or obtain the signature of an opposition party president.

Generally, the expectation is that contemporary lawmaking will resemble the federal stimulus package in early 2009. On the heels of an impressive victory in the 2008 elections, House Democrats passed their version of the American Recovery and Reinvestment Act (ARRA; Pub. L. 111-5) without a single Republican vote.[3] In the Senate, Democratic leaders and the White House negotiated with a small cadre of moderate Republicans, adjusting the size and scope of the package to win the support of three Republican senators: Susan Collins (R-ME), Olympia Snowe (R-ME), and Arlen Specter (R-PA). The votes of those three moderates were just enough to invoke cloture[4] and move the package through the chamber, giving Democrats a major victory in their efforts to jump-start the economy after the 2008 financial collapse. Generally, when contemporary majority parties are able to break free of stalemate and pass items on their agenda, they are expected to enact proposals along party lines, making only the concessions necessary to bring along the requisite number of opposing party votes.

The previous chapters should already raise doubts about this narrative. As shown in chapter 2, high levels of bipartisanship persist in congressional lawmaking, and majority parties rarely get most of what they want on their agenda priorities. Moreover, as shown in chapter 3, majority parties often fail to enact their agendas because of challenges building consensus within their own ranks, not just because of opposition-party-controlled veto points.

This chapter again draws on our dataset of majority party agenda priorities, as well as our interviews, to take a close look at congressional majority party successes. We find that the pathways by which majority parties succeed in the contemporary Congress run contrary to the expectations of partisan theories. Today's majority parties are not achieving lawmaking victories by steamrolling the opposing party. In fact, if anything, our data suggest that they may be becoming slightly *less* efficacious at getting most of what they want on their agenda items.

Rather, we find that even in the contemporary, partisan Congress majority parties succeed mostly by cultivating bipartisanship early in the legislative process or by making concessions to the other party and backing off key goals in order to gain bipartisan support later in the process. While majority parties often appear to be *trying* to overwhelm the opposition and enact partisan laws, our interviewees observe that party leaders and key negotiators typically still plan for and negotiate toward a bipartisan outcome behind the scenes. Despite all the partisan rancor in the contemporary Congress, successful lawmaking typically involves elements of what Warren and Mansbridge (2015, 152–65) term "deliberative negotiation": seeking common ground on the merits, finding zones of agreement, compromising in the face of intractable conflicts, and negotiating policy trades and logrolls within and across the parties. Regardless of the specific techniques employed, the dominant pathway to legislative victory is still to develop bipartisan support.

Overall Patterns of Majority Party Success

As we discussed in chapter 2, we distinguish between two categories of success: those in which the majority achieved *most* of what it set out to achieve— what we might think of as *strong* or *clear* victories; and those in which the majority was able to achieve only *some* of what it set out to achieve—what we might think of as *partial* victories.

Among the subset of successful cases in our data, figure 4.1 shows the distribution of successes categorized as achieving *most* or *some* of the party's goals. Across the Congresses we analyze, majority party victories were a variable mix of "most" and "some." In some Congresses, parties more often achieved "most" outcomes, and in other Congresses "some" outcomes were more common. However, there was no clear trend over time.[5] Majorities during the last six years of the Obama presidency (2011–16, or the 112th– 114th Congresses) struggled to achieve clear victories. Proportions of clear and partial victories returned to the historical norm in the Republican unified government of the 115th Congress (2017–18). Despite growing party unity on roll-call votes and increased party organizational strength, congressional majority parties have not become more efficacious in their legislative efforts.

Neither party has a stronger record in realizing its policy agenda items. Over the full time period, Democrats succeeded on 54 percent of their agenda items while Republicans did so on 50 percent, a difference that is not statistically significant.[6] Nor are there meaningful differences in the parties' rates of getting most of what they wanted. Democrats did so on 19 percent of their priorities over the full time series, and Republicans did so on 23 percent.[7] Other dynamics of party control also made little difference. Congressional majorities achieved similar success rates when controlling both

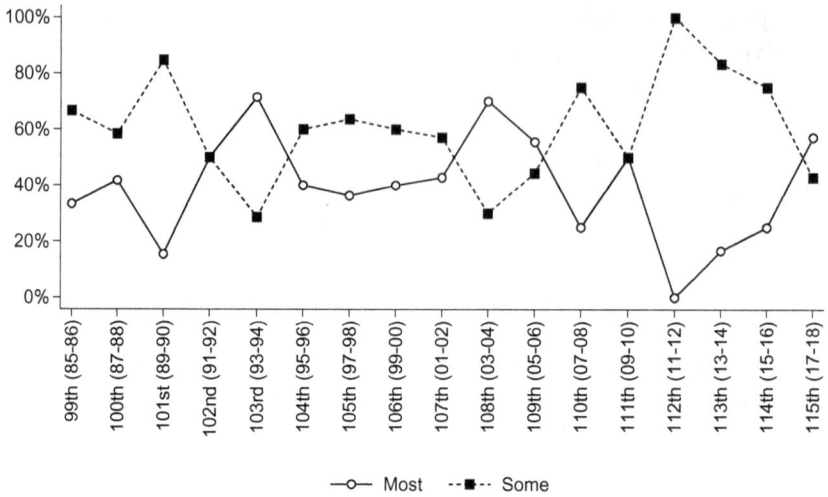

Figure 4.1. Percentage of successes achieving "most" and "some," 99th–115th Congresses

chambers of Congress (54 percent) or when control of the chambers was split (44 percent)[8] and when party control of national government was unified (57 percent) or divided (51 percent).[9]

As we discussed in chapter 2, majority parties in control of both chambers and unified government do achieve more strong victories. Parties controlling both chambers of Congress won most of what they set out to accomplish on 24 percent of their agenda priorities, compared with only 11 percent when party control was split.[10] Majority parties in unified government achieved strong victories on 35 percent of their agenda items, compared with just 16 percent in divided government.[11] Nonetheless, rates of strong victories were relatively low in all these configurations of institutional control.

Most important, there is no evidence in our data that today's congressional majority parties have leveraged their increased roll-call voting cohesion and greater party organizational strength into more success on their policy agendas. Success rates have remained generally steady, even as significant partisan and procedural change has occurred in Congress.

Pathways of Success

Congressional majority parties have not seen increases in their agenda success. But what about the *means* by which they succeed? Have congressional majority parties more often turned to partisan approaches to making law?

Drawing on our interviews and the legislative histories we compiled for each partisan agenda priority, we identified four pathways to majority party success from 1985 to 2018. These paths are not mutually exclusive. Congressional majority parties can, and do, sometimes follow more than one to get their agenda items across the finish line. However, these categories are exhaustive of the approaches majority parties employed in the years we studied. We identified no other approach of note either in our interviews or in our analyses of cases of majority party success. These pathways are:

1. Bipartisan logroll. In these cases the majority party had to logroll with opposition party lawmakers in order to obtain enough votes to get the final legislative package passed. Logrolls exploit the fact that parties often prioritize different policy goals without entirely disagreeing with one another. It can thus be possible to build support for legislation by aggregating priorities from each party, thereby "exploiting differing valuations of the different aspects of the negotiation" (Warren and Mansbridge 2015, 157). Logrolls typically involve giving the minority party things on its wish list so as to secure votes sufficient for passage of a majority party priority.

2. Seek broad support. Cases in this category come in one of two forms.
    a. The majority makes a modest/popular proposal. These are cases in which the majority makes a modest or bipartisan proposal that finds broad support across the political spectrum at the very start of the process. These are cases of agreement "on the merits" (Warren and Mansbridge 2015, 165). In other words, the majority is trying to pass something that is popular and lacks partisan controversy. Reauthorizations of existing programs often take this pathway.
    b. The majority engages in a process to find bipartisan agreement even though the issue might provoke partisan conflict if handled differently. These are cases in which the majority party sets out at the very start of the legislative process to develop a bipartisan and uncontentious proposal. Rather than proposing something partisan and making changes along the way to gain votes, the majority seeks to find out what *can* pass with broad support and then writes that bill. This approach involves "problem solving," in which the majority listens to the minority and takes input so as to put together a legislative package both can support (Warren and Mansbridge 2015, 158).

3. Back down. In these cases the majority starts out by making a strong partisan proposal. As the process unfolds, however, the majority backs down on some of the more contentious aspects of its proposal in order to secure votes, or it yields to a determined opposition party on some of its positions

and proposals. These are cases of compromise, in which the majority "offer[s] concessions that involve sacrificing something of value" in order to reach a mutually acceptable outcome (Warren and Mansbridge 2015, 159).

4. Steamroll. In these cases the majority proposes a policy that is strongly opposed by the other party, but the majority is able to bludgeon the opposition into submission or otherwise pass the bill in spite of clear opposition. The majority party makes few concessions to the minority party along the way. Negotiations and compromises that do take place are primarily among majority party members.

Overall, we coded 87 percent of cases into just one of these four pathways (120 in total), with the remaining 13 percent (18 in total) coded into two pathways, reflecting the use of two approaches by the majority party. Appendix table A.3 identifies and briefly explains the coding of each case.

Our findings underscore that even in the contemporary, partisan Congress, majority parties overwhelmingly succeed by pursuing bipartisanship. Often bipartisan intent is apparent from the very start. In other cases the majority appears to seek a more partisan outcome early on but is forced to back down as the legislative effort unfolds and, in the end, settles for bipartisanship. In many of these latter cases, majority coalition leaders were well aware from the start that a bipartisan compromise would be necessary, but they pushed partisan-sounding proposals early on to set the tone for cross-party negotiations or to placate their own hard-liners by demonstrating that they were "fighting hard."

Figure 4.2 presents the overall frequency of each pathway of success for 1985–2018. As shown, on 38 percent of successes ($n = 52$) the majority party succeeded by *seeking broad support*, looking to develop or advance a policy proposal that would find strong support on both sides of the aisle. In these cases the majority never seriously entertained or even feigned a partisan approach but sought bipartisanship in earnest from the very beginning. On another 54 percent of cases ($n = 74$), the majority started by making a strong partisan proposal but ultimately *backed down* and settled for something less ambitious and typically bipartisan. On another 8 percent of cases ($n = 11$), the majority engaged in a *bipartisan logroll* with the minority. Unable to pass the proposal alone, the majority coupled its preferred policies with the other party's priorities in order to secure the votes needed for passage. Finally, the majority *steamrolled* the minority and passed a strong partisan proposal in just 14 percent of cases ($n = 19$). In these instances the majority party found no need to compromise across the aisle.

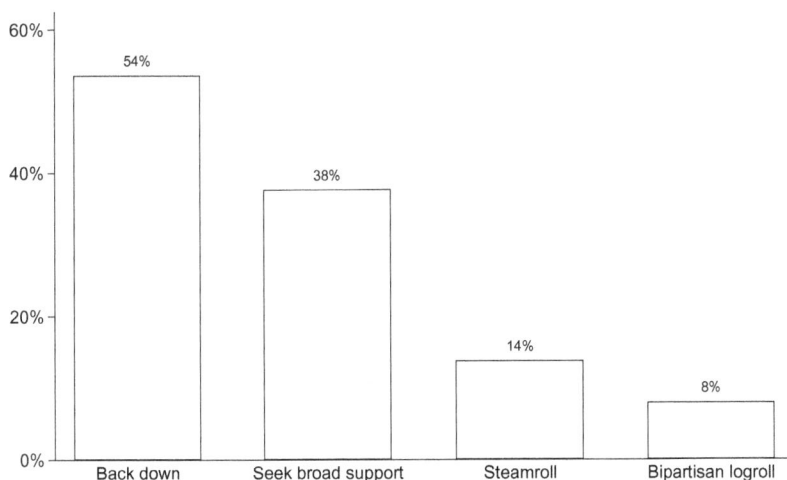

Figure 4.2. Pathways of majority party success, 99th–115th Congresses

Figure 4.3 presents the prevalence of these pathways over time. The most important takeaway is that none of the trends over time are statistically significant.[12] Congressional majority parties have not become more or less likely to pass laws addressing their partisan priorities by steamrolling the opposition. Nor have they become more or less likely to do so by seeking broad support, backing down, or logrolling. In all but three Congresses, the majority's most common pathway to success (though sometimes combined with other pathways) was to *back down*. Among the three Congresses during which a different pathway was most common, in two (the 106th and the 114th—the final two years of the Clinton and Obama presidencies, both featuring divided government) *bipartisan logrolls* were the most common. In the third (the 108th Congress, featuring unified government) the most common pathway was to *seek broad support*. There was not a single Congress during the entire period we studied in which *steamroll* was the most common pathway to success. In fact, in most Congresses, including those with unified party control, *steamrolls* were the least or second-least common.

Successes achieved by seeking broad support from the outset appear across a wide spectrum of issues, and they occur throughout the period studied. Some were relatively modest proposals to reauthorize or expand programs with broad political support, including child nutrition programs (99th Congress, Democrats); clean water (100th Congress, Democrats) and

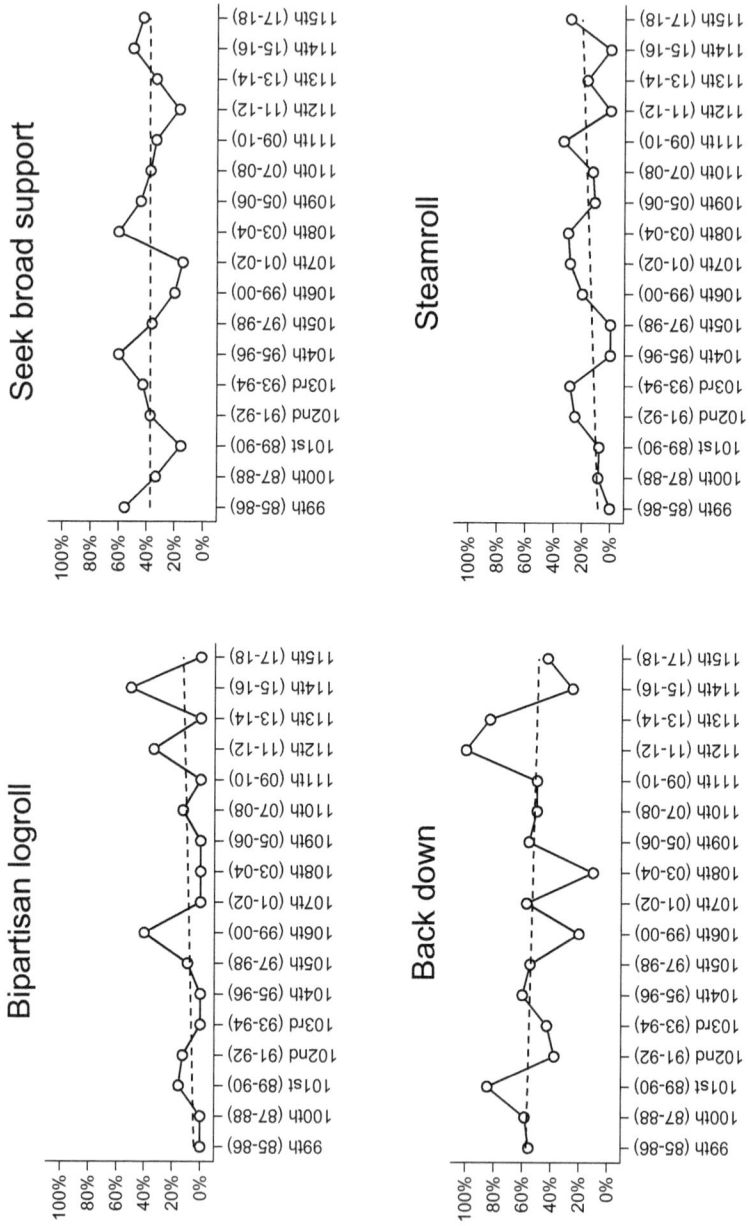

Figure 4.3. Pathways of majority party success over time

clean air programs (101st Congress, Democrats); vocational and applied technical education programs (102nd Congress, Democrats, and 109th Congress, Republicans); the National Institutes of Health (103rd Congress, Democrats); the Individuals with Disabilities Education Act (105th Congress, Republicans); federal surface transportation programs (109th and 112th Congresses, Republicans); the Children's Health Insurance Program (111th Congress, Democrats); and the farm bill (113th and 115th Congresses, Republicans). With each of these items, and others, the majority party made it a priority to renew federal programs popular in both parties.

Proposals integrally connected to a party's reputation or electoral efforts are included among these successes. For example, the Republicans' 1994 Contract with America and the Democrats' 2006 Six for '06[13] agendas were major efforts at developing nationalized party platforms for congressional action, but both included some proposals selected and finely calibrated to attract broad bipartisan support during the legislative efforts that followed. Several Contract planks fit this bill, including successful efforts to establish a line-item veto, reform congressional rules, enact various tough-on-crime proposals, reform private securities litigation, and limit federal unfunded mandates. Some of the Democrats' Six for '06 agenda items were also designed in this manner, including efforts to reduce student loan interest rates and enact congressional ethics and lobbying reforms.

In other years we can observe clear party priorities addressed by the broad bipartisan support pathway as well. The Democrats' long-sought success passing the Family and Medical Leave Act in the 103rd Congress, for example, had found substantial support among both Democrats and Republicans in the 1980s and 1990s but was opposed by both President Reagan and President H. W. Bush. Republicans' successes in expanding free trade deals with Central America and Southeast Asia in the 108th Congress had likewise found strong support from members of both parties, but it reinforced the GOP's reputation as the pro-business party.

Of course, the conditions have to be right for seeking broad support from across the aisle. Not every issue lends itself to this pathway. Before participating in bipartisan efforts, both parties have to think about their electoral reputations and consider whether their party base will be satisfied with compromise. According to our interviewees, congressional leaders have to make a choice:

> If you think bipartisanship is possible—and it's true bipartisanship—you go for it. But on something like tax reform, where both sides have drawn clear lines in the sand for decades, then, no, you just can't do this in a bipartisan manner. It would have been great to do so, but you can't, so you take a different approach.[14]

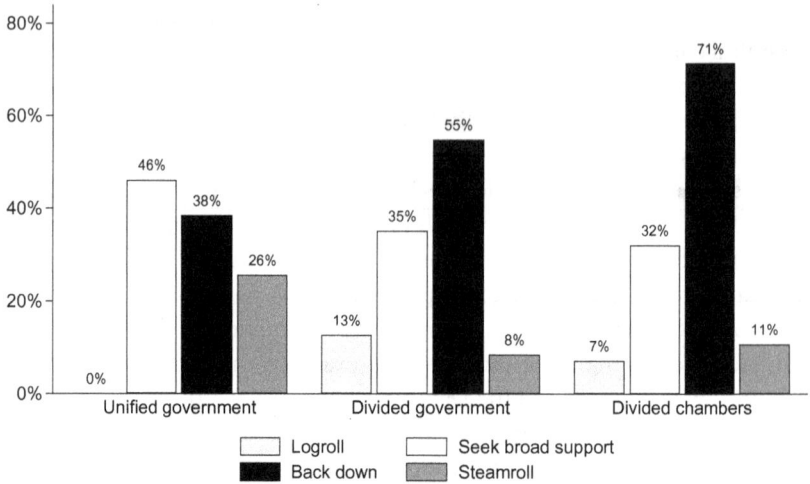

Figure 4.4. Pathways of majority party success by party control

Divided government seems to play a role in the salience of this pathway as well. Only five of the seventeen Congresses we studied featured unified party government, and the realities of divided government, including periods of split party control of the House and Senate, dispose congressional leaders to think about policymaking in bipartisan terms:

> For four years [2011–14], we had split control of Congress, and I think it created better opportunities for bipartisanship. Democrats in the Senate knew they needed sixty votes, so they wouldn't try to cut a deal that would fuck over Republicans. And we couldn't be difficult and try to push for something that didn't have any support from Democrats.[15]

Or as another staffer put it, "With Obama, we knew from the beginning that if we wanted a law we had to involve the Democrats. It's difficult to not involve them at the beginning but try to bring them in later in the process."[16]

However, our data do *not* show that seeking broad support is more likely under divided government (see fig. 4.4). If anything, the pattern runs in the opposite direction. About 46 percent of successes under unified party government occurred when the majority sought broad support, compared with 35 percent under divided government and 32 percent under divided chambers.[17] Nonetheless, the frequency with which modern congressional parties face conditions of divided government may broadly shape the way congressional actors think about how to achieve legislative accomplishments.

On a substantial percentage of successes, congressional majority parties take approaches that end in bipartisanship but start out on more partisan terms. Indeed, as shown in figure 4.2, the most prominent pathway of majority party success was to *back down*. More than half of majority party successes—54 percent—were coded this way. These are successes in which the majority party started the process by making or advancing a strong partisan proposal but backed off from, watered down, or otherwise dropped some of the most controversial aspects of that proposal in order to win broad enough support—typically bipartisan support—for passage. Cases categorized as *bipartisan logrolls* are similar in some respects. In these cases, rather than backing off key goals, the majority pairs its priorities with minority party priorities to build a bipartisan coalition. With both pathways, the majority initially seeks a partisan bill but has to make important concessions and compromises and build bipartisan support for enactment.

Both of these pathways were more common under divided control of government than under unified party government. *Backing down* was by far the most common approach under divided government and divided chambers, as shown in figure 4.4, and the differences between each of these conditions of divided party control and unified government are statistically significant.[18] *Bipartisan logrolls* occurred only under conditions of divided government, with none of these cases of success happening during periods of unified party government. That the parties demonstrate a penchant for more conflictual lawmaking under divided government is not a surprise. With each party holding some claim to government control, neither can simply roll over and submit. It is in each party's interest to put up a visible fight before they agree to a deal.

The individuals we interviewed said that members of Congress know that early, partisan legislative efforts will often yield to bipartisanship. "Just from a basic negotiating point of view, that's the way to approach it sometimes. You start out trying to get as much as you can. But in the end, you know you're going to need the votes," one staffer told us.[19] Especially on issues that might animate their party's base, members of Congress cannot appear to simply cave in to the demands from the other side of the aisle. "You have to show a fight."[20]

Particularly in the House, the majority party will sometimes advance or even pass partisan proposals on a party-line vote, knowing they will not have the votes to get them through the Senate or win bicameral agreement.

This is often a strategy for placating hard-liners ahead of eventual compromises and disappointments:

> Some of it is feeding the raw meat to the troops. You let them vote on these partisan bills. You let them vote fifty times to repeal Obamacare even though you know it's not going anywhere in the Senate. You also sometimes let them add these amendments to the bill because you know [they are] going to get dropped before the thing becomes law. Those votes give those members sufficient cover to vote for the bill, even if everyone knows those crazy amendments never are part of the final law.[21]

To some degree, congressional parties will put on an almost scripted show of partisan enmity in the lead-up to a bipartisan deal. Even after both sides back down and a deal is reached, there are discussions about how to stage the bipartisan acquiescence:

> At the end of the day, we also have to come out of negotiations with our talking points. We have to plan out how we are going to talk about this thing and how we are going to explain it and sell it to the conference: We won on A, B, and C. We screwed the Democrats on 1, 2, and 3. . . . Messaging is key. There's always going to be this week after the deal is final and everything is in place where we have to brief everyone, get ready for the floor, let the staff finish drafting the language. While this is happening, we have to keep selling the deal to the conference, and it could easily break down at any time. Holding these agreements together is hard, and you need your messaging ready to try to pull it off.[22]

However, backing down and logrolling are not always scripted. Sometimes the parties take a hard line either out of a hope that they can steamroll the minority or simply to see how far they can push the other side and find out how good a deal they can cut at the close of the negotiations. One staffer described the 2017–18 legislative fight over reauthorizing and extending CHIP (Children's Health Insurance Program) as a good example of Republicans' pushing the Democrats as far as they could before agreeing to a deal:

> I think the CHIP example is a rare good example where you push the minority. Republicans were smart. They knew if Democrats wanted children's health they would have to come to the table eventually. So they ratcheted up the pressure to get them to come to the bargaining table. . . . The Republicans

decided to . . . go through regular order with a very partisan bill. The Republicans' thought was, Democrats won't want to be seen as opposing children's health. But with the Republicans' offsets [funding mechanisms] in the bill, it put Democrats in a position where they had to oppose something they usually like. Republicans put the squeeze on them, and now the Democrats are willing to come back to the table. There are a lot of strategic decisions like that.[23]

Ultimately, "under current conditions, each side has leverage. This means you have to deliver a compromise at the end of the day."[24] Even when the majority wants to push something partisan, or does so early in the process, they almost always know they will eventually give in: "As the saying goes, pain is inevitable; suffering is optional."[25]

Congressional majority parties have used backing down and bipartisan logrolling as pathways to success on some of the most notable laws passed since the mid-1980s. Cases of backing down include the 1986 tax reform package (99th Congress, Democrats), on which Democrats accommodated Republicans by acceding to lower marginal rates than they had initially wanted; Welfare reform (104th Congress, Republicans), on which Republicans gave up on their hopes of overhauling Medicaid and several other social welfare programs in order to pass a narrower bill replacing Aid to Families with Dependent Children (AFDC) with Temporary Assistance for Needy Families (TANF); No Child Left Behind (107th Congress, both parties), on which Republicans agreed to higher spending levels than they wanted and Democrats agreed to tying more of that funding to student testing; the 2001 and 2003 Bush tax cuts (107th and 108th Congresses, Republicans), both of which saw Republicans back down on the size and scope of their proposed cuts and tilt more of the cuts toward low-income Americans than they initially proposed; and the 2009 federal stimulus package (ARRA, 111th Congress, Democrats), which saw the Democrats agree to a package hundreds of billions of dollars smaller than they originally sought.

A number of bipartisan logrolls are also among the most notable laws enacted during 1985–2018. These include the Balanced Budget Act of 1997 (105th Congress, Republicans), which saw Republicans agree to include several Democratic proposals—including the Children's Health Insurance Program and the restoration of some welfare benefits; the Fair Minimum Wage Act of 2007 (110th Congress, Democrats), which saw Democrats agree to larger small-business tax breaks sought by Republicans in order to secure the first federal minimum wage increase in a decade; and the 21st Century Cures Act (114th Congress, Republicans), on which Republicans had to agree to Democratic priorities of boosting National Institutes of Health spending and several other health care initiatives in order to secure their proposed overhaul of Federal Drug Administration drug approval processes.

Among our four pathways, only one represents successful efforts at purely partisan lawmaking—*steamrolls*. In steamrolling the minority, the majority advances something that is partisan, or that engenders strong opposition from the other party, and finds a way to enact that proposal making few, if any, compromises. Steamrolling occurred just nineteen times on party priority legislation since 1985 (14 percent of cases). Our interviewees spent little time talking about efforts at partisan steamrolling. Nevertheless, it appears that the ability to steamroll starts with getting the majority unified around a proposal: "Either you have overwhelming support [within your party] behind what you want to do, or you're going to have to do it on a bipartisan basis."[26] As shown in the previous chapter, building intraparty unity is no small feat. Even then, a close look at the nineteen steamrolls suggests that these partisan outcomes are very situational. As shown in figure 4.4, steamrolls were far more likely under unified government.[27] In total, ten of nineteen steamrolls (53 percent) occurred during periods of unified party government, despite party control being unified less than 30 percent of the time in our study.

Some of the steamrolls in our data are notable as controversial and consequential acts of lawmaking, including the Affordable Care Act (Democrats, 111th Congress), the Dodd-Frank financial sector reforms (Democrats, 111th Congress), the Medicare Modernization Act (Republicans, 108th Congress), and the Tax Cuts and Jobs Act (Republicans, 115th Congress). But as we discussed in chapter 2, other such cases are less notable or impactful, including the PAYGO budgetary reforms (Democrats, 110th Congress) and the National Voter Registration Act of 1993 (Democrats, 103rd Congress).

A few steamrolls included cases in which the minority waved the white flag, reluctantly caving to political pressure and dropping their opposition. As we discuss later in this chapter, congressional Democrats dropped their opposition, and were steamrolled, on several Republican proposals to increase military spending and military projects in the aftermath of the September 11 terrorist attacks. Republicans, for their part, were steamrolled in a few instances in which they dropped their opposition to Democrats' social policy proposals related to race or gender when it became clear to GOP leaders that continued obstruction might cast their party in a negative light.

There are few differences between the parties in their propensity to use different pathways to success. Democrats and Republicans used bipartisan logrolls on nearly identical percentages of successes (7 percent and 9 percent, respectively). Democrats were more likely to back down on their way to success (61 percent of Democratic successes compared with 45 percent of Republican successes) and less likely to seek broad support (35 percent of Democratic successes compared with 41 percent of Republican successes), but only the first of these differences is statistically significant.[28] Most important, however, neither party was more likely to steamroll the other. Both took this pathway on 14 percent of their successes.

Other partisan dynamics also appear to have little effect on the pathways used. A multivariate regression analysis, found in appendix table B.1, assesses the effect of party distance, majority party unity, and the number of seats held by the majority party in the House and Senate on the likelihood that each pathway was used on each successful agenda item. These variables, measured in the same manner as in chapter 2, almost never have significant effects. The degree of party distance, party unity, and number of seats held by majorities in the House never have statistically significant effects. The unity of Senate majority parties predicts lower likelihood that the majority seeks broad support, and higher likelihood that the majority backs down. However, none of the measures predict increased or decreased likelihood of steamrolling. Among all the variables included in the analyses, only divided government has a consistent effect: this configuration increases the likelihood that a majority party will succeed by backing down from controversial positions, as already highlighted in figure 4.4.

Generally, clear partisan victories are rare and have not become more common over the period studied. Partisan pathways to majority party success have not become more or less likely as the partisan dynamics inside Congress has changed. Bipartisanship continues to be the primary means of success for House and Senate majority parties. Contrary to prominent theories of party power and the general perceptions of congressional observers, the more unified majorities and polarized parties of recent years have not increased the likelihood of steamrolls. When contemporary majority parties succeed in enacting legislation on their priority agenda items, they do so primarily by cultivating broad bipartisan support in the House and Senate.

Clear Victories or Settling for Less

To understand further how majority parties succeed in the contemporary Congress, it is important to take stock of the relationship between *paths* to success and *degrees* of success. Below we take a look at how majority parties win clear victories on their agenda priorities and how they win partial victories.

These deeper dives yield and reinforce a few key insights. First, in both clear victories and partial victories, congressional majority parties largely

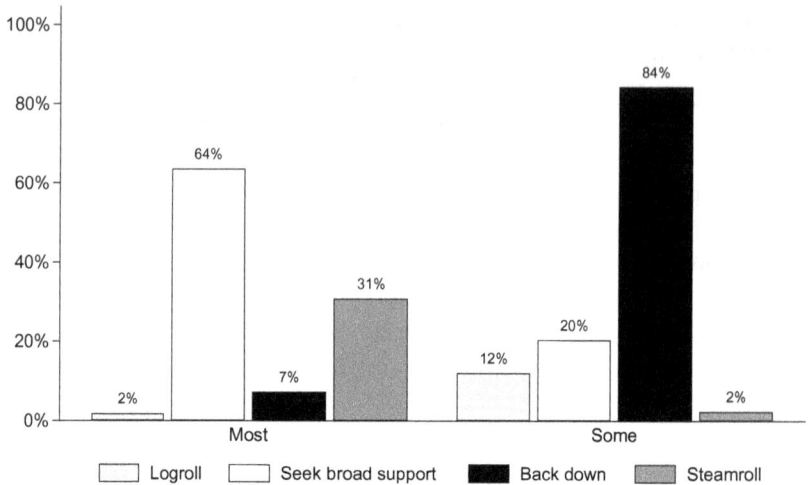

Figure 4.5. Pathways and degrees of success, 99th–115th Congresses

adopt approaches of seeking or agreeing to bipartisan compromises. Majority parties occasionally steamroll the opposition on their way to getting most of what they want, but they more often seek to advance broadly popular proposals that simply do not engender strong partisan opposition. Second, barriers to success do not always involve the other party. In many cases the majority party has to settle for less owing to recalcitrance *within its own ranks*, just as majorities often fail on their agenda items owing to intraparty disagreement (see chapter 3). Third, there is some evidence that in recent years some congressional majority parties have been more willing to try to steamroll the minority party. However, this approach has coincided with higher rates of majority party failure.

Figure 4.5 provides an initial look at the pathways of success employed for "most" and "some" successes in our data. The figure makes it clear that while majorities achieve different kinds of success in different ways, both overwhelmingly involve efforts ending in bipartisanship. Clear victories in which the majority gets most of what it set out to achieve are primarily achieved by seeking broad support, with almost two-thirds of such successes, 64 percent, achieved in this manner. By comparison, only 31 percent of these clear majority party victories occurred by steamrolling. These two means of success make up 95 percent of all clear victories for congressional majority parties. Partial victories, on the other hand, are overwhelmingly achieved when the majority party backs down. All together, 84 percent of such successes came by this pathway, with another 20 percent achieved through seeking broad support. Note that the differences in the use of each pathway between cases of majority parties achieving clear victories versus partial victories are statistically significant for all four pathways.[29] Different ends were reached by different paths.

There is some evidence that the paths to success may be shifting over time. Figure 4.6 shows the percentage of cases in which the majority achieved most of what it set out to achieve across each Congress using each pathway.[30] The data demonstrate that congressional majority parties are achieving slightly smaller shares of successes by seeking broad support and instead are adopting approaches that are more confrontational over time. Indeed, before the end of the 106th Congress (1999–2000) at least 50 percent of clear majority party successes in every Congress were achieved by seeking broad support. However, that share has met or exceeded 50 percent in only four Congresses since that time. Instead, the combined percentage of these successes achieved by backing down or by steamrolling matches or exceeds those achieved by seeking broad support in most Congresses since the end of the Clinton administration. Nevertheless, this shift has occurred as congressional majority parties have achieved fewer strong victories and fewer successes overall. Moreover, these trends over time for seeking broad support and for steamrolling are not statistically significant.[31] Majority parties are not becoming better at getting most of what they want by steamrolling the opposition. They may be *trying* more frequently to win out over the objections of the minority, but they are not succeeding more frequently.

Pathways for achieving partial victories demonstrate less change over time. Figure 4.7 shows the percentage of cases in which the majority achieved some of what it set out to achieve by each pathway in each Congress. Across time, backing down persists as the dominant path. In all but three Congresses, it was the most common route to success, and the slight downward trend over time is not statistically significant.[32] However, there is some evidence that seeking broad support has become a more common pathway for majority parties achieving partial victories in recent years. Following a spike in this approach during the 108th Congress, the percentage of cases seeking broad support (30 percent) plateaued at a higher level than before the 108th (10 percent), and the shift approaches conventional levels of statistical significance.[33] Nevertheless, seeking broad support remains far less common than backing down. Generally, the dominant approach to achieving partial victories for congressional majority parties has been, and remains, to back down from the most controversial aspects of the party's proposal and seek a compromise.

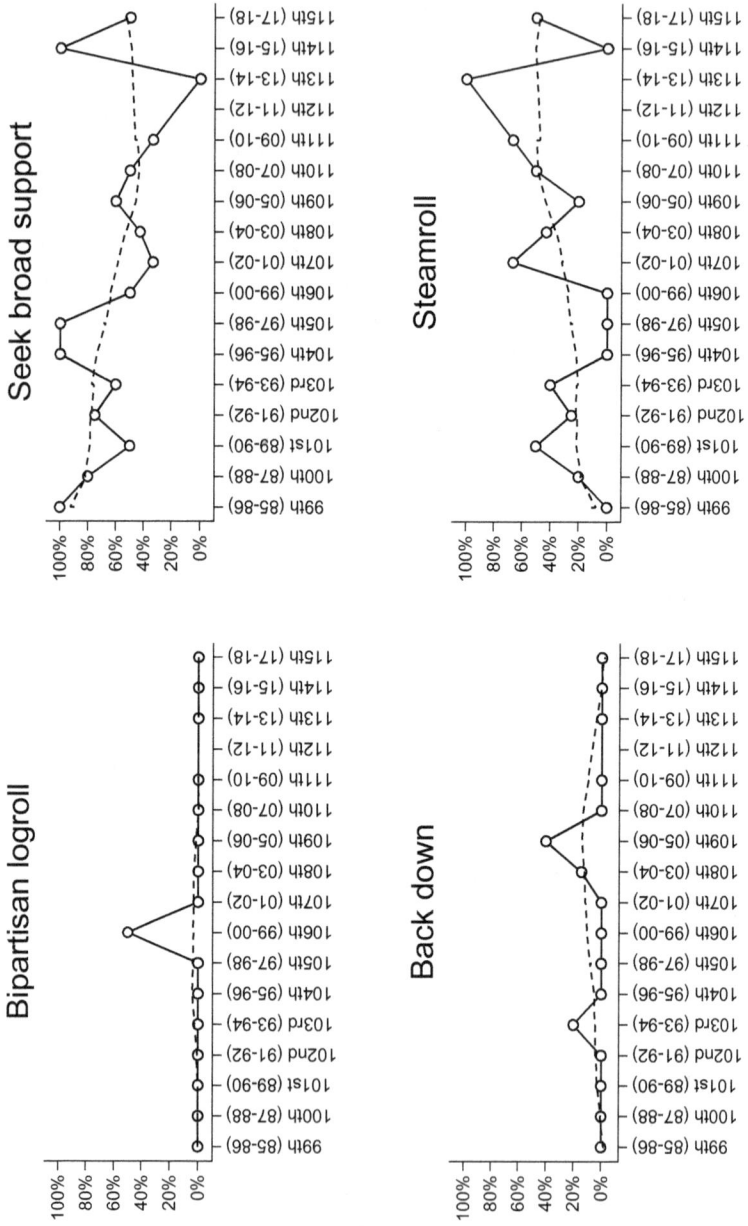

Figure 4.6. Pathways of achieving "most" successes over time

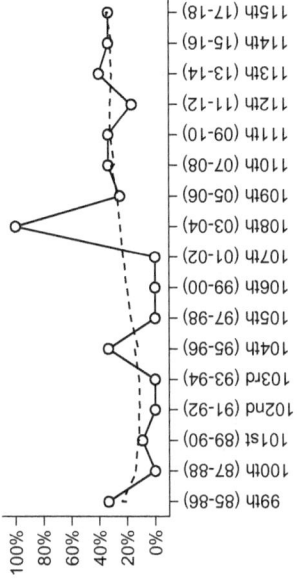

Bipartisan logroll

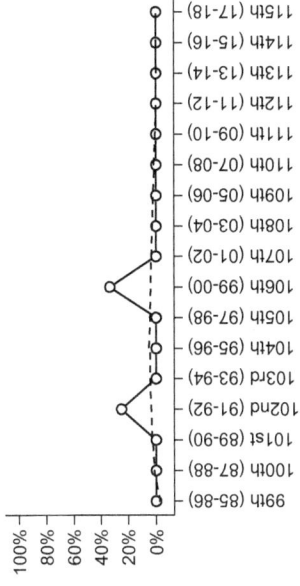

Seek broad support

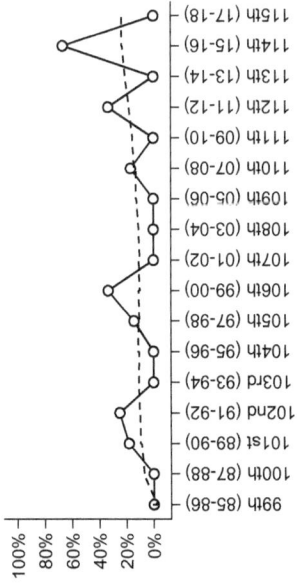

Back down

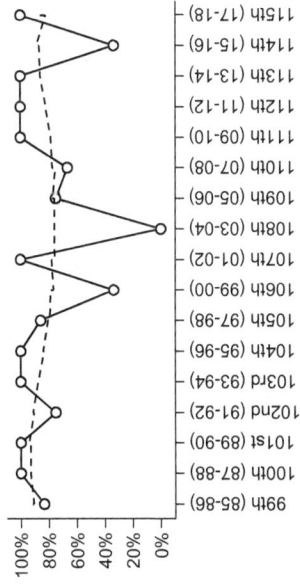

Steamroll

Figure 4.7. Pathways of achieving "some" successes over time

Together, these data reveal that congressional majority parties achieve different kinds of success on their agenda items by different paths, but both primarily involve compromise rather than partisan steamrolling. Closer examination of cases of majority party success underscores the importance of bipartisan compromise.

Clear Victories: Pursuing Popular Policies and Occasionally Steamrolling

Clear majority party successes come in various forms, but they predominantly involve the majority party's seeking broad support for popular proposals that the other party either agrees with or lacks the political will to oppose. In all but a handful of cases, when the majority was able to get most of what it wanted, it did so in this manner rather than by advancing a contentious proposal. Moreover, clear partisan victories do not always result in clearly partisan passage votes. Across the fifty-five successes where the majority got most of what it wanted, just seventeen (31 percent) were enacted by final passage votes that we coded as *partisan outcomes*—in which the majority party enacted its proposal over the opposition of a majority of the opposition party in both chambers. Even fewer cases (22 percent, $n = 12$) passed without the support of an opposition party leader in at least one chamber. Figure 4.8 shows that bipartisanship was especially common when the majority party sought broad support on the way to victory. Just 17 percent of these cases (six in total) resulted in a partisan outcome, and only two cases (6 percent) passed without the support of opposition party leaders in at least one chamber.

Among clear victories following a pathway of seeking broad support, two general types emerge: those in which the majority party sought to take advantage of broad political support for a relatively modest policy proposal; and those in which the majority party sought to construct a bipartisan legislative package that could win passage.

One example of the former is the Democrats' efforts on college affordability during the 110th Congress. In one of several "rather bland . . . poll-tested proposals that would provide few targets for Republicans" (Peters and Rosenthal 2010, 61) composing the Six for '06 platform, Democrats aimed to cut student loan interest rates and expand Pell Grants. Additional pressure to reform lending practices came early in 2007 after a report found colleges were receiving kickbacks for directing students toward certain private lenders[34] and the Department of Education found at least one lender had kept hundreds of millions of dollars in improper federal subsidies.[35] Generally, in 2007 there was public and bipartisan support for some level

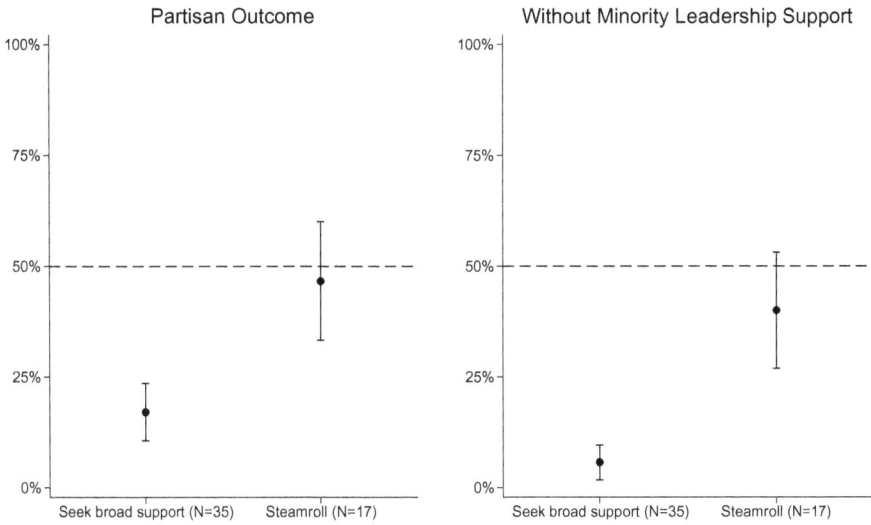

Figure 4.8. Percentage of "most" successes by pathways of success, passed with a partisan outcome or without minority leadership support (with standard errors)

of reform. Even President Bush included a plan in his fiscal year 2008 budget proposal to redirect nearly $20 billion in private lender subsidies to the Pell Grant program.[36]

House Democrats moved quickly. H.R. 5, which slashed student loan interest rates for those qualifying for subsidized loans, passed the House on January 17 with over 60 percent of Republicans voting in support.[37] And in July both the House and the Senate passed legislative packages cutting billions from lender subsidies and redirecting that money to various loan and student aid programs.[38] Differences between House and Senate packages, and a veto threat from President Bush over the specifics of how the money was to be redirected, extended negotiations through the summer.[39] However, the eventual outcome was never in doubt. There was broad support for redistributing billions in student loan funds. Negotiations focused on how, not if, those dollars would be reallocated.[40] By September, lead negotiators had persuaded enough members to sign on, and later in the month President Bush signed the bill into law. The final conference report on H.R. 2669 passed the House by a 292–97 vote with seventy-seven Republicans in support (44 percent of the conference), and passed the Senate 79–12 with most Republican senators (73 percent) in support. This was a clear victory for Democrats, but on a modest proposal with broad political appeal.

At least two items from the Republicans' Contract with America platform in 1994 were similar. Though not without opposition, a proposal to give the president a line-item veto had found substantial support in both parties well before the 104th Congress convened. As early as 1992, a modified line-item veto measure had passed a Democratic Party–controlled House with broad support,[41] and Bill Clinton publicly endorsed the effort before he was sworn in as president.[42] The challenge facing congressional Republicans was not to gin up support for a line-item veto in general, but to determine what specific mechanism could be enacted. The House proposal, H.R. 2, empowered the president to rescind spending decisions in appropriations laws, providing Congress with the power to overturn those decisions by a two-thirds vote in both chambers. This bill moved through the House with great speed and, reflecting its broad appeal, seventy-one Democrats joined nearly every Republican in passing the bill on February 6, 1995.[43]

In the Senate, three line-item veto mechanisms were considered. Senator McCain's proposal (S. 206) reflected the "enhanced rescissions" approach in the House bill, but Budget Committee chair Pete Domenici (R-NM) favored an "expedited rescissions" approach (S. 14) under which Congress would have to approve of the president's proposed rescissions, and Sen. Bob Dole (R-KS), the majority leader, preferred a proposal by which appropriations bills would be enrolled as hundreds of separate measures before being sent to the president for a signature or veto (S. 2).[44] An eventual compromise took parts from all three proposals, garnering not only unanimous Republican support, but also the yea votes of nineteen Democratic senators, passing the chamber 69–29.[45] While conference negotiations took time, final passage in March 1996 again reflected significant bipartisan support. The House never took a clean vote on the conference report but viewed it as popular enough to couple it with a debt ceiling increase so as to induce members to support raising the ceiling.[46] The final vote in the Senate was as sweeping as the first, passing 69–31, with nineteen Democrats again in support.

Unfunded mandates reform followed a similar track and was one of the first Contract with America planks signed into law. Heading into the 104th Congress, there was broad support among bipartisan organizations of state and local officials, and Democratic and Republican officeholders, to limit the federal government's ability to impose unfunded requirements on state, local, and tribal governments.[47] Throughout its first two years the Clinton administration had tried to curb unfunded mandates through executive action, and Clinton called for the passage of an unfunded mandates bill in his 1995 State of the Union address. Persistent opposition would emerge only from the most liberal Democrats.

House and Senate Republicans introduced identical bills on the subject at the start of the 104th Congress (H.R. 5 and S. 1). The proposal was fairly modest, barring new unfunded mandates but taking no action on existing ones,[48] and it quickly garnered broad support, undercutting the arguments of liberal Democrats that unfunded mandates reform was a veiled attempt at curbing existing entitlement and welfare programs. By February 1995 the House and Senate had passed their respective bills,[49] and only minor differences between the two versions needed to be ironed out in conference.[50] In March the conference report was cleared for the president's signature.

In addition to pursuing popular proposals, majority parties also won clear victories by using the legislative process to construct bipartisan bills. With these items, the majority party either was not at all specific at the start of the Congress about what it wanted to achieve with its legislative effort, or it entered into the new Congress ready to drop demands that had hampered success in previous years. Rather than achieving ideological aims, the primary goal was simply to pass *something* addressing the issue. These cases often involved reauthorizing federal programs, with a goal of getting the reauthorization done but with no clear desire for major or sweeping changes to those federal programs.

One example was the Republicans' goal of reauthorizing federal surface transportation policies during the 109th Congress. After failing to pass an ambitious and expensive "highway bill" in the previous Congress, Republicans entered the 109th Congress with more modest expectations and a willingness to settle for a smaller package than the $375 billion behemoth that had drawn President Bush's ire during the 108th.[51] With a temporary extension of transportation programs set to expire in May 2005, all sides were motivated to find an agreement.

Able to pick up where conference negotiations left off in late 2004, congressional Republicans had an idea of what might pass and win White House approval. Aiming to keep the overall price tag under the administration's stated $300 billion limit, the final hurdle was to mollify representatives of states paying significantly more into the Highway Trust Fund than they were getting out of it.[52] Once an agreement was reached, the bill (H.R. 3) sailed through the House, 417–9.[53] The Senate passed its version two months later by a similarly lopsided vote, 89–11. The outstanding issue between the chambers' bills was an $11 billion difference in total cost, which left the Senate bill above the president's red line. But with victory close and both congressional Republicans and the White House tired of delays,[54] negotiators were able to finish the job before the August recess, passing the conference report on H.R. 3 with well over 90 percent of each chamber in support.

This was a clear victory for Republicans, meeting their stated goal of getting the reauthorization done after three years of delays, but it worked in large part because of the modest and bipartisan nature of their policy objectives. They wanted to complete a surface transportation reauthorization, not fundamentally alter those policies or programs.

Republicans' goal of pension reform, also in the 109th Congress, displays similar dynamics. Having attempted reform of private-sector pensions for years, congressional Republicans were determined to get the job done and set aside internal party squabbles that had hindered previous efforts. In the 108th Congress, for instance, Senate Republicans and the Bush administration clashed over a plan to bail out some private pension plans.[55] But by 2005, several high-profile defaults of private retirement benefit plans brought new urgency to pension reform and created an atmosphere of crisis.

In January the Bush administration unveiled a proposal for shoring up the finances of the Pension Benefit Guaranty Corporation (PBGC)—which insures private pension plans and by 2004 was running a $23 billion deficit[56]—by phasing in increases in companies' contributions to the PBGC fund and instituting even higher premiums on companies that did not meet their pension obligations. In summer the House and Senate advanced their separate plans, both similar in approach to the administration's.[57] House Democrats showed some willingness to try to make a political issue out of the Republicans' pension reform efforts, unanimously opposing the plan in committee, but when it reached the floor seventy Democrats backed it,[58] and the Senate's similar plan passed with overwhelming bipartisan support, 97–2.[59] Conference negotiations dragged on for five months, largely because Republicans hoped to attach the pension reform bill to a series of tax breaks and retirement security proposals. Once the decision was made to move pension reform separately, the Pension Protection Act of 2006 (H.R. 4) passed easily, 279–131 in the House, and 93–5 in the Senate.

These four cases share important similarities. In each there was broad support throughout the political system for action on an issue. Members of both parties agreed legislation was needed, and there was agreement on the broad contours of the policy solution. Often there was urgency to act, with a looming crisis or failure of previous Congresses to take legislative action on the issue at hand. And in each case the majority either made a modest proposal or sought a modest outcome. Legislative negotiations focused on hammering out the details of a plan rather than adjudicating major disagreements. Once those details were settled, these legislative efforts sailed to easy passage, giving the majority party clear victories on priority agenda items.

In the remaining seventeen cases in which the majority party got most of what it wanted, it steamrolled the opposition.[60] However, even many of these cases ended in bipartisan votes. In eight of the seventeen steamrolls the opposition party waved the white flag, yielding to public pressure or support for the majority's proposal and reluctantly conceding defeat and voting for it on the House and Senate floors despite clear dissatisfaction.

In our dataset, all cases of Democrats giving in on Republican proposals involved military policy in the aftermath of the September 11 terrorist attacks. Twice in the 107th Congress, and once each in the 108th and 109th Congresses, Democrats dropped their previous opposition to new or expansive military funding. As late as summer 2001, top Senate Democrats were demanding increases in social spending in return for supporting some of the Bush administration's requests on defense spending and military projects,[61] and others were pointing to declining revenue projections (after the tax cuts package passed earlier that year) as necessitating cuts to the Department of Defense.[62] But after the terrorist attacks in New York and Washington, Democrats dropped their opposition to several defense buildup measures, including the largest increase in military spending since the Vietnam War[63] and aggressive new spending to back the Bush administration's ambitious missile defense system plan[64]—an agenda priority that Democrats had opposed in previous Congresses.[65] These same dynamics continued during the 108th and 109th Congresses as most Democrats voted to pass large supplemental spending bills for the war on terror and military operations in Afghanistan and Iraq.[66] In the security-minded years following 2001, Democrats were wary of appearing weak on defense.

Republicans, for their part, waved the white flag when opposition might have made them appear heartless or indifferent to vulnerable populations (as noted above). The most recent such case was the reauthorization of the Violence against Women Act in 2013 (the 113th Congress). Throughout the 112th Congress, Senate Democrats advocated a renewed and expanded law, including new provisions covering gay and lesbian victims, expanding visa access to immigrant victims of domestic abuse, and extending the law to tribal lands.[67] House Republicans balked at these new proposals, passing a more restrictive measure along party lines. After the 2012 elections, attempts to find a compromise ran afoul of Republican hard-liners, even as some Democrats appeared willing to negotiate.[68] As the 113th Congress convened, Senate Democrats again pushed their expansive measure and won bipartisan support.[69] This time House Republican leaders acquiesced. Unwilling to let their party take any more body blows for conducting a "war on women,"[70] the House Republican leadership put the Senate's bill on the floor, where it passed 286–138, with eighty-seven Republicans joining all Democrats in support.

A similar case occurred twenty-two years earlier, during the 102nd Congress, when Republicans dropped their opposition to the Democrats' antidiscrimination proposals in the aftermath of the Anita Hill testimony. In the late 1980s, several rulings by the Rehnquist-led Supreme Court limited the reach and effectiveness of federal antidiscrimination laws and placed new burdens on plaintiffs alleging racial or sexual discrimination in the workplace.[71] In the 101st Congress, President George H. W. Bush vetoed the Civil Rights Act of 1990, which included new antidiscrimination language (S. 2104), calling the provisions burdensome and saying they would "introduce the destructive force of quotas into our Nation's employment system."[72] House and Senate Republicans had joined President Bush in opposition, voting overwhelmingly against S. 2104 in both chambers and blocking a veto override in the Senate.[73]

In the first several months of the 102nd Congress, the battle lines appeared unchanged as Democrats again pushed for strong antidiscrimination policies and congressional Republicans and the White House stood in opposition. H.R. 1 met the same stiff Republican opposition as its predecessor bill, and it passed the House with just twenty-two Republican votes in support. Republicans maintained their rhetorical opposition as well. Henry Hyde (R-IL), for instance, said the bill was "about dividing people—tribalizing and balkanizing our society." Newt Gingrich (R-GA), then minority whip, chastised Democrats for earning fewer Republican votes for their proposal than they had in the previous Congress, predicting that "a long-term trend is against the bill."[74]

Throughout the summer, negotiations in the Senate and between Democrats and President Bush proved fruitless. A breakthrough came only with allegations of sexual misconduct against the president's Supreme Court nominee Clarence Thomas and the controversy surrounding Anita Hill's testimony before the Judiciary Committee. With Ku Klux Klansman David Duke's strong showing as a Republican in a gubernatorial race in Louisiana, Republicans began to fear that their continued opposition to a civil rights and antidiscrimination bill would paint them in a negative light. As *CQ Magazine* described it, "Sensing that Bush could no longer count enough Senate Republicans to sustain another veto, White House officials cut a deal with Senate bill proponents."[75] The final bill, S. 1745, on which the Democrats gave in very little and the White House sacrificed a lot, passed overwhelmingly, 93–5 in the Senate, and 381–38 in the House.

These cases are clear partisan victories, won when the minority party conceded defeat. Only the remaining nine steamroll victories in our dataset represent clear partisan successes over unrelenting opposition. These successes—which account for just 3 percent of all the party agenda priorities in our data—represent the kind of partisan lawmaking envisioned by party government theorists, in which the majority party achieves most of what it set out to achieve and does so by passing its proposals with a majority of the other party opposed in both chambers and without the support of opposition party leaders in either chamber.[76]

In many ways these cases are an exceptional bunch. Two of them—the ACA and the Dodd-Frank financial sector reforms—were possible only because of the Democrats' unusually large Senate majority during the 111th Congress. Two relied on budget reconciliation procedures that allowed the majority to sidestep the usual supermajoritarian rules of the Senate: the Republicans' 2017 tax reform effort (115th Congress) and the ACA (111th Congress). Moreover, all but one took place under unified government, a rare condition during our period of study, and the one exception (PAYGO reforms) did not require a presidential signature.

These steamroll victories did not always move policy in the ideological direction one might expect (as we discussed in chapter 2). The tougher sentencing requirements in the Democrats' 1994 crime bill did not constitute a leftward move in criminal justice. Likewise, the Republicans' Medicare Modernization Act creating Medicare's prescription drug benefit program was a major unfunded expansion of a Great Society entitlement program, hardly a major conservative shift. In other cases the policy changes achieved by these steamroll victories were rather modest. The PAYGO rules enacted in the 110th Congress did not survive a change in party control of the House in the 112th Congress. Although it was a hard-fought victory at the time, the passage of Motor Voter did not have the expected effect on voter registration and participation.

These nine steamroll victories are a controversial and unrepresentative bunch. They show that congressional majority parties can achieve clear partisan victories, but rarely. Even when they do so, there is no guarantee that the legislation will endure or prove to be a good talking point for the party's electioneering in the future.

For the most part, when majority parties achieve clear victories, they do so by seeking bipartisanship or inducing the other party to drop its opposition. Among these fifty-five clear victories, just nine look like the partisan steamrolling that political pundits and theories of party government usually envision. Even in today's hyperpartisan Congress, strong and clear victories on majority party agenda priorities usually involve bipartisanship.

Settling for Less: Backing Down and Seeking Bipartisanship

Partial successes—in which congressional majority parties achieve only some of what they set out to achieve—are largely stories of backing down. On 84 percent of these successes, the majority party succeeded by giving in to the opposition on significant aspects of its proposal. On 20 percent of partial successes, the majority party sought broad support from the beginning, and on another 12 percent bipartisan logrolls were a pathway to success.

These eighty-three outcomes were typically enacted by strong bipartisan majorities, regardless of the pathway. Across all the cases, just 14 percent were enacted with partisan final passage votes in the House and Senate, and just 13 percent were opposed by the opposition party's leaders in both chambers. In the end, each pathway resulted in similarly low levels of partisanship on final passage (see fig. 4.9).

Despite being less complete victories for the parties, these efforts were no less significant in the importance of the policies produced. Almost identical percentages of clear (49 percent) and partial (53 percent) successes in our dataset are included in Mayhew's list of landmark laws. Table 4.1 directly compares lists of thirteen notable clear and partial successes. Both columns are composed exclusively of landmark legislation, and the lists rival each other in terms of major lawmaking efforts and broad impact on American public policy. Table 4.1 is reminiscent of table 2.3, which displayed lists of laws enacted on partisan and bipartisan votes. Rather than comparing laws based on extent of support on final passage, table 4.1 classifies them based on policy outcomes, comparing laws on which the majority got most versus some of what it set out to achieve. As is evident here, partial party victories may be less fulfilling to implacable partisans, but they are of roughly equal weight in major congressional policymaking since the 1980s.

The primary distinctions among the cases of partial success are how much the majority party compromised on its initial goals and whether it primarily made concessions across the aisle or also had to make important concessions to its own members to get them on board.

In some cases the majority conceded a lot to the opposition to seal the deal, even giving away the farm in order to claim "victory." One example was the Republicans' effort to replace No Child Left Behind (NCLB) in the 114th Congress (2015–16). Legislators had been working since 2007 to

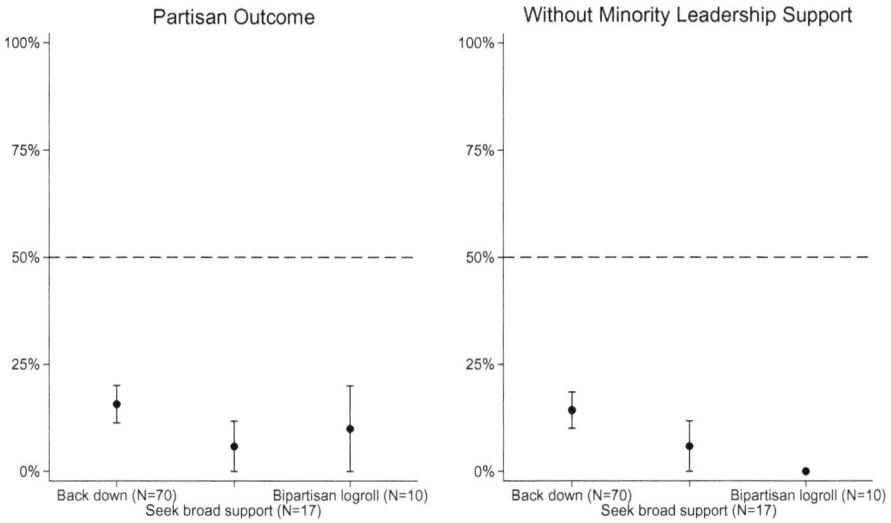

Figure 4.9. Percentage of "some" successes by pathways of success, passed with a partisan outcome or without minority leadership support (with standard errors)

Table 4.1 Notable clear and partial majority party successes

Notable clear successes	Notable partial successes
Tax Cuts and Jobs Act (115th)	Dodd-Frank rollback (115th)
Violence against Women Act renewal (113th)	21st Century Cures Act (114th)
Children's Health Insurance Program increase (111th)	American Taxpayer Relief Act (fiscal cliff, 112th)
Affordable Care Act (111th)	2009 financial stimulus (111th)
Dodd-Frank (111th)	2008 FISA amendments (110th)
PAYGO (110th)	Bush tax cuts part 1 (107th)
Medicare Modernization Act (108th)	No Child Left Behind (107th)
Partial-birth abortion ban (108th)	Gramm-Leach-Bliley (106th)
Bush tax cuts part 2 (108th)	Balanced Budget Act of 1997 (105th)
Unfunded mandates reform (104th)	Welfare reform (104th)
National Voter Registration Act/Motor Voter (103rd)	Clinton budget (103rd)
Omnibus crime bill (103rd)	Clean Air Act amendments (101st)
Family and Medical Leave Act (103rd)	1986 tax reform (99th)

reauthorize the law but had come up empty on previous efforts. Both parties disliked aspects of NCLB and agreed it was "too prescriptive and had unintended consequences."[77] But it was not so easy to find agreement on what to change. Since 2011, House Republicans had pushed to devolve as much power as possible to the states. During the 113th Congress, H.R. 5

proposed to give states flexibility to develop their own systems of student accountability, combine most federal education grants into one flexible block grant, and make it easier for students to use federal dollars to attend private schools. Democrats opposed most of these provisions and opposed H.R. 5 unanimously in committee and on the floor as the bill squeaked through the House 221–207. The Democrats' proposal that year (S. 1094) was very different. Senate Democrats proposed to give the states some additional flexibility but placed more stringent federal requirements on standards, and maintained the existing structure for federal grants.

The two sides fought to a draw in the 113th Congress, and they appeared headed in the same direction in the 114th. In 2015 the House passed a bill similar to that from the 113th Congress,[78] and again it passed by the narrowest of margins, 218–213, without any Democratic votes. But in the now Republican-controlled Senate, Lamar Alexander (R-TN), chair of the Health, Education, Labor, and Pensions Committee, recognized the need to compromise.[79] With just a three-seat majority, Senate Republicans needed Democratic votes to move forward with any bill. Alexander worked with Sen. Patty Murray (D-WA) to construct a compromise that could earn Democratic and Republican votes (S. 1177). The compromise increased federal K-12 education spending to appeal to Democrats, but to appeal to Republicans it also gave states more flexibility in setting standards and spending federal funds. The Senate bill did not contain some of the more controversial provisions of the House bill, including the move to block grants, and as a result it passed easily, 81–17. Alexander sacrificed a lot of Republican priorities with the compromise, which earned more Democratic votes (40) than Republican votes (39). But the compromise showed that an agreement could be reached.

In conference, the question was whether House Republicans would hold firm or accept the Senate's bipartisan approach. Ultimately they did the latter, backing off nearly all of their most contentious proposals to reach a deal.[80] Conservative Republicans were clearly unhappy with the final deal, which garnered unanimous Democratic support in both chambers but saw sixty-four House Republicans and twelve Republican senators oppose it on the floor. In making concessions, Republicans succeeded on one of their top priorities for the 114th Congress, but they had to give up on many of their partisan goals for reforming federal K-12 education policy.

A very similar situation took place during the 115th Congress. A Republican priority for this Congress was reauthorizing the farm bill. Specifically, Republican leaders hoped to use the reauthorization effort to make broad changes to the food stamp program (Supplemental Nutrition Assistance

Program, or SNAP), including stricter work requirements for beneficiaries along with other conservative proposals on commodity trading, conservation programs, and forestry programs.[81] In June 2018 the House passed a partisan bill (H.R. 2) including this wish list, and it received a predictably partisan vote. After an earlier failed passage vote, the bill narrowly passed, 213–211, with no Democrats in support and twenty Republicans joining them in opposition.

In the Senate, Agriculture Committee chairman Pat Roberts (R-KS) worked with ranking member Debbie Stabenow (D-MI) to forge a more bipartisan path forward. As in other cases, they avoided all of the land mines that created controversy in the House bill. But the result was a measure that achieved none of what Republican leaders stated they wanted to accomplish at the start of the Congress, including new work requirements tied to SNAP.[82] In conference, House negotiators and conservatives folded. With little time left in the 115th Congress and an incoming Democratic House majority threatening the work Republicans had put in over the previous two years, the House largely accepted the Senate's language. According to one conservative insider, there was not "a single significant conservative win to be found in the entire 800-page monstrosity."[83] Republicans passed a farm bill reauthorization, but they gave up on nearly everything they wanted to get it done.

Democrats have experienced similarly hollow victories, such as their effort to revise the Foreign Intelligence Surveillance Act (FISA) in the 110th Congress. After the Bush administration's secret wiretapping program was uncovered in late 2005,[84] Democrats made revamping FISA provisions a major priority when they took back the majority in the 2006 elections. Democrats wanted to increase oversight of surveillance ordered under FISA and opposed the Bush administration's plans to give "retroactive immunity" to telecommunications companies that had cooperated with the secret program after September 11.

Ahead of a February 1, 2008, deadline to reauthorize FISA authorities, Democrats began moving on an overhaul. In November 2007 House Democrats passed H.R. 3773, which required the Justice Department to oversee actions taken under FISA, revoked immunity for telecommunications companies, and required warrants for collecting information involving persons in the United States.[85] House Republicans almost unanimously opposed the bill, and President Bush threatened to veto any legislation that did not provide retroactive as well as prospective immunity or did not provide the tools for eavesdropping he requested.[86] In the other chamber, after a lengthy standoff during which a similarly strong Democratic proposal failed to win enough votes to secure cloture,[87] Senate Democrats caved and supported a compromise measure drafted by Sen. Jay Rockefeller (D-WV) and backed by Senate Republicans and the White House.

House Democrats initially stuck to their guns and refused to pass the compromise legislation, letting FISA authorities lapse. In mid-March, feeling public pressure, House Democrats tried to put together a measure with softer language on retroactive immunity, but Republicans held firm and opposed the measure on the House floor.[88] Not wanting to imperil their 2008 election hopes, House Democrats surrendered and, on June 19, announced that they had struck a deal. The compromise, which had been endorsed by the White House, placed far fewer restrictions and less oversight on government surveillance than Democrats had wanted. They were able to get the Bush administration to agree to let a federal court decide the issue of retroactive immunity,[89] but Republicans saw this change as a mere formality, and the courts ultimately upheld the immunity given to these companies.[90]

Technically, Democrats could claim "victory" in addressing one of their priority agenda items for the 110th Congress—revising FISA laws—but they came up empty on almost everything they wanted to get done. They wanted increased oversight but did not get it. They wanted telecommunications companies to be liable for secretly cooperating with the Bush administration, but they did not get that. In this case and others in our data, the majority party gave up a lot of what it hoped to accomplish to cut a deal and pass the legislation.

Cases of backing down were not always so unfortunate for the majority. Often, majority parties find more favorable compromises. The "fiscal cliff" standoff during the 112th Congress is one example. The fiscal cliff—a looming combination of dramatic tax increases and across-the-board spending cuts that would go into effect on January 1, 2013—spurred Democratic and Republican efforts to promote their competing visions for federal budgetary policy. House Republicans wanted to preserve Bush-era tax cuts while cutting nondefense discretionary spending. Senate Democrats wanted to end the Bush-era cuts for the richest Americans—those earning more than $250,000 annually—while preserving nondefense discretionary spending.[91]

Both parties advanced partisan measures as the cliff loomed.[92] In July 2012, Senate Democrats passed their proposal (S. 3412) 51–48, with every Republican lined up in opposition. House Republicans responded in August, passing their bill (H.R. 8) along mostly partisan lines, 256–171. Several months of dramatic negotiations ensued, especially after President Obama won reelection. It seemed neither side would budge as hard-line Republicans refused to consider any tax increases and hard-line Democrats balked at any significant nondefense spending cuts. At the last moment, on New Year's Eve, both sides backed down and agreed to a compromise under which each side got some of what it wanted and sacrificed other priorities. Democrats saw Bush-era tax rates increase for Americans making over $450,000—higher than their $250,000 target but lower that the $1 million threshold Republicans had offered in negotiations. Republicans, for their part, got some cuts to discretionary spending—$12 billion in total—about half of the $24 billion they wanted. Neither side was thrilled, but each could claim a partial victory as the American Taxpayer Relief Act (H.R. 8) passed each chamber with support from both Democrats and Republicans.

The Republican priority of welfare reform in the 104th Congress was similar. In a plank of the Contract with America, Republicans wanted to turn various social welfare programs into block grants, shifting control to the states. Their far-reaching reform proposal (H.R. 4) reflected Republican priorities. The bill proposed to give states control over a host of federal social programs, including Medicaid, foster care, adoption programs, school lunch programs, nutritional assistance for pregnant women and children, and food stamps.[93] It passed the House 234–199, with just five Democrats in favor. Twice, congressional Republicans sent proposals of this nature to President Clinton's desk, and twice he vetoed them.[94]

After costly budget standoffs with Clinton, Republicans began to narrow the scope of the welfare reform proposals. In May the GOP unveiled a proposal that included only provisions reforming the AFDC welfare program and Medicaid. But with Clinton again inclined to veto the measure, Republicans agreed to drop the Medicaid provisions as well.[95] When Republicans reworked the bill to replace only AFDC with a block grant (TANF), Clinton—who had campaigned on a promise to "end welfare as we know it"—finally agreed to sign.[96] The legislation was a big win for Republicans, but they had significantly narrowed the scope of their proposal to get it done.

Cases of backing down did not always involve making concessions primarily to the minority party. Sometimes the majority party had to grant important concessions to its own members or internal factions, who were the bigger obstacles to legislative success. With the Republicans' goal of cutting taxes in the 107th Congress, for instance, important concessions had to be made to fiscally moderate Republican senators, including Jim Jeffords (R-VT) and Olympia Snowe (R-ME), to keep them on board.[97] In several other cases concessions within the majority party were crucial to legislative victory. The passage of No Child Left Behind (107th Congress) hinged on accommodations the Bush administration and conservative Republicans made for moderates in their own party, especially dropping their proposal to create a private school voucher program.[98] In the 106th Congress, passage of the Gramm-Leach-Bliley financial services reforms largely hinged on compromises between the conservative Phil Gramm (R-TX), who chaired the Senate Banking Committee, and the moderate Jim Leach (R-IA), who chaired the House Banking Committee.[99]

Backing down and making concessions is not the only way majorities can claim partial victories. A subset of our cases are coded as *bipartisan logrolls*. In these cases the majority, rather than giving up on its priorities, paired them with minority party priorities to win support from across the aisle. A recent case exemplifies this pathway to success: the legislative drive resulting in the 21st Century Cures Act in the 114th Congress. Republicans wanted to pass a biomedical innovations bill, with a focus on streamlining Food and Drug Administration (FDA) approval of new drugs and treatments. But to get the job done they had to incorporate the Democrats' priorities on medical research. In the House, Energy and Commerce Committee chair Fred Upton (R-MI) worked with Rep. Diana DeGette (D-CO) to build a package that both parties could support by coupling streamlined FDA drug approval processes with increases in funding for medical research through the National Institutes of Health. The bill (H.R. 6) passed the House with ease but ran into disagreements that slowed its progress in the Senate.[100] The deal got done only as Republican leaders worked to add even more provisions that would build support on each side of the aisle, including funding for several of the Obama administration's health initiatives, such as Vice President Biden's "moonshot" cancer initiative and money for states to combat the growing opioid epidemic. The final package (H.R. 34) passed both chambers with broad bipartisan support.[101] Both sides would find things to complain about with the final package, but both parties also got things they wanted, and Republicans could claim victory on one of their agenda priorities.

When congressional majority parties achieve partial victories, they do so primarily by dropping provisions in their proposals that draw strong opposition or adding provisions that build bipartisan support. Throughout the Congresses we studied, we find examples of congressional majority parties making concessions to achieve legislative successes. Even in today's hyperpartisan politics, compromise, rather than intransigence, remains a key to party success.

Majority Party Success in a Partisan Era

Majority parties in the contemporary Congress take various paths to succeed on their agenda items, but most of those paths end in bipartisanship. Across the 138 party agenda successes we analyze in this chapter, only 14 percent saw the majority steamroll its opposition, just 21 percent saw a law enacted over the resistance of the opposing party in both chambers, and just nine cases (7 percent) saw the majority get most of what it set out to achieve while doing both of those things. Even as the parties have become more homogeneous and as conflict between the parties has ramped up since the 1980s, strategies of building broad support still predominate when majority parties succeed in accomplishing their legislative goals. Majority parties today and in previous decades overwhelmingly achieve successes either by seeking to advance broadly supported proposals or by backing down and giving up on the more contentious and partisan aspects of their agendas.

These findings have clear implications for how we understand party influence in congressional lawmaking. First, they clearly do not fit with the general expectations of theories of congressional party government. We do not find that contemporary majority parties are able to marshal their impressive roll-call voting unity or their considerable organizational and procedural advantages to regularly push through clear partisan victories on their agenda priorities. Instead, we find that party proposals are often not very controversial but are modest, broadly supported ideas that do not engender significant opposition. These cases of seeking broad support were found throughout the Congresses we studied and accounted for almost 40 percent of majority party victories in our dataset.

More commonly, in more than half of all the cases we studied, the majority party had to back down on key aspects of its proposals, making concessions to either the opposition party or holdouts within its own ranks in order to enact legislation. In some cases majority parties succeeded in legislating on agenda items only after giving way on almost everything they sought to achieve. Such hollow victories bear out Rep. Richard Bolling's (1968, 24) observation:

> There is a point at which supporters of a particular bill must decide whether or not to compromise the bill into ineffectiveness in order to score a nominal victory or to refuse to do so and to suffer obvious defeat, only to return to the task of mustering the public and governmental majority necessary to pass meaningful legislation.

We found examples of such cases even in very recent Congresses, illustrating that majority parties today face the same dilemmas Bolling described in a much less partisan era. Sometimes majority parties get much less than half a loaf and have to confront the question of just how little is acceptable.

Throughout our analyses we find remarkable continuity over the decades. From the mid-1980s through 2018, there were no significant changes to the pathways congressional majority parties followed to achieve victories on their agenda priorities, the degree to which majorities achieved complete or partial victories, or levels of partisanship on final passage votes to enact majority party proposals. Congressional majority parties in the 2010s achieved legislative victories on their priority items in much the same way such parties did during the Reagan administration—by cultivating bipartisan support, backing off contentious items, or otherwise finding ways to build coalitions broad enough to overcome the considerable hurdles that characterize the process.

If our findings do not fit with partisan theories, they also do not fit neatly with a pivotal politics model of congressional lawmaking. Consistent with pivotal politics models, we find lawmaking is generally bipartisan and enacting coalitions are generally large. But in most of the legislative histories we investigated, pivotal actors were not prominent players, and outcomes usually garnered support beyond what would have been necessary to clear pivot points. Furthermore, the individuals we interviewed did not describe coalition building as a process of routinely seeking to placate key moderates in the House and Senate. Rather, congressional negotiators think about lawmaking in terms of the parties as the central units, seeking to identify what can engender the support of most of both parties, or at least not draw strong partisan opposition.

As we discussed in chapter 2, majority parties in the current polarized era often have to negotiate directly with minority party leaders rather than try to pick off support from among the minority party's rank and file. Today's cohesive minority parties limit opportunities for majority party leaders to construct policy proposals that will pull in just enough minority party moderates to subvert Senate filibusters. Rather, negotiators usually work to determine what minority leaders and ranking members can sign off on and legislate from there. Even in the House, where single-party lawmaking is always a possibility based on the majoritarian rules of the chamber, lawmakers frequently seek to develop bipartisan agreement as early as possible in the legislative process rather than waiting until it becomes necessary in the later stages, attempting to develop proposals that have a chance to earn Senate passage and a presidential signature well before they clear the chamber initially. In most cases when congressional parties are able to break free of gridlock and achieve legislative successes, the process involves various techniques of "deliberative negotiation" in which the parties seek zones of agreement and engage in logrolling or compromise (Warren and Mansbridge 2015).

Finally, these findings have implications for party accountability, and for accountability in the American political system more broadly. We find here that congressional majorities can sometimes steer the ship of state, enacting legislation addressing their party priorities, but the rudder is rarely turned decisively. Mostly, to earn victories congressional parties have to compromise, concede, or otherwise advance watered-down proposals. They most often get only some of what they want, and in many cases their proposals are humble to begin with. Generally speaking, the more unified parties of the contemporary period have not ushered in more programmatic party lawmaking, as party reformers of earlier eras would have envisioned, and have not created the conditions for the public to hold the majority party accountable for its policy actions. While parties are unmistakably central units in congressional lawmaking, they are rarely able to legislate their partisan visions into law; and voters, in turn, are unable to then hold a congressional majority party accountable for the direction of public policy. Despite decades of partisan change, the US political system continues to frustrate partisan ambitions and continually limits what either party can accomplish on its own.

FIVE

Bipartisanship and the Decline
of Regular Order

Under regular order, bipartisanship and compromise flourish.

—Rep. Justin Amash (I-MI, 2011–)[1]

The problem is not the process; the problem is the problem.

—Rudolph Penner, former Congressional Budget Office director[2]

Picking up where the previous chapter left off, here we continue to investigate *how* congressional majority parties succeed in enacting laws. In particular, we assess the often-made argument that congressional majority parties bypass traditional legislative processes as a means of enacting their partisan agendas. Since the 1970s, Congress has increasingly departed from "regular order" or "traditional" processes under which legislation is developed in committee, is subjected to open floor amendment, then traverses other legislative steps. Instead, it has frequently turned to unorthodox, behind-the-scenes processes that centralize decision making in congressional leaders (Sinclair 2016; Tiefer 2016). Parallel to these changes, congressional partisanship and party conflict have intensified (Barber and McCarty 2015; Lee 2016). Many contend that these two trends are causally linked.

Indeed, members of Congress and journalists frequently maintain that unorthodox processes make lawmaking more partisan and that a return to regular order would promote more bipartisanship. This perspective was on stark display during Republicans' 2017 push to repeal and replace the Affordable Care Act. Current and former lawmakers on both sides of the aisle lamented that the secretive, behind-the-scenes approach to writing the bill was responsible for the intensity of partisan discord.[3] Political scientists likewise often portray traditional, decentralized legislative processes as central to careful deliberation, conflict resolution, and bipartisan consensus building (Fenno 1962; Lewallen, Theriault, and Jones 2016; Mann and Ornstein 2012; Polsby 1975). Unorthodox processes are often presented as tools of congressional majority party power, used to ram through partisan laws (Aldrich and Rohde 2000a, 2000b; Cox and McCubbins 2005; Monroe and Robinson 2008; Young and Wilkins 2007).[4]

This chapter takes stock of these claims in two steps. First, we assess the relation between violations of "regular order" (the use of unorthodox processes) and the levels of partisan disagreement on the passage of 621 important laws passed by Congress from 1987 to 2016. Second, drawing again on our interviews, we seek to understand leaders' motivations for employing unorthodox processes. We find little evidence that the use of unorthodox legislative processes is a leading indicator of partisan lawmaking. Congressional leaders often turn to unorthodox approaches not to pass partisan programs, but to resolve impasses in enacting bipartisan legislation. The flexibility and secrecy permitted by these more streamlined, centralized procedures help with negotiations and can be necessary to legislate successfully in the contemporary political environment, even with highly bipartisan legislation. Rather than being tools of party power used to enact partisan laws, unorthodox processes are largely just different means to achieving legislative ends.

Legislative Processes and Party Power

A half-century ago, congressional procedure almost always adhered to what we refer to today as "regular order." Although there is no single consensus definition of the concept, Sinclair (2016) offers the most systematic characterization. She describes regular order as a formal, sequential process featuring a decentralized division of labor in the development of legislation and broad opportunities for rank-and-file members to participate during consideration of bills on the floor.

Generally, when scholars and observers write about regular order, they focus on committee-led policy development and open floor consideration (e.g., Bendix 2016a; Aldrich and Rohde 2000b; Rohde 1991). Typically, a bill is introduced and referred to a committee, where it is scrutinized in committee hearings. Subsequently, committee "markups" are held during which the bill is subjected to debate and amendment before it is voted on and reported to the floor. On the chamber floor, it is again subjected to open debate and amendment before a final vote on passage. The process repeats itself in the other chamber. If the bill passes there, a conference committee hammers out House and Senate agreement before it is voted on again and sent to the president.

Congressional scholarship routinely portrays these traditional legislative processes as designed to promote meaningful deliberation and to build bipartisan policymaking coalitions. The foundations of these perspectives stem from pioneering works of Richard Fenno and Nelson Polsby, among others. Fenno (1962, 310) described committee-led processes as important for "integration" in Congress. Committees' formal processes and norms were found to help reduce conflict and build consensus around action, particularly on the House Appropriations Committee (Fenno 1966). More broadly, Polsby (1975) conceived of "transformative" legislatures as those that were well institutionalized and followed routine processes with a complex and decentralized division of labor. For Polsby, internal organization and processes strengthen legislatures and mute external pressures, including those from parties. Contemporary scholarship also reinforces the view that committees are critical to the development of bipartisan consensus. For instance, the informational committees model describes committees as agents of the chamber rather than of the majority party (Gilligan and Krehbiel 1990; Krehbiel 1991; see also Kiewiet and McCubbins 1991).

Today, rather than following these traditional approaches, Congress frequently operates by what Sinclair (2016) terms "unorthodox" processes. These centralized, informal, leadership-led, and often secretive approaches to legislating include bypassing traditional committee consideration, closing off amendment and debate on the floor, and moving legislative development and negotiations behind the scenes, where they are managed by congressional party leaders (Bendix 2016a; Curry 2015; Hanson 2014; Tiefer 2016; Wallner 2013). In chapter 1, figure 1.4 documented how much policy development occurs outside the committee process in the contemporary Congress. Likewise, figures 1.5 and 1.6 illustrated the marked decline of floor amending in both the House and the Senate.

Theories of congressional party government see unorthodox legislative procedures largely as instruments of party power. Leaders are thought to use such maneuvers to ram through partisan legislation, exacerbating partisan conflict in the House and Senate (Aldrich and Rohde 2000a; Cox and McCubbins 2005). Harbridge (2015) further contends that party leaders use their procedural control over the House agenda to undercut bipartisan agreement among the rank and file. In a vicious cycle, hyperpartisanship is understood to lead to unorthodox legislating, which in turn fuels deeper partisan conflict (Lewallen, Theriault, and Jones 2016). Members of

Congress themselves often describe centralized processes as sapping committee autonomy and reducing opportunities for bipartisanship (Crespin and Madonna 2016).

In short, there is a clear sense that regular order promotes broadly supported and bipartisan laws, whereas unorthodox and centralized processes are used by the majority party to pass partisan laws.

There are reasons to be skeptical of this narrative. The superiority of regular order rests on the assumption, often unspoken, that members will employ open processes to deliberate about public policy in good faith. But open processes in the contemporary Congress can be exploited not to work out policy disagreements, but for obstruction, partisan grandstanding, and scoring points. When there is tight competition for party control of governing institutions (Lee 2016), members of Congress have incentives to push messaging votes rather than substantive proposals (Egar 2016; Gelman 2017). Open processes also permit more opportunities for legislative obstruction (Smith 2014). Given such incentives, "regular order" in the contemporary Congress can frequently hamper serious legislative efforts rather than aid them.

Consider, for example, the fate of House Republicans' top legislative priority in 2011.[5] Fresh off their impressive victory in the 2010 elections, House Republicans were determined to cut federal spending by billions of dollars. GOP backbenchers, in particular, wanted opportunities to offer their own particular cuts for consideration on the House floor. The leadership relented, putting an omnibus appropriations bill on the floor open for amendment.[6] What resulted was the most freewheeling amending process seen on the House floor in decades. Democratic and Republican members offered over four hundred amendments to the bill across almost four days.[7] However, the bill that finally passed, on an almost perfect party-line vote, 235–189,[8] hardly reflected the bipartisan agreement that is often lauded as a benefit of such open amending.

Similarly, a 2016 energy and water appropriations bill was defeated on the floor of the House largely because the leadership allowed an open process.[9] Bowing to pressure, the leadership ruled in order Rep. Sean Maloney's (D-NY) amendment to ban federal contractors from discriminating based on sexual orientation or gender identity.[10] The amendment passed 223–195, drawing support from forty-three Republicans. But the amendment was a poison pill. Democrats were still unwilling to support the underlying appropriations measure and voted overwhelmingly against the final package. Conservative Republicans, opposed to the LGBT protections language, also turned in opposition. The bill failed 112–305.[11] As these cases show, allowing more open processes does not necessarily translate into bipartisan consensus.

Nothing about regular order guarantees bipartisan cooperation. Recent legislative efforts provide clear examples. The Affordable Care Act[12] and Dodd-Frank[13] were subject to dozens of committee hearings and markups but were enacted with little minority party support. Meanwhile, nearly every omnibus spending deal to avert a government shutdown in recent years was negotiated behind the scenes by party leaders, and each one passed with a bipartisan majority.[14] Legislation ending the fiscal cliff standoff of 2011–12 was also negotiated behind closed doors without any traditional process but was enacted by a cross-party coalition.[15] In the end, the use of particular *processes* may neither generate nor preclude bipartisanship.

Assessing Process and Partisanship

We take stock of whether unorthodox processes appear to be tools of partisan lawmaking in two steps. First we ask a straightforward descriptive question: Are laws passed using more unorthodox processes more partisan than laws passed under regular order? This has been studied surprisingly little. Work positing a connection typically analyzes action in just one chamber, focuses on selected examples, or does not track whether efforts actually resulted in the enactment of laws (Aldrich and Rohde 2000a, 2000b; Cox and McCubbins 2005; Monroe and Robinson 2008; Young and Wilkins 2007).

Scholars may have steered away from investigating the relation between process and outcomes because of thorny problems with causal inference. Even if unorthodox legislative processes correlate with partisanship, correlation alone would not establish causation. Indeed, leaders may turn to centralized processes in response to heightened partisan conflict, rather than the processes' themselves driving partisanship. If centralized processes *do* correlate with more partisan outcomes, scholars would still need to determine whether partisanship drives process, process drives partisanship, or the two interact. The next section of this chapter delves into the motives behind the use of unorthodox procedures. However, at present scholars have not even established that there is a *correlation* between processes and partisan lawmaking. Questions of causal inference present themselves only if there is a correlation. No one would posit a causal relation in the absence of any correlation.

To assess any such relation, we assembled a dataset of important laws passed by Congress from 1987 to 2016 (100th–114th Congresses). This dataset is different from that used in the previous chapters. Here we are not just interested in understanding how congressional majorities pursue their agenda priorities. We want to understand whether they employ unorthodox tactics to maximize partisan advantage, and partisan lawmaking, on the full range of important laws enacted by the Congress.

To compile this dataset of important laws, drawing on an approach used by Sinclair (2016), we made note of every House or Senate bill in *CQ Magazine*'s recurring lists of important legislation. Following Curry (2015), we added all appropriations measures to the list. This list is composed of bills deemed important by close contemporaneous congressional observers. Minor and noncontroversial measures are therefore excluded, which should bias our data toward identifying more partisan efforts.[16]

To focus our analyses on *lawmaking*, we filtered out bills that did not become law, leaving us with a dataset of 621 important laws.[17] We researched the legislative history of each law to assess how closely processes followed "regular order." We identified eleven dichotomous indicators of important violations of regular order processes—five in the House, five in the Senate, and one for bicameral reconciliation efforts. Each was coded to one if regular order was violated and to zero otherwise. Throughout, our data collection recognized that the path to a new law might involve several bills. In other words, we did not focus solely on the House or Senate measure that was enacted but also considered relevant related legislation.[18]

We conceptualize the lawmaking process in two stages—*bill development* and *bill management*. The former involves efforts to develop legislation, which traditionally occur in committees and involve hearings and markup sessions aimed at drafting, scrutinizing, and redrafting legislation. The latter—bill management—involves efforts to manage the consideration of legislation on the floor. These include regulating floor debate and amendment processes, overcoming efforts at obstruction, and reconciling the differences between House-passed and Senate-passed versions of the measure. Under "regular order," bill development and management are relatively distinct, with committees leading the development of legislation and party leaders playing a larger role in managing floor consideration. For these reasons we created separate indexes capturing the degree of "unorthodoxy" in each stage of the process. This approach helps us better understand which aspects of regular order, when violated, might relate to heightened partisanship.

For the *unorthodox development* indexes, we draw on combinations of four indicators:

· No House committee hearings: Committee hearings are typically seen as important initial steps in the regular order consideration of bills. We used data from Congress.gov, the Government Publishing Office, ProQuest Congressional Publications, and committee reports to determine if a law or its topic was subject to a House committee hearing.

· No House committee report: Regular order expects legislation to receive floor consideration only after it is reported by at least one committee. Data from Congress.gov were used to determine if a law received any committee reports in the House.

· No Senate committee hearings: Using the same data sources, we determined if a law or its topic was subject to Senate committee hearing.

· No Senate committee report: Using the same data sources, we identified any committee reports in the Senate.

For the *unorthodox management* indexes, we draw on combinations of seven indicators:

· Considered under a closed rule (House): Under regular order, relatively open amending processes are expected on the House floor. This indicator notes if the initial bill considered in the House was closed to floor amendments by a special rule, drawing on Congress.gov data and the House Rules Committee's published surveys of its activities.

· Bill layover less than seventy-two hours (House): Under House rules, bills are supposed to "lay over" for three calendar days before floor consideration so members have time to read them (Rybicki 2017). We use seventy-two hours as a rough indicator. Bills laid over for less time than this represent efforts by the majority party leadership to rush the proposal through the chamber (Curry 2015).

· Late-stage adjustment (House): This indicator notes whether adjustments were made to legislation by key party or committee leaders late in the House's initial consideration of the law (not pursuant to bicameral agreement). Such adjustments include Sinclair's (2016) "post-committee adjustments," but we also include last-minute changes made to bills that bypassed committee consideration. This frequently occurs through self-executing special rules. It also includes cases in which the leadership introduced new legislation after initial chamber or committee consideration, making major changes to the bill reflecting behind-the-scenes negotiations. For this indicator we drew on data from Congress.gov and from descriptions of the legislative process in *CQ Magazine*.

· Cloture invoked (Senate): Using Congress.gov data, we determine if cloture was invoked on the law during its initial consideration in the Senate. The cloture process, once rare, has become a common violation of "regular order," requiring the Senate to muster sixty votes or otherwise strike a bipartisan agreement to move forward.

· Amendment tree filled (Senate): In recent years, Senate majority leaders have taken steps to "fill" the amendment tree on a bill to effectively block floor amendments (see Smith 2014). Using data collected by the Congressional Research Service (Davis 2017), we note legislation on which the Senate majority leader filled the amendment tree.

· Late-stage adjustment (Senate): As with House consideration, we identify whether late-stage adjustments were made in the Senate during a law's initial consideration. For this determination, we relied on the *Congressional Record* and coverage in *CQ Magazine*. Typically, these changes were made by a party or committee leader's offering a bill substitute during floor debate, or by introducing a new bill to replace earlier legislative language.

· No conference committee (bicameral): This indicator notes when no conference committee was held to reconcile bicameral differences. Under regular order, the House and Senate convene a conference to hammer out differences in their bills. However, more unorthodox approaches, including behind-the-scenes negotiations among leaders, can be used instead (see Ryan 2018).

In total, we created six indexes. Each is additive and standardized to range from zero to one, with one representing a fully unorthodox process and zero a fully "regular order" process:

· *House unorthodox development index* using the two House development indicators;
· *Senate unorthodox development index* using the two Senate development indicators;
· *House unorthodox management index* using the three House management indicators;
· *Senate unorthodox management index* using the three Senate management indicators;
· *All unorthodox development index* using all four development indicators;
· *All unorthodox management index* using all seven management indicators.

Figure 5.1 shows the mean level of "unorthodoxy," or how greatly regular order was violated, according to each index across the Congresses we study. Two patterns are worth noting. First, these data clearly show that both bill development and management processes have become more unorthodox in both chambers. In fact, both appear to increase in similar ways over

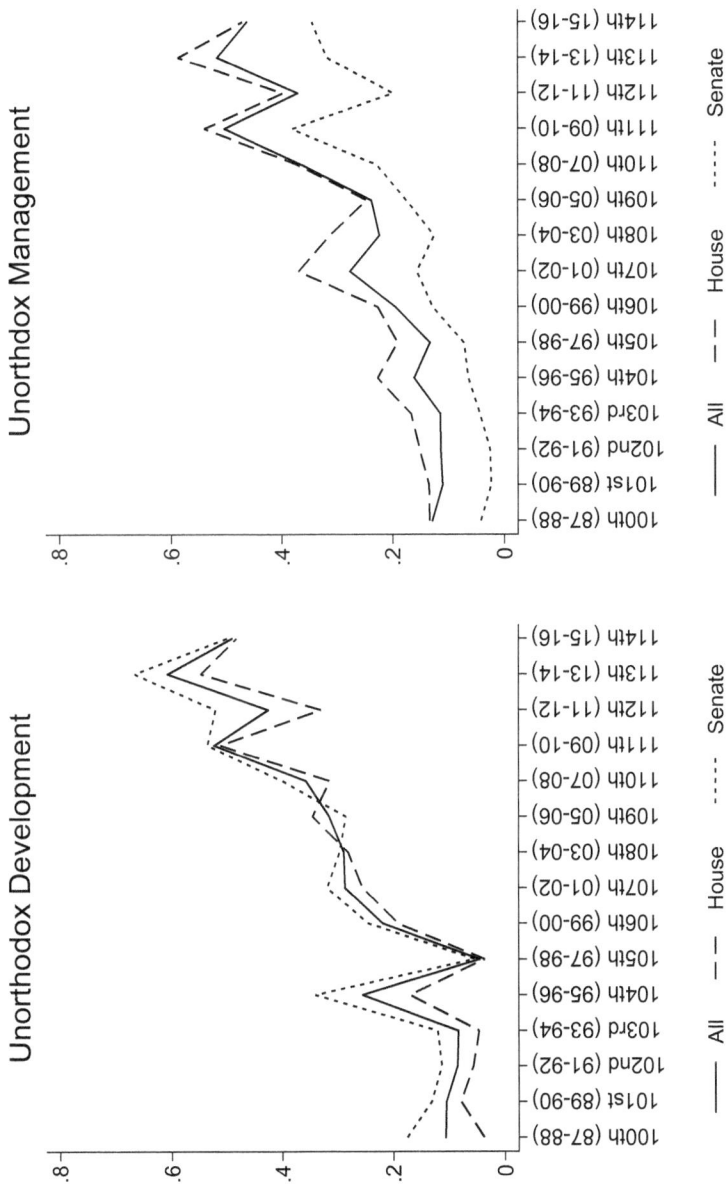

Figure 5.1. Unorthodox development and management indexes, 1987–2016
Note: A modified version of this figure appears in Curry and Lee (2020).

time. Development and management remained fairly orthodox for the first several Congresses, averaging about 0.1 through the 105th Congress (with a bump during the 104th). However, all the indexes rise steadily starting in the 106th Congress and climb through the most recent Congresses. The second pattern of note, however, is that regular order processes also continue to be used, even in recent years. The indexes never exceed 0.5–0.6, on average, for a Congress. Were every law considered using a completely unorthodox process, the indexes would be equal to one.

Using these indexes, we conducted several multivariate analyses to assess the relation between violations of regular order and levels of partisanship on the passage of important new laws. We measure partisanship as levels of partisan disagreement on the initial and final passage votes in each chamber for each new law.[19] *Initial passage* is the first passage vote taken in each chamber, and *final passage* is the final vote taken in each chamber after bicameral reconciliation. Sometimes a chamber took only one passage vote on a law, and in those cases the initial and final passage votes are recorded as the same.[20] We created three dependent variables for each of the four passage votes taken on each new law:

- A dichotomous *50 percent party vote* indicator (a majority of each party in opposition to the other);
- A dichotomous *90 percent party vote* indicator (at least 90 percent of each party opposed to the other);
- A continuous measure of bipartisanship, *percentage minority party* in favor of passage.

The primary independent variables are the indexes of process unorthodoxy. In each test we also included a dummy variable indicating whether the measure dealt with appropriations (which typically draw more bipartisan support). Our regression models are multilevel mixed-effects models that calculate random effects parameters for each Congress and for the policy area addressed by each new law.[21]

Table 5.1 presents the results for passage votes in the House.[22] The results, first, show that there is no meaningful statistical relationship between bill development unorthodoxy and levels of partisanship on initial and final passage votes. Across the six analyses, the coefficients for unorthodox development either are not statistically significant or, in the case of *percentage minority party* support, predict *more* bipartisanship on final passage, with more minority members in support. In contrast, the results show a consistent relation between unorthodox bill *management* and levels of partisanship.

Table 5.1 Predicting levels of partisanship on passage votes in the House, 1987–2016

	Initial passage			Final passage		
	(1) % minority party	(2) 50% party vote	(3) 90% party vote	(4) % minority party	(5) 50% party vote	(6) 90% party vote
Bill-level variables						
House unorthodox development index	0.110** (0.037)	−0.138 (0.274)	0.079 (0.425)			
House unorthodox management index	−0.291** (0.048)	1.701** (0.362)	1.897** (0.591)			
All unorthodox development index				0.083* (0.035)	−0.083 (0.330)	−0.347 (0.705)
All unorthodox management index				−0.283** (0.065)	2.056** (0.590)	2.507* (1.205)
Appropriations bill	−0.104** (0.031)	0.256 (0.235)	0.397 (0.378)	−0.003 (0.027)	−0.241 (0.268)	−0.685 (0.694)
Constant	0.785** (0.038)	−1.438** (0.262)	−3.557** (0.376)	0.837** (0.042)	−1.851** (0.317)	−6.169** (1.416)
Random-effects parameters						
Congress	0.008 (0.004)	0.253 (0.143)	0.160 (0.241)	0.015 (0.006)	0.419 (0.216)	5.293 (5.199)
Policy issue	0.006 (0.003)	0.311 (0.188)	0.296 (0.288)	0.005 (0.002)	0.337 (0.211)	0.893 (0.921)
N	621	621	621	621	621	621

Note: Columns 1 and 4 are multilevel mixed-effects linear regressions; columns 2, 3, 5, and 6 are multilevel mixed-effects logistic regressions. $*p < .05$; $**p < .01$.

Across the six analyses, the coefficients for the unorthodox management index all predict more partisanship: less minority party support and higher likelihood of party votes.

Perhaps more important, *to what degree* does partisanship relate to unorthodox processes? Figure 5.2 shows the predicted effects of the indexes from each analysis as they increase from least to most unorthodox. The results indicate that while partisan voting is more likely when floor management processes are more unorthodox, a substantial amount of bipartisanship exists under any kind of process. Even under maximally unorthodox floor management, the models still predict that, on average, 50 to 60 percent of the minority party will support *initial* and *final* passage. The largest effects are with 50 percent party votes. Under the most unorthodox management

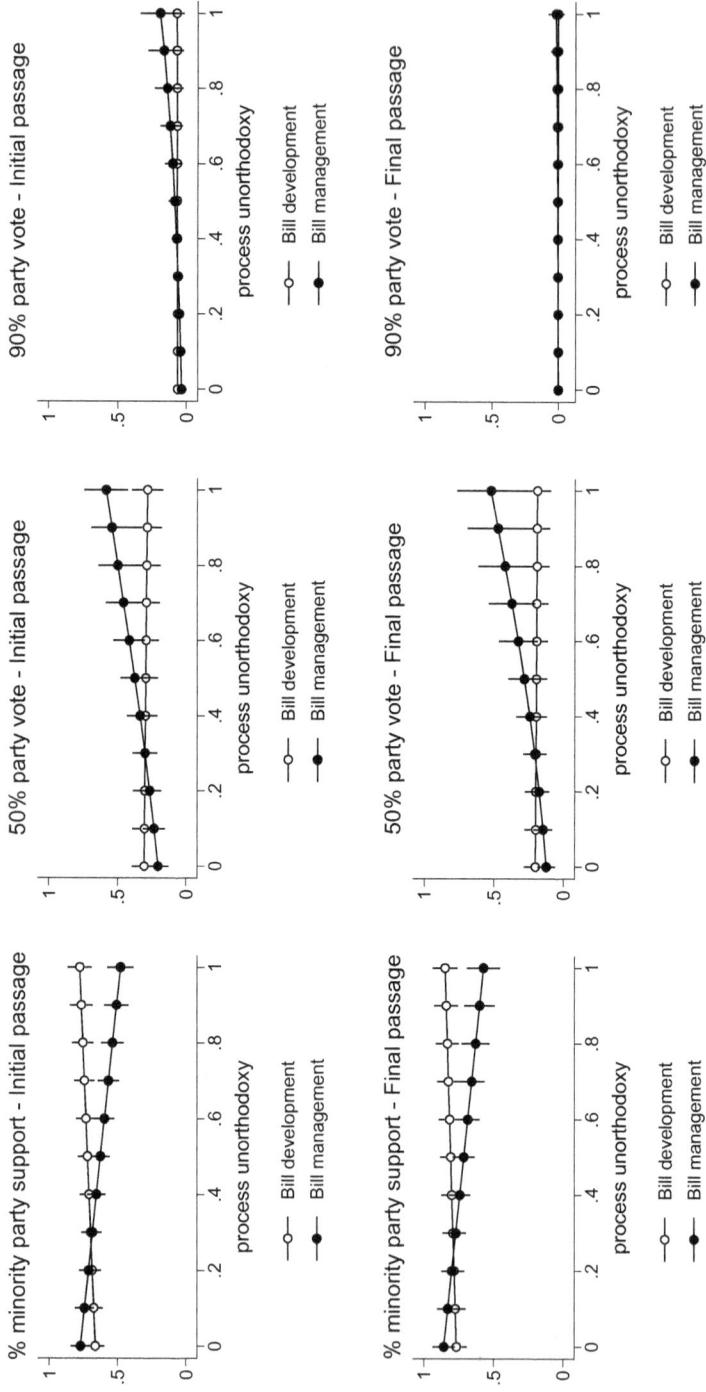

Figure 5.2. Effect of process unorthodoxy on passage vote partisanship in the House
Note: A modified version of this figure appears in Curry and Lee (2020).

processes, the likelihood of a 50 percent party vote rises to 58 percent on initial passage and 52 percent on final passage. Although the increases are notable with this metric, the predicted likelihoods still indicate that roughly half of laws considered under the most unorthodox management processes will fail to reach even the lowest threshold definition of a party vote. Moreover, highly partisan votes on passage—90 percent party votes—appear unlikely under any kind of process. Even in the House, where the majority has strong procedural control and the ability to pass anything along partisan lines, the likelihood of a 90 percent party vote never exceeds 19 percent on initial passage and 2 percent on final passage.

Table 5.2 reports similar findings for the Senate. There is limited evidence of a relationship between unorthodox development processes and partisanship—only one such coefficient predicts significantly more partisanship. However, the management indexes predict more partisanship in four of six analyses. Nevertheless, as shown in figure 5.3, while the results

Table 5.2 **Predicting levels of partisanship on passage votes in the Senate, 1987–2016**

	Initial passage			Final passage		
	(1) % minority party	(2) 50% party vote	(3) 90% party vote	(4) % minority party	(5) 50% party vote	(6) 90% party vote
Bill-level variables						
Senate unorthodox	−0.030	0.741*	0.999			
development index	(0.023)	(0.321)	(0.746)			
Senate unorthodox	−0.174**	1.889**	1.155			
management index	(0.039)	(0.498)	(1.016)			
All unorthodox				0.011	0.390	0.800
development index				(0.029)	(0.398)	(0.895)
All unorthodox				−0.190**	2.215**	−0.383
management index				(0.053)	(0.710)	(1.770)
Appropriations	−0.010	−0.330	−0.794	−0.009	−0.219	−1.420
bill	(0.022)	(0.351)	(0.955)	(0.022)	(0.352)	(1.220)
Constant	0.892**	−2.870**	−6.409**	0.904**	−3.167**	−8.057**
	(0.031)	(0.418)	(1.343)	(0.034)	(0.459)	(2.565)
Random-effects parameters						
Congress	0.007	0.591	3.552	0.010	0.908	11.734
	(0.003)	(0.353)	(3.408)	(0.004)	(0.540)	(15.212)
Policy issue	0.004	0.854	1.931	0.003	0.652	3.612
	(0.002)	(0.511)	(1.753)	(0.002)	(0.482)	(3.189)
N	621	621	621	621	621	621

Note: Columns 1 and 4 are multilevel mixed-effects linear regressions; columns 2, 3, 5, and 6 are multilevel mixed-effects logistic regressions. *$p < .05$; **$p < .01$.

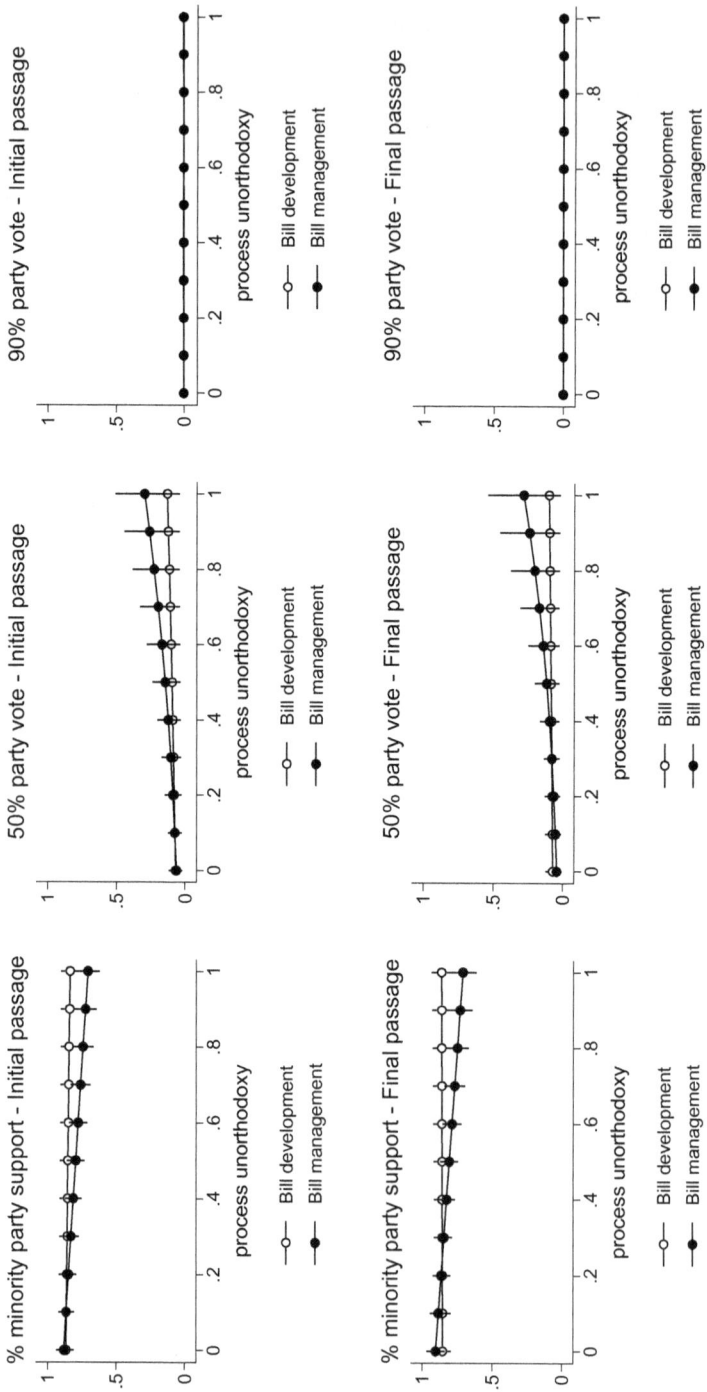

Figure 5.3. Effect of process unorthodoxy on passage vote partisanship in the Senate
Note: A modified version of this figure appears in Curry and Lee (2020).

indicate that partisan voting is more likely when management processes are more unorthodox, a substantial amount of bipartisanship exists under any kind of process. The most unorthodox management processes still result in, on average, 75 percent of the minority party's voting in support of passage, and just 30 percent and 28 percent of initial and final passage votes, respectively, expected to be 50 percent party votes. Moreover, the effect of unorthodox processes on 90 percent party votes is substantively nonexistent. In short, even egregious violations of regular order frequently end in bipartisan voting patterns in the Senate.

The takeaway from these analyses is that violations of regular order do not clearly relate to higher levels of partisanship in the ways scholars, observers, and practitioners typically expect. We find only a weak relationship between departures from regular order in bill management and partisanship on passage votes, and we find no relationship between partisanship and the process by which bills are developed. That unorthodox bill development processes do not weaken bipartisan support for bills undercuts any inference that regular order yields broader consensus building, since the substance of legislation is rarely altered in a significant way on the floor.

These findings are reinforced by additional regression models (see appendix B) that include each of the eleven separate indicators of violations of regular order. These models find that only "closed rules" and "cloture invoked" consistently predict higher than average levels of partisanship on passage votes. Notably, these processes are not relevant to the development of policy proposals, but rather are for managing their consideration on the House and Senate floors. From our analyses, it appears that the specific procedures used to enact laws in the contemporary Congress are simply not that strongly related to the levels of partisanship observed.[23]

Nonpartisan Reasons for Centralized Legislative Processes

What accounts for the lack of a relationship between process and partisanship? We draw on our interviews with long-serving members of Congress and senior congressional staff to investigate the considerations that inform decisions to follow regular order or use unorthodox processes to develop and consider legislation.

Our interview subjects emphasize that unorthodox processes are often used simply because they *work* to achieve a legislative outcome in today's political environment. Although Congress can and does use unorthodox procedures in efforts to pass partisan legislation, it also frequently opts to do so on bills with broad support. Congressional leaders commonly depart from regular order just because doing so can be helpful in resolving legislative deadlocks. These processes provide pathways to success in passing laws, often with substantial bipartisan buy-in.

Our interviewees consistently point to three reasons the contemporary Congress turns to unorthodox and centralized processes: they are more efficient; they afford more secrecy; and they allow more flexibility than regular order processes. Drawing on our interviews, we discuss these reasons in general terms and apply them to a particular case example of a significant law that some of our interview subjects participated in negotiating: the Medicare Access and CHIP Reauthorization Act of 2015 (the permanent "doc fix").[24]

Efficiency

Our interviewees frequently described regular order processes as inefficient and prone to deadlock in the current political environment. Open, decentralized legislative processes often fall victim to obstruction and grandstanding. Committee markups and open floor proceedings create opportunities for obstructionists to throw a monkey wrench into the proceedings, causing unnecessary headaches and delays. According to one staffer, "[If] you try to work through an open markup or something, the bill gets weighed down in partisan attacks and nothing happens."[25] Faced with these prospects, leaders instead often opt for tightly managed procedures: "When the other side isn't really trying to legislate through the process but is just putting up these partisan gotcha amendments, you have to move on. You have to close it down."[26]

Others echoed these sentiments, noting that attempting to move legislation through regular order these days is just untenable, since members of the minority, and sometimes the majority, are inclined to play games. As a result, the process can drag on indefinitely, or the bill's survival might be imperiled by poison pill amendments. As one staffer told us, "Part of the reason we started doing structured rules was the Democrats were getting some of their amendments passed, and it would kill the bill because the Democrats still wouldn't vote for the final bill, but the amendments would kill Republican support."[27] Striking a more bipartisan tone, he noted, "A more polarized House of Representatives led to the process breaking down. Both sides were motivated to push gotcha amendments, and it made using an open rule impossible."[28] Another staffer put it this way: "Something like the Labor-H appropriations bill just can't be done in a totally open rule on the floor. There will be hundreds of amendments and debates for hours. It would take weeks of floor time, at least!"[29]

Nevertheless, party leaders prefer a decentralized process provided it can achieve a result. Most rank-and-file lawmakers are happier if legislation can be worked up in that manner (Crespin and Madonna 2016). Indeed, despite increases in unorthodox processes (fig. 5.1), much legislation still proceeds under regular order. But when decentralized approaches cannot achieve legislative success, leadership intervenes. "If you can do regular order, you do it," summarized one staffer.[30] But as a committee staffer put it, "When we just couldn't resolve things with the Democrats, we'd have to kick it to the leadership to work it out."[31]

Centralization can happen in a number of ways and for various reasons, but "the number one reason it happens is timing."[32] When facing a deadline, the leadership is expected to step up:

> It's a crisis model. Leadership steps in when backs are against the wall and something has to be done. Expiring tax provisions, debt limit has to be raised. . . . These days most of what's getting done is happening only in states of crisis. The leadership doesn't *want* these crises. . . . But the pressures just keep pushing issues up the food chain to the leadership.[33]

> There is legislation done at the end when crisis looms. The House has passed something extreme. The Senate is log-jammed or passed something really different. In these processes, the leadership takes the lead.[34]

Sometimes "there just isn't time to work through the traditional process."[35] This is not anyone's ideal: "It's a shame you can't do things differently. . . . The time cycles we are working in speed things up so you can't."[36]

Even without a deadline or crisis, there are some issues that at the outset do not seem amenable to regular order. In such cases the leadership may preempt committees.[37] As one staffer described it, leadership will sometimes work around a committee: "They essentially create ad hoc committees because they don't believe the regular committees can do it anymore. And they're right. They can't."[38] Referring to the 2011 debt limit standoff, another staffer noted: "It's not as though the Ways and Means Committee had moved a debt limit bill. Even if they'd tried to do so, there was no way to pass it. . . . The story was the same with the payroll tax extension at the end of 2011 and the tax cliff of 2012."[39]

In many cases committee chairs themselves will "punt to the leadership to make key decisions."[40] In using centralized processes, leaders do not seek to undercut the authority of committee chairs per se. A staffer explained the approach: "If committee leaders couldn't work [the issues] out, they get kicked up to the leadership. It's usually just a handful of things—hot-button issues that neither side is budging on and leadership has to get involved."[41] Describing Pelosi, one long-serving member said, "She would meet with the chairs. She would meet with members. . . . It was more centralized, but this did not mean committee chairs were excluded."[42] Concerns about the capacity of decentralized processes to achieve a legislative result are a critical consideration rather than leaders' desire to arrogate committee power or impose a partisan outcome.

Interview subjects emphasized that chairs have come to accept departures from regular order as a normal way of doing business in the contemporary Congress:

> Chairmen are now acculturated to the reality that they will be negotiating with the leadership on everything. No one has the old bull attitude to tell the leader to go away. Even someone like [Sen.] Grassley [R-IA] won't push back like a [Sen.] John Tower [R-TX, 1961–85] or something. He's a miserable person to deal with, but he doesn't play hide the football.[43]

Along similar lines, another staffer explained, "As a committee guy, I don't see increased leadership involvement as challenging committees. I see it as assisting us. Leadership is our ally helping clear the way for our committee initiatives."[44]

Whether the leadership takes the initiative to centralize or intervenes as the behest of a committee, concerns about the capacity of decentralized processes to achieve a legislative result are often the critical consideration. Our interviews did not turn up examples of members or staffers complaining that leadership was usurping power that appropriately resided elsewhere. Centralization was generally portrayed as a second-best alternative that is adaptive to contemporary challenges. "Chairmen don't want to surrender their power," summed up one staffer. "But if it's the only way they can get what they want they'll go along with it."[45] The implication is that decentralized processes may have worked well in the past but do not fare well in today's challenging legislative environment.

Secrecy

The reduced transparency of centralized processes also creates efficiencies. Traditional processes not only make it easier for opponents to obstruct, they can also make it harder for a bill's proponents to engage in meaningful deliberations. As one staffer put it, "Transparency is a good thing in principle, but it makes Congress more dysfunctional."[46] Consistent with

Warren and Mansbridge (2015), our interview subjects argued that closed-door interactions facilitate negotiation on politically sensitive issues. For negotiators, "private interactions behind closed doors provide the moments, sheltered from publicity . . . in which opposition parties can share their perspectives freely and come to understand the perspectives of others" (Warren and Mansbridge 2015, 174). Doing things in a more secretive manner helps lawmakers find common ground, compromise, and hash out mutually beneficial deals in several ways.

Centralized processes allow lawmakers to conduct sensitive negotiations out of the view of lobbyists. Traditional processes—including freewheeling committee meetings and open floor debate and amendment—allow well-financed interest groups to monitor the proceedings and use their clout to influence reelection-minded legislators. As Arnold (1990, 275) put it, "Open meetings filled with lobbyists, and recorded votes, on scores of particularistic amendments serve to increase the powers of special interests, not to diminish them." These efforts can bog down a legislative effort: "I know transparency is good, but it's very difficult with an issue like health care. There are so many interested parties on the outside. There is so much money involved; 15,000 lobbyists who want to be involved."[47] Another noted, "Once K Street knows you have a train leaving the station, they have umpteen things they want to get on it."[48] To make a deal, "you need the back-room discussions outside the view of the lobbyists, even if that's sacrilege to the open-government people."[49]

Centralized processes also enable Congress to mute pressures from the parties' activist bases, who can make it difficult for negotiators to agree to any concessions: "The right to petition means these days you have a lot of petitioners who can blow things up."[50] A zealous party base can spur rank-and-file lawmakers to react negatively to a potential deal, even when objections focus on only a few issues: "Hyperpartisans on both sides will turn everything into a wedge."[51] When negotiations unfold in public view, issues "get tribalized in the media," explained a longtime staffer and Hill insider. "If you can keep things out of the view of the public, that's the best way to actually do something."[52] While regular order processes may have allowed Congress to resolve conflicts in the past, today openness and transparency are often seen as threats to legislative success: "Regular order is too messy, and it's covered instantly in the media and it can create problems."[53]

Information disclosures present a risk to ongoing negotiations because they "run the risk of some members' getting all riled up and the snowball starting rolling down the mountain and picking up steam."[54] Today "the politics of each party's base has made [regular order] impossible."[55] Lawmakers find it difficult to engage in give-and-take when exploratory offers can be interpreted as capitulations. "Complete and total transparency makes it very hard to negotiate and have conversations," one staffer told us. "It's impossible to have a quiet, candid conversation except at the leadership level."[56]

If congressional leaders often appear overly secretive in their approach, they often feel they have to be:

> There's so much divisiveness inside in the parties' caucuses that you render yourself pretty vulnerable if you're putting out your gives publicly. I'll admit there is an increasing trend toward opaqueness and nondisclosure to the broader group, but part of it is this sense that the broader group will not handle the information responsibly.[57]

Behind-the-scenes processes allow negotiators to explore opportunities, float ideas, and manage sensitive issues with confidence that their counterparts will not leak the details. "Secrecy is very important" because it allows negotiators to explore whether a deal is possible and, if so, what it needs to look like:

> If there was mutual interest in pursuing legislation, you can close the door and ask questions like, "How far are you willing to go?" "Where do you draw the line?" . . . [You can] figure out where you need to be, reach an agreement, and then you can do the dog and pony show, beat each other up, and so on. But you know where it was going to end up because you had worked it out behind closed doors.[58]

Negotiators often "need to have a theoretical discussion" to ascertain whether any agreement is possible.[59] They also need the freedom to reverse course. Negotiations may involve "blind alleys" that become apparent only once possibilities have been explored in some detail.[60] But "if you try to do all this out in the open, it makes it hard to do U-turns."[61]

Meanwhile, disclosures during the process can "short-circuit the negotiations."[62] As a staffer explained,

> If a piece of the negotiation gets reported, it'll be seen in isolation from everything else we're trying to do, all the other moving parts. . . . Social media will start churning information—all about one little piece. It spreads like wildfire. And all this even before you can have a discussion with the skeptics. By the time you can reach them, they've already made up their minds. They're not listening to you.[63]

However, if a deal can be reached and negotiators emerge unified around a single legislative package, it will become hard to oppose. Instead, everyone can say, "Well, this or that part of it stinks, but at least it solves the overall problem."[64] Simply put, in today's Congress "it's in the backroom where the deal is made."[65]

Flexibility

The flexibility of centralized processes enables leaders to negotiate broader legislative packages than might otherwise be possible. Several of our interviewees noted that some deals, and some decisions, are just too big for committees to take the lead.

Committees are often hemmed in by jurisdictional boundaries. When looking for trades or logrolls across issues to build legislative support, committees can work only within their jurisdictions. "The committee process chops issues up, making larger negotiations impossible," one staffer explained.[66] Another noted that "committee chairs are always a bit too in the weeds to some extent," and speaking of one committee chair in particular, "[He] has proven he is the smartest guy in the room, but he gets lost in the bark of the tree and can't see the forest." Party leaders are often better suited to strike "grand bargains," since they can explore policy solutions across policies, programs, and jurisdictions to put together legislative packages that can draw broad support for passage:

> Leadership can open up the universe of policy to find the solution, taking into account the whole picture—the politics, the budget. These decisions get chased up to the leaders. . . . There's no other decision maker who can get a deal to do things like keep the government open.[67]

In the contemporary Congress, "all the big deals tend to be leadership driven."[68]

Flexibility is particularly valuable in figuring out how to pay for legislation. "Pay-fors" are often a sticking point for enacting legislation. Identifying necessary offsets requires creativity and an ability to look across jurisdictional boundaries:

> For anything you do, you have to find the money. Handling things at the leadership level allows you to go outside the relevant committee to find the money. Whatever problem you're trying to resolve—FAA, highway trust fund, whatever. The committee may not have jurisdiction over the policies that

would allow you to get the pay-fors. So the leadership needs to step in. The leadership is the place you go when you need to find offsets.[69]

In short, "leadership has more flexibility to find the pay-fors" because it can work "outside the jurisdiction of any particular committee."[70]

Party leaders are often the only members of Congress who have the clout necessary to cut high-level deals. One committee staffer noted that only the leadership could resolve jurisdictional conflicts among committees and "clear the path for our committee. Leadership can work with the other committees and get them to back down, figure out what deals can be made. They can break, or maybe interpret, the rules in a certain way to help out."[71] Moreover, party leaders are the only individuals who can claim to speak for the entire caucus in these high-level talks. Speaking about Senate Minority Leader Chuck Schumer's (D-NY) involvement in major budget negotiations, one staffer emphasized that "no one else could have jurisdiction over everything—no one chairman could do that."[72] Another emphasized that committee chairs just do not have that level of authority:

> So many big things have to be negotiated trilaterally—between the House, Senate, and President—and committee chairs just aren't empowered to do those negotiations. You don't send a committee chair to do that, just like you wouldn't hear about cabinet secretaries being empowered to go negotiate with the Hill. The House majority isn't going to send a chairman to negotiate with the president.[73]

When issues need to be worked out between the House and Senate or with the White House, the task will fall to party leaders rather than committee chairs.

Finally, party leaders are often the only ones willing to take the heat for making the tough decisions and trade-offs associated with big legislative deals. Finding offsets to pay for legislation entails political pain—cuts have to be imposed or revenue raised: "When pain is involved, the leadership has to handle it."[74] During the 2011–13 budget fights, one Republican staffer told us, "Anytime anything was getting signed into law by Obama it fell to [the leadership]. No one else wanted to make decisions because it was going to be less than perfect. Leadership were the only ones who could be the bad guy and were willing to take the blame."[75]

Ultimately, centralizing processes in the leadership helps achieve a legislative outcome because it makes resolution and decisiveness easier. At some point decisions have to be made, and "that's why you have leaders. You have to let people air their opinions and all that, but you [also] have to have someone to ultimately make a decision."[76]

Medicare Access and CHIP Reauthorization Act of 2015

Our interviews offered insight into an informative case of lawmaking that was highly unorthodox, but also highly bipartisan: the 2015 effort to repeal and replace the Medicare Sustainable Growth Rate (SGR). It was a GOP priority going into the 114th Congress (see appendix A), and the parties' top leaders negotiated this deal in secret. Most rank-and-file members of both parties did not even know negotiations were under way. There was no committee process whatever. The final package was presented to the Democratic and Republican caucuses only after it was finished and key interest groups had endorsed it. Despite this centralized, secretive process, the legislation passed both chambers of Congress by overwhelming margins.[77]

The Medicare SGR policy had been put in place by the Balanced Budget Act of 1997 to control Medicare costs by tying increases in providers' payments to economic growth. Starting in the late 1990s, however, health spending outpaced economic growth. If Congress allowed the SGR caps go into effect, Medicare doctors would have faced dramatic pay cuts. So every year, Congress passed a "doc fix" lifting the cap and allocating billions of dollars to maintain payments to medical providers. Congress had tried repeatedly to resolve this problem,[78] but every attempt failed:

> We had been trying to do this fix since before Pelosi became Speaker. We tried to do it with CHIP in '97. We tried to do it as part of the ACA. But the problem was the $300 billion price tag. We'd done a short-term fix something like seventeen times. Members were tired of it. Even the doc lobbyists were tired of it.[79]

Another noted, "We had tried to get that done in the ACA but the price tag was too high. But we had told the American Medical Association that we'd get that done. Everybody wanted to get it done, and the Republicans were sick of it too."[80] After repeated failures to deal with the issue through the regular committee process, party leaders took the initiative to negotiate a solution. One former staffer described how the process got under way:

> Boehner had told us that he wanted a permanent doc fix as a legacy for his Speakership. So I went to [Pelosi's point person] and said, "Can we talk?" He

said he thought we could do this, but no one could know. Through the process [Pelosi's point person] and I met two times a day every day.[81]

The top negotiators in both parties emphatically portrayed the secrecy of the process as crucial to their success in resolving the issue. Secrecy afforded numerous advantages. First, it protected the legislation from attacks from hard-liners. As one put it, "My side would be so mad if they knew the two leaders were working together!"[82] Leaders worked hard to preserve secrecy throughout the months of negotiations: "On occasions when Boehner and Pelosi would need to meet during the negotiation, we made up reasons to cover for them."[83]

Second, secrecy let negotiators control the number of demands placed on them and allowed them to protect the legislative vehicle from attracting too many varied provisions important to lobbyists and individual members. Secrecy also helped negotiators work around recalcitrant legislators, especially those sitting on a committee of jurisdiction, who might have acted as barriers to action: "If we involved the committee members, there would be too many demands to accommodate. . . . Different groups would begin to impose their litmus tests on the package—'We can't support it unless it has this or that feature.'"[84]

By keeping negotiations secret, Boehner, Pelosi, and their staff negotiators could decide which legislators—and which stakeholders—would be involved in the negotiations and when. It also allowed them to have confidential discussions with stakeholder groups such as the AMA, AARP, and the hospital industry. Everyone leadership staffers spoke to was pledged to secrecy. Word that a deal was being negotiated could not be let out:

When we talked to outside experts, we pledged them to secrecy. We had technical assistance from the Centers for Medicare and Medicaid Services. We had to figure out how and where to come up with $175 billion. We reached out to the hospital industry looking for help. The key to this was absolute secrecy.[85]

Everyone we talked with, we pledged them not to tell anyone. We talked with the hospital industry. [Boehner's staffer] dealt with the American Hospital Association and the GOP lobbyists there. I talked with the people at the Federation of American Hospitals. These folks were very discreet.[86]

The negotiators "spent a lot of time gaming out when we'd loop people in. You talk with the people you trust most first and then you expand the circle."[87] Individuals and groups who might pose a problem were not consulted until late in the process, once a deal was already formed. This put pressure on them to get on board or be run over. Some key members, such as Rep. Sander Levin (D-MI), ranking member on Ways and Means, and Rep. Fred Upton (R-MI), chair of Energy and Commerce, were not brought into the discussions.

In addition to secrecy, centralized processes allowed leaders more flexibility to construct the legislation and build a supportive coalition. According to our interviewees, the committees had not been able to close a deal to replace the SGR policy because they had been unable to move beyond preexisting ideas, policies, and avenues of negotiation. The leadership, less ingrained in these debates, could be more creative in developing solutions without getting bogged down in details:

> Before we started work on the negotiation, we held a meeting with the committee staffs. It was obvious why they hadn't gotten it done before. They were so focused on the little pieces. They had something like seventeen meetings on just the nursing home provisions. They'd debate two lines, a comma, etc. It's just too much detail![88]

The unorthodox process also allowed leadership to identify and shoulder the blame for the pay-fors. The committees had been working on solutions to the doc fix for years, but "the problem was the pay-fors, and that's where the leadership had to come in. . . . The committees had done the bulk of the SGR fix itself. But they understood that leadership had to figure out how to pay for it."[89] As another committee staffer put it, "There is no way we could come up with offsets for that. There's no way anyone else could! It had to be a leadership decision to say that it was only going to be partially offset."[90]

Before the leaders' deal could be announced to their respective party caucuses, negotiators recognized that they had to bring in one key member who would vouch for the package—Rep. Paul Ryan (R-WI), then chair of Ways and Means: "We had to work with Ryan. We had no choice. We needed Ryan not so much because he was chair of Ways and Means, but because of his standing in the conference."[91] Ryan was not particularly happy with the final deal, but with everything finished, he was persuaded not only to go along, but to play a central role in the bill's unveiling: "We made Ryan present the deal. He didn't want to do it. He said he didn't even like it all that much! But we told him he had to do it. We knew that everyone would want to know what he thought."[92]

Once the negotiations concluded, the deal was announced concurrently with the key outside groups' giving their endorsement. The Democrats' primary negotiator recalled: "[Boehner's staffer] got her conservative think tanks to bless it. I got the Center on Budget on board. The day the package was unveiled there was a wonderful Center paper blessing the deal."[93] The primary Republican negotiator explained, "When we unveiled the package, I held a meeting with industry groups. They were all asking, 'You gave away all that money for QI [qualifying low-income seniors]? All that money for community health centers? Is this really a good deal for conservatives?' I was thinking to myself: 'I'm glad I didn't tell you further in advance!'"[94]

After almost fifteen years of failed attempts to replace the Medicare SGR, in three months of secret negotiations Boehner, Pelosi, and their staffs cut a deal that garnered overwhelming support in both chambers. As one of the longtime staffers involved in this effort explained, this was something that could be achieved only through unorthodox and leadership-led processes:

> A negotiation like this could only really happen at the leadership level. Committee chairs just think about how to get bills out of committee. They don't think about the whole conference at large. You need to get out of the committee to take a broader view. You have to have a sense for the whole Democratic caucus, the whole Republican conference, not just members of a particular committee.[95]

Taken together, this case study and our interviewees' perspectives comport well with the statistical analyses. The quantitative analyses revealed that centralized processes are not much more likely than regular order processes to result in the passage of partisan laws. Consistent with those data, our interviewees emphasized that congressional leaders frequently turn to centralized, behind-the-scenes processes for nonpartisan reasons. Unorthodox processes are often used not to push through partisan laws but instead because such processes can help Congress succeed legislatively. Leaders often employ centralized and behind-the-scenes processes to resolve legislative conflicts, not necessarily to force a partisan outcome.

Alternative Paths to the Same Ultimate Ends

> There are many paths to legislation. Some are more difficult than others. When you want to drive across the country, say from Washington to San Francisco, the easiest way to do it is straight across I-80. But if there's something in the way, you can find some ways around.[96]

Contrary to the expectations of many scholars and observers, this chapter finds that the unorthodox legislative processes that have developed in the contemporary Congress are not tools majority parties use to ram through partisan laws. Our quantitative analyses find little correlation between legislative processes and outcomes. Bypassing the traditional committee-led bill development process does not relate to the level of partisan conflict on passage votes at all, and more restrictive floor consideration bears only a modest relationship. The processes used are a poor leading indicator of whether a new law will garner bipartisan support in Congress.

Our in-depth interviews with long-serving members and staff offer an explanation for these nonfindings: unorthodox processes are often adaptations aimed at achieving legislative success in the contemporary political environment. Regular order and committee-led processes may have functioned well for successful legislating in earlier eras of muted partisanship and large majority parties (Fenno 1962; Polsby 1975), but they fare poorly under today's conditions. Leaders often find themselves faced with resolving impasses that cannot be worked out at the committee level. Centralized processes have advantages—efficiency, secrecy, and flexibility—that help Congress reach legislative resolutions in an era of polarization and intense competition for majority control.

Reformers focused on bringing back regular order as a means of restoring bipartisanship are likely misguided. Our data show that regular order processes are not much more likely to result in bipartisan legislation than are centralized, leadership-driven ones. Both partisan and bipartisan laws are passed using both traditional and unorthodox approaches.

For their part, scholars should reconsider the centrality of unorthodox processes to theoretical and empirical work on congressional party power. Most theories of congressional party government expect that party leaders will use the procedural powers at their disposal to enact partisan laws. Our results indicate that the use of these procedural tactics largely does not correlate with more partisanship in enacting laws. This does not mean party leaders do not use (and attempt to use) these processes to achieve partisan laws. Indeed, clearly they sometimes do. However, as with the Medicare SGR effort, they also use unorthodox approaches to cultivate bipartisanship.

The specific procedural pathway to a law's enactment does not reliably predict the extent of partisanship on the final legislative product. As one of our interview subjects explained, the key question is the majority party's goals, not its choice of procedure: "Sometimes the majority wants to make law; in those cases they might violate regular order and engage the [minority party]. In other instances they might want to send a message or satisfy a base constituency. In those cases they may choose to violate regular order and produce a very partisan bill."[97] In other words, the process used is much less important than whether the majority party chooses to constructively negotiate with the minority party in developing the legislation. Our findings in this chapter are clear: bipartisan legislation regularly emerges from unorthodox processes. Indeed, process simply bears little meaningful relation to the level of partisan conflict on final passage.

SIX

Credit Claiming and Blaming: How Members React to Legislation in Public

But the trouble with bipartisan compromises—one rarely advertised by advocates of bipartisanship like me—is that they are no fun. They are, by definition, disappointing.

—Doyle McManus, *Los Angeles Times*[1]

The art of compromise is rarely appreciated fully by men of principle.

—C. Vann Woodward, *Commentary*[2]

The preceding chapters show that there has been considerable continuity in congressional lawmaking over the past several decades, despite much partisan change in American politics more broadly. Contrary to perceptions, the laws Congress enacts remain as bipartisan as they were in the 1970s, today's congressional majority parties are no more efficacious at enacting their programmatic party agendas than those of less partisan eras, and majority party successes continue in most cases to involve reaching across the aisle. Congress has adopted more centralized legislative processes to pass laws, but those processes appear to be an adaptive means to the same ultimate, and typically bipartisan, ends.

Nonetheless, Americans still perceive contemporary lawmaking as deeply and increasingly partisan. Given the persistently high levels of bipartisanship apparent in the outcomes of congressional lawmaking, what drives these perceptions? Why is Congress perceived as routinely passing legislation on a partisan basis, even by close congressional observers, while bipartisanship is thought to be a rare bird? One possibility is that lawmakers' public statements in reaction to successful legislative action create a different impression than is found by looking at roll-call breakdowns and the substance of legislative accomplishments. In other words, lawmakers' public reactions and messages around congressional action may create an impression of conflict, partisan division, and general acrimony even in cases of overwhelming bipartisan agreement.

After all, congressional parties and their members have incentives to communicate divisive messages to constituents and the public. All members of Congress invest considerable resources and energy communicating with constituents and the general public (Fenno 1978; Grimmer 2013). Over recent decades, congressional party organizations have likewise developed robust, institutionalized communications operations to convey political messages (Lee 2016). Members and leaders see these efforts as central to affecting the narrative around congressional action and influencing the outcomes of upcoming elections. Legislators of both parties work to shape news coverage of congressional action through strategic public statements and try to "win" policy debates by shaping public opinion around policy issues and legislation (Evans 2001; Evans and Oleszek 2002; Sellers 2010; Schaffner and Sellers 2009).

These messaging efforts often center on shaping party reputations, or brands (Groeling 2010). Party leaders work to coordinate the development of reputations (Green 2015; Harris 2013) that can serve as cues for voters (Butler and Powell 2014). To do so, they seek to draw attention to differences between the parties, including deliberately setting up roll-call votes designed to put partisan conflict on display (Egar 2016; Gelman 2017). They not only draw distinctions on substantive questions of public policy but also try to undercut the reputations of their partisan opponents. Indeed, members of both parties in Congress have strong incentives not only to bolster their own party, but to denigrate the other party as inept, corrupt, and out of touch (Lee 2009). In reacting to legislative action in the House or Senate, lawmakers can try to shape these impressions for the public, touting their own accomplishments or attacking their opponents' efforts as misguided or worse. And there is evidence that these efforts have measurable effects on vote shares in subsequent elections (Butler and Powell 2014; Woon and Pope 2008).

News media coverage of congressional action typically reinforces the parties' messaging efforts by focusing on partisan combat. More controversial legislative efforts receive more news coverage, promoting an appearance of conflict and creating an avenue by which lawmakers with something negative to say about congressional action will be overemphasized in media stories (Bennett 2012). This kind of coverage, in turn, undermines public faith in Congress, the parties, and even the laws enacted (Atkinson 2017; Curry 2019; Harbridge and Malhotra 2011; Jones 2013; Mutz 2015; Ramirez 2009).

In general, congressional parties and their members, and the news media that communicates their messages, have incentives to accentuate partisan conflict, especially as party competition for control of Congress has intensified in recent years (Lee 2016). In this chapter we ask if these combined patterns shed light on the public's perceptions of partisanship in congressional lawmaking. Do lawmakers' public reactions to congressional action, as relayed in the news media, create a perception of negativity, acrimony, and partisan conflict? Do members emphasize partisan disagreement over agreement? Have patterns in members' public statements changed over time? In particular, we want to know if contemporary majority party members are more pleased with legislative outcomes than were their counterparts in the less partisan Congresses of the 1970s. We also want to know whether contemporary minority party members are less pleased with legislation than their predecessors.

Assessing Lawmakers' Reactions to Congressional Action in the News Media

To assess the impressions conveyed through lawmakers' reactions to congressional action in the news media, we assembled a unique dataset of *New York Times* and *Washington Post* articles covering successful legislative action in Congress from 1975 to 2016 (the 94th–114th Congresses).[3] Specifically, using ProQuest, we searched for all articles published in these two periodicals during this period that included in their titles one of the following phrases:

1. "Congress passes"
2. "Congress approves"
3. "House passes"
4. "House approves"
5. "Senate passes"
6. "Senate approves"

These searches yielded 1,667 relevant articles over the forty-two years (twenty-one Congresses), with the number of articles ranging from 45 to 120 per Congress.

Working with a team of four research assistants, we identified each quotation from a representative or senator included in each article. We compiled a total of 4,132 such quotations from within 1,541 of the articles. Each quotation was then coded for its *tone* (positive, negative, or mixed) as well as its *content* (credit claiming, blaming, or position taking) into seven combined categories inspired by Mayhew (1974):

1. Positive credit claiming. Quotations in this category include those in which actors claim credit for the legislation passed by Congress as good, great, or important. The credit claimed could be individual or collective, but these quotations generally portray the action taken by Congress as good, or even historic, in the face of a national challenge.

2. Mixed credit claiming. These quotations are similar to positive credit claiming but decidedly less positive. In these quotations the actor claims credit but is less enamored with the result, describing the legislation as better than nothing or better than some worse alternative. In many cases actors describe the final product as falling short of their hopes but a step in the right direction, or as necessary to avoid some further calamity.

3. Blaming for losing. Quotations in this category include those in which opponents of the legislation blame its proponents for passing something bad. These actors indicate that they find the passed legislation unacceptable or predict that it will have negative consequences. Sometimes they suggest the proponents are up to no good, mistaken in their actions, or even knowingly doing damage to the country or the public with their actions.

4. Blaming despite winning. Quotations in this category include those in which proponents of the legislation, rather than touting their success, attack those who were opposed. This category also includes quotations in which actors warn against further opposition, including criticizing the president for promising to veto the legislation or condemning other actors for their reluctance to get on board.

5. Positive position taking. Quotations in this category include those in which the actors take a supporting position on an issue or policy related to the legislation. For instance, actors may state that they support policies contained in the bill or other policies or government actions related to the bill and its topic.

6. Negative position taking. Quotations in this category include those in which the actors take an opposed position on an issue or policy related to the legislation. For instance, actors may state that they oppose policies contained in the bill or other policies or government actions related to the bill and its topic.

7. Mixed position taking. Similar to mixed credit claiming, these quotations are qualified statements of position. They include quotations in which the actors note that they are somewhat ambivalent about a policy or issue,

perhaps seeing it as problematic, but see no viable alternative. In other words, these statements take positions of some dissatisfaction, but not opposition.

Each quotation was coded by at least one research assistant and one author. Where there were disagreements between the research assistant's and author's coding decisions, the author reconsidered the coding and made a final determination. Almost 87 percent of the quotations were coded into one of the seven categories above, with the remaining 13 percent unassigned.[4]

The result is a unique dataset of media-covered lawmaker reactions to successful legislative action on Capitol Hill. We know of no other dataset of its kind. While other research looks closely at parties' or legislators' messaging efforts across the board (e.g., Sellers 2010; Grimmer 2013), our data allow us to focus specifically on how lawmakers are portrayed in the media as reacting to the passage of legislation and to assess the impression created from the accumulation of these statements.[5]

With these data, we conduct three sets of analyses. First, we look at the overall impression created by these quotations throughout the whole period from 1975 to 2016. We assess whether the quotations largely create an impression of *negativity* or *positivity*—whether lawmakers' reactions are generally negative or positive in tone. We also assess the combined content *and* tone of the quotations. The key question is whether representatives and senators are touting the accomplishments of Congress—making positive statements and claiming credit—or providing quotations that create a less than positive impression of legislative action.

Second, we assess the amount of partisan disagreement within these publicly disseminated reactions. Primarily, we want to know: Does the content and tone of these quotations differ meaningfully between members of the majority and minority parties in Congress? Are majority party members more positive in their statements, and do they attempt to claim credit? Are minority party members more negative about legislative action, frequently casting blame? Such patterns would suggest a clear partisan divide in how lawmakers react to legislative success. In contrast, convergence between the parties, with members of the majority and minority parties providing similar reactions to legislative actions, would give a very different impression.

Third, we assess whether patterns in lawmakers' reactions to legislative action have *changed over time*. Have reactions become more negative? Have partisan differences become more pronounced? In other words, did the tone and content of these quotations change between 1975 and 2016 in ways that would create the impression that congressional lawmaking has become more partisan and divisive? Do contemporary majority party members express more satisfaction with legislative outcomes than majority party members in the 1970s and 1980s? Do today's minority party members voice more dissatisfaction? Combined, these three sets of analyses provide insight into the impressions created by lawmakers' publicly disseminated reactions to congressional action and how much they convey conflict, frustration, and partisan division over time.

Patterns in Lawmakers' Reactions to Congressional Action

What impressions do lawmakers' reactions to congressional action in the news media convey? Across our analyses we find, first, that lawmakers provide a wide array of reactions, but negativity is prevalent among members of both parties. Second, we find that during the period studied here there are marked partisan differences among lawmakers' reactions. Members of the majority party are much more likely to be positive and to claim credit for the legislation being passed, while members of the minority party are more likely to be negative and to cast blame across the aisle. However, we find a significant amount of negativity and blaming from both the majority and the minority. It seems both parties find a lot to complain about. Finally, we find only weak evidence that lawmakers' reactions to congressional action have become more negative or more divided along partisan lines since 1975. There is a lot of acrimony and partisanship in the public statements we study, but at best statements have become only slightly more acrimonious and partisan over the past four decades.

Overall Patterns

Do lawmakers' statements present an overall impression of negativity or conflict about congressional action? What is the tone and content of lawmakers' quotations during the period we study (1975–2016)? First, figure 6.1 shows the frequency of quotations in each of our seven categories. As shown, most quotations reflect lawmakers' efforts to either claim credit for legislation or cast blame for its passage. Fully 57 percent of the quotations are categorized as either "positive credit claiming" or "blaming for losing," in relatively equal proportions. Another combined 16 percent fall into either the "mixed credit claiming" or the "blaming despite winning" category, meaning 73 percent of all quotations are either credit claiming or blaming in content. The remaining quotations are position taking.

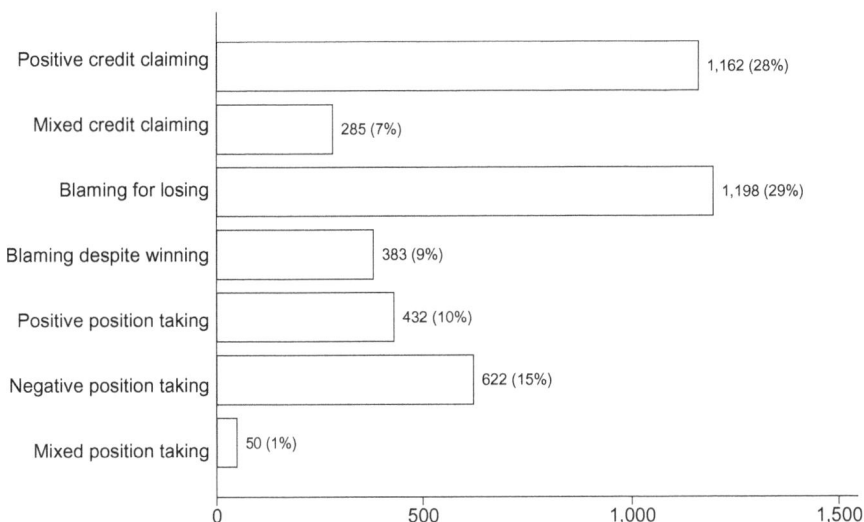

Figure 6.1. Content of quotations, 1975–2016

Figure 6.2 breaks down the quotations specifically by tone—positive, negative, or mixed—and shows the share of quotations across each category of tone from members of the majority and minority parties. The figure shows, first, that lawmakers' comments on legislative action are largely negative. A majority of all quotations (54 percent) were negative in tone. Another 8 percent were mixed in tone—indicating at least some dissatisfaction by the speaking lawmaker. Consequently, just 38 percent of lawmakers' quotations reacting to *successful* legislative action in the House or Senate were positive. In other words, lawmakers reacting to the passage of legislation from 1975 to 2016 predominantly expressed negativity or dissatisfaction. Legislative success does not translate into positive reactions.

The figure also shows that negativity and dissatisfaction are bipartisan. While positive quotations come primarily from lawmakers in the majority party, negative and mixed quotations come in relatively equal proportions from majority and minority lawmakers. Indeed, the percentages of negative reactions from majority and minority lawmakers are almost identical. From these data it is clear that the public frequently hears negativity about congressional action from lawmakers on both sides of the aisle.

Figure 6.3 further characterizes the content of positive, negative, and mixed quotations. As shown, positive quotations are mostly credit claiming, with a smaller proportion aimed at position taking. When lawmakers make

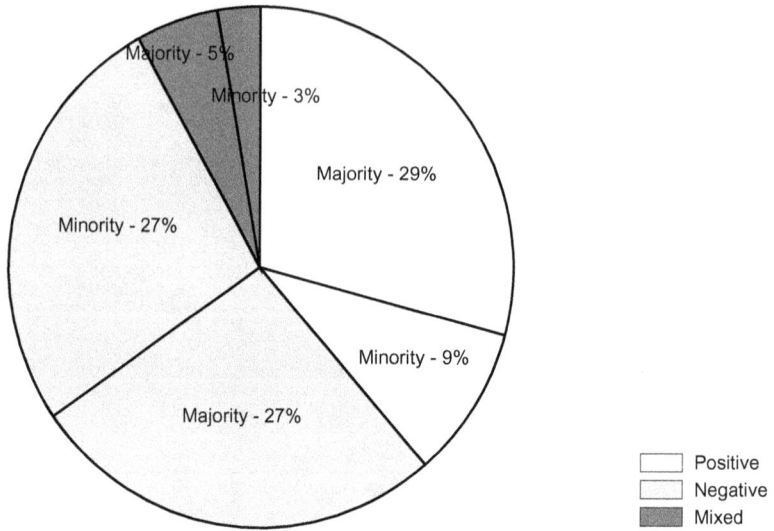

Figure 6.2. Percentage of quotations by tone, 1975–2016

positive statements in reaction to legislative success, they are typically touting the achievements of the legislation. Negative quotations, on the other hand, are mostly blaming, with lawmakers attacking the legislation passed as bad in some way. Moreover, this figure reinforces the prevalence of negativity and blaming in lawmakers' statements. In our data, there were nearly as many blaming quotations (1,581) as all types of positive quotations combined (1,594). Negativity well outpaces positivity in the frequency of lawmaker reactions.

Examples from our data illustrate the nature of these statements. When a bill's proponents react positively and claim credit for legislation, they frequently do so unambiguously, referring to legislative accomplishments as great, historic, or unprecedented, sometimes bordering on hyperbole. Numerous examples appear throughout the years covered in our dataset.

Speaking about the passage of the Reagan budget in 1981, House Minority Leader Bob Michel (R-IL) stated, "Let history record that we provided the margin of difference that changed the course of American government."[6] Regarding a bill restructuring the United States Commission on Civil Rights in 1983, Sen. Joe Biden (D-DE) remarked, "It's a tremendous victory for the civil rights community."[7] Of the sweeping 1986 tax reform law, Sen. Bill Bradley (D-NJ) said, "This is the most significant tax bill since 1954 and maybe since 1913."[8] Three decades later, we can observe similar rhetoric.

On the imminent passage of the 21st Century Cures Act in 2016, Rep. Fred Upton (R-MI) stated, "We are on the cusp of something special—a once-in-a-generation opportunity to transform how we treat disease. . . . With this vote, we are taking a giant leap on the path to cures."[9] Sen. Lamar Alexander (R-TN) similarly described the Every Student Succeeds Act, which replaced No Child Left Behind in 2015, as "the single biggest step toward local control of public schools in 25 years."[10] Members of Congress also credit claim by describing the good the new law will do. Rep. Al Gore (D-TN) argued that the passage of an organ donor bill in 1984 had "the potential to save thousands of lives each year,"[11] just as Sen. Mike DeWine (R-OH) said about a bill targeting cigarette advertising in 2004: "A lot of lives will be saved by this bill."[12]

The blaming statements in our data are frequently as damning as the credit-claiming statements are effusive. Representatives and senators do not hold back in their criticisms, and incendiary statements are found throughout the period we study. In the early years of our data, we can find various examples of legislators describing enacted legislation in stark, sometimes harrowing terms. Of a bill to limit fishing rights in 1976, Sen. Mike Gravel (D-AK) predicted, "It will produce anarchy of the seas."[13] Rep. Ron Dellums (D-CA) called a 1978 bill to regulate ocean mining a "horrible piece of legislation" that would, among other things, provide a license to "rape and plunder."[14] Rep. Ted Weiss (D-NY) labeled the Reagan budget "the 'Drop

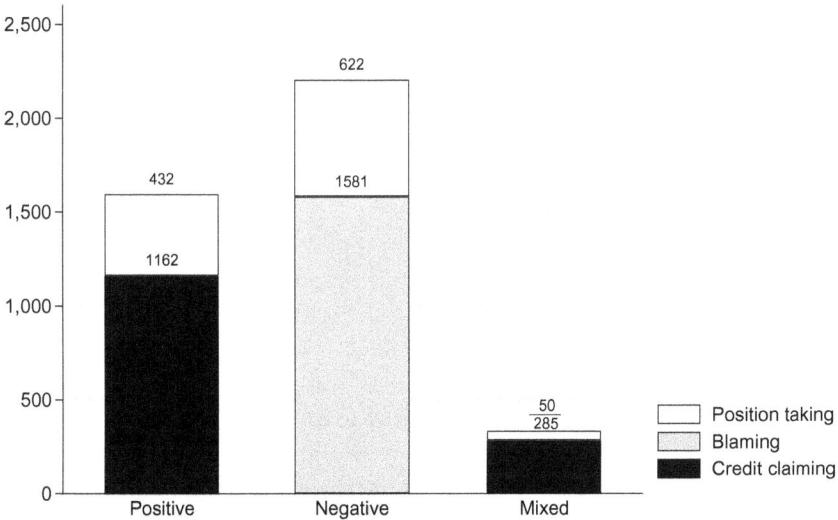

Figure 6.3. Quotations by tone and content, 1975–2016

dead, America' budget" in 1981,[15] and Sen. Ernest Hollings (D-SC) called approval of the Reagan administration's 1981 plan to fund the B1 bomber a "$400 million monstrosity."[16] Rep. Jack Fields (R-TX) dismissed the Democrats' 1994 omnibus crime bill as "a touchy-feely piece of legislation that gives new meaning to the phrase hug-a-thug."[17] The rhetoric is similar in recent years. Sen. Debbie Stabenow (D-MI) called a farm bill passed in 2013 "extremely flawed" and "an insult to rural America."[18] Rep. Steve La-Tourette (R-OH) derided the American Taxpayer Relief Act of 2012 (which resolved the fiscal cliff standoff) as "a package put together by a bunch of sleep-deprived octogenarians on New Year's Eve."[19] Rep. Emanuel Cleaver (D-MO) called the Budget Control Act of 2011 a "Satan sandwich."[20] And Rep. John Boehner (R-OH) called a House-passed 2009 budget resolution an "audacious move to a big socialist government" that piles "debt on the backs of our kids and our grandkids."[21]

Blaming goes beyond attacking the legislation at hand. Blaming throughout the years also singles out the proponents of legislation, attacking them as wrong, misguided, or worse. About cutting funding for a congressional delegation to travel to the United Kingdom to receive a facsimile of Magna Carta in 1976, Sen. Mike Mansfield (D-MT) shouted, "You should be ashamed of yourselves. . . . You are making a ridiculous spectacle of yourselves . . . and fools of your institution."[22] In 1989 Rep. Henry Hyde (R-IL) called Democrats supporting a bill providing funds for abortion "the pro-killer crowd—the death squads of the left."[23] On the passing of a farm bill without funding for food stamps in 2013, Rep. Corinne Brown (D-FL) admonished Republicans, "This is a sad day for the House of Representatives. Shame on the Republicans. . . . Mitt Romney was right; you all do not care about the 47 percent. Shame on you!"[24]

Though less frequently, representatives and senators also often express ambivalence about legislation in the quotations we coded as mixed. In many of these quotations, legislation is described as imperfect, as having fallen short of expectations, or as the only option and better than nothing at all. In others, lawmakers describe their support as tepid or unenthusiastic. For instance, Rep. Gillis Long (D-LA) noted that he would "hold his nose" while voting for a railroad aid bill in 1975.[25] About a 1983 bill raising taxes, Rep. Chalmers Wylie (R-OH) noted, "It is not a good bill, but I am absolutely convinced there is no alternative to this bill."[26] Rep. Claude Pepper (D-FL) said of a 1983 Social Security reform measure, "This bill gives us all something to complain about."[27] Rep. John Dingell (D-MI) noted that he was allowing himself "to be dragged kicking and screaming," into supporting a 1988 banking bill.[28] About the 1994 crime bill, Rep. William

Hughes (D-NJ) said, "some of the provisions are absolutely awful . . . [but it's] time to stop fiddling and pass a crime bill."[29] Sen. Tom Daschle (D-SD) concluded about the 1996 welfare reform law, "It's not the bill I would have drafted [but it's] the best bill we are going to get."[30] About a 2004 law pairing tobacco regulations with a farmer relief package, Sen. Jim Bunning (R-KY) said, "I think FDA regulation is a very steep price to pay for a buyout. . . . But if that's the only way to get my growers relief, this senator will vote to pay it," while Sen. Dick Durbin (D-IL) noted about the relief provisions, "If that is the only way that we can get FDA regulation of tobacco products, all right I will buy that compromise."[31] Disappointment continues to be on display in recent years, with Speaker John Boehner (R-OH) saying of a 2011 budget deal, "Is it perfect? No. . . . I'd be the first to admit it's flawed. But welcome to divided government,"[32] Rep. Paul Ryan saying of a 2015 budget deal, "As with any budget agreement, this one has some good, some bad, and some ugly,"[33] and Rep. Tim Murphy (R-PA) saying of 2016 drug research legislation, "We didn't get everything we needed . . . but we needed everything we got."[34]

The overall takeaway is that the data present an overall impression of conflict, with roughly three-quarters of quotations coded to the credit claiming or blaming categories, and a strong impression of negativity, with a majority of quotations coded as negative in tone and another substantial proportion communicating disappointment. As shown, these quotations are typically stark in their appeals. It is easy to gain an impression from them. Given that these quotations follow *successful* legislation, it is clear that the contemporary Congress frequently feeds into a narrative of conflict and dissatisfaction over legislative outcomes.

Partisan Divisions

Do lawmakers' statements create an impression of *partisan* disagreement in tone and content? In other words, do majority and minority lawmakers meaningfully differ in how they react to legislative success? Our data indicate that lawmakers' descriptions of congressional action are somewhat, but not overwhelmingly, partisan. Figure 6.4 shows the percentage of quotations from majority and minority party lawmakers that were positive, negative, or mixed in tone. Echoing the data in figure 6.2, the data show that positive statements about legislative successes are highly partisan. Positive reactions to legislative successes came primarily (75 percent) from majority party lawmakers. Even mixed reactions appear partisan, with almost twice as large a proportion of qualified or ambivalent-reaction quotations coming

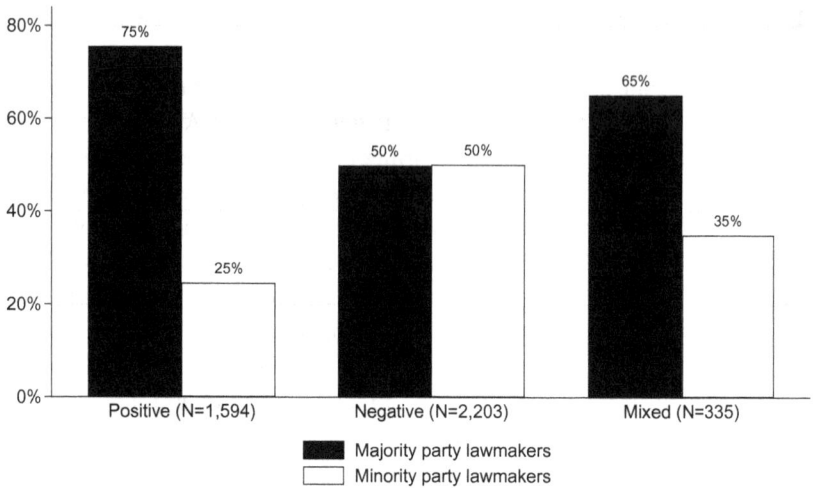

Figure 6.4. Quotations by tone and majority/minority party status, 1975–2016

from lawmakers in the majority (though the overall share of quotations coded as mixed is small). Generally, there is a clear partisan division between those quoted as giving positive and mixed reactions to legislative successes on Capitol Hill.

Negative reactions tell a different story. While positive reactions only rarely come from minority party lawmakers, negative reactions are a bipartisan affair. The share of negative quotations coming from majority and minority lawmakers is almost identical, with 50.1 percent coming from those in the minority party and 49.9 percent from those in the majority party. Majority and minority party lawmakers are frequently negative in the face of legislative success.

Figure 6.5 cuts the data with more precision, showing the percentage of quotations by each category of content and tone coming from majority and minority party lawmakers. Statements in both categories of positive reactions—"positive credit claiming" and "positive position taking"—far more frequently come from majority party lawmakers. Overall, 77 percent of positive credit-claiming statements are made by those in the majority, and 71 percent of positive position-taking statements come from majority party members of the House or Senate. Again, being positive and taking credit is largely a majority party activity.

Partisan differences on blaming are more nuanced. Both parties frequently cast blame in the wake of legislative successes, but in different ways.

Quotations categorized as "blaming despite winning" are far more likely (81 percent) to come from majority party lawmakers. In other words, when the majority casts blame, it is typically attacking the minority party or other opponents for opposing legislation or trying to derail it. In contrast, the minority party casts blame primarily by "blaming for losing." Two-thirds of all blaming for losing quotations came from members of the minority party in the House or Senate. When the minority casts blame, it is typically taking aim at a bill's proponents, usually the majority party, and arguing that the legislative action was a bad choice.

These differences in the manner of blame are apparent in the quotations in our dataset. Blame casting from the majority is very different in form from the aspersions cast on legislation and its proponents in the previous section. When the majority casts blame, it attacks the opposition, often impugning its motives. Across the years in our data these types of statements are readily found. About the Carter administration's welfare plan, Rep. Pete Stark (D-CA) said opposition to the bill came from "those who would starve children."[35] After passing a bill providing emergency assistance to low-income Americans in 1982, Rep. David Bonior (D-MI) attacked the Reagan administration: "It's time that this Administration spend less time with blue bloods and more

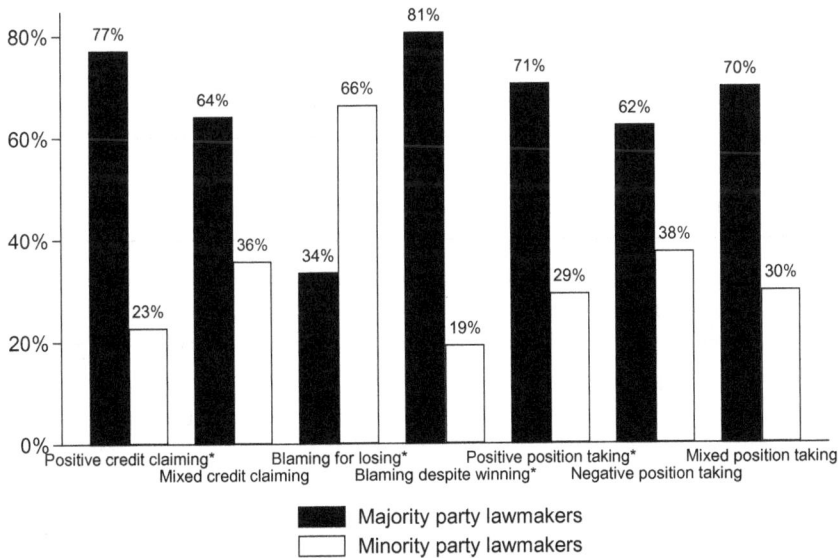

Figure 6.5. Quotations by tone and content and majority/minority party status, 1975–2016
Note: Asterisk means the difference is statistically significant ($p < .05$).

time with blue collars."[36] Attacking opponents of a bill establishing a federal death penalty, Sen. Strom Thurmond (R-SC) shouted, "How would senators feel about their daughter killed in that way? Strangled, mutilated, cut, killed, and a man serving a life term. Maybe someday he will be paroled and kill others."[37] In 1994 Sen. Ted Kennedy (D-MA) attacked opponents of a school aid bill as "against education . . . against an increase in federal aid to hard-pressed local schools . . . against teachers and students . . . against major reforms and improvements in the most important federal assistance for schools in every city, town and village in America."[38]

Similar quotations are found in recent years. On Democratic opposition to the House Republicans' budget proposal in 2013, Rep. Paul Ryan (R-WI) noted that it "clarifies the divide between [the parties]. . . . We want to balance the budget. They don't. . . . We want to restrain spending. They want to spend more."[39] In 2015 Speaker John Boehner (R-OH) argued, "With all the threats our troops face and the sacrifices they make, Democrats' opposition to this defense bill is in fact indefensible."[40]

These "blaming despite winning" quotations often involve presidential veto threats, with congressional majority party members reacting to that possibility or warning the president that a veto would be a bad idea. "Understand, Mr. President, we are going to pass this bill by a very wide margin," Rep. Thomas Downey (D-NY) said of a Reagan veto threat to a Superfund bill in 1986. "If you veto it, we will override you. If you want to pocket the veto, we'll stay in town so you can't do it."[41] Of a possible 1990 veto by President Bush of a civil rights bill, Sen. Ted Kennedy (D-MA) warned, "The President has to do more than pay lip service to civil rights."[42] Of a threatened Clinton veto of a Republican spending bill in 1996, Speaker Newt Gingrich (R-GA) stated, "President Clinton and his party in Congress have refused for four years to make or allow others to make those needed changes that could balance the Federal budget for the first time in a generation."[43] And of President Obama's threat to veto a Republican Keystone XL pipeline approval bill in 2015, Speaker John Boehner (R-OH) said, "Instead of listening to the people, the president is standing with a bunch of left-fringe extremists and anarchists. . . . The president needs to listen to the American people and say 'yes, let's build the Keystone pipeline.'"[44] In general these quotations are just as negative as those coming from opposition lawmakers casting blame after losing legislative battles, but they are different in form. Nonetheless, both kinds of quotation convey significant negativity around successful legislative action.

All together, the data show clear partisan divisions in a willingness to be positive about legislative action. Lawmakers in the majority are far more likely than those in the minority to make positive statements in response to legislative action and to claim credit in the aftermath of successful passage. Negative reactions are a bipartisan tradition on Capitol Hill, though manifest in different forms. In any case, these patterns convey two important points. First, there are noticeable divides between majority and minority parties in the kinds of statements made in response to congressional action. Second, negativity and blame abound in both parties. These combined patterns indicate that lawmakers' reactions to legislative action in the news media exhibit clear partisan differences, but also substantial overall negativity.

Assessing Change over Time

A final set of questions focuses on whether there have been changes in patterns of lawmakers' reactions to successful congressional action that would create an impression of more conflict or more partisan disagreement since the 1970s. The data above indicate that for the full period we study a notable amount of negativity, acrimony, and partisan division is apparent in lawmakers' public statements. But have these trends become more prevalent in recent years? Across the data presented below, the answer is *not really*.

Figure 6.6 presents the percentage of quotations by tone for each Congress from 1975 to 2016 (the 94th–114th Congresses). As shown, there are

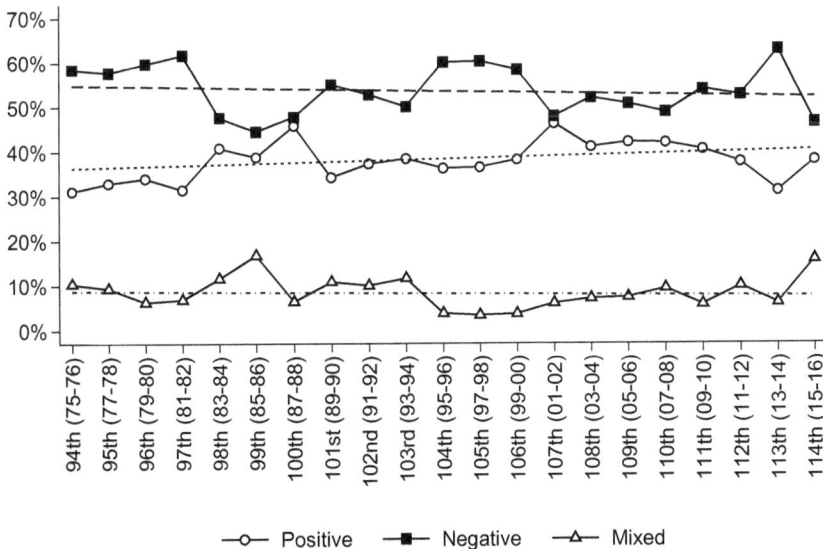

Figure 6.6. Tone of quotations over time

no clear trends in the data. The percentage of quotations categorized as positive or negative fluctuates from Congress to Congress, but trend lines for both are not statistically significant,[45] as is the trend line for mixed quotations.[46] In every single Congress, negative quotations outpace positive quotations, but negativity has not become more prevalent over time. Where tone is concerned, there is simply no evidence that members of Congress are portraying successful congressional action in a more negative light in recent years than in the 1970s. The rhetoric of those less partisan years was every bit as negative as the rhetoric today.

Figure 6.7 presents similar findings looking at the content of quotations over time. Focusing on credit claiming and blaming (the most prevalent categories), this figure again shows no significant trends over time. "Positive credit claiming" and "blaming for losing" were the most common categories in every Congress, but neither has noticeably increased or decreased in frequency over time. Neither trend is statistically significant.[47] The trends for "mixed credit claiming" and "blaming despite winning" are also unremarkable. Both have relatively flat trends that are also not statistically significant.[48] There is no evidence that the content of lawmakers' statements has changed in a way that would convey greater overall negativity or acrimony in more recent years.

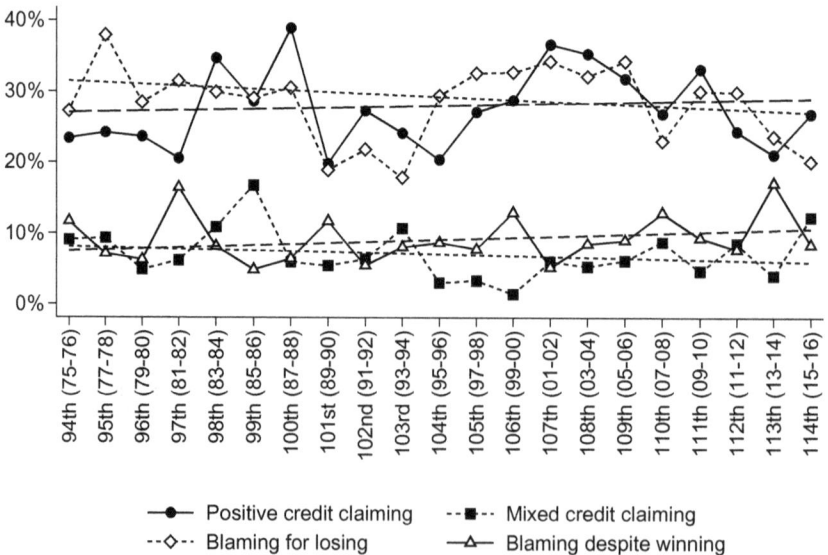

Figure 6.7. Content of quotations over time

Nor is there evidence that partisan divisions in lawmakers' reactions have changed or increased appreciably over time. Figure 6.8 shows the tone of quotations from members of the majority and minority parties, separately, across the Congresses we studied. The data primarily reflect the patterns highlighted in the section above: majority party lawmakers are more positive, but both parties express substantial negativity. However, these patterns have not changed much over the four decades analyzed. For majority party lawmakers, quotations reflect a mix of positive and negative reactions in every Congress. While linear time trends suggest that majority party quotations are becoming more positive and less negative over time,[49] the LOWESS trends shown in figure 6.8 show that most of that change occurred from the 1970s to the 1980s as competition for majority control intensified and the parties developed more sophisticated and combative messaging operations (see Lee 2016). Since the 1980s, the proportion of quotations from majority party lawmakers that were positive or negative has varied from Congress to Congress, but the trend line is generally flat over time.[50] Over the post-1980 period, majority party members were more positive than negative in most but not all Congresses, but they consistently expressed substantial negativity.

For minority party lawmakers, any trends are equally unimpressive. Minority party reactions are overwhelmingly negative over time. Negative quotations account for over 50 percent of the minority party's quotations in every Congress but one (the 98th Congress, 1983–84). A linear time trend does not suggest any increase in negativity among the minority over time,[51] and the LOWESS trend line shown in figure 6.8 similarly indicates that while the amount of negativity varies from Congress to Congress, there is no obvious trend over time. Similarly, the proportion of positive quotations has not changed over time among minority party lawmakers. Finally, mixed quotations have not significantly increased or decreased over time for either party, and quotations expressing ambivalence are the least common in almost every Congress for both parties.

Figure 6.9 shows the content of quotations by majority and minority party status over time for three key categories of credit claiming and blaming: "positive credit claiming," "blaming for losing," and "blaming despite winning." Again the primary takeaway is a lack of clear trends over time. Majority party lawmakers primarily claim credit for legislative successes. In all but two Congresses, "positive credit claiming" is the most common category of quotation for members of the majority, and there is no clear trend over time, either with a linear time trend[52] or in the LOWESS trend shown

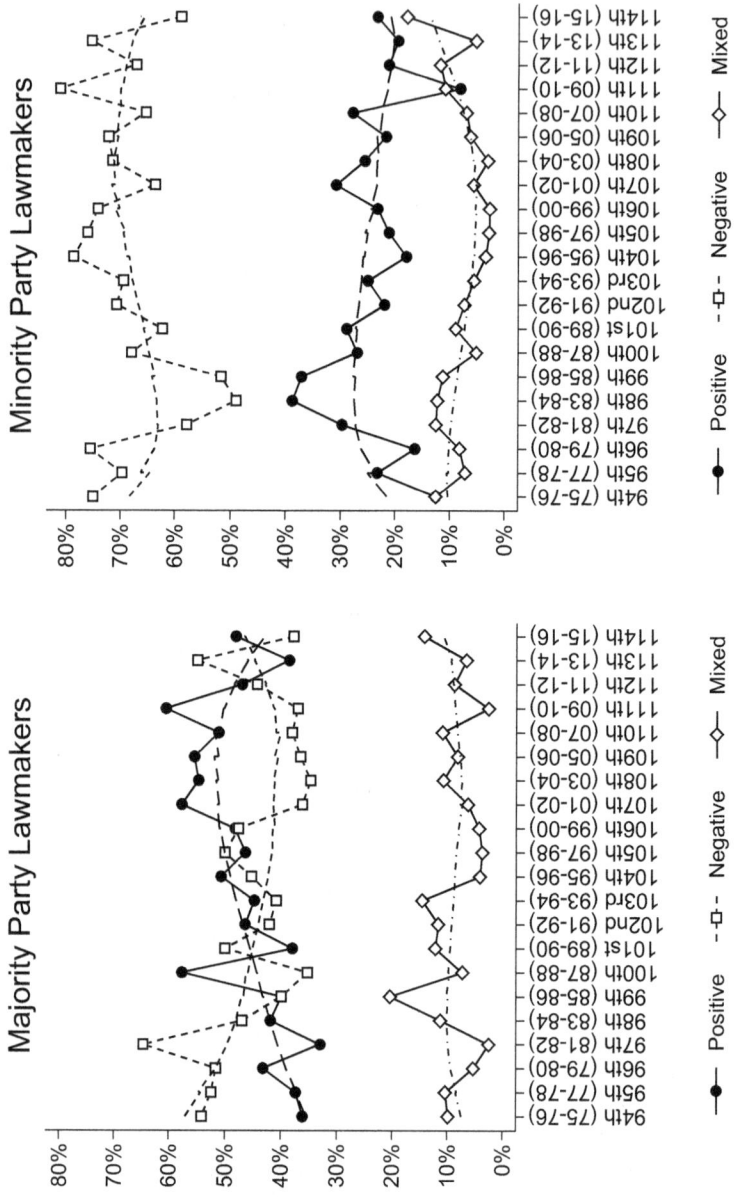

Figure 6.8. Tone of quotations over time by majority/minority status

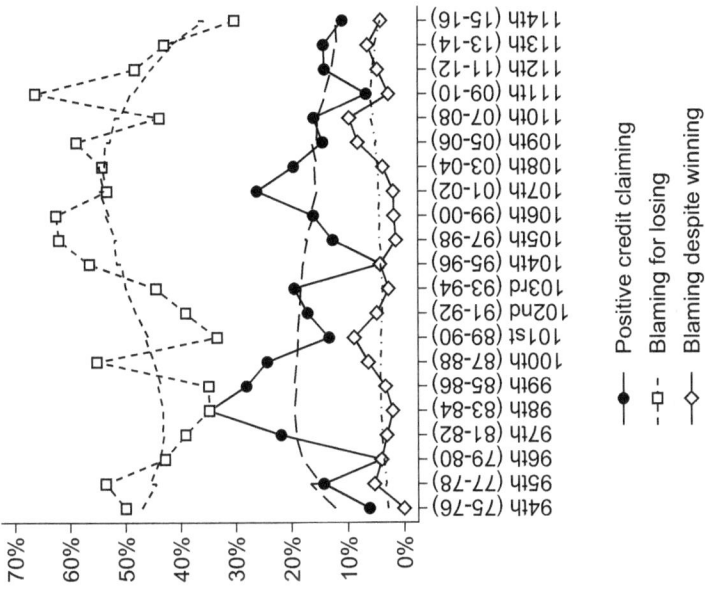

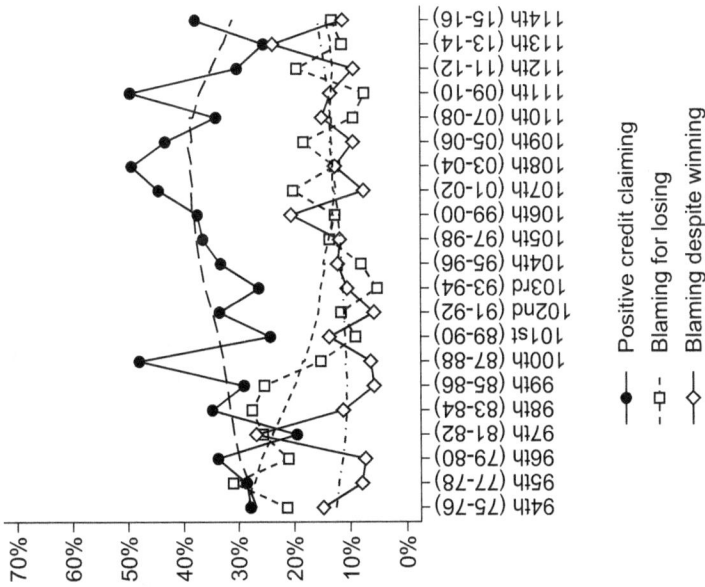

Figure 6.9. Content of quotations over time by majority/minority status

in figure 6.9. There is some evidence that majority party lawmakers have offered fewer "blaming for losing" reactions over time. A linear time trend suggests a statistically significant decline in such quotations over time.[53] But again, the LOWESS trend shows that most of this decline took place from the 1970s to the 1980s. After 1980, a linear time trend is flat and not statistically significant.[54] Generally, majority party lawmakers both claim credit and cast blame after legislation is passed.

Among minority party lawmakers there is even less change over time. In every Congress, more quotations from minority party lawmakers are categorized as "blaming for losing" than any other category. Moreover, linear trends over time are not statistically significant for either category, and the LOWESS trends similarly show no appreciable change. There is some fluctuation from Congress to Congress, but more than anything there is remarkable consistency. The data simply do not demonstrate any large increase in partisan divisions among lawmakers' reactions, in either tone or content, that would have created a clear impression within the public that lawmaking has become more partisan in recent years.

Multivariate analyses confirm that increases in partisan conflict and party strength have not had much effect on majority and minority party reactions to legislative successes. Table 6.1 presents logistic regression analyses predicting the likelihood that quotations from majority and minority party lawmakers are positive, negative, or mixed in tone. The unit of analysis for each regression is each quotation in our dataset, and the analyses are split between majority and minority lawmakers (House and Senate combined). The key independent variables are measures of House and Senate polarization and House and Senate majority party unity in each chamber during each Congress. The former measures are the difference between the first-dimension DW-NOMINATE party medians in each chamber. The latter measures are the inverse of the standard deviation of first-dimension DW-NOMINATE scores among members of the majority party in each chamber. These variables, which capture the amount of party conflict and party homogeneity in each chamber, would predict more positive statements among majority party lawmakers and more negative statements among minority party lawmakers if lawmakers' reactions to congressional action correlate with these broader partisan changes in Congress since the 1970s.

As controls, the models also include variables indicating whether the source of each quotation held a party leadership position (Speaker, majority and minority leaders, assistant leaders, and whips in the House; majority and minority leaders, assistant leaders, and whips in the Senate), or a committee leadership position (chair or minority ranking member), whether

Table 6.1 Party polarization and predicting likelihoods of quote tones among lawmakers

	Positive		Negative		Mixed	
	Majority	Minority	Majority	Minority	Majority	Minority
House	0.036	1.543	0.034	0.437	−0.209	−5.067
polarization	(1.641)	(3.171)	(1.468)	(3.006)	(3.799)	(3.742)
House majority	16.19**	4.303	−18.17**	5.771	6.065	−28.45*
party unity	(5.021)	(7.031)	(6.616)	(8.869)	(16.130)	(13.080)
Senate	−2.117	−5.606	2.897	−0.257	−2.461	14.28*
polarization	(2.519)	(4.742)	(3.242)	(4.608)	(8.332)	(6.070)
Senate majority	1.421	−1.442	−0.814	1.723	−1.754	0.187
party unity	(1.674)	(2.179)	(2.042)	(2.987)	(5.581)	(4.778)
Divided	−0.169*	0.340*	0.153*	−0.362**	0.061	0.258
government	(0.082)	(0.160)	(0.074)	(0.141)	(0.233)	(0.167)
Party leader	0.189	−0.267	−0.193	−0.024	0.019	0.674*
	(0.116)	(0.175)	(0.134)	(0.191)	(0.176)	(0.288)
Committee	0.507**	0.048	−0.533**	−0.086	0.050	0.136
leader	(0.089)	(0.139)	(0.087)	(0.142)	(0.182)	(0.265)
Representative	0.170	−0.466**	−0.098	0.342*	−0.224*	0.192
	(0.091)	(0.155)	(0.092)	(0.146)	(0.105)	(0.179)
Constant	−13.80**	−0.885	13.99**	−5.636	−4.092	14.97*
	(3.874)	(6.178)	(4.298)	(6.594)	(10.530)	(6.805)
N	2,515	1,611	2,515	1,611	2,515	1,611

Note: Robust standard errors calculated correcting for clustering by Congress. $*p < .05$; $**p < .01$.

the statement was made during a Congress featuring divided government, and whether the quotation came from a representative rather than a senator.

The results provide minimal evidence that lawmakers' public statements about congressional action convey more partisanship and partisan conflict when the parties are more internally homogeneous or more polarized. Across the analyses of positive and negative quotations, none of the party polarization measures have statistically significant effects. The likelihood that positive or negative quotations come from majority or minority lawmakers is indistinguishable between Congresses with high or low levels of polarization in each chamber. House majority party unity appears to have some effect on the tone of majority party quotations, but the effect is not great. At one standard deviation below the mean of House majority party unity, a majority party lawmaker has a 41 percent likelihood of providing a positive quotation, whereas at one standard deviation above the mean of House majority party unity a majority party lawmaker has a 54 percent likelihood. The effects are similar for negative quotations, with the likelihood of a negative quotation 37 percent at one standard deviation above the mean of House majority party unity and 51 percent at one standard deviation

below the mean. In all cases, the likelihood that a lawmaker gives both positive and negative statements remains high. Moreover, while House majority
party unity has an effect, Senate majority party unity does not. Generally
there is little relation between measures of party conflict or party unity and
the positive or negative tone of lawmakers' reactions to legislation.

Both party polarization and party unity appear to sometimes affect the
likelihood that minority party lawmakers provide mixed statements, but
the results are inconsistent. Minority party lawmakers are *less* likely to be
quoted making ambivalent statements when the House majority is more
unified, but they are *more* likely to be quoted doing so when the Senate is
more polarized, providing a truly contradictory set of findings. Overall, the
results in table 6.1 suggest that changes to party polarization and majority
party unity over time have not meaningfully affected the tone of lawmakers'
reactions to congressional action.

While continuity is the key takeaway from the analyses above, at least
one change reflecting the growing importance of parties and partisanship in
American politics since the 1970s is worth discussing. The most prominent
change in our data is a steady increase in quotations coming from lawmakers holding party leadership positions. Figure 6.10 shows the percentage of
quotations coming from party leaders in either chamber. In both majority
and minority parties, the trends show a marked increase. In the 1970s and
1980s, leaders' quotations typically made up less than 15 percent of lawmakers' quotations published in the articles we studied. By contrast, in recent years leaders' quotations constitute 30 percent or more of such quotations. This trend reflects the heightened role contemporary party leaders are
playing in every facet of congressional lawmaking (e.g., Curry 2015; Hanson
2014; Sinclair 2016) and party communications (Lee 2016).

Note that our data also show that the increase in the share of quotations
coming from party leaders has not come at the expense of quotations from
committee leaders. Among majority party lawmakers, the share of quotations from committee chairs has not declined since the 1970s. Among minority party lawmakers, the trend has been relatively flat since the 1980s.
Our results mirror Bekafigo (2014) in documenting a long-term increase in
the visibility of party leaders in news stories, but we do not find a decline in
coverage of committee leaders. Our data indicate that it is mostly rank-and-
file lawmakers who have been squeezed out.

Moreover, quotations from those in the party and committee leadership,
compared with the rank and file, differ only slightly in tone and content.
Figure 6.11 compares the percentage of quotations by tone for leaders and
nonleaders in each party. The figure shows that within the majority party

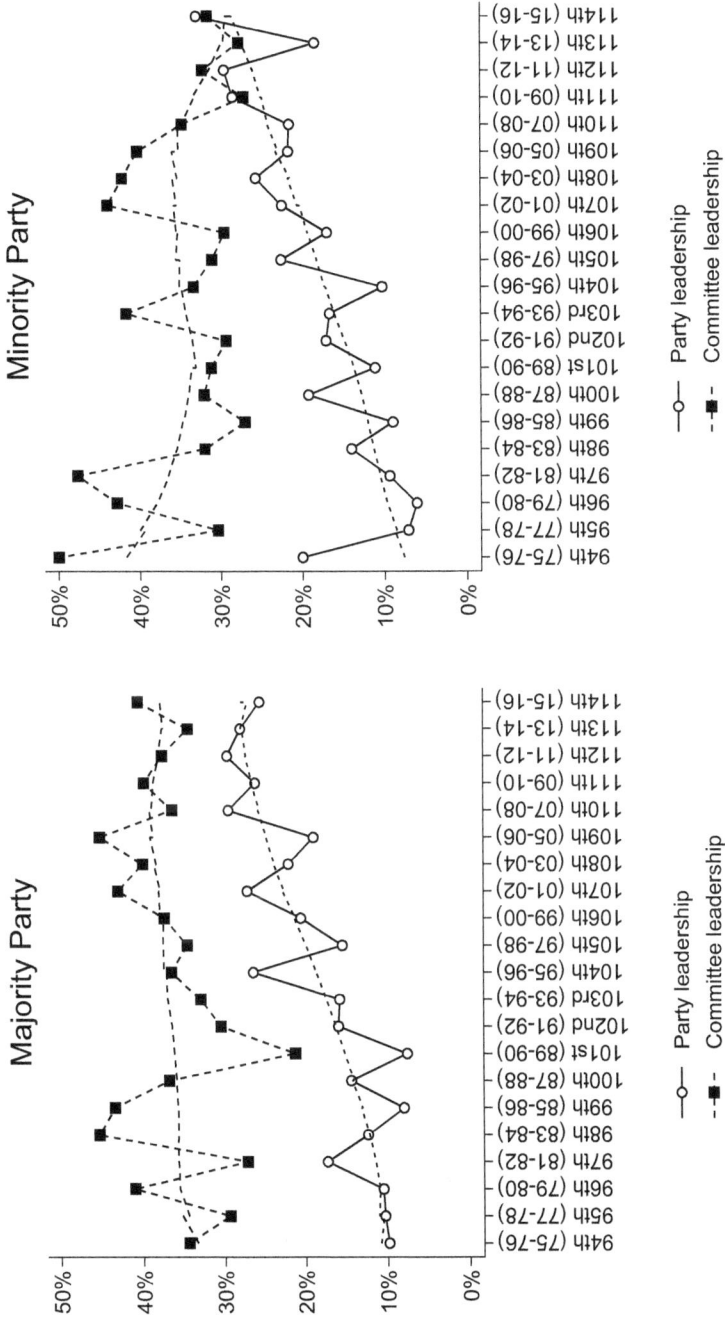

Figure 6.10. Percentage of lawmakers' quotations from those in leadership positions over time

there are some slight differences in the proportion of quotations from rank-and-file lawmakers, party leaders, and committee chairs that are positive, negative, or mixed in tone. Both party leaders and committee leaders are generally more positive than rank-and-file members. About 48 percent of quotations from party leaders and 54 percent of those from committee chairs are positive, compared with just 42 percent among rank-and-file law-makers.[55] So, if anything, an increasing share of quotations coming from majority party leaders likely has a *positive* effect on the tone of congressional reactions in the news media. Among minority party members, the differences between leaders and rank-and-file members are all very small. Party leaders in the minority are slightly less likely to be positive in their statements than their rank and file or committee leaders, and slightly more likely to be negative. However, for all groups of minority lawmakers the preponderance of quotations is negative in tone—from 66 percent to 70 percent. Generally, minority party lawmakers in and outside the leadership provide quotations that are overwhelmingly negative.

Taken together, the preceding analyses largely convey continuity rather than change over time. Lawmakers' published reactions to congressional action in the news media have not become more positive or negative. In fact, the overall tone and content of these quotations has remained remarkably

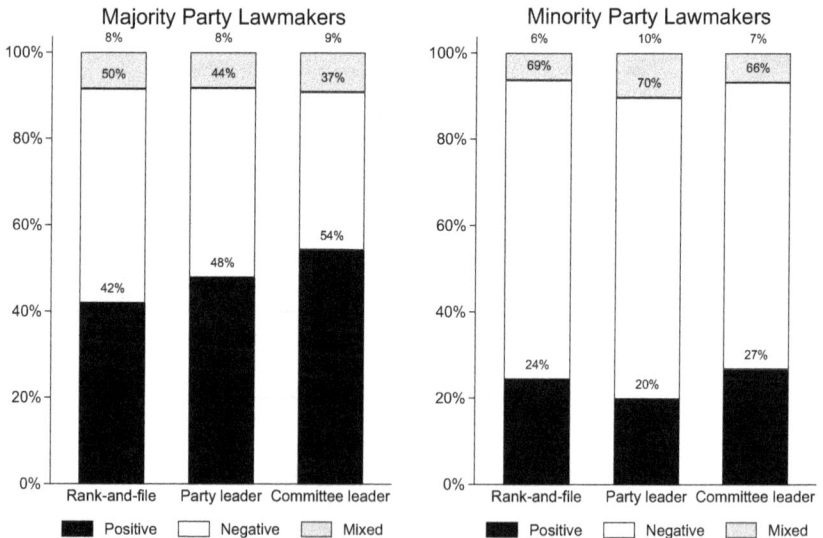

Figure 6.11. Tone of quotations among leaders and rank-and-file members of the majority and minority parties, 1975–2016

stable. Within the majority and minority parties, stability is also the rule—majority lawmakers talk about legislative successes today much as they did in the 1980s, as do minority party lawmakers. Quotations from party leaders have increased in quantity and proportion, but quotations from leaders do not differ substantially from those coming from other lawmakers. Overall, while notable negativity and partisan disagreement are apparent in lawmakers' reactions to legislative action, such statements have not become more negative, conflictual, or partisan than they were thirty years ago.

Constant Negativity and Discord

The analyses here present lawmakers' reactions to successful legislative action in the media as prominently featuring negativity and discord. The quotations appearing in *New York Times* and *Washington Post* articles covering House or Senate passage of legislation largely find representatives and senators making statements that are negative in tone. Members frequently react to legislative action by casting blame on each other. Moreover, there are clear partisan differences in these reactions. Majority party lawmakers are far more likely to make positive statements regarding the action and to claim credit, touting legislative achievements. Minority party lawmakers far less frequently have anything positive to say about legislative enactments and are more likely to cast blame.

Consequently, consumers of media coverage are left with a clear impression of negativity and partisan discord around congressional action. Indeed, the acrimony apparent in these quotations stands in contrast to the continued patterns of bipartisanship we find in members' roll-call support for legislative enactments. However, we also find very little evidence that any of this has changed in ways that would create an impression of *more* partisanship in congressional lawmaking in recent years. Our data show remarkable continuity in the content and tone of quotations over time. Media-covered lawmaker reactions have not become more negative or conflictual. Lawmakers fight it out in public today just as they did during the Ford administration. There is simply no evidence that lawmakers' public reactions to successful congressional action present more partisanship or party conflict than in the past.

To some degree these findings reflect the reality of congressional lawmaking in today's partisan era. Despite a dramatic intensification of partisan conflict since the 1970s, marked increases in party cohesion on roll-call voting, and increased party organizational strength in both the House and the Senate, legislative enactments have continued to garner high levels of bipartisan support. In that respect, legislative outcomes have been consistent throughout the period we analyze. It thus makes sense that lawmakers' reactions to successful legislating have also remained consistent. When it comes to legislation that passes Congress, lawmakers' public reactions have not changed in a way that would contribute to a perception of rising partisanship.

Any perceptions that legislative outcomes are more partisan than in the past must rely on sources other than members quoted in media coverage. Overall patterns in roll-call voting probably stand at the root of many of these perceptions. As is well established, roll-call votes break down on partisan lines far more often than they did thirty years ago (see fig. 1.1), and members are much more likely to vote with their party on such votes (see fig. 1.2). Patterns of gridlock likely also contribute. A significant amount of congressional gridlock is caused by party differences (Binder 2003, 2014), even if much of it is also rooted in intraparty disagreements (see chapter 3). The partisan acrimony and finger pointing that occur with legislative stalemate likely also color the public's perceptions of partisanship in congressional lawmaking. But in the end, the data presented here indicate more continuity than change. In reacting to legislative action members are fighting to shape public perceptions, but they did the same thing forty-five years ago.

Constancy and Continuities

An effective party system requires, first, that the parties are able to bring forth programs to which they commit themselves and, second, that the parties possess sufficient internal cohesion to carry out these programs.

—American Political Science Association, Committee on Political Parties (1950, 17–18)

Now we have just the kind of political-party system Roosevelt and the political scientists envisioned. We are living the future, and it does not work.

—David Shribman, *Pittsburgh Post-Gazette*[1]

To demand more of the parties—to ask that they become governing instruments—is to run them up against components of the American regime as fundamental as the party system itself. . . . In this complicated, multi-component setting, British-style governing by party majorities does not have much of a chance.

—David Mayhew (2005, 199)

James Madison, warning of the danger of majority factions, argued that the structure of the American political system as laid out in the Constitution would provide a necessary bulwark. No faction or party would be able to dominate the federal government because the Constitution would ensure that the political system represents a "multiplicity of interests" and would "divide and arrange the several offices in such a manner as that each may be a check on the other" (*Federalist Papers* #51). As Paul Ryan (R-WI) and his party gaveled in the 115th Congress in January 2017, many observers thought, and perhaps many Republicans hoped, that the strengthening of congressional parties that had occurred over the previous decades had eroded Madison's famous checks and balances. They anticipated that the GOP would be able to marshal parliamentary-style discipline to advance a party platform through Congress, where a newly installed Republican president, Donald Trump, would be ready and willing to sign their bills into law. But, as for partisans of so many past eras, reality was disappointing.

This study has taken stock of the capacity of congressional majority parties to steer the American ship of state in a party-polarized era. We have analyzed levels of partisanship on legislative enactments from the 1970s through the 2010s, as well as the efforts of congressional majority parties to pass their agenda items since the 1980s, looking at how majority parties succeed and why they fail. Our data span a period of substantial partisan change in Congress and elsewhere in the American political system. Since the 1970s, Congress has evolved away from the muted partisanship and decentralized legislative processes characteristic of the mid-twentieth century. Legislative parties now exhibit almost parliamentary levels of discipline on roll-call votes (see figs 1.1 and 1.2), organize and staff elaborate whip and messaging operations, and employ legislative processes centralized around party leaders (Sinclair 2016; Tiefer 2016).

Despite these changes, we find remarkable constancy and continuity in the limits on congressional majority party influence over public policy. At the start of this book we asked six questions about majority party capacity in congressional lawmaking. In light of the preceding chapters, we can revisit each with some answers.

1. Is lawmaking less bipartisan in the contemporary Congress than in the past? Are more laws enacted on party-line votes? The data analyzed in chapter 2 showed that levels of partisan disagreement on lawmaking votes have remained relatively unchanged since the 1970s. In the first six years of our data, from 1973 to 1978, on average 82 percent of minority party House members and 82 percent of minority party senators supported the passage of new laws, while 72 percent of minority party House members and 80 percent of minority party senators supported the passage of new landmark laws. In the most recent six years we analyze, from 2013 to 2018, those rates of House minority party support were 90 percent and 72 percent, respectively, for all laws and for landmark laws, and 68 percent and 77 percent for minority party senators. Across the years and all the partisan change, minority party support for new laws remains substantial and unchanged.

2. Are majority parties in Congress better able to enact their legislative priorities? Chapter 2 assessed congressional majority party agenda success and

failure across every Congress from 1985 through 2018, drawing on our data tracking the legislative outcomes of majority party priorities. Our analyses reveal that majority parties have become neither more nor less efficacious in enacting their agenda priorities over time. Majority parties succeeded on 52 percent of their agenda items and failed on 48 percent, and those rates of success and failure have not changed substantially over time. Congressional majority parties certainly have not become better at getting most of what they want on their agenda items or winning clear partisan victories. Since the 1980s, parties have found more success when compromising, and getting half a loaf, than when trying to obtain a full loaf. There has been no notable change or trend in these outcomes.

3. When congressional majority parties fail in enacting their agendas, when and why do they do so? Chapter 3 shows that the etiology of majority party failure on priority agenda items has also not changed. Today's congressional parties are far more ideologically coherent than those of thirty years ago, but intraparty disagreement remains a persistent obstacle to majority party success. Recent majority parties are not much better at getting their members to coalesce behind party proposals in order to avoid failure. Internal disagreement continues to be just as prominent a reason for failure in recent Congresses as it was in the 1980s. Similarly, legislative veto points controlled by the opposing party, such as the Senate's sixty-vote cloture requirement, do not account for an increasing share of majority party agenda failures. Veto points are a significant obstacle, but they have not become a bigger problem over time. There are simply no trends in how and why congressional majority parties fail. Majority parties still fail for the same mix of reasons as in the 1980s.

4. When congressional majority parties succeed in passing their agendas, how do they do so? Do they win by steamrolling or co-opting the minority party? Chapter 4 finds similar continuities among party successes. Today's majority parties do not achieve more victories by partisan legislative pathways than the majorities of less partisan eras. Rather, they continue to achieve legislative victories on priority items primarily by seeking to advance broadly popular and bipartisan policy proposals or by compromising across the aisle and backing down from their controversial policy demands. Simply put, the how and why of both majority party success and failure have remained remarkably constant since the Reagan administration.

5. Do more centralized legislative procedures and departures from "regular order" promote the passage of more partisan laws? Chapter 5 further demonstrates that the more frequent use in recent years of centralized legislative policymaking directed by party leaders also has not affected levels

of partisanship in congressional lawmaking. Members of Congress have centralized power in party leaders not to achieve more partisan lawmaking victories, but because the secrecy, efficiency, and flexibility of unorthodox and centralized legislative processes smooth the path to lawmaking successes in a difficult political environment. Writing legislation in party leaders' offices is no more likely to result in a law passed on party lines than writing legislation in open committee markup. Indeed, unorthodox, centralized procedures have been and continue to be used to enact even highly bipartisan laws.

6. When Congress succeeds in passing legislation, how do members discuss their achievements in public? Are contemporary majority party members more pleased with legislative outcomes than their counterparts in the less partisan Congresses of the 1970s? Are contemporary minority party members less pleased? Chapter 6 explored whether Republicans and Democrats are more divided in their assessments of congressional legislation than they were in earlier, less partisan periods. In particular, we wanted to know whether contemporary majority party members expressed more satisfaction with legislative outcomes today than in the 1970s and 1980s and whether contemporary minority party members expressed more dissatisfaction. To answer these questions, we examined the statements members made about lawmaking successes over the decades from the 1970s through the 2010s. Again, we found no changes along these lines. When Congress passes laws, lawmakers tend to react in negative and partisan ways, but these patterns are no more prevalent or pronounced today than in the 1970s or 1980s.

One simple fact is apparent and unavoidable: in American policymaking the parties' ability to enact their platforms has been and remains highly limited. Changes to party discipline and party organizational strength inside Congress since the 1970s have not perceptibly altered levels of partisan conflict over the enactment of federal laws. Nor have organizational changes and increased party cohesion in roll-call voting improved the capacity of majority parties to achieve their stated aims and fulfill their campaign promises.

Rather, Madisonian limits to party influence remain as robust in today's era of party polarization as they were in eras when parties were more internally divided and weakly organized. The American policymaking system—characterized by constitutional checks and balances, separation of powers, and the decentralizing force of individualized elections for members of Congress—frustrates and moderates efforts at partisan lawmaking. The political system imposes constancy and continuity on party influence despite dramatic partisan change inside Congress. Parties remain as limited as ever as instruments of governance in American politics. This conclusion has important implications for how political scientists and observers should think about the roles congressional parties play in our political system.

Revisiting Responsible Parties

Historically, scholars and political observers saw the parties' decentralized structure, fragmentation, and lack of internal organization and discipline as the primary obstacles to programmatic party lawmaking. Deep divisions within both the Democratic and Republican parties for much of the twentieth century impeded their capacity to steer the ship of state in any coherent partisan direction (Polsby 2004; Sundquist 1968). Party reformers as far back as James Bryce (1888) and Woodrow Wilson (1908) saw weak parties as a problem not just for party government but for American governance in general (Wickham-Jones 2018). Schattschneider (1948, 1) called this state of affairs "an invisible governmental crisis."

Scholars of party government in the mid-twentieth century saw responsible parties as "the most practicable and feasible solution of the problem of organizing American democracy" (Schattschneider 1942, 207). These political scientists argued for a system in which American parties would be cohesive enough to put coherent platforms before voters and the victorious party would have the institutional power necessary to enact its policy program. The report of the American Political Science Association's Committee on Political Parties (1950) has come to be seen as an archetypal representation of the reforms many scholars of that era had in mind.[2] Where Congress is concerned, the report recommended, among other things, stronger legislative party organizations with party leaders possessing more tools and resources to encourage party discipline, including more power over committees and committee chairs. These new arrangements, it was thought, would allow for party programmatic lawmaking in the halls of Congress.

As centralizing changes along these lines subsequently came about in Congress, legislative scholars contended that stronger, more cohesive congressional parties would be better able to approximate the party government model. *Conditional party government* theory argues that when legislative parties are internally homogeneous and sharply polarized, they will endow their party organizations with the kind of authority Schattschneider and other responsible parties advocates hoped for. Such parties will use their powers to "enact as much of the party's program as possible" (Aldrich and Rohde 2000a, 38). Even the more static *procedural cartel* understanding of congressional party power includes an expectation that empowered legislative party organizations and leaders will make majority parties "more able . . . to fashion a favorable [legislative] record" (Cox and McCubbins 2005, 7).

But the recent history analyzed in this book suggests that the hopes of responsible parties theorists were misplaced and the expectations of later legislative scholars were not borne out. To be sure, the more polarized politics of recent years have seen majority parties exhibit internal discipline and empower their legislative organizations. This much is true, but these changes have not translated into more *partisan lawmaking*. Today's congressional parties are no better at executing a party program than those of earlier eras. Laws garner roughly as much bipartisan support in the contemporary Congress as they did in the far less partisan 1970s. Majority parties continue to struggle with internal disagreements when attempting to advance party proposals. When we take a close look at legislative outcomes, many of the dynamics that frustrated party government scholars in the 1930s and 1940s are just as apparent today.

Given this, we have to question whether a responsible parties model of American government is possible under any plausible set of political conditions. Even today, with ideologically coherent parties and party organizational strength rivaling or exceeding that of any other period in congressional history, majority parties still have very limited capacity to effectively steer the ship of state in a partisan direction.

The discipline that party members evince on roll-call voting often seems to evaporate when Congress gets down to the brass tacks of making laws. Parties hold together well on messaging vehicles, but when legislation is being proposed or written, representatives and senators still regularly buck their party and frustrate party goals. As we discussed in chapter 3, every majority party in control of unified government since the 1980s has seen at least one of its highest legislative priorities stymied by intraparty disagreement. Intraparty consensus cannot be taken for granted in the contemporary Congress, no matter how impressive its roll-call party cohesion scores.

More broadly, majority parties fail on their agenda priorities just as often in unified government as in divided government. Thus, even highly unified majority parties cannot deliver the programmatic policymaking envisioned by a responsible party government model. The constitutional system of legislative bicameralism and separate executive and legislative branches almost always requires the majority party to reach across the aisle and compromise, even when its members are able to coalesce behind a specific proposal. And our system of individually elected representatives and senators seems to ensure that coalition building within the majority will itself commonly be a challenge.

Our findings comport well with research in comparative politics showing that political parties operate differently in parliamentary and presidential systems (Samuels and Shugart 2010; Shugart and Carey 1992). The responsible parties model favored by reformers of the 1950s and 1960s emerged during a time when most other democracies around the world were parliamentary systems. In that context, scholars compared the US Congress with the more disciplined, cohesive parties of parliamentary democracies—especially the British model that Americanists were most familiar with—and found congressional parties wanting. In light of such comparisons, congressional parties failed to exhibit collective responsibility and seemed incapable of bearing the burdens of governance (Fiorina 1980; Schattschneider 1942). By the twenty-first century, however, most democracies have directly elected presidents (Samuels and Shugart 2010, 4–6), allowing comparative scholars to ascertain that, across the board, political parties tend to be more fragmented in systems with separation of powers. Legislative parties exhibit lower levels of cohesion in presidential systems than in parliamentary systems (Carey 2007). Presidents also achieve less of their legislative agendas than prime ministers do, after taking into account the size of the executive's legislative coalition (Cheibub, Przeworski, and Saiegh 2004, 578). In conjunction with this comparative work on presidentialism, our results suggest that scholars need to benchmark congressional parties not against parliamentary parties but against parties in political systems more comparable to the United States.

Our findings have implications for public understanding of Congress as well. Voters also need to come to terms with the limits of party in the US political system. Instead of creating the conditions for party government, highly partisan eras like today's may instead just serve to inflate public expectations and end in even more disappointment with the parties and with Congress.

Contemporary congressional parties are homogeneous enough to make bold promises—to repeal and replace the Affordable Care Act or reform major federal entitlement programs (Republicans, 115th Congress), to prohibit federal funding for abortions (Republicans, 114th Congress), to enact comprehensive immigration reform (Democrats, 113th Congress), to dramatically reduce federal spending (Republicans, 112th Congress), or to address global climate change (Democrats, 111th Congress). They can schedule symbolic messaging votes on these issues and proposals and achieve parliamentary levels of party discipline on those substantively inconsequential votes. They can then use their considerable communications and messaging operations to broadcast the partisan divide on those votes and cultivate strong and clear party reputations among voters. But they can rarely follow through and enact these agenda items over the other party's opposition. Except for unusual breakthroughs—on less than 5 percent of the 265 agenda items we studied—majority parties either fail outright or have to make considerable concessions in order to pass a law. Most of the time, majority parties successfully legislate only with bipartisan support.

As a consequence, partisans in the electorate face a reality of constant disappointment. Their party will almost never be able to fully deliver on its goals or satisfactorily fulfill its campaign promises. Most of the time only half-measures will be possible as parties have to water down their proposals to clear the many hurdles of the policymaking process. As longtime Hill staffer and former White House congressional liaison Gary Andres observes, parties seem to be enmeshed in endless cycles of "over-promising and under-delivering." "Lawmakers talk like they operate in a parliamentary system . . . and proffer their platforms as if the other party doesn't exist," he writes. But "[their] campaign promises will likely hit a wall of immovable institutional constraints."[3]

With respect to majority party "underdelivering," it is important to note that even the handful of clear partisan victories we identified entailed some serious watering down. The ACA passed the House of Representatives in 2009 only after Democratic leaders gave up on a public option for health care coverage. Republicans passed the Tax Cuts and Jobs Act (TCJA) in 2017 only after they gave up on offsetting the cost of their tax cuts by reducing tax breaks and expenditures and had to settle for a temporary tax cut that would expire after ten years.

Even though these were both major partisan wins by the standards of American politics, both Republicans and Democrats subsequently discovered that their achievements cut little ice with voters. With many in the party's liberal base viewing the ACA's compromises as a sellout to pharmaceutical firms and other corporate interests,[4] Democrats found themselves unable to campaign on the achievement. They began to campaign on the legislation only seven years after enactment when the Trump administration sought to repeal and replace the program.[5] For their part, Republicans were unable to extract electoral mileage from the TCJA in the 2018 midterms and eventually abandoned the issue entirely in their campaign messaging.[6] Rather than claiming credit for the tax cuts it had enacted, the Trump administration shifted gears to promise a new tax cut more focused on the middle class.[7] In short, even some of the best-case examples of majority parties accomplishing their agenda items over minority party opposition reveal parties struggling to manage voter disappointment rather than trumpeting their successes.

In sum, we are a long way from parliamentary-style governance. When it comes to lawmaking in Congress, the choice between the parties today is clearer in terms of symbols than in policy consequences. When voters support the Democratic or Republican party in contemporary congressional elections, they know what issue positions they are voting for (Hetherington 2001) and what the parties will fight for, but they will rarely see those positions translated into new laws. They are almost certain to be disappointed.

Even so, it is not clear that political leaders have much incentive to be honest with voters about the limits parties confront. As a case in point, presidential candidate Joe Biden angered Democratic activists when he said that Republicans and Democrats would need to work together to solve important problems in American politics.[8] "The fact of the matter is," Biden said, "if we can't get a consensus, nothing happens except the abuse of power by the executive. Zero."[9] Our data show that his claim about the need for broad consensus for lawmaking rests on a strong empirical foundation. Honesty, however, does not necessarily make this frustrating reality any more palatable for activists. Politicians likely get more electoral mileage out of telling their base that they will get what they want without compromise, thereby inflating unrealistic hopes even at the cost of later disappointment.

The American political system remains a disruptive force for congressional parties. The "multiplicity of interests" represented by members of each chamber promotes a lack of party discipline despite the best efforts of empowered party leaders. And the policymaking system's various checks, balances, and veto points almost always require bipartisan adjustments and partisan concessions for anything to become law. To date, it seems that no amount of party polarization or party strength has been able to breach these Madisonian barriers.

Reconceptualizing Party Influence

Does this mean parties are weak, inconsequential, or unimportant in Congress? No. Far from it. Even though congressional parties seldom enact programmatic agendas in the manner sought by advocates of responsible parties, we should not conclude that they are unimportant. For the past several decades, and possibly longer, political scientists have debated the nature of party power in Congress in ways that center on outputs and outcomes, especially lawmaking outcomes. As Keith Krehbiel (1998, 228) framed the debate, "The important issue in studies of lawmaking, however, is not whether parties matter generally but rather how majority-party status matters specifically, and whether it ultimately matters in ways that are predictable and *outcome consequential.*" Congressional scholars have absorbed this conceptualization of party power, debating and testing for party influence by assessing whether party status results in empirically identifiable partisan shifts in policy outcomes. Indeed, as our data show, partisan shifts in policy outcomes are not easily identified. But conceiving of party influence in terms of the prevalence of partisan policy outcomes is simply too narrow an understanding of parties' place in congressional politics.

Nothing about the findings of this study should be viewed as making a case that parties do not matter. Just because the parties cannot typically legislate their partisan ambitions through the lawmaking process does not mean they do not play a vital role. To the contrary, the parties, and the parties' legislative leaders, are the central units and actors driving the lawmaking efforts we have analyzed. Scholars need to reconceptualize party influence, how it matters, and how it is important.

One way congressional parties play a vital role is in *conflict-clarifying representation* (Curry and Lee 2019b).[10] Today's parties deliberately bring forward messaging bills and encourage their members to hold the party line in position taking (Evans 2001; Evans and Oleszek 2002). By taking sides among various political interests and publicly displaying their coalitions, congressional parties thus help clarify the lines of political conflict for the public and enable the "ventilation of opinion for the education of the country at large" (Polsby 1975, 281). Contemporary parties are clearly better at this than parties of the past, as demonstrated by the rise in partisan voting on the numerous measures that never become law and the extensive growth and institutionalization of party message operations in both chambers and both parties (Lee 2016, 112–17). It is likely that the public's improved understanding of party differences (Hetherington 2001) owes something to the congressional parties' strengthened capacities for conflict-clarifying representation. This is an important development, and one that likely would have pleased responsible party government theorists of earlier eras.

But party influence is not restricted to representation and messaging. Congressional parties play a vital role in making law, just not in the way typically conceived. Our findings clearly indicate that majority parties usually succeed (when they do succeed) by co-opting support from the minority party rather than rolling the opposition. Today's legislative processes put party leaders at the center of the legislative negotiations that produce these bipartisan outcomes. Leaders negotiate across branches, chambers, and parties with the aim of winning the necessary support to enact laws in a challenging political system. Once those agreements are reached, leaders then work to persuade rank-and-file members to set aside partisan or ideological inclinations and support the compromise. Getting party members, many of whom represent uncompetitive and heavily skewed partisan districts and constituencies (Abramowitz, Alexander, and Gunning 2006), to support partisan messaging bills is not an onerous task. Rather, persuading hard-liners on both sides of the aisle to accept unsatisfactory compromises and vote for negotiated bipartisan agreements is frequently the true test of party leadership and party influence in contemporary lawmaking.

Our findings suggest that often only parties and party leaders can accomplish these vital tasks in the contemporary Congress. Our interviewees, especially those highlighted in chapter 5, described party leaders as the only actors in Congress who "can open up the universe of policy to find the solution, taking into account the whole picture,"[11] and they think that "no one else could have jurisdiction over everything" to cut grand bargains with the other chamber, the other party, or the president.[12] Today, "so many big things have to be negotiated trilaterally—between the House, Senate, and president—and committee chairs just aren't empowered to do those negotiations."[13] When the going gets tough—when negotiations are difficult, complicated, and important to the parties, committees "punt to the leadership to make key decisions."[14] Ultimately, "Everyone wants to be led. They want someone to lead them."[15] In the contemporary Congress, party leaders play this role (Wallner 2013). The fighting, wrangling, negotiating, and legislating in the cases analyzed for this book, which include many of the most consequential acts of policymaking from the past three or more decades, were to a great extent conducted by the parties and by party leaders. In most cases they are the key players leading the negotiations that result in the policy outcomes we observe.

Majority parties do not have to get what they want out of the lawmaking process for parties to matter or to be "outcome consequential." Parties and party leaders affect outcomes by setting the congressional agenda around partisan goals, taking the lead in brokering the necessary intra- and inter-party compromises, and having the authority to marshal backbench support to enact laws. Even when not making laws, parties leave a substantial mark on our politics by orchestrating conflict-clarifying representation and by shaping party messaging and patterns of roll-call voting, and thus public debates, through their symbolic actions. Indeed, contemporary congressional action is "unthinkable save in terms of the parties" (Schattschneider 1942, 1).

Rethinking Centralization in Congress

Political scientists and congressional observers have long viewed centralized and party-led unorthodox legislative processes as tools to enact partisan laws. This view exists in part because decentralized and committee-led "regular order" processes were used by Congress and studied by scholars during a mid-twentieth-century era of far more muted partisanship. Fenno (1962), Polsby (1975), and others illuminated how, at the time, decentralized processes were the primary tools of deliberation and an effective means of legislative conflict resolution, such that they became synonymous with how a legislature *should* work to build bipartisanship and enact laws.

Newer processes—those termed centralized or unorthodox—similarly became synonymous with partisanship and partisan legislating, in part because they emerged as partisan conflict escalated on Capitol Hill and elsewhere in the political system, and because they centralized decision making in party leaders. It became natural to interpret these emerging patterns as party leaders' asserting new procedural powers to enact partisan legislation. But as chapter 5 clearly shows, this is mistaken. Bypassing the traditional committee-led bill development process does not relate to the level of partisan conflict on passage votes at all, and more restrictive floor consideration bears only a modest relation to it. The legislative procedures employed along the path to enactment are poor leading indicators of whether a new law will garner bipartisan support in Congress. Most laws, including landmark laws, still pass with large, bipartisan majorities, even as regular order legislative processes have declined.

Writing during that midcentury period, Fenno (1962, 317) observed that committee-led processes would not work well under highly partisan conditions: "Nothing would be more disruptive to the Committee's work than bitter and extended partisan controversy." That disruption has come to pass. Congress operates today in a state of almost constant partisan controversy. As our interviewees emphasized, this has made regular order impossible on many bills. Decentralizing and opening up the process, trying to navigate bills through freewheeling committee markups and open floor debate, often only exposes bills to attacks, dilatory tactics, and general chicanery on the part of individual members and a minority party looking to score political points (Green 2015; Lee 2016). The transparency involved in regular order processes also can make otherwise reasonable legislators on both sides of the aisle more responsive to the parties' activist bases, who demand ideological purity and attack compromises as signs of weakness or betrayal. Today's politics are different from those of the 1950s or even the 1970s. Achieving bipartisanship and successful lawmaking likewise requires different tactics.

Centralized and party-led processes, of course, come with costs and trade-offs relative to decentralized "regular order" processes, and they have wide-ranging implications for Congress and its members. Among other things, decentralized processes may be superior for utilizing Congress's full institutional capacity. Centralized processes necessitating the leadership's intimate involvement make it difficult for Congress to do as many things at once as it could with a more robust division of labor among the committees. Decentralized processes can also provide more direct power and input to rank-and-file members of both parties. With centralized decision making, backbenchers can more easily be cut out of deliberations and negotiations (Curry 2015), and leaders have much more flexibility in determining who will and will not be part of the discussions (see chapter 5; Curry and Lee 2019b). Members and leaders still seem to prefer decentralized processes when they can be made to work, and "regular order" may have certain normative advantages. But if using traditional processes hamstrings Congress's ability to build legislative coalitions and enact laws in today's political climate, then trade-offs must be made.

Our findings should spur scholars and observers to reconsider how they think about procedures and congressional action. Let's put to rest any infatuation with the "textbook" legislative processes of the mid-twentieth century. Legislative processes have seen near constant evolution across congressional history, and these changes often occur purposefully and in response to pressures from the political environment (see Binder 1996; Cooper and Brady 1981; Polsby 1968; Schickler 2001; Smith 1989). The trend toward centralization across recent decades is no different. Today's unorthodox and party-led processes should be understood as new paths that allow Congress to continue doing what it has long done: building broad bipartisan support to enact laws.

Reconsidering Congressional Capacity and Gridlock

The findings in this book also speak to debates about the role parties play in patterns of congressional gridlock and productivity and in Congress's capacity as a lawmaking institution. Scholars and observers in recent years have been deeply concerned about Congress's institutional capacity and its ability to overcome stalemate and pass legislation (see, e.g., Binder 2015; Drutman 2016; Mann and Ornstein 2012). There is a general sense that rising partisanship has mired national politics in gridlock (Binder 2003, 2014) and that the centralization of power and process in the hands of party leaders has led to dysfunction and an inability to address policy problems (Lewallen, Theriault, and Jones 2016; Bendix 2016b).

Our results are largely consistent with Binder's (2003, 2014) in that today's cohesive political parties collide with the constitutional system of separation of powers and checks and balances in ways that obstruct legislative action and frequently end in stalemate. Our analyses in chapter 3 show that about half of majority party agenda failures were the result of the opposing party's leveraging veto points in the policymaking process to block action. Indeed, party conflict frequently is a barrier to successful congressional action, and the constitutional system regularly frustrates what the parties want to accomplish. But our broader findings show that parties can also be a driver of, and an important force in, legislative productivity.

Again, our interviewees emphasized that in the contemporary Congress, party leaders and party influence were often crucial to successful congressional action. Many of the individuals we spoke with, as quoted above and in chapter 5, were convinced that a number of legislative deals and enactments were possible only owing to leadership intervention and a centralized, party-led approach. But perhaps more important, the cases of legislative success analyzed in this book, such as those in chapter 4, were achieved only at the behest and through the efforts of the congressional parties. These cases, about half of them landmark laws as defined by Mayhew, were efforts initiated by congressional majority parties. The parties played a key role in moving the legislation through the House and the Senate. In most cases party leaders brokered the important deals and compromises necessary for passage. And the party also managed the legislative processes employed to get the job done. Across the cases of legislative success we analyzed, parties are a constant force in congressional action.

Moreover, we do not find evidence that Congress, or congressional majorities, achieves dramatically less today than in the less partisan decades of the 1970s and 1980s. As shown in chapters 2 and 3, although recent congressional majority parties succeeded on their agenda items at slightly lower rates than those of the 1980s, the decline was small. Some recent Congresses, including the 111th (2009–10) and 115th (2017–18), under unified party control achieved levels of success typical for the post-1985 period.

Although no one can deny that the contemporary Congress struggles to address many pressing social, fiscal, and environmental problems, recent Congresses pass more legislation by sheer volume than the less polarized Congresses of the 1970s and roughly the same amount as in the 1980s. As shown in figure 2.4, the number of pages of legislation enacted is higher than in the 1950s, 1960s, and 1970s and has stayed relatively flat since the 1980s, even while the number of laws Congress passes is down markedly (see also Taylor 2013). Congress still achieves a lot, even though it falls short of public expectations and demands.

The public, journalists, close congressional observers, and political scientists are quick to blame the parties for inaction and stalemate. We are continually told that bipartisanship is dead and that Congress is broken and incapable of completing its most basic functions. Analysts tend to focus on party conflict and gridlock in the halls of Congress (Atkinson 2017; Bennett 2012), but they rarely give Congress or the parties much credit when successes do occur. Nevertheless, majority parties navigate a lot of bipartisan legislation through Congress every two years. These achievements frequently go unrecognized and uncelebrated. Indeed, as we show in chapter 6, even members of Congress themselves typically offer negative assessments of congressional action.

Near the end of the 115th Congress, key communications staffers for Republican Party leaders complained on Twitter that bipartisan legislation receives too little acknowledgment. Responding to a reporter who had called the criminal justice reform bill a "rare" bipartisan success for the 115th Congress, Senate Majority Leader McConnell's (R-KY) spokesman tweeted:

"rare?" Maybe you missed:
Opioids
Water infrastructure
Aviation infrastructure
Farm bill
Drug pricing transparency
Veterans bills
Safe medications
Banking reform
Preventing sex trafficking
Longest SCHIP extension in history
School safety legislation
Appropriations
to name a few.[16]

As gauged by the data assembled for this study, McConnell's spokesperson was unquestionably correct. The 115th Congress had indeed passed bipartisan legislation in all these areas, many of which had been flagged as party agenda priorities (see appendix table A.1). Furthermore, party leaders had taken a leading role in the negotiations that allowed these bills to traverse the process to enactment. Just a few days later Mike Ricci, Speaker Paul Ryan's (R-WI) communications director, similarly tweeted, "Like criminal justice reform, most of what Congress passes is bipartisan. Not an old saw, check the record. Bipartisanship isn't rare; it's just rarely noted."[17] Indeed, the contemporary Congress continues to enact bipartisan legislation, just as it did in the 1970s, 1980s, and 1990s. While parties contribute to conflict and stalemate, they also regularly contribute to legislative productivity, bipartisan compromise, and consequential congressional action.

Constancy and Continuity in Congressional Lawmaking

We have shown in this book that party government in the halls of Congress, even in an era of strong and cohesive parties, remains limited. Even when provided with unified control over both the legislative and executive branches, today's ideologically coherent and cohesive parties, with immense procedural power in both the House and the Senate, cannot achieve responsible party government. Majority parties still strain to steer the ship of state in a partisan direction.

Across all the analyses in this study, our most striking finding is simply how little congressional lawmaking has changed. The parties may be more polarized, but laws continue to be enacted with broad bipartisan support. Majority parties may enjoy more institutional power, but they are not able to achieve more of their policy goals. Party cohesion and unity may be more apparent on roll-call votes, but majority parties continue to struggle with internal disunity on major legislative efforts. At its core, congressional lawmaking has changed little over the past half-century.

When scholars and observers think about party influence in Congress, they should keep these facts in mind. The parties today may be able to "clothe themselves in a dogmatic and argumentative garment of high public purpose" (Schattschneider 1942, 129) via constant party messaging and communications efforts. But rhetoric and position taking conceal the truth about parties' capacity to change public policy. Even today, congressional parties remain profoundly constrained in what they can accomplish, particularly over partisan opposition. American national lawmaking remains a process of bipartisan accommodation.

ACKNOWLEDGMENTS

Our collaboration on this project began with a paper we drafted for a conference hosted in 2016 by the Social Science Research Council's (SSRC) Anxieties of Democracy program. For that paper we asked what we thought was a simple question: How has the approach members of Congress take to make a law—or get something done—on Capitol Hill changed over the past several decades? To our surprise, we found that the tremendous changes in congressional partisanship and legislative processes on Capitol Hill have had little effect on actual lawmaking. Enacted laws are just as bipartisan today as they were in much less partisan eras.

As we continued to develop this project, we kept coming up with similar findings of constancy over time. Congressional majority parties are not better at enacting their agendas than they were in less partisan eras. Majority parties fail on their initiatives for much the same reasons as in the past. When majority parties succeed, they do so by cultivating bipartisanship, very rarely by steamrolling the opposing party. Members of Congress even talk about congressional action in similar ways over time. Despite vast changes to congressional procedures and parties—and to our political system more generally—lawmaking remains remarkably the same.

As we have worked on this project since 2016, we have incurred numerous debts. We owe the greatest debt to the current and former members of Congress and congressional staffers who took time out of their busy schedules to be interviewed. These men and women certainly had other important things to do with their time. However, many of the insights in this book would not have been possible without their knowledge and perspective.

We thank the Department of Government and Politics at the University of Maryland and the Department of Political Science at the University of Utah for giving both of us time off to research and write. We benefited from excellent research assistance from graduate students at both institutions: SoRelle Wyckoff and Sara Browning at the University of Maryland and Zachary Stickney and Charles Turner at the University of Utah. We are grateful to Daniel Stid, Jean Bordewich, and the Hewlett Foundation's Madison Initiative for their generous support of this project. The Library of Congress's John W. Kluge Center, under the direction of John Haskell, provided space, support, and a wonderful environment for research and writing.

Although most of what follows has not previously been published, parts of two chapters have appeared in other publications. The groundwork for chapters 2 and 5 was laid in a chapter in *Can America Govern Itself?*, edited by Nolan McCarty and Frances E. Lee (New York: Cambridge University Press, 2019), 181–219. Some material in chapter 2 was published in "Nonparty Government: Bipartisan Lawmaking and Party Power in Congress," *Perspectives on Politics* 17, no. 1 (2019): 47–65. Parts of chapter 5 were published in "What Is Regular Order Worth? Partisan Lawmaking and Congressional Processes," *Journal of Politics* 82, no. 2 (2020): 627–41. We are grateful to anonymous reviewers for helping improve these earlier pieces as well as the subsequent development of the research in this book.

This book benefited from comments and criticisms we received at numerous workshops and presentations, including the aforementioned SSRC conference, the Brookings Institution, New America, and political science departments at Vanderbilt University, Duke University, University of Michigan, University of Georgia, Yale University, University of California, Irvine, University of North Carolina, Brigham Young University, and Princeton University. We also received helpful feedback at Congress and History conferences held at the Library of Congress and Princeton University, and the American Politics Workshop at the University of Maryland. Many people at these presentations and elsewhere provided helpful comments, guidance, and feedback, including Doug Arnold, Sarah Binder, Stuart Butler, Scott de Marchi, Lee Drutman, Peter Hanson, David Karol, Keith Krehbiel, Thomas Mann, Jenny Mansbridge, David Mayhew, Molly Reynolds, Jason Roberts, Ruth Bloch Rubin, Allen Schick, Eric Schickler, Wendy Schiller, Ian Shapiro, Sarah Treul, and James Wallner. The reports from anonymous readers secured by the University of Chicago Press were also enormously helpful.

We are grateful to our editor Chuck Myers for taking an early and sustained interest in the project, supervising a constructive review process, and offering guidance and encouragement that helped us write a better book. We thank Alice Bennett for her skillful and careful copyediting.

Finally, we are grateful to our families, without whose love and support this book would not have been possible. It is to them that this book is dedicated. As always, Frances's husband, Emery, read and commented on everything. Emery and Frances's daughter, Beverly, unfailingly took an interest in the project as it progressed, even when it was, in Beverly's succinct assessment, "boring." Jim thanks his wife, Jill, for her constant love and unbending optimism about this project, and his children, Louise and Henry, for their inquisitiveness, creativity, and humor, which keep him on his toes. All three provided welcome, and much needed, distractions from working on this book.

Majority Party Agenda Priorities

This appendix includes the full list of majority party agenda priorities analyzed in this book.

Table A.1 gives a short description of the priority, the outcome on each (most, some, none; see chapter 2) and a short description, plus information about the final votes taken in the House and Senate (where applicable) and whether opposition party leaders in each chamber voted for (yes) or against (no) passage on successful cases.

Table A.2 gives additional information about each of the cases of failure (those on which the majority party achieved none of what it set out to achieve). It includes information about the category(s) of failure for each case, a short description, and the summary failure coding (see chapter 3).

Table A.3 gives additional information about each case of success (those on which the majority party achieved some or most of what it set out to achieve). It includes information about the pathway(s) of success each case was coded to and a short description.

Table A.1 Majority party agenda priorities, 1985–2018

Priority	Outcome (1=Most of what they want; 2=Some of what they want; 3=None of what they want)	Final House vote	Final Senate vote	House opposition leadership support	Senate opposition leadership support
99th Congress 1985–96 (Republicans)					
Reduce the federal budget/cut spending	2—A compromise budget resolution left Republicans having to embrace defense cuts and a cap on Social Security. Democrats were unsuccessful in their attempts to restore Medicare and Medicaid funding and impose a minimum corporate tax (S. Con. Res. 32).	309–119: D 182–67; R 127–52	67–32: D 30–17; R 37–15	O'Neill—n/a Wright—Yes Foley—Yes	Byrd—Yes Cranston—No
Reform the Senate committee system (Quayle Committee recommendations)	3—Despite multiple proposals, no reforms of the committee system were passed.				
99th Congress 1985–86 (Democrats)					
Tax reform/Reduce the budget deficit	2—The Tax Reform Act of 1986 (H.R. 3838) reflected compromises made on both sides of the aisle. And a compromise budget resolution left Republicans having to embrace defense cuts and a cap on Social Security. Democrats were unsuccessful in their attempts to restore Medicare and Medicaid funding and impose a minimum corporate tax (S. Con. Res. 32).	292–136: D 176–74; R 116–62	74–23: D 33–12; R 41–11	Michel—Yes Lott—Yes	Dole—Yes Simpson—No
Revise and extend housing programs for the poor	3—Pervasive differences between House and Senate conferees stymied enactment of a housing authorization bill.				

Issue	Description	House vote	Senate vote	Michel / Lott	Dole / Simpson
Reauthorize the farm bill	2—A comprehensive compromise over subsidies and price supports allowed both sides to claim victory (H.R. 2100).	325–96: D 194–49; R 131–47	55–38: D 22–23; R 33–15	Michel—No Lott—Yes	Dole—Yes Simpson—Yes
Reduce unemployment through job training	1—The Job Training Partnership Act was amended to help youths and unskilled adults find work and to aid displaced workers (S. 2069).	Voice	Voice	No roll call	No roll call
Pursue arms control with the Soviets	2—A compromise measure on arms control was claimed as a victory by both Reagan's conservative supporters and his liberal critics (S. 1160).	Voice	94–5: D 44–3; R 50–2	No roll call	Dole—Yes Simpson—Yes
Increase child nutrition programs	2—Scaled-back provisions increasing child nutrition programs were attached to the 1987 defense authorization bill and passed (H.R. 7).	367–59: D 243–1; R 124–58	Voice	Michel—Yes Lott—No	No roll call
Reauthorize the Water Resources Development Act	1—Senate leaders and the White House eventually struck a compromise to reauthorize the Water Resources Development Act (H.R. 6).	329–11: D 186–3; R 143–8	84–2: D 41–1; R 43–1	Michel—No Lott—Yes	Dole—Yes Simpson—Yes
Renew Water Quality Programs	3—Legislation authorizing billions of dollars to clean up lakes and streams was pocket-vetoed by the president (S. 1128).	UC	Voice	No roll call	No roll call
Pass armor-piercing bullet ban	1—Congress passed a ban on so-called cop-killer bullets with minimal party contention (H.R. 3132).		Voice	No roll call	No roll call
Reauthorize programs under the Coastal Zone Management Act	2—Congress reauthorized the Coastal Zone Management Act after agreeing to an amendment freezing the bill's FY 1986 authorization at the FY 1985 appropriation level (H.R. 3128).	331–76: D 234–2; R 97–74	Voice	Michel—No Lott—No	No roll call

(continued)

Table A.1 (*continued*)

Priority	Outcome (1=Most of what they want; 2=Some of what they want; 3=None of what they want)	Final House vote	Final Senate vote	House opposition leadership support	Senate opposition leadership support
100th Congress 1987–88 (Democrats)					
Pass a trade bill to reduce the trade deficit	3—President Reagan struck a final blow after three years of congressional efforts by vetoing the Omnibus Trade and Competitiveness Act.				
Reduce the budget deficit with budget reforms	2—Legislation set spending and revenue limits for 1988 and 1989, but congressional Democrats were upset that it did not raise taxes or cut defense spending as much as they would have liked (H. Con. Res. 93).	215–201: D 212–34; R 3–167	53–46: D 50–3; R 3–43	Michel—No Lott—No	Dole—No Simpson—No
Reauthorize the Elementary and Secondary Education Act	1—Both chambers had passed an omnibus education bill to extend until 1993 nearly every program the federal government supported for elementary, secondary, and adult education (H.R. 5).	397–1: D 229–0; R 168–1	Voice	Michel—Yes Lott—Yes	No roll call
Reauthorize clean water programs	1—President Reagan vetoed the bill but both chambers overrode the veto (H.R. 1).	401–26: D 254–0; R 147–26	86–14: D 54–1; R 32–13	Michel—Yes Lott—Yes	Dole—No Simpson—Yes
Reauthorize the Clean Air Act	3—The efforts stalled over disagreements on whether to tighten controls on ozone and acid rain precursors.				
Reorganize Farm Credit System and provide aid to farmers	1—H.R. 3030 passed with a clear majority in both chambers.	365–18: D 214–7; R 151–11	85–2: D 44–1; R 41–1	Michel—Yes Lott—Yes	Dole—No Simpson—Yes
Campaign finance reform for Senate elections	3—Democrats failed to break through Republican opposition to state-by-state spending limits for Senate campaigns.				

		House vote		Senate vote	
Ratify two US-Soviet treaties limiting nuclear weapons (INF treaty and ABM treaty)	2—The Senate ratified the INF treaty with broad bipartisan support, but no movements were made on an ABM treaty.	n/a	n/a	93–5: D 51–1; R 42–4	Dole—Yes Simpson—Yes
Reauthorize surface transportation programs	1—Overriding Reagan's veto, Democrats seemed to get most of what they wanted, with the overall price tag matching that of a bill passing the House in the previous Congress (H.R. 2).	407–17: D 249–1; R 158–16	Michel—Yes Lott—Yes	79–17: D 51–1; R 28–16	Dole—No Simpson—No
Enact legislation to address and fix the country's savings and loan crisis	2—Congress passed $10.8 billion bailout for the S&L industry in 1987. By 1988 the bailout appeared insufficient, but Congress was unable to take any further action.	382–12: D 223–8; R 159–4	Michel—Yes Lott—Yes	96–2: D 52–0; R 44–2	Dole—Yes Simpson—Yes
Establish a national policy to deal with the AIDS crisis	2—Congress cleared an omnibus health package that contained the first significant federal policies for dealing with the deadly AIDS epidemic. Some provisions preferred by congressional Democrats (including confidentiality and antidiscrimination language) were dropped to ease passage and obtain Reagan's support (S. 2889).	Voice		Voice	
Reauthorize and reform housing assistance programs	2—Congressional Democrats settled for the less ambitious Senate version of bill, which carried a smaller price tag and focused on renovating existing public housing structures rather than constructing new ones (S. 825).	Voice	No roll call	71–27: D 51–2; R 20–25	Dole—No Simpson—No
Establish "effective schools" and "even start" programs	1—Passed as part of a larger omnibus education package (H.R. 5). The provisions mirror those in H.R. 6 establishing "effective schools" and "even start" programs.	397–1: D 229–0; R 168–1	Michel—Yes Lott—Yes	Voice	No roll call

(continued)

Table A.1 (*continued*)

Priority	Outcome (1=Most of what they want; 2=Some of what they want; 3=None of what they want)	Final House vote	Final Senate vote	House opposition leadership support	Senate opposition leadership support
Pass the Sunset Act of 1987	3—No legislation requiring ten-year sunsets on all new authorizations was enacted.				No roll call
Address national air transportation problems (e.g., delays, safety, and concerns over mergers) by reauthorizing and revising airline policies	2—Congress successfully reauthorized federal airline policies, increasing FAA funding and addressing user fee concerns (H.R. 2310). To ease passage, consumer protection measures favored by Democrats were dropped. A separate bill on airline consumer protections (H.R. 3051) failed to pass.	410–1: D 238–1; R 172–0	Voice	Michel—Yes Lott—No vote	
Take action on pay equity, reducing discrimination and inequities in both pay and federal benefits (including Social Security)	2—A massive welfare overhaul represented a compromise for both Democrats and Republicans. The final bill created a Commission on Equitable Pay Practices, but both sides had to accept provisions they did not like to get the reform package enacted (H.R. 1720).	347–53: D 205–34; R 142–19	96–1: D 52–0; R 44–1	Michel—No Lott—No	Dole—Yes Simpson—Yes
Creation of state-run child care assistance programs	3—A $2.5 billion child care initiative died in the waning days of the Congress, the victim of bipartisan discord in the Senate and concern in the House over church-state questions (S. 2488/H.R. 3660).				

101st Congress 1989–90 (Democrats)

Pass a new clean air bill	2—The bill emerged as a compromise between Democratic senators and the White House. The final provisions were less sweeping than many Democrats had hoped in order to get the Bush administration on board (S. 1630).	401–25: D 248–5; R 153–20	89–10: D 50–5; R 39–5	Michel—Yes Gingrich—Yes	Dole—Yes Simpson—Yes
Renew low-income housing assistance and homelessness programs	2—House Democrats had to accept provisions in a Senate-passed bill that represented a compromise between the Senate and White House (H.R. 3789).	Voice	Voice	No roll call	No roll call
Raise the minimum wage	2—After Bush vetoed H.R. 2, which more closely hewed to Democrat's wishes, H.R. 2710 represented a compromise that could garner bipartisan support and Bush's signature.	382–37: D 247–2; R 135–35	89–8: D 53–0; R 36–8	Michel—Yes Gingrich—Yes	Dole—Yes Simpson—Yes
Pass affordable child care legislation	2—After a long battle, compromise child care policies, including both grants, tax credits, and some federal standards, were included in an omnibus budget reconciliation package (H.R. 5835).	228–200: D 181–74; R 47–126	54–45: D 35–20; R 19–25	Michel—Yes Gingrich—No	Dole—Yes Simpson—Yes
Pass congressional ethics reform, including honorarium ban	2—Congress enacted an ethics reform package, but one that fell short of the lofty goals of a House task force (H.R. 3660).	Voice	Voice	No roll call	No roll call
Campaign finance reform	3—The House and Senate passed different campaign finance reform packages but could not come to an agreement				
Budget deficit reduction	2—Bipartisanship won out over House Democrats' "soak the rich" bill. The final deficit reduction package, passed in late 1990, reflects a compromise that was acceptable to both parties and the Bush administration (H.R. 5835).	228–200: D 181–74; R 47–126	54–45: D 35–20; R 19–25	Michel—Yes Gingrich—No	Dole—Yes Simpson—Yes

(continued)

Table A.1 (*continued*)

Priority	Outcome (1=Most of what they want; 2=Some of what they want; 3=None of what they want)	Final House vote	Final Senate vote	House opposition leadership support	Senate opposition leadership support
Trade legislation to reduce the deficit	3—Congress was unable to pass legislation to reduce the trade deficit				
Combat drugs on streets and in schools/fully fund existing antidrug programs	2—Congress and the Bush administration agreed to increase funding for antidrug programs by more than 50%, and passed bills authorizing new antidrug programs. However, other efforts stalled in bicameral negotiations, giving Democrats a partial win on antidrug policies.	Voice	Voice	No roll calls	No roll calls
Pass legislation improving enterprise zones	3—No action was taken to expand or improve urban enterprise zones				
Pass legislation requiring Congress to be notified of any covert military action within forty-eight hours of its being planned	2—Democrats pushed for legislation requiring the president to inform Congress about any CIA covert operations within forty-eight hours of their being planned, but settled for an informal deal in which Bush promised to keep Congress apprised.				
Establish a program of voluntary national service	2—The final bill was a compromise worked out between Kennedy and Hatch. It slashed the total authorization from more than $300 million in the version approved by the committee to $125 million and included Bush's "Points of Light" foundation in an effort to make the package more palatable to the White House (S. 1430).	235–186: D 213–41; R 22–145	75–21: D 52–1; R 23–20	Michel—No Gingrich—No	Dole—Yes Simpson—Yes

(continued)

Pass a uniform poll closing law	3—The House and Senate could not reconcile different uniform poll closing proposals.				No roll calls
Improve the quality of US health care	2—Democrats secured modest increases to Medicaid but fell short of lofty goals to expand the program dramatically (H.R. 3299).	272–128: D 186–47; R 86–81	Voice	Michel—Yes Gingrich—Yes	
Increase government investment in research and development	3—Congress was unable to pass the American Technology Preeminence Act or take any other major action expanding US R&D.				
Increase investment in early childhood education	1—Congress passed legislation increasing authorization levels for Head Start over several years (H.R. 4151).	Voice	Voice		
Improve education standards and teacher quality	3—The Educational Equity and Excellence Act (H.R. 5932) passed the House but did not move forward in the Senate.	Voice			
Restrict foreign ownership/ acquisitions	2—Unable to move legislation to restrict foreign ownership, Congress passed legislation improving the Commerce Department's data collection of foreign investments in the US (S. 2516).	Voice	Voice		
Expand vocational and applied tech educational programs	1—Congress passed the Carl D. Perkins Vocational Education Act, which reauthorized and expanded federal funds for vocational education programs (H.R. 7).	Voice	Voice	No roll calls	No roll calls
102nd Congress 1991–92 (Democrats)					
Provide a cost-of-living increase to disabled veterans	1—Congress quickly passed a COLA increase for disabled veterans (H.R. 3).	421–0: D 254–0; R 164–0	99–0: D 55–0; R 44–0	Michel—Yes Gingrich—Yes	Dole—Yes Simpson—Yes

Table A.1 (*continued*)

Priority	Outcome (1=Most of what they want; 2=Some of what they want; 3=None of what they want)	Final House vote	Final Senate vote	House opposition leadership support	Senate opposition leadership support
Improve and track progress on nationwide education standards	3—Several disagreements between House and Senate Democrats derailed an effort to pass a national education standards bill.				
Campaign finance reform	3—President Bush vetoed the Democrats' campaign finance bill, which would have provided public funding for campaigns and incentives for candidates to limit their spending.				
Expand health care coverage to all Americans	3—Democrats advanced several ambitious health care plans that quickly drew opposition from Republicans and the Bush White House. At the same time, some liberal Democrats criticized the plans for not going far enough.				
Pass legislation guaranteeing family and medical leave	3—The House could not override President Bush's veto of the Family Leave Act of 1991.				
Reform the bank insurance deposit system	2—After an aggressive FDIC overhaul failed on the House floor (H.R. 6), the Senate took the lead in negotiating a less ambitious compromise bill acceptable to the White House (S. 543).	Voice	68–15: D 36–13; R 32–2	No roll call	Dole—Yes Simpson—Yes
Expand child welfare programs for low-income children	3—Congressional Democrats made several attempts to expand federal child welfare programs, each of which failed. President Bush vetoed an omnibus urban tax aid measure (H.R. 11) that had several related proposals attached to it.				

Restore antidiscrimination employment laws	1—Vetoing a similar measure in 1990, the Bush White House and most Republicans were willing to make a deal after the Anita Hill hearings. Democrats made some concessions, including allowing for caps on litigation damages. However, this was seen as a major win (S. 1745).	381–38: D 251–5; R 127–33	93–5: D 55–0; R 38–5	Michel—Yes Gingrich—Yes	Dole—Yes Simpson—Yes
Reauthorize surface transportation programs	2—The final bill emerged from behind-the-scenes compromises between congressional Democrats and the White House. Both sides claimed victory, but both sides gave up proposals they had hoped to include in the bill (H.R. 2950).	372–47: D 241–14; R 129–33	79–8: D 47–4; R 32–4	Michel—Yes Gingrich—Yes	Dole—Yes Simpson—Yes
Economic stimulus via tax incentives for enterprise zones	3—Efforts to expand tax incentives in enterprise zones failed to advance. Congressional Democrats attached some related proposals to an omnibus urban aid tax measure (H.R. 11) that was pocket vetoed by President Bush.				
Reform the unemployment compensation system	2—With unemployment rates rising, Democrats were able to get President Bush to relent and agree to a broad unemployment compensation amendments bill (H.R. 5260). A win for Democrats, it still required compromises.	396–23: D 253–2; R 142–21	93–3: D 56–0; R 37–3	Michel—Yes Gingrich—Yes	Dole—Yes Simpson—Yes
Expand federal job training programs	1—A bill amending the Job Training Partnership Act was hailed as a major accomplishment, winning broad support on both sides of the aisle (H.R. 3303).	Voice	Voice	No roll call	No roll call

(continued)

Priority	Outcome (1=Most of what they want; 2=Some of what they want; 3=None of what they want)	Final House vote	Final Senate vote	House opposition leadership support	Senate opposition leadership support
Make it easier for people to afford long-term care for elderly and disabled relatives	3—Efforts providing supplemental coverage for long-term care through Medicare stalled in the Senate.				
Pass energy independence legislation, including energy conservation policies	2—After two years of negotiations, Congress passed a national energy strategy bill seen as a compromise among Democrats and Republicans (H.R. 776).	363-60: D 239–20; R 123–40	Voice	Michel—Yes Gingrich—No	No roll call
Tax deadline extension for troops in Iraq	1—A bill granting the extension was quickly passed and signed by the president (H.R. 4).	415–0: D 250–0; R 164–0	99–0: D 55–0; R 44–0	Michel—Yes Gingrich—Yes	Dole—Yes Simpson—Yes
Prohibit the permanent replacement of labor strikers	3—Legislation banning employers from permanently replacing strikers passed the House but never received a vote in the Senate (H.R. 5).				
Pass the Brady Handgun Violence Prevention Act	3—The Brady bill was included as part of an omnibus crime bill (H.R. 3371) that never made it to the president's desk.				
Eliminate some antitrust exemptions for insurance companies	3—Democrats' insurance antitrust measures (H.R. 9 and S. 430) never made progress in the face of stiff Republican opposition.				
103rd Congress 1993–94 (Democrats)					
Pass legislation guaranteeing family and medical leave	1—With a Democratic president, the Family and Medical Leave Act was passed and signed into law.	247–152: D 210–29; R 36–123	71–27: D 55–2; R 16–25	Michel—No Gingrich—No	Dole—No Simpson—No

Goal	Description	House vote	Senate vote	House leaders	Senate leaders
Expand national voter registration/Enact Motor Voter	1—(H.R. 2) Democrats passed a bill similar to the Motor Voter law vetoed by President Bush in the previous Congress.	259–164: D 238–14; R 20–150	62–36: D 56–0; R 6–36	Michel—No Gingrich—No	Dole—No Simpson—No
NIH reauthorization	1—With a Democratic president, Congress easily passed an NIH reauthorization no longer bogged down over disagreements with the Bush and Reagan administrations over the use of aborted fetal tissue in research.	290–130: D 230–16; R 59–114	Voice	Michel—No Gingrich—No	No roll call
Pass comprehensive health care reform	3—Clinton's controversial health care reform effort was never considered on the floor of either chamber.				
Reduce the federal deficit	2—(H.R. 2264) The Clinton budget just got across the finish line. It gave Democrats a win on deficit reduction, but at the cost of displeasing liberals over the balance of tax increases and spending cuts.	218–216: D 217–41; R 0–175	51–50: D 50–6; R 0–44	Michel—No Gingrich—No	Dole—No Simpson—No
Revise and reauthorize the Elementary and Secondary Education Act	2—A five-year reauthorization gained enough support for passage only after Democrats agreed to important compromises, including limiting mandatory standards and requirements on states.	262–132: D 230–4; R 31–128	77–20: D 54–0; R 23–20	Michel—No Gingrich—No	Dole—No Simpson—No
Campaign finance reform	3—Legislation to limit spending on congressional campaigns and provide candidates with partial public funding was killed in the 103rd Congress.				
Increase federal infrastructure investment	3—Senate Republicans successfully blocked two Democratic attempts to pass infrastructure investment legislation.				

(continued)

209

Table A.1 (*continued*)

Priority	Outcome (1=Most of what they want; 2=Some of what they want; 3=None of what they want)	Final House vote	Final Senate vote	House opposition leadership support	Senate opposition leadership support
Enact legislation combating crime, drugs, and violence	1—Congress passed a major crime bill including most of what Democrats wanted to achieve (H.R. 3355).	235–195: D 188–64; R 46–131	61–38: D 54–2; R 7–36	Michel—No Gingrich—No	Dole—No Simpson—No
Prohibit the permanent replacement of labor strikers	3—A bill banning employers from permanently replacing striking workers was killed by objections on both sides of the aisle.				
Reform housing assistance programs	3—The House passed a bill reforming federal housing programs, but the Senate's bill did not advance.				
Reauthorize child nutrition and school lunch programs	1—Congress reauthorized these programs with little controversy.	Voice	Voice		
Elimination of some antitrust exemptions for insurance companies	3—Little action was taken to advance legislation lifting the insurance industry's antitrust exemptions.				
Pass congressional rules reforms and reorganization	3—A Joint Committee on the Organization of Congress made a series of recommendations in 1993, but no further action was taken.				
Pass the National Competitiveness Act (improve US competitiveness in tech innovation)	3—Both chambers advanced versions of the National Competitiveness Act along party lines, but differences could not be resolved in conference.				
104th Congress 1995–96 (Republicans)					
Establish a line-item veto	1—Congress passed S. 4, which granted the president a line-item veto starting in the 105th Congress.	232–177: D 11–173; R 221–3	69–31: D 19–28; R 50–3	Gephardt—No Bonior—No	Daschle—Yes Ford—No

Pass congressional rules reforms and reorganization	2—The House passed various procedural and organizational reforms (H.R. 6), but broader bicameral reforms, including lobbying reform, were not passed.	416–12: D 191–12; R 224–0	n/a		
Pass tough on crime legislation	2—Congressional Republicans were able to pass half of the party's tough on crime agenda, addressing victim restitution, criminal aliens, and tough death penalty appeals rules. Other proposals (prison construction and block grants) were scrapped, and still others were watered down in order to pass.	193–133: D 105–86; R 188–46	91–8: D 40–7; R 51–1	Gephardt—Yes Bonior—No	Daschle—Yes Ford—Yes
Enact tax cuts	3—Republicans aimed for over $200 billion in tax cuts, but in the end were able to secure only small cuts tied to other policies, including a $20 billion business tax cut tied to a ninety-cent minimum wage increase (H.R. 3448).				
Regulatory overhaul	3—An omnibus regulatory overhaul bill (H.R. 9) passed the House but was stopped in the Senate. By the end of the 104th Congress, Republicans were committed to taking an incremental approach in the next Congress.				
Unfunded mandates reform	1—Congress passed a bipartisan bill (S. 1) to deter the federal government from imposing requirements on state, local, and tribal governments without providing funding.	394–28: D 168–28; R 225–0	91–9: D 38–9; R 53–0	Gephardt—Yes Bonior—No	Daschle—Yes Ford—Yes
Pass a balanced budget amendment	3—Senate Democrats successfully blocked efforts to pass a balanced budget amendment (H.J. Res. 1) in 1995 and 1996.				

(continued)

Table A.1 (*continued*)

Priority	Outcome (1=Most of what they want; 2=Some of what they want; 3=None of what they want)	Final House vote	Final Senate vote	House opposition leadership support	Senate opposition leadership support
Welfare reform	2—To try to get Clinton to sign on, Republican leaders narrowed the scope of their bill (H.R. 3734), dropping all proposed changes to Medicaid. This step got some Democrats on board and pressured Clinton into signing it.	328–101: D 98–98; R 230–2	78–21: D 25–21; R 53–0	Gephardt—No Bonior—No	Daschle—No Ford—Yes
Expand NATO/Reduce US payments to UN and involvement in UN peacekeeping	2—House Republicans passed a bill to promote the expansion of NATO to include several Soviet bloc countries (H.R. 3564), but efforts to substantially reduce US payments for and involvement in UN peacekeeping efforts failed.	370–37: D 167–13; R 202–24	Voice	Gephardt—Yes Bonior—Yes	No roll call
Raise the Social Security senior citizens earnings limits	1—Congress passed an increase in the Social Security earnings limit (H.R. 3136). The proposal had bipartisan support and was attached to a debt limit increase to help the debt limit increase pass.	328–91: D 127–60; R 201–30	UC	Gephardt—Yes Bonior—Yes	No roll call
Securities litigation reform	1—Congress overrode President Clinton's veto of a popular securities litigation reform package.	320–102: D 90–101; R 230–0	65–30: D 19–26; R 46–4	Gephardt—No Bonior—No	Daschle—No Ford—Yes
Establish congressional term limits	3—A constitutional amendment (H.J. Res. 73) to impose term limits on members of Congress failed in both chambers.				

Enact broad spending cuts	2—Republicans were unable to advance their ambitious plans for drastic cuts to domestic spending. Republicans were able to secure some cuts for FY 1996 (H.R. 3019), but nowhere near the ambitious plans during the 1994 campaign.	399–25: D 184–5; R 214–20	88–11: D 47–0; R 41–11	Gephardt—Yes Bonior—Yes	Daschle—Yes Ford—Yes
Expand and speed up completion of missile defense system	2—Republicans pushed to get larger budgets and a firmer deployment timetable for antimissile defenses, but were able to secure only some increases in spending (in H.R. 3610). Clinton's deployment plan remained untouched.	370–37: D 167–13; R 202–24	Voice	Gephardt—Yes Bonior—Yes	No roll call
Protect private property owners	3—The House passed a bill (H.R. 925) allowing landowners to demand compensation for some federal regulatory actions diminishing the value of their property, but it did not advance in the Senate.				

105th Congress 1997–98 (Republicans)

Enact tax cuts	2—Taxpayer Relief Act (H.R. 2014) split the difference between what Republicans hoped to cut and what the Clinton administration said it would accept.	389–43: D 164–41; R 225–1	92–8: D 37–8; R 55–0	Gephardt—No Bonior—Yes	Daschle—Yes Ford—Yes
Deficit reduction/balanced budget	2—The final budget deal was something on which both parties could claim victory, fulfilling Republican promises to balance the budget while including key Democratic priorities on child tax credits and child health care.	346–85: D 153–52; R 193–32	85–15: D 42–3; R 43–12	Gephardt—No Bonior—Yes	Daschle—Yes Bonior—No

(continued)

Table A.1 (*continued*)

Priority	Outcome (1=Most of what they want; 2=Some of what they want; 3=None of what they want)	Final House vote	Final Senate vote	House opposition leadership support	Senate opposition leadership support
Enact education reform including school aid and school choice	2—Republicans passed several bipartisan initiatives including boosting charter schools and supporting Clinton's "America Reads" program. More partisan initiatives, on education savings accounts and school choice, failed to pass.	369–50: D 160–40; R 208–10	85–15: D 42–3; R 43–12	Gephardt—Yes Bonior—No	Daschle—Yes Ford—Yes
Working Families Flexibility/comp time and flex time for working families	2—Republicans achieved some of their goals including a $500-per-child tax credit (in H.R. 2014), but the Working Families Flexibility Act failed to pass Congress (H.R. 1 and S. 4).	389–43: D 164–41; R 225–1	92–8: D 37–8; R 55–0	Gephardt—No Bonior—Yes	Daschle—Yes Ford—Yes
Surface transportation reauthorization	2—Republican leaders had to compromise with their own committee chair (Rep. Shuster R-PA) in order to put together a reauthorization bill (TEA-21) that could gain passage.	297–86: D 153–30; R 143–56	88–5: D 39–1; R 49–4	Gephardt—Yes Bonior—Yes	Daschle—Yes Ford—No vote
Expand war on drugs/tougher penalties for drug lords	3—Congressional Republicans failed in their efforts to impose penalties on Mexico related to the drug trade.				
Enact tough-on-crime legislation	3—The House passed tough-on-crime legislation (H.R. 3), but it did not advance in the Senate.				
Partial-birth abortion ban	3—President Clinton vetoed a bill that would have established a partial-birth abortion ban (H.R. 1122)				

Goal	Status	House vote	Senate vote	House leaders	Senate leaders
Expand and speed up completion of a national missile defense system	2—Congressional Republicans secured funding increases for national missile defense, but the Clinton administration adopted a missile defense plan that was less ambitious than Republicans hoped.	373–50: D 166–38; R 207–11	96–2: D 43–2; R 53–0	Gephardt—Yes Bonior—No	Daschle—Yes Ford—Yes
Pass the Paycheck Protection Act	3—Republican leaders could not muster the votes to pass the Paycheck Protection Act, but they were able to block other campaign finance reform proposals they opposed.				
Balanced budget amendment	3—Republicans were unable to pass a balanced budget amendment.				
Increased NAFTA and WTO oversight	3—Congress did not take any action to increase oversight of NAFTA or the WTO.				
Military modernization	3—Unable to close bases to free up funds, no action was taken to dramatically modernize the military.				
TEAM Act/weakening labor unions	3—Vetoed in the previous Congress, Republicans did not take steps to pass the TEAM Act again.				
Individuals with Disabilities Education Act reauthorization	1—IDEA was reauthorized with a bipartisan effort (H.R. 5). Republican leaders pushed for a broadly bipartisan and universally appealing bill after failure to reauthorize IDEA in the 104th Congress.	420–3: D 198–0; R 221–3	98–1: D 54–1; R 44–0	Gephardt—Yes Bonior—Yes	Daschle—Yes Ford—Yes
Regulatory overhaul (particularly for small businesses)	3—Conservative regulatory overhaul bills could not garner the support for passage, and conservative opposition killed a bipartisan compromise (S. 981).				

(continued)

Table A.1 (*continued*)

Priority	Outcome (1=Most of what they want; 2=Some of what they want; 3=None of what they want)	Final House vote	Final Senate vote	House opposition leadership support	Senate opposition leadership support
Streamline child adoption processes	1—Congress passed a bipartisan bill (H.R. 867) to streamline the adoption of children in foster care.	406–7: D 193–2; R 212–5	UC	Gephardt—No vote Bonior—Yes	Daschle—Yes Ford—Yes
Public housing reform	2—A bipartisan Senate bill replacing public housing programs with block grants won out over a House Republican bill that would have repealed the Housing Act of 1937.	409–14: D 195–5; R 213–9	96–1: D 43–0; R 53–1	Gephardt—Yes Bonior—Yes	Daschle—Yes Ford—Yes
Higher education reauthorization and reform	1—Republicans set out to reauthorize federal higher education policies with a bipartisan effort and were successful (H.R. 6).	Voice	96–0: D 43–0; R 53–0	No roll call	Daschle—Yes Ford—Yes
Citizenship Reform Act (reform birthright citizenship)	3—Congress did not pass the Citizenship Reform Act.				
Pass the Border Smog Reduction Act, prohibiting foreign vehicles from repeatedly crossing the border	1—The Border Smog Reduction Act of 1998 (H.R. 8) became law with bipartisan support.	Voice	Voice	No roll call	No roll call
Financial services reform and reauthorization	3—The House passed a very partisan bill (H.R. 10), but no action was taken in the Senate.				
Product liability reform	3—Republicans and the White House engaged in negotiations, but no action was taken.				
Superfund cleanup acceleration	3—Congress did not complete work on an overhaul of the superfund hazardous waste cleanup program.				

106th Congress 1999–2000 (Republicans)

Use the budget surplus for tax cuts and debt reduction	3—Congressional Republicans were unable to get several bills committing parts of the budget surplus to debt reduction through the Senate.			
Expand and speed up completion of missile defense system	3—Congress passed a bill declaring it a US policy to deploy a national missile defense system, but the GOP was never able to get the Clinton administration to accept proposals to speed up or beef up its plans for missile defense.			
ESEA overhaul, including education savings accounts	3—Congress was unable to pass an ESEA reauthorization.			
Social Security reform and solvency	3—Republican leaders and the Clinton administration negotiated plans for a broad Social Security overhaul but came up short.			
Complete Clinton impeachment proceedings	2—Impeachment proceedings were completed, but Republicans did not get the outcome they wanted, since Clinton was acquitted.	n/a	50–50: D 0-45; R 50-5	n/a	Daschle—No Ford—No
Managed care reform (health care)	3—The House and Senate both advanced managed care reform packages but could not agree in conference on reconciling the bills.			
Medicare reform	3—No action was taken on comprehensive Medicare reform.			
Bankruptcy reform	3—Congress passed a major bankruptcy overhaul bill, drawing some bipartisan support, but it was pocket vetoed by Clinton.			

(continued)

217

Table A.1 (*continued*)

Priority	Outcome (1=Most of what they want; 2=Some of what they want; 3=None of what they want)	Final House vote	Final Senate vote	House opposition leadership support	Senate opposition leadership support
Supporting faith-based charities	2—Some action was taken to support "charitable choice." An antipoverty bill included a provision allowing federal funding for faith-based anti–substance abuse programs (H.R. 4577).	292–60: D 157–9; R 133–51	Voice	Gephardt—Yes Bonior—No vote	No roll call
Enact partial-birth abortion ban	3—The House and Senate passed partial-birth abortion bans, but no final action was taken following a SCOTUS ruling that a similar law in Nebraska was unconstitutional.				
Repeal Social Security earnings test	1—Congress passed a bill eliminating the Social Security earnings test, removing the limit on how much outside income retirees age sixty-five through sixty-nine may earn and still collect full Social Security benefits (H.R. 5).	419–0: D 207–0; R 210–0	100–0: D 45–0; R 55–0	Gephardt—Yes Bonior—Yes	Daschle—Yes Reid—Yes
Financial services reforms and reauthorization	2—Congress passed the Gramm-Leach-Bliley Act (S. 900). The final bill was seen as a bipartisan compromise.	362–57: D 155–51; R 207–5	90–8: D 38–7; R 52–1	Gephardt—Yes Bonior—Yes	Daschle—Yes Reid—Yes
Federal elections reform	3—No action was taken to reform federal elections administration.				
Increase spending to fight the drug trade	1—Republicans were able to include $1.3 billion to fight the drug trade in South America in a supplemental spending bill (H.R. 4425).	306–110: D 135–64; R 171–44	Voice	Gephardt—Yes Bonior—Yes	No roll call

107th Congress 2001–2 (Republicans)

		House vote	Senate vote		
Revise and reauthorize the Elementary and Secondary Education Act	2—No Child Left Behind reflected a bipartisan compromise that kept federal education spending higher than Republicans has hoped but tied that funding to student achievement on state-developed testing, as was a priority for Republicans and the Bush administration (H.R. 1).	381–41: D 198–6; R 183–33	87–10: D 43–6; R 44–3	Gephardt—Yes Bonior—Yes	Daschle—Yes Reid—Yes
Enact broad tax cuts	2—The final deal included $1.35 billion in tax cuts, but they were tilted more toward the lower end of the income spectrum than Republicans initially wanted (H.R. 1836). Democrats were unhappy with the size and scope of the cuts but secured phaseouts and a few of their priorities.	240–154: D 28–153; R 211–0	58–33: D 12–31; R 46–2	Gephardt—Yes Bonior—No	Daschle—No Reid—No
Health care reform via market solutions and Medicare prescription drug coverage	3—Democrats and Republicans were ultimately unable to come to an agreement on joint priorities—managed care and Medicare prescription drug coverage.				
Social Security reform	3—A bipartisan commission on Social Security reported recommendations for incorporating personal retirement accounts, but Congress did not act.				
Expand and speed up completion of missile defense system	1—After 9/11 Democrats dropped their opposition, and the full amount Bush sought to develop a missile defense system was authorized (S. 1438).	382–40: D 171–34; R 209–6	96–2: D 48–1; R 47–1	Gephardt—Yes Bonior—Yes	Daschle—Yes Reid—Yes
Pass a domestic energy plan to reduce energy costs and increase oil and gas drilling	3—A House-passed energy bill stalled in the Senate.				

(*continued*)

Table A.1 (*continued*)

Priority	Outcome (1=Most of what they want; 2=Some of what they want; 3=None of what they want)	Final House vote	Final Senate vote	House opposition leadership support	Senate opposition leadership support
Increase military funding	1—In the post-9/11 climate, Congress passed the largest increase in military spending since Vietnam, granting Bush nearly all of the funds requested (H.R. 4546).	Voice	Voice	No roll call	No roll call
Pass CARE Act of 2002—charitable giving	3—The House passed a stripped-down version of the CARE Act, but Democratic opposition sank the bill in the Senate (S. 592).				
Pass the Railroad Retirement and Survivors' Improvement Act of 2001	1—A bipartisan bill easily passed the House and the Senate.	369–33: D 196–2; R 170–31	90–9: D 49–0; R 40–9	Gephardt—No vote Bonior—Yes	Daschle—Yes Reid—Yes
107th Congress 2001–2 (Democrats)					
Broad tax reform	2—The final deal included $1.35 billion in tax cuts, but they were tilted more toward the lower end of the income spectrum than Republicans initially wanted (H.R. 1836). Democrats were unhappy with the size and scope of the cuts but secured phaseouts and a few of their priorities.	240–154: D 28–153; R 211–0	58–33: D 12–31; R 46–2	Hastert—Yes Armey—Yes Delay—Yes	Lott—Yes Nickles—Yes
Health care—patients' bill of rights and Medicare prescription drug coverage	3—Democrats and Republicans were ultimately unable to come to an agreement on joint priorities—managed care and Medicare prescription drug coverage.				

(continued)

Revise and reauthorize the Elementary and Secondary Education Act	2—No Child Left Behind reflected a bipartisan compromise that kept federal education spending higher than Republicans had hoped but tied that funding to student achievement on state-developed testing a priority for Republicans and the Bush administration (H.R. 1).	381–41: D 198–6; R 183–33	87–10: D 43–6; R 44–3	Hastert—Yes Armey—Yes Delay—No	Lott—Yes Nickles—Yes
Working families relief (including minimum wage increase, reducing gender pay gap, CHIP expansion)	3—No progress was made by congressional Democrats on these priorities.				

108th Congress 2003–4 (Republicans)

Establish Medicare prescription drug coverage	1—Republicans were finally able to pass their Medicare Part D proposal over the objections of most Democrats.	220–215: D 16–189; R 204–25	54–44: D 11–35; R 42–9	Pelosi—No Hoyer—No	Daschle—No Reid—No
Pass Bush tax cuts part 2/ tax reform	1—Republicans were able to pass another major tax cut bill over the objections of most Democrats (H.R. 2).	231–200: D 7–198; R 224–1	51–50: D 2–46; R 48–3	Pelosi—No Hoyer—No	Daschle—No Reid—No
Make some Bush tax cuts permanent (especially estate tax)	3—The House passed a bill to permanently repeal the estate tax, but action was not taken in the Senate.				
Welfare law reauthorization	3—The House passed a welfare overhaul with tougher work requirements, but legislation did not achieve cloture on the Senate floor.				
Pass a domestic energy plan to reduce energy costs and increase oil and gas drilling	3—Omnibus energy bills passed the House and Senate and a conference report passed the House but failed to clear the Senate.				

Table A.1 (*continued*)

Priority	Outcome (1=Most of what they want; 2=Some of what they want; 3=None of what they want)	Final House vote	Final Senate vote	House opposition leadership support	Senate opposition leadership support
Expand war on terror/provide war spending	1—Congress passed a large supplemental to fund wars in Iraq and Afghanistan (H.R. 3289).	298–121: D 82–115; R 216–5	87–12: D 37–11; R 50–0	Pelosi—No Hoyer—Yes	Daschle—Yes Reid—Yes
Health care liability and lawsuit reform	3—The House passed a bill to cap noneconomic and punitive damages in medical malpractice lawsuits (H.R. 4520), but it could not overcome a filibuster in the Senate.				
Regulatory and tax relief for businesses	2—The Senate put together a largely bipartisan bill that repealed an export subsidy, cut corporate taxes, and curbed some tax shelters.	280–141: D 73–124; R 207–16	69–17: D 25–14; R 43–3	Pelosi—No Hoyer—No	Daschle—Yes Reid—Yes
Enact unemployment benefits extension	2—Congress extended unemployment benefits (H.R. 2185), but the GOP allowed the supplemental benefits to expire at the end of the year.	409–19: D 204–0; R 204–19	Voice	Pelosi—Yes Hoyer—Yes	No roll call
Homeland security amendments	2—Congress provided generous funding for the new DHS but did not take other steps to improve its organization or increase congressional oversight (H.R. 2555).	417–8: D 196–6; R 220–2	Voice	Pelosi—Yes Hoyer—Yes	No roll call
Class-action lawsuit reform	3—Republicans were unable to get a tort reform bill through the Senate.				
Expand K-12 school choice and enact higher education improvements	3—Congress was unable to take action on K-12 or higher education legislation.				

Promote US trade and exports	1—Trade agreement with Singapore (H.R. 2739) was easily approved.	272–155: D 75–127; R 197–27	66–32: D 22–24; R 44–7	Pelosi—Yes Hoyer—Yes	Daschle—Yes Reid—No
Promote US trade and exports	1—Trade agreement with Chile (H.R. 2738) was easily approved.	270–156: D 75–128; R 195–27	65–32: D 22–24; R 43–7	Pelosi—Yes Hoyer—Yes	Daschle—Yes Reid—No
Reduce taxes on charitable foundations but apply new regulations	3—The House and Senate were unable to reconcile different versions of legislation that would have created a charitable tax deduction for individuals who do not itemize.				
Intelligence reform and counter terrorism/enact 9/11 Commission's recommendations	1—Congress passed legislation overhauling the nation's intelligence agencies as spurred by the 9/11 Commission's recommendations (S. 2845).	336–75: D 183–8; R 152–67	89–2: D 44–1; R 44–1	Pelosi—Yes Hoyer—Yes	Daschle—Yes Reid—Yes
Pass the partial-birth abortion ban	1—Republicans finally passed a long sought partial-birth abortion ban (S. 3)	281–142: D 53–137; R 218–4	64–34: D 17–30; R 47–3	Pelosi—No Hoyer—No	Daschle—Yes Reid—Yes

109th Congress 2005–6 (Republicans)

Pass a domestic energy plan to reduce energy costs and increase oil and gas drilling	2—Congress passed a domestic energy plan, but ANWR drilling, a top priority, did not survive the process (H.R. 6).	275–156: D 75–124; R 200–31	74–26: D 25–19; R 49–6	Pelosi—No Hoyer—No	Reid—No Durbin—Yes
Enact a tax overhaul and make Bush tax cuts permanent	2—Republicans were unable to make the Bush tax cuts permanent, but they were able to extend them for more years through budget reconciliation (H.R. 4297).	244–185: D 5–182; R 229–2	54–44: D 3–40; R 51–3	Pelosi—No Hoyer—No	Reid—No Durbin—No
Reauthorize surface transportation programs	1—Congress was able to pass a major surface transportation reauthorization with bipartisan support (H.R. 3).	412–8: D 194–0; R 217–8	91–4: D 42–0; R 48–4	Pelosi—Yes Hoyer—Yes	Reid—Yes Durbin—Yes

(continued)

Table A.1 (*continued*)

Priority	Outcome (1=Most of what they want; 2=Some of what they want; 3=None of what they want)	Final House vote	Final Senate vote	House opposition leadership support	Senate opposition leadership support
Pass class-action lawsuit and tort reform	1—Republicans passed an aggressive class-action and tort reform bill making limited concessions to Democrats (H.R. 5). This had been an important Republican goal for years.	279–149: D 50–147; R 229–1	72–26: D 18–26; R 53–0	Pelosi—No Hoyer—No	Reid—No Durbin—No
Limit medical malpractice litigation	3—Senate Democrats successfully filibustered a bill proposing to limit medical malpractice liability.				
PATRIOT Act partial reauthorization	2—Republicans successfully extended various provisions of the PATRIOT Act, but only after agreeing to compromises, including imposing sunsets on some of the provisions (H.R. 3199).	251–174: D 44–155; R 207–18	89–10: D 34–9; R 55–0	Pelosi—No Hoyer—Yes	Reid—Yes Durbin—Yes
Continue Iraq and Afghanistan war spending	1—Congress passed an emergency supplemental fully funding continuing military operations in Iraq and Afghanistan (H.R. 1268).	368–58: D 143–54; R 225–3	99–0: D 44–0; R 55–0	Pelosi—Yes Hoyer—Yes	Reid—Yes Durbin—Yes
Social Security overhaul	3—President Bush's top priority to overhaul Social Security never got off the ground.				
Enact broad entitlement reform	3—Congress did not take any steps to reform federal entitlement programs.				
Pass workforce training and related education legislation	2—Congress passed bipartisan legislation renewing federal vocational and technical education programs (S. 250).	99–0: D 43–0; R 55–0	399–1: D 186–0; R 212–1	Pelosi—Yes Hoyer—Yes	Reid—Yes Durbin—Yes

		House vote	Senate vote	House leaders	Senate leaders
Enact pension reform	1—Negotiations were protracted, and Republicans were unable to couple the pension bills with various tax measures, but a bill addressing the looming pension crises was passed (H.R. 4).	279–131: D 76–114; R 203–16	93–5: D 40–2; R 52–3	Pelosi—No Hoyer—No	Reid—Yes Durbin—Yes
Reauthorize the Voting Rights Act	1—Congress cleared a bipartisan renewal of the Voting Rights Act (H.R. 9).	390–33: D 197–0; R 192–33	98–0: D 44–0; R 53–0	Pelosi—Yes Hoyer—Yes	Reid—Yes Durbin—Yes
Trade rights and litigation policy	3—No action was taken on trade rights.				
Reform teen pregnancy and abortion policies	3—The House passed two different bills requiring parental consent for teen abortions, but no action was taken in the Senate.				
110th Congress 2007–8 (Democrats)					
Student loan interest rate reduction	1—The final bill included most of the Democrats' priorities despite initial Republican opposition and veto threats from the Bush administration (H.R. 2669).	292–97: D 215–0; R 77–97	79–12: D 43–0; R 34–12	Boehner—No Blunt—No	McConnell—No Lott—Yes
Repeal oil industry tax breaks and bolster renewable energy	2—Democrats had to drop a number of their key priorities, including some tax provisions and renewable energy standards, to get the bill to President Bush's desk (H.R. 6).	314–100: D 219–4; R 95–96	86–8: D 44–1; R 40–7	Boehner—No Blunt—Yes	McConnell—Yes Lott—Yes
Pass congressional ethics/ lobbying reform	2—After making some concessions, congressional Democrats were able to push through an ethics and lobbying reform package with bipartisan support (S.1).	411–8: D 221–6; R 190–2	83–14: D 47–0; R 34–14	Boehner—Yes Blunt—Yes	McConnell—Yes Lott—No
Pass a minimum wage increase coupled with small-business tax breaks	2—Democrats had to accept small-business tax breaks three times larger than they initially proposed in order to gain enough Republican support to increase the minimum wage to $7.25/ hour (H.R. 2206).	280–142: D 86–140; R 194–2	80–14: D 37–10; R 42–3	Boehner—Yes Blunt—Yes	McConnell—Yes Lott—Yes

(continued)

Table A.1 (continued)

Priority	Outcome (1=Most of what they want; 2=Some of what they want; 3=None of what they want)	Final House vote	Final Senate vote	House opposition leadership support	Senate opposition leadership support
Enact 9/11 Commission recommendations alongside port security funding increase	2—Democrats had to make many concessions to Republicans along the way, including over labor rights for TSA agents and the distribution of DHS grants, but the bill enacted the remaining 9/11 Commission recommendations left out of the 2004 bill (H.R. 1).	371–40: D 221–1; R 150–39	85–8: D 46–0; R 37–8	Boehner—No vote Blunt—Yes	McConnell—Yes Lott—No vote
Establish federal funding for stem cell research	3—President Bush vetoed Democratic efforts to establish federal funding for stem cell research.				
Medicare drug price negotiation	3—Democrats were unable to pass a bill requiring the HHS secretary to negotiate prescription drug prices for Medicare Part D providers over strong Republican opposition and a veto threat.				
Establish a new direction on Iraq War	3—Democrats were unable to pass stand-alone bills setting withdrawal timetables in Iraq. Defense authorization and spending bills did little to change the course of the conflict.				
Comprehensive immigration reform	3—Despite a number of bipartisan efforts and presidential support, no immigration bill made its way out of the Senate				
Pass PAYGO	1—Not needing a presidential signature, Democrats in the House and Senate were able to establish PAYGO rules along party lines (S. Con. Res. 21).	212–207: D 212–12; R 0–195	52–47: D 48–0; R 2–47	Boehner—No Blunt—No	McConnell—No Lott—No

Goal	Description	House vote	Senate vote	House leaders	Senate leaders
Rebuild and modernize the military	2—Democrats were never specific on what rebuilding and modernizing the military meant, but the accomplishments seem to be a bit of a mixed bag (H.R. 1585).	370–49: D 182–45; R 188–4	90–3: D 41–2; R 48–0	Boehner—Yes Blunt—Yes	McConnell—Yes Lott—Yes
Health care reform/health care costs and access	3—Democrats were unable to take meaningful action on health care. A bill expanding SCHIP was vetoed by President Bush.				
Retirement security	3—No action was taken on this priority.				
Increase congressional oversight of the executive branch	3—No specific action was taken to expand congressional oversight.				
Enact FISA reforms	2—After a six-month battle, FISA policies were amended and extended; Republicans were viewed as getting more of what they wanted in the end (H.R. 6304).	293–129: D 105–128; R 188–1	69–28: D 21–27; R 47–0	Boehner—Yes Blunt—Yes	McConnell—Yes Kyl—Yes
111th Congress 2009–10 (Democrats)					
Pass an economic stimulus package	2—The final stimulus bill (ARRA) was not as expansive as many Democrats envisioned, but compromises were necessary to get the bill through the Senate (H.R. 1).	246–183: D 246–7; R 0–176	60–38: D 57–0; R 3–38	Boehner—No Cantor—No	McConnell—No Kyl—No
Enact comprehensive health care reform	1—Democrats made two key compromises, eliminating a government-run health plan and allowing for restrictions on spending for abortion services. Nonetheless, the ACA represents most of what the Democrats wanted to achieve (H.R. 3590).	219–212: D 219–34; R 0–178	60–39: D 60–0; R 0–39	Boehner—No Cantor—No	McConnell—No Kyl—No

(continued)

Table A.1 (*continued*)

Priority	Outcome (1=Most of what they want; 2=Some of what they want; 3=None of what they want)	Final House vote	Final Senate vote	House opposition leadership support	Senate opposition leadership support
Energy independence/climate change legislation	3—The House cleared a climate change bill (H.R. 2454), but with over forty Democrats opposing the plan, Republican votes were needed for passage. Action in the Senate never got off the ground as Democratic senators were unable to coalesce behind a specific plan.				
Broad financial sector reform and mortgage relief (Dodd-Frank)	1—Democrats passed a broad finance regulatory bill (Dodd-Frank) with the support of just a few Republicans. Obama described the final bill as "90 percent of what I proposed when I took up this fight" (H.R. 4173).	237–192: D 234–19; R 3–173	60–39: D 57–1; R 3–38	Boehner—No Cantor—No	McConnell—No Kyl—No
SCHIP reauthorization	1—Democrats passed an expansion of the SCHIP program after removing some of the compromise measures they had included in 2007 to try to gain more Republican support and avoid President Bush's veto (H.R. 2).	290–135: D 250–2; R 40–133	66–32: D 57–0; R 9–32	Boehner—No Cantor—No	McConnell—No Kyl—No
New direction with war on terror/Iraq and Afghanistan wars	3—Democrats continued war funding, despite reluctance. The 2002 AUMF was not repealed or amended. Generally, the 111th Congress did not cause a shift in policy on the wars.				

		House vote	House leaders	Senate vote	Senate leaders
Address college costs and affordability	2—The Democrats' bill made broad changes to federal student loan policy but proposed that funding for community college be cut drastically after the CBO downgraded potential savings meant to help pay for the bill (H.R. 4872).	220–211: D 220–33; R 0–178	Boehner—No Cantor—No	56–43: D 56–3; R 0–40	McConnell—No Kyl—No
Gender pay equity legislation	2—Congress passed the Lilly Ledbetter Fair Pay Act (S. 181), but Democrats were unable to advance a measure making it easier for individuals to file sex discrimination cases over wage claims by putting the legal onus on employers to prove that pay discrepancies between women and men were not discriminatory (S. 3772/H.R. 12).	250–177: D 247–5; R 3–172	Boehner—No Cantor—No	61–36: D 56–0; R 5–36	McConnell—No Kyl—No
Comprehensive immigration reform	3—Congress was unable to pass legislation overhauling the nation's immigration laws.				
Modernize and rebuild the military	3—Democrats were unable to make broad sweeping changes in defense or military policy.				
Retirement security	3—There seemingly was no room on the agenda to address retirement policies or Social Security.				
Oppose Bush administration midnight regulations	3—Democrats did not take any action on this or use the Congressional Review Act to stop any Bush regulations from the end of his term.				
112th Congress 2011–12 (Republicans)					
Cut federal spending and preserve Bush-era tax cuts (for deficit reduction)	2—Across several fights (FY 2011 spending, the Budget Control Act, and the fiscal cliff) Republicans took steps to reduce federal spending, but never by as much as they hoped. The fiscal cliff bill (H.R. 8) extended some Bush-era tax cuts, but not all.	257–167: D 172–16; R 85–151	Pelosi—Yes Hoyer—Yes	89–8: D 49–3; R 40–5	Reid—Yes Durbin—Yes

(continued)

Table A.1 (*continued*)

Priority	Outcome (1=Most of what they want; 2=Some of what they want; 3=None of what they want)	Final House vote	Final Senate vote	House opposition leadership support	Senate opposition leadership support
Repeal and replace the Affordable Care Act	3—Republicans were unable to repeal and replace the ACA.				
Reauthorize surface transportation programs/reform the Highway Trust Fund	2—The final bill (MAP-21) did not enact the broad changes Republicans had hoped for. The final deal was a short-term compromise that could get through the House and Senate (H.R. 4348).	373–52: D 187–0; R 186–52	74–19: D 50–0; R 24–19	Pelosi—Yes Hoyer—Yes	Reid—Yes Durbin—Yes
Broad tax overhaul	2—Republicans got some of what they wanted, extending some Bush-era tax cuts. However, they were unable to reform the tax code or expand the tax base (H.R. 8).	257–167: D 172–16; R 85–151	89–8: D 49–3; R 40–5	Pelosi—Yes Hoyer—Yes	Reid—Yes Durbin—Yes
Congressional process reforms	2—House Republicans enacted some reforms, including replacing PAYGO with CUTGO (H.R. 5). However, they were unable to enact broader bicameral reforms, such as changes to the budget process or CBO accounting.	238–191: D 0–191; R 238–0	n/a	Pelosi—No Hoyer—No	n/a
Social Security solvency	3—Cuts and changes to entitlement programs were floated by Republicans as part of a fiscal "grand bargain," but nothing of the sort was enacted.				
Restrict taxpayer funding for abortions	3—The House passed a permanent ban on federal abortion funding, but it went nowhere in the Senate. House Republicans pushed various riders related to abortion funding (including on H.R. 1), but none ended up in final legislation.				

Regulatory reform	3—House Republicans passed a bill requiring congressional approval for major regulations issued by the executive branch, but it was not taken up in the Senate (H.R. 10, REINS Act).			
Cut taxes on small businesses	3—House Republicans passed a small business tax cut bill, but it went nowhere in the Senate (H.R. 9).			
112th Congress 2011–12 (Democrats)				
Pass a second economic stimulus and job creation bill	3—Some jobs initiatives passed, but not a new stimulus, and nothing that looked like the Obama administration's $447 billion blueprint (S. 1660).			
End Bush-era tax cuts for rich and preserve federal spending	2—The fiscal cliff deal ended Bush-era tax cuts for the richest Americans, but Democrats had to accept more nondefense spending cuts than they would have liked (H.R. 8).	257–167: D 172–16; R 85–151	89–8: D 49–3; R 40–5	Boehner—Yes Cantor—No McCarthy—No	McConnell—Yes Kyl—Yes
Comprehensive immigration reform	3—Limited legislative action was taken on immigration in the 112th Congress.			
Climate change/renewable energy legislation	3—Senate Democrats were unable to move any major climate change or renewable energy policies.			
Replace No Child Left Behind (Elementary and Secondary Education Act reauthorization)	3—Committees in the House and Senate advanced NCLB reform bills, but no further action occurred.			
Reauthorize surface transportation programs/ reform the Highway Trust Fund	2—The final bill (MAP-21) was a short-term compromise that could get through the House and Senate (H.R. 4348).	373–52: D 187–0; R 186–52	74–19: D 50–0; R 24–19	Boehner—No vote Cantor—Yes McCarthy—Yes	McConnell—Yes Kyl—Yes

(continued)

Table A.1 (*continued*)

Priority	Outcome (1=Most of what they want; 2=Some of what they want; 3=None of what they want)	Final House vote	Final Senate vote	House opposition leadership support	Senate opposition leadership support
Broad cybersecurity reform	3—The House and Senate advanced very different cybersecurity bills. Neither became law.				
Filibuster reform	3—Reid and McConnell made a "gentlemen's agreement" on the filibuster, but it faded throughout the two-year session. Other proposals fell short of the necessary votes to reform the rules.				
DISCLOSE Act reforms	3—The bill, which would have required more groups spending money in elections to disclose their donors, was filibustered by Senate Republicans.				
Help women in the workforce (pay equity, family leave, child care, etc.)	3—Senate Democrats were unable to force through any legislation on these issues.				
113th Congress 2013–14 (Republicans)					
Deficit reduction (tied to debt limit)	3—Republicans wanted major policy reforms in exchange for raising the debt limit but did not get them.				
Replace No Child Left Behind (Elementary and Secondary Education Act reauthorization)	3—The House passed a Republican-backed bill, but no further action occurred.				
Increase energy independence and domestic energy production	3—House Republicans passed several energy bills, but no action was taken in the Senate.				

232

Broad tax overhaul	3—Republicans on the House Ways and Means Committee introduced a draft bill, but it went no further.				
Health entitlement reform (Medicare)	3—Republicans did not make any progress reforming entitlement programs.				
Restrict taxpayer funding for abortions	3—The House passed a bill to prohibit use of federal funds to pay for abortions or health insurance that covers abortions. No action taken in the Senate.				
113th Congress 2013–14 (Democrats)					
Reauthorize the Violence against Women Act	1—Both the Senate and the House passed the Democrats' bill reauthorizing the VAWA (S. 47).	286–138: D 199–0; R 87–138	78–22: D 53–0; R 23–22	Boehner—No vote Cantor—No McCarthy—Yes	McConnell—No Cornyn—No
Replace No Child Left Behind (Elementary and Secondary Education Act reauthorization)	3—The House passed a K-12 education bill, but the Senate did not take up a version advanced by the HELP Committee.				
Pass new gun control legislation	3—Modest gun control measures were introduced in Senate following the Newtown shooting but failed cloture (S. 649).				
Voting and campaign finance reform	3—No action taken on voting rights or campaign finance reform.				
Comprehensive immigration reform	3—The Senate passed a bipartisan immigration reform bill, but it was not taken up in the House.				
Deficit reduction (vague)	3—No further steps were taken to reduce the deficit.				
Reauthorize the farm bill	2—The farm bill was reauthorized after a contentious partisan fight over SNAP and several compromises (H.R. 2642).	251–166: D 89–103; R 162–63	68–32: D 44–9; R 22–23	Boehner—No vote Cantor—Yes McCarthy—Yes	McConnell—Yes Cornyn—No

(continued)

Table A.1 (*continued*)

Priority	Outcome (1=Most of what they want; 2=Some of what they want; 3=None of what they want)	Final House vote	Final Senate vote	House opposition leadership support	Senate opposition leadership support
Increase workers' wages and compensation	3—A minimum wage increase bill fell short of cloture in the Senate (S. 2223).				
Bolster US tech innovation	3—A package of Democratic proposals did not advance in the House or Senate.				
Pass Hurricane Sandy relief and aid	2—Proponents had to accept a smaller relief package after resistance from conservatives who wanted the costs offset by spending cuts elsewhere (H.R. 152).	241–180: D 192–1; R 49–179	62–36: D 52–0; R 9–36	Boehner—No vote Cantor—Yes McCarthy—Yes	McConnell—No Cornyn—No
Reauthorize surface transportation programs	2—Congress was able to pass only a short-term extension, despite initial optimism about a long-term highway bill (H.R. 5021)	367–55: D 186–10; R 181–45	81–13: D 51–1; R 30–12	Boehner—No vote Cantor—No vote McCarthy—Yes	McConnell—Yes Cornyn—Yes
Expand veterans' benefits	2—Spending on veterans' health care increased as part of an omnibus spending bill (H.R. 83).	219–206: D 57–139; R 162–67	56–40: D 32–22; R 24–18	Boehner—Yes McCarthy—Yes Scalise—Yes	McConnell—Yes Cornyn—Yes
Climate change/renewable energy legislation	2—Existing tax breaks for renewable energy were extended temporarily (H.R. 678), but no further action was taken.	416–7: D 188–7; R 228–0	Voice	Boehner—No vote Cantor—Yes McCarthy—Yes	No roll call
114th Congress 2015–16 (Republicans)					
Keystone XL. pipeline approval	3—Congress could not override the Obama veto to force approval of Keystone pipeline (S. 1).				
Repeal and replace the Affordable Care Act	3—Republicans could not override the Obama veto of ACA repeal (H.R. 3762).				
Broad tax overhaul	3—No progress was made on tax reform.				

Goal	Description	House vote	Senate vote	House leaders	Senate leaders
Pass an infrastructure and energy bill expanding domestic energy production	3—The House passed a large energy and transportation bill that would streamline export of liquefied natural gas, expedite gas pipeline permits, and improve smart grid and efficiency technologies. No action was taken in the Senate.			Pelosi—Yes Hoyer—Yes	Reid—Yes Durbin—Yes
Replace No Child Left Behind (Elementary and Secondary Education Act reauthorization)	2—A bipartisan Senate bill, rather than the more partisan House bill, formed the basis of the first long-term ESEA reauthorization in well over a decade (S. 1177).	359–64: D 181–0; R 178–64	85–12: D 44–0; R 40–12	Pelosi—Yes Hoyer—Yes	Reid—Yes Durbin—Yes
Expand federal health care research policies and streamline drug approval (21st Century Cures Act)	2—A bipartisan compromise to streamline the process for new drug approval and increase funding for the NIH and the FDA passed at the end of the Congress (H.R. 34).	392–26: D 174–6; R 218–20	94–5: D 41–3; R 52–1	Pelosi—Yes Hoyer—Yes	Reid—Yes Durbin—Yes
Permanent Medicare sustainable growth rate (SGR) repeal	2—A bipartisan compromise permanently repealed the Medicare SGR and extended SCHIP for two years (H.R. 2).	392–37: D 180–4; R 212–33	92–8: D 44–0; R 46–8	Pelosi—Yes Hoyer—Yes	Reid—Yes Durbin—Yes
Approve Trans-Pacific Partnership trade deal	3—Congress did not act to approve the TPP.				
Pass a veterans' job bill	1—"Hire More Heroes Act" enacted as part of a larger bill—H.R. 3236, Surface Transportation and Veterans Health Care Choice Improvement Act.	385–34: D 170–9; R 215–25	91–4: D 45–0; R 46–4	Pelosi—Yes Hoyer—Yes	Reid—Yes Durbin—Yes
Prohibit federal funding for abortion	3—A House bill prohibiting federal funds for insurance plans covering abortion passed the House but did not receive Senate action.				
Patent reform	3—No floor action in either chamber on pension reform.				

(continued)

Table A.1 (*continued*)

Priority	Outcome (1=Most of what they want; 2=Some of what they want; 3=None of what they want)	Final House vote	Final Senate vote	House opposition leadership support	Senate opposition leadership support
115th Congress 2017–18 (Republicans)					
Obamacare repeal and replace	3—House passed an Obamacare repeal and replace bill (H.R. 1628), but the Senate was unable to clear one.				
Tax cuts/tax reform	1—The TCJA (H.R. 1) sharply and permanently lowered tax rates for corporations, limited and eliminated many tax deductions for individuals while raising the standard deduction, exempted more taxpayers from the alternative minimum tax and the estate tax, and temporarily lowered individual income tax rates. The TCJA also opened the Arctic National Wildlife Refuge to oil and natural gas drilling and abolished the Affordable Care Act's individual mandate.	224–201: D 0–189; R 224–12	51–48: D 0–48; R 51–0	Pelosi—No Hoyer—No	Schumer—No Durbin—No
Domestic spending cuts	3—House passed a bill (H.R. 3) rescinding $15 billion in budget authority, a White House priority. The Senate rejected it.				
FAA reauthorization	2—Five-year reauthorization of the FAA. To secure House passage, Republicans had to drop their bid to privatize air traffic control.	398–23: D 187–3; R 211–20	96–3: D 45–1; R 49–2	Pelosi—Yes Hoyer—Yes	Schumer—Yes Durbin—Yes

Policy area	Description	House vote	Senate vote	House leaders	Senate leaders
Reform of agency rule making	3—The House-passed bill (H.R. 3) would revise rule-making procedures under the APA to consider more than seventy new criteria when issuing rules and to limit judicial deference to agencies on rule making. The Senate declined to advance a companion bill.				
Opioid crisis response	1—The legislation brought together many smaller proposals sponsored by hundreds of lawmakers. It created a grant program for addiction recovery centers, allowed Medicaid to cover thirty days of residential treatment, and included efforts to block fentanyl from being imported through the mail.	393–8: D 178–0; R 215–8	98–1: D 49–0; R 49–1	Pelosi—No vote Hoyer—Yes	Schumer—Yes Durbin—Yes
End taxpayer funding of abortion	3—The House-passed bill (H.R. 7) prohibits qualified health plans under the ACA from covering abortions. The Senate declined to take up a companion measure.				
Water resources development	1—The legislation (S. 3021) authorizes new Army Corps projects and studies and changes how such projects are vetted.	Voice	Voice	No roll call	No roll call
Rollback of financial regulations (Dodd-Frank)	2—The legislation (S. 2155) exempted community and regional banks from stringent regulatory oversight, though the effort fell far short of the Dodd-Frank repeal.	258–159: D 33–158; R 225–1	67–31: D 16–31; R 50–0	Pelosi—No Hoyer—No	Schumer—No Durbin—No

(continued)

Table A.1 (*continued*)

Priority	Outcome (1=Most of what they want; 2=Some of what they want; 3=None of what they want)	Final House vote	Final Senate vote	House opposition leadership support	Senate opposition leadership support
Farm bill	2—Congress passed a five-year reauthorization after House Republicans dropped their demands for adding additional work requirements to SNAP and other conservative proposals (H.R. 2).	369–47: D 187–3; R 182–44	87–13: D 47–0; R 38–13	Pelosi—Yes Hoyer—Yes	Schumer—Yes Durbin—Yes
Obama administration rules rollback	1—Rolled back a series of fourteen Obama-era agency regulations (H.J. Res. 41; H.J. Res. 38; H.J. Res. 40; H.J. Res. 37; H.J. Res. 44; H.J. Res. 57; H.J. Res. 58; H.J. Res. 42; H.J. Res. 83; H.J. Res. 43; H.J. Res. 67; H.J. Res. 66; H.J. Res. 111; H.J. Res. 57)	All passed on party-line votes.	All passed on party-line votes.	All passed over the opposition of Pelosi and Hoyer.	All passed over the opposition of Schumer and Durbin.

238

Table A.2 Descriptions of majority party priority failure cases and coding

Priority	Outcome 1 = Senate's sixty-vote threshold; 2 = presidential veto; 3 = only one chamber passes; 4 = no formal action; 5 = committee report, no floor action; 6 = House and Senate cannot reconcile their bills	Summary coding 1 = veto player problems; 2 = internal party dissent
99th Congress 1985–86 (Republicans)		
Reform the Senate committee system (Quayle Committee recommendations)	4—The Senate Republican Conference endorsed several recommendations produced by the Temporary Select Committee to Study the Senate Committee System (the Quayle Committee) in 1984. However, no action was taken by Majority Leader Dole or Senate Republicans to move forward with these proposals.	2
99th Congress 1985–86 (Democrats)		
Revise and extend housing programs for the poor	3—House Democrats rejected watered-down housing measures proposed by the Senate as part of a larger budget reconciliation bill (H.R. 3128). The Senate did not take up the more aggressive House-passed measure (H.R. 1).	2
Renew Water Quality Programs	2—Congress passed legislation reauthorizing and strengthening the Clean Water Act by overwhelming margins, but the bill was pocket vetoed by President Reagan (H.R. 8/S. 1128).	1
100th Congress 1987–88 (Democrats)		
Pass a trade bill to reduce the trade deficit	2—Congress passed the Omnibus Trade and Competitiveness Act (H.R. 3) with mostly Democratic votes. Republicans objected to various provisions including a requirement that businesses provide workers with advance notice of plant closings. President Reagan vetoed the bill, and congressional Democrats could not muster enough votes for an override.	1
Reauthorize the Clean Air Act	5—The Senate's Committee on Environment and Public Works reported a bill to revise clean air standards (S. 1894), but House Democrats were unable to resolve their internal disagreements over various issues and move a bill (H.R. 3054/ H.R. 2666). The major lines of disagreement were between Energy and Commerce Committee chair John Dingell (D-MI) and Subcommittee on Health and the Environment chair Henry Waxman (D-CA) and their respective allies over how much to tighten controls on ozone, carbon monoxide, and acid-rain precursors.	2

(*continued*)

Priority	Outcome 1 = Senate's sixty-vote threshold; 2 = presidential veto; 3 = only one chamber passes; 4 = no formal action; 5 = committee report, no floor action; 6 = House and Senate cannot reconcile their bills	Summary coding 1 = veto player problems; 2 = internal party dissent
Campaign Finance Reform for Senate elections	1—Majority Leader Robert Byrd kept the Senate in session for two all-night debates, but Senate Republicans blocked cloture on a broad campaign finance reform package eight times (S. 2), objecting to state-by-state spending limits on Senate campaigns.	1
Pass the Sunset Act of 1987	4—The "Sunset Act," requiring ten-year sunsets on all new legislative authorizations, was introduced in the House (H.R. 7, H.R. 602), but no action was taken on the proposal.	2
Creation of state-run child care assistance programs	1—Both liberals and conservatives found things to dislike about the Act for Better Child Care Services (the "ABC bill," H.R. 3660/S. 1885). The House measure never advanced owing to objections on both sides. Cloture on a Senate measure combining the "ABC bill" with a paid parental leave measure failed, with Democrats split over the proposal.	2
101st Congress 1989–90 (Democrats)		
Campaign finance reform	6—President Bush promised to veto the package, but House and Senate Democrats were unable to reconcile the differences between their separate campaign finance proposals in any case (H.R. 5400 and S. 137). Among other things, disagreements over how to treat political action committees left a wide gap between the two bills, and there was not enough time before the 1990 midterm elections to work out a compromise.	2
Trade legislation to reduce the trade deficit	4—No legislative action was taken on legislation to reduce the country's trade deficit.	2
Pass legislation improving enterprise zones	4—No legislative action was taken on improving enterprise zones.	2
Pass a uniform poll-closing law	3—The House passed a bill to establish a uniform poll-closing time across the continental United States with some bipartisan support, but efforts stalled in the Senate over objections from eastern and midwestern senators from both parties (H.R. 18/S. 136).	2

Priority	Outcome 1 = Senate's sixty-vote threshold; 2 = presidential veto; 3 = only one chamber passes; 4 = no formal action; 5 = committee report, no floor action; 6 = House and Senate cannot reconcile their bills	Summary coding 1 = veto player problems; 2 = internal party dissent
Increase government investment in research and development	6—Despite bipartisan agreement that more should be done to spur research and development, negotiators could not resolve differences between House- and Senate-passed versions of the American Technology Preeminence Act (S. 1191/H.R. 4329) as time ran out before the 1990 midterms.	2
Improve education standards and teacher quality	1—Senate Republicans, led by Senator Helms, blocked action on the Educational Equity and Excellence Act (H.R. 5932),	1
102nd Congress 1991–92 (Democrats)		
Improve and track progress on nationwide education standards	1—Senate Democrats passed a bipartisan bill (S. 2), while House Democrats passed a more partisan version of the Neighborhood Schools Improvement Act (H.R. 4323). After protracted negotiations the House and Senate reached an agreement on a conference report, but the agreement was highly objectionable to Senate Republicans, who threatened a filibuster. Majority Leader Mitchell did not schedule a vote in the Senate before the Congress ended.	1
Campaign finance reform	2—House and Senate Democrats passed a measure setting voluntary spending limits for congressional candidates and providing public funding and other benefits to those who comply. With most congressional Republicans opposed to the measure, Congress was unable to override President Bush's veto (S. 3).	1
Expand health care coverage to all Americans	4—Republicans and liberal Democrats alike raised objections to H.R. 5502, promoted by the Democratic leadership as a "first step" bill for comprehensive health care reform. Ultimately, liberal Democrats remained unhappy that the bill did not guarantee health care access to all Americans, and moderate Democrats were unwilling to back something that aggressive. A markup was never scheduled in committee.	2

(*continued*)

Priority	Outcome 1 = Senate's sixty-vote threshold; 2 = presidential veto; 3 = only one chamber passes; 4 = no formal action; 5 = committee report, no floor action; 6 = House and Senate cannot reconcile their bills	Summary coding 1 = veto player problems; 2 = internal party dissent
Pass legislation guaranteeing family and medical leave	2—House and Senate Democrats passed the Family Leave Act of 1991 with some Republican support, but an override of President Bush's veto fell short in the House in the face of strong Republican opposition (S. 5).	1
Expand child-welfare programs for low-income children	3—Democrats made several attempts to expand child-welfare programs (H.R. 2571, S. 4) with only one (H.R. 3603) passing the House with strong opposition from Republicans over its funding mechanism. President Bush later pocket vetoed an omnibus tax bill (H.R. 11) that included watered-down versions of some of that bill's provisions.	2
Economic stimulus via tax incentives for enterprise zones	2—Unable to move a stand-alone bill to expand tax incentives for enterprise zones (H.R. 10), Democrats attached some provisions to an omnibus tax bill (H.R. 11) that was pocket vetoed by President Bush.	1
Make it easier for people to afford long-term care for elderly and disabled relatives	5—House and Senate bills to help people afford long-term care made little progress during the 102nd Congress despite ongoing efforts. In the Senate, Senator Kennedy was unable to cull enough Republican support to move forward, despite offering to drop a controversial provision that would have required all policies to include inflation-protection clauses.	1
Prohibit the permanent replacement of labor strikers	1—House Democrats passed a bill banning employers from permanently replacing workers who are on strike with few Republicans votes in support (H.R. 5). Senate Republicans blocked cloture on Senate Democrats' version of the bill (S. 55).	1
Pass the Brady Handgun Violence Prevention Act	1—The House passed the Brady Handgun Violence Prevention Act (H.R. 7) despite the objections of most Republicans and some Democrats. The Senate was unable to advance its stand-alone measure (S. 257) owing to similar opposition. Later, Senate Republicans blocked cloture on the conference report for an omnibus anticrime bill that included the Brady Handgun Violence Prevent Act (H.R. 3371).	1

Priority	Outcome 1 = Senate's sixty-vote threshold; 2 = presidential veto; 3 = only one chamber passes; 4 = no formal action; 5 = committee report, no floor action; 6 = House and Senate cannot reconcile their bills	Summary coding 1 = veto player problems; 2 = internal party dissent
Eliminate some antitrust exemptions for insurance companies	5—House Judiciary Committee Democrats worked up and reported the Insurance Competitive Pricing Act of 1992 (H.R. 9). Committee Republicans unanimously opposed the bill, but some Democrats were uneasy as well, concerned that the provisions would negatively affect small insurers. As a result, the bill advanced no further in either chamber.	2

103rd Congress 1993–94 (Democrats)

Pass comprehensive health care reform	5—The Clinton health care plan faced opposition from Republicans as well as many Democrats. Rather than unifying behind the plan, several Democrats offered their own, and opposition to the plan came from both moderates, who saw too much government involvement, and liberals, who preferred a single-payer system. After a year of debate, Senate Majority Leader Mitchell pulled the plug.	2
Campaign finance reform	1—Democrats passed campaign finance reform measures through both the House and Senate, though the bills differed in various respects (S. 3 and H.R. 3). Sidetracked by other agenda items, Democrats were unable to forge a compromise between the House and Senate bills until late in 1994, and Senate Republicans were able to filibuster attempts to convene a conference with the House.	· 1
Increase federal infrastructure investment	1—Senate Republicans blocked cloture on a stimulus proposal including substantial infrastructure investments even after Clinton offered to reduce its price tag by 25 percent (H.R. 1335).	1
Prohibit the permanent replacement of labor strikers	1—The House passed its version (H.R. 5) of a bill banning employers from permanently replacing striking workers in June 1993. Republicans twice blocked cloture on the Senate bill (S. 55) in July 1994.	1
Reform housing assistance programs	3—The House passed a bipartisan federal housing reform bill (H.R. 3838), but with a crowded agenda the Senate never brought its bill to the floor (S. 2049).	2

(*continued*)

Priority	Outcome 1 = Senate's sixty-vote threshold; 2 = presidential veto; 3 = only one chamber passes; 4 = no formal action; 5 = committee report, no floor action; 6 = House and Senate cannot reconcile their bills	Summary coding 1 = veto player problems; 2 = internal party dissent
Eliminate some antitrust exemptions for insurance companies	5—Democrats seemingly could not find agenda space for this long-held priority. The House Judiciary Committee reported a bill eliminating antitrust exemptions for the insurance industry (H.R. 9), but it was never scheduled on the floor.	2
Pass congressional rules reforms and reorganization	5—Proposals for various congressional reforms (including to shift to a two-year budget and appropriations cycle, discourage extra committee assignments, reduce the opportunities for Senate filibusters, and end Congress' exemptions from various workplace laws) moved through committees in the House and Senate (e.g., S. 1824) but remained controversial with members of both parties and never received floor time.	2
Pass the National Competitiveness Act (improve US competitiveness in tech innovation)	6—Both chambers advanced versions of the National Competitiveness Act along party lines (H.R. 820 and S. 4), but differences could not be resolved in conference. One source of internal disagreement among Democrats was a provision barring the involvement of foreign firms in certain programs, which some viewed as too protectionist and possibly in violation of international trade agreements.	2
104th Congress 1995–96 (Republicans)		
Enact tax cuts	2—Republicans' ambitious tax cut plan (H.R. 2491) was vetoed by Clinton after bipartisan talks collapsed. Small tax cuts tied to a minimum wage increase passed later on (H.R. 3448).	1
Regulatory overhaul	1—Senate Democrats blocked cloture on several attempts to pass a regulatory overhaul bill (e.g., H.R. 9 and S. 343).	1
Pass a balanced budget amendment	3—Senate Democrats successfully blocked efforts to pass a balanced budget amendment (H.J. Res. 1) in 1995 and 1996 (two-thirds vote required), though the amendment passed the House.	1
Establish congressional term limits	5—Democrats in the House and Senate united in enough opposition to block a constitutional amendment establishing the congressional terms limits from achieving the two-thirds necessary to pass either the House or the Senate (H.J. Res. 73 and S.J. Res. 21).	1

Priority	Outcome 1 = Senate's sixty-vote threshold; 2 = presidential veto; 3 = only one chamber passes; 4 = no formal action; 5 = committee report, no floor action; 6 = House and Senate cannot reconcile their bills	Summary coding 1 = veto player problems; 2 = internal party dissent
Protect private property owners	3—The House passed a bill (H.R. 925) allowing landowners to demand compensation for some federal regulatory actions diminishing the value of their property, but it faced opposition from members of both parties in the Senate.	2
105th Congress 1997–98 (Republicans)		
Expand war on drugs/ tougher penalties for drug lords	5—A bipartisan group of senators voted down a resolution (S.J. Res. 42) that would have imposed sanctions on Mexico and rolled back Clinton's approval for Mexican efforts to combat drug trafficking.	2
Enact tough on crime legislation	6—House Republicans passed a juvenile crime bill with opposition from a majority of Democrats (H.R. 3). Liberals opposed the bill, but so did many conservative Republicans over concerns that the bill would curb gun rights. Consequently the Senate could not move a similar package (S. 10) but instead passed a much narrower, bipartisan measure (S. 2073). House Republicans refused to compromise, dooming conferees to failure.	2
Partial-birth abortion ban	2—The Senate failed to override Clinton's veto of a ban on partial-birth abortions (H.R. 1122).	1
Pass the Paycheck Protection Act	5—Differing from Democrats as well as some of their own rank and file about how to address campaign finance reform, Republican leaders favored the Paycheck Protection Act, which would have barred corporations and unions from using dues and fees paid by employees or members for political activities. This bill failed (H.R. 2608) on the Senate floor, however, Senate Republican leaders were also able to block a coalition of Democrats and Republicans from advancing more ambitious campaign finance reform, including H.R. 2183, which passed the House with primarily Democratic votes.	2
Balanced budget amendment	5—The balanced budget amendment (S.J. Res. 1) failed by one vote in the Senate (two-thirds required).	1

(*continued*)

Priority	Outcome 1 = Senate's sixty-vote threshold; 2 = presidential veto; 3 = only one chamber passes; 4 = no formal action; 5 = committee report, no floor action; 6 = House and Senate cannot reconcile their bills	Summary coding 1 = veto player problems; 2 = internal party dissent
Increased NAFTA and WTO oversight	4—With a crowded agenda, no legislative action was taken with respect to NAFTA or the WTO.	2
Military modernization	4—Congressional Republicans sought to balance modernizing the military and military weaponry against cuts to bases and personnel that might be necessary to pay for that modernization. But by the end of the Congress, many Republicans were unwilling to close more bases or increase defense spending dramatically, so little was done to advance modernization.	2
TEAM Act/weakening labor unions	1—House Republicans narrowly passed a bill aimed at undercutting labor unions (H.R. 1) over nearly unanimous opposition from Democrats. Senate Democrats were able to block floor action on similar bills in the Senate (S. 4 and S. 295).	1
Regulatory overhaul (particularly for small businesses)	5—Conservative Republicans opposed a bipartisan measure (S. 981) easing some federal regulations, while conservatives faced opposition from both Democrats and Republicans on their more aggressive proposals.	2
Citizenship Reform Act (reform birthright citizenship)	4—Hearings were held on the Citizenship Reform Act (H.R. 7), but no other action occurred. While the Citizenship Reform Act had some support among Republicans, lack of unanimity on the issue within the GOP, coupled with strong opposition from Democrats, spelled the end for the proposal.	2
Financial services reform and reauthorization	3—House Republicans narrowly passed a Republican-backed bill to revise financial services laws (H.R. 10), but time ran out before the 1998 midterms as the Senate tried to move forward on a bipartisan substitute. This effort paved the way for the Gramm-Leach-Bliley Act in the following Congress.	2
Product liability reform	1—Senate Democrats blocked cloture on a partisan product liability reform measure (S. 648), and no movement was made on a compromise effort.	1

Table A.2 (*continued*)

Priority	Outcome 1 = Senate's sixty-vote threshold; 2 = presidential veto; 3 = only one chamber passes; 4 = no formal action; 5 = committee report, no floor action; 6 = House and Senate cannot reconcile their bills	Summary coding 1 = veto player problems; 2 = internal party dissent
Superfund cleanup acceleration	5—Both chambers began work on Superfund cleanup legislation (S. 8, H.R. 2727, and H.R. 3000), but no measure received floor time in a busy Congress.	2
106th Congress 1999–2000 (Republicans)		
Use the budget surplus for tax cuts and debt reduction	1 and 2—Republicans repeatedly attempted to force through debt reduction and tax cut legislation. Most of the bills were ignored by the Senate (e.g., H.R. 4601, H.R. 3859, H.R. 4866, H.R. 5173, H.R. 5203), and several tax bills were vetoed by President Clinton (e.g., H.R. 8 and H.R. 2488). Another omnibus package (H.R. 2614) was killed by Democratic opposition in the Senate.	1
Expand and speed up completion of missile defense system	4—Congress passed a bill declaring it a US policy to deploy a national missile defense system, but the GOP was never able to get the Clinton administration to accept proposals to speed up or beef up its plans. The annual defense authorizations did not include any proposals to beef up a missile defense system or substantially increase defense spending.	1
ESEA overhaul, including education savings accounts	5 and 2—Congress was unable to pass an ESEA reauthorization. Senate Republicans reported a bill out of committee (S. 2) but pulled it from the floor amid partisan acrimony. House Republicans passed three parts of a larger reauthorization but could not muster enough Republican support in committee to move forward on the rest. On education savings accounts, the Senate passed a bill (S. 1134) with mostly Republican support that would have allowed parents to set aside $2,000 annually in tax-free accounts for educational expenses. A similar House bill (H.R. 7) passed committee but not the chamber amid a Clinton veto threat.	1
Social Security reform and solvency	1—A bill to create a "lockbox" for Social Security funds passed the House with bipartisan support (H.R. 1259), but Democrats blocked cloture on the Senate's bill (S. 557).	1

(*continued*)

Table A.2 *(continued)*

Priority	Outcome 1 = Senate's sixty-vote threshold; 2 = presidential veto; 3 = only one chamber passes; 4 = no formal action; 5 = committee report, no floor action; 6 = House and Senate cannot reconcile their bills	Summary coding 1 = veto player problems; 2 = internal party dissent
Managed care reform (health care)	6—Congress was unable to pass managed care reform/patients' bill of rights legislation as a partisan bill (H.R. 2990/ S. 1344), and a bipartisan package (H.R. 2723) competed for attention and support among Republicans. The partisan package ultimately went to conference but did not emerge among pressure to support the bipartisan alternative and in the face of the looming presidential election.	2
Medicare reform	4—No legislative action was taken in either chamber on broad Medicare reform. The only provision to pass was a "doc fix" as part of an omnibus spending bill (H.R. 4577)	2
Bankruptcy reform	2—A bankruptcy overhaul was passed by Congress with some bipartisan support but was pocket vetoed by President Clinton.	1
Enact partial-birth abortion ban	6—After a SCOTUS ruling that a similar law in Nebraska was unconstitutional, the House (H.R. 3660) and Senate (S. 1692) abandoned bicameral negotiations over their respective bills.	2
Federal elections reform	4—No action taken on a proposal to create an Election Administration Commission to study local, state, and federal voting procedures and election administration, recommend improvements, and provide grants (S. 1).	2
107th Congress 2001–2 (Republicans)		
Health care reform via market solutions and Medicare prescription drug coverage	1 and 6—Two major legislative efforts died different deaths. House Republicans and Senate Democrats passed largely partisan patients' bill of rights proposals and could not reconcile their differences in conference (H.R. 2563 and S. 1052). A bill establishing a Medicare prescription drug program passed the House (H.R. 4954), but Democrats blocked the bill in the Senate.	1
Social Security reform	4—A bipartisan commission on Social Security made recommendations for incorporating personal retirement accounts, but Congress took no action.	2
Pass a domestic energy plan to reduce energy costs and increase oil and gas drilling	6—The Republican-led House and Democratic-led Senate passed very different bills (H.R. 4 and S. 517) and could not reconcile the differences.	1

Priority	Outcome 1 = Senate's sixty-vote threshold; 2 = presidential veto; 3 = only one chamber passes; 4 = no formal action; 5 = committee report, no floor action; 6 = House and Senate cannot reconcile their bills	Summary coding 1 = veto player problems; 2 = internal party dissent
Pass CARE Act of 2002—charitable giving	3—The House passed the CARE Act (H.R. 7), but Democratic opposition to the possibility of religious-based job discrimination essentially sank the bill in the Senate (S. 592), with the Democratic leadership never bringing it to a vote.	1
107th Congress 2001–2 (Democrats)		
Health care—patients' bill of rights and Medicare prescription drug coverage	1 and 6—Two major legislative efforts died different deaths. House Republicans and Senate Democrats passed largely partisan patients' bill of rights proposals and could not reconcile their differences in conference (H.R. 2563 and S. 1052). A bill establishing a Medicare prescription drug program passed the House (H.R. 4954), but Democrats blocked the bill in the Senate.	1
Working families relief (including minimum wage increase, reducing gender pay gap, CHIP expansion)	4—No legislative action took place in a Congress that had its agenda hijacked by the 9/11 terrorist attacks and the war on terror.	2
108th Congress 2003–4 (Republicans)		
Make some Bush tax cuts permanent (especially estate tax)	3—The House passed an estate tax repeal (H.R. 8), but no action was taken in the Senate in the face of opposition from Democrats as well as moderate Republicans concerned about the deficit.	2
Welfare law reauthorization	1—A Republican-backed bill imposing tougher work requirements for welfare passed the House (H.R. 4), but Democrats blocked cloture in the Senate.	1
Pass a domestic energy plan to reduce energy costs and increase oil and gas drilling	1—The Senate was unable to invoke cloture on the conference report for an omnibus domestic energy bill (H.R. 6). Senate Republicans were able to muster only forty-four votes for the measure, demonstrating considerable intraparty disunity on the proposal.	2
Health care liability and lawsuit reform	1—Senate Democrats blocked cloture on three Republican-backed medical malpractice liability bills (S. 11, S. 2061, and S. 2207)	1

(continued)

Priority	Outcome 1 = Senate's sixty-vote threshold; 2 = presidential veto; 3 = only one chamber passes; 4 = no formal action; 5 = committee report, no floor action; 6 = House and Senate cannot reconcile their bills	Summary coding 1 = veto player problems; 2 = internal party dissent
Class-action lawsuit reform	1—Senate Democrats blocked cloture on a Republican-backed bill to move class-action lawsuits to federal courts (H.R. 1115/S. 1751).	1
Expand K-12 school choice and enact Higher Education improvements	4—Some committee action took place on a Higher Education reauthorization, but no other action occurred. Partisan disagreement was apparent from the start on what is typically a bipartisan effort, especially over how to rein in the cost of college tuition, the ability of students to consolidate their student loans, and support for for-profit colleges. Republicans were able to pass only a narrow private school voucher program for the District of Columbia as part of an omnibus spending package (H.R. 2673), with strong opposition from most Democrats.	1
Reduce taxes on charitable foundations but apply new regulations	6—The House and Senate both passed bills to increase charitable deductions for taxpayers (H.R. 7 and S. 476) but were unable to resolve disagreements over funding for the measure. The Senate bill was paid for by closing various business tax loopholes. The House bill contained no offsets.	2
109th Congress 2005–6 (Republicans)		
Limit medical malpractice litigation	1—House Republicans passed a medical malpractice liability bill (H.R. 5), but Democrats blocked cloture on a similar measure in the Senate (S. 22).	1
Social Security overhaul	4—President Bush's top priority to overhaul Social Security never got out of committee in the House or Senate as Republicans could not coalesce behind a plan in the face of strong public pressure.	2
Enact broad entitlement reform	5—Several measures aimed at entitlement and related budgetary reforms were approved by House and Senate committees (e.g., S. 3521, H.R. 4890, H.R. 4297), but none received further action, with limited Democratic support available and internal disagreements within the GOP.	2
Trade rights and litigation policy	4—No action was taken in either chamber on legislation addressing trade rights.	2

Priority	Outcome 1 = Senate's sixty-vote threshold; 2 = presidential veto; 3 = only one chamber passes; 4 = no formal action; 5 = committee report, no floor action; 6 = House and Senate cannot reconcile their bills	Summary coding 1 = veto player problems; 2 = internal party dissent
Reform teen pregnancy and abortion policies	1—The House passed two different bills requiring parental consent for teen abortions (H.R. 748 and S. 403). Senate Democrats blocked cloture on both measures.	1
110th Congress 2007–8 (Democrats)		
Establish federal funding for stem cell research	2—The House and Senate passed a mostly Democratic-backed stem cell research bill (S. 5) but couldn't override President Bush's veto.	1
Medicare drug price negotiation	1—The House passed a Democratic-backed bill (H.R. 4), but Senate Republicans blocked cloture on a more modest Senate measure (S. 3).	1
Establish a new direction in Iraq War	1 and 2—Democrats made several failed attempts to "end" the war in Iraq. H.R. 1591 set a timetable for removing troops from Iraq but was vetoed by President Bush. A couple of attempts to either attach troop withdrawal dates to spending bills or strip funding for military action in Iraq failed cloture in the Senate (including H.R. 4156 and H.R. 2764).	1
Comprehensive immigration reform	1—The Senate was unable to invoke cloture on several bipartisan immigration measures backed by President Bush, including those to create a guest worker program, to create a path to citizenship, and to protect undocumented children of immigrants (e.g., S. 1348, S. 1639, and S. 2205). Senate Democrats were split on all three measures, which denied proponents the necessary sixty votes.	2
Health care reform/health care costs and access	2 and 4—A Democratic push to expand SCHIP (H.R. 979 and H.R. 3963) was vetoed by President Bush. No legislative action was taken in either chamber on broader health care reform measures.	1
Retirement security	4—No legislative action was taken on this priority in either chamber.	2
Increase congressional oversight of the executive branch	4—No legislative action taken on legislation to improve congressional oversight of the Bush administration.	2

(*continued*)

Priority	Outcome 1 = Senate's sixty-vote threshold; 2 = presidential veto; 3 = only one chamber passes; 4 = no formal action; 5 = committee report, no floor action; 6 = House and Senate cannot reconcile their bills	Summary coding 1 = veto player problems; 2 = internal party dissent
111th Congress 2009–10 (Democrats)		
Energy independence/ climate change legislation	3—The House passed comprehensive climate change legislation, but with over forty Democrats opposing it and needing Republican votes for passage (H.R. 2454). Senate efforts stalled as Democrats were unable to coalesce behind specific proposals (including S. 1462 and S. 1733).	2
New direction with war on terror/Iraq and Afghanistan	4—No action taken to establish a new direction in Iraq or Afghanistan. Democrats ended up reluctantly backing continued war funding. The 2002 AUMF was not repealed or amended. Generally, Democrats did not make a serious attempt to shift policy in Iraq or Afghanistan during the 111th Congress.	2
Comprehensive immigration reform	1—No action was taken on a broad path- to-citizenship measure in either chamber (H.R. 1751). A bill to provide legal status to undocumented children of immigrants (H.R. 5281) passed the House, but Republicans blocked cloture in the Senate.	1
Modernize and rebuild the military	4—Several controversies unrelated to military spending, including a proposed "don't ask, don't tell" repeal and various domestic spending provisions tacked on by House Democrats dragged negotiations over the 2010 defense bill into December. Ultimately, congressional Democrats made no attempt to use the bill to modernize or rebuild the military because the legislative agenda was consumed by other issues.	2
Retirement security	4—With an overcrowded agenda, House and Senate Democrats did not make any progress on retirement security.	2
Oppose Bush administration midnight regulations	4—No action was taken in either chamber to block or roll back late Bush-era regulatory actions.	2
112th Congress 2011–12 (Republicans)		
Repeal and replace the Affordable Care Act	3—The House passed several Republican- backed measures to dismantle the ACA, but none were considered in the Democratic-controlled Senate.	1

Table A.2 (*continued*)

Priority	Outcome 1 = Senate's sixty-vote threshold; 2 = presidential veto; 3 = only one chamber passes; 4 = no formal action; 5 = committee report, no floor action; 6 = House and Senate cannot reconcile their bills	Summary coding 1 = veto player problems; 2 = internal party dissent
Social Security solvency	4—Cuts and changes to entitlement programs were floated by Republicans as part of a fiscal "grand bargain," but nothing of the sort was enacted. Ultimately Social Security reforms were not seriously considered in either chamber.	2
Restrict taxpayer funding for abortions	3—Several Republican-backed efforts to prohibit federal funding for abortions passed the House (including H.R. 3) but were not considered in the Democratic-controlled Senate.	1
Regulatory reform	3—House Republicans passed a bill requiring congressional approval for major regulations issued by the executive branch, but it was not taken up in the Democratic-controlled Senate (H.R. 10, REINS Act).	1
Cut taxes on small businesses	3—House Republicans passed a small-business tax cut bill, but it went nowhere in the Democratic-controlled Senate (H.R. 9).	1
112th Congress 2011–12 (Democrats)		
Pass a second economic stimulus and job creation bill	1—Senate Republicans successfully filibustered the Obama administration's $447 billion stimulus plan (S. 1660).	1
Comprehensive immigration reform	4—No formal action on any "comprehensive" immigration reform measures took place in either chamber, as the congressional agenda was consumed by spending and fiscal crises.	2
Climate change/renewable energy legislation	4—Senate Democrats took no formal steps to advance climate change or renewable energy proposals with a congressional agenda lurching from fiscal crisis to fiscal crisis.	2
Replace No Child Left Behind (Elementary and Secondary Education Act reauthorization)	5—Committees in both chambers advanced replacements for No Child Left Behind. The Senate HELP Committee forwarded a bipartisan measure (S. 3578), while the House Committee on Education and the Workforce advanced two Republican-backed measures (H.R. 3989 and H.R. 3990). The parties remained far apart on this issue, but House Republicans were also divided, unable to find the support even to bring their committee bill to the floor for a vote.	2

(*continued*)

Priority	Outcome 1 = Senate's sixty-vote threshold; 2 = presidential veto; 3 = only one chamber passes; 4 = no formal action; 5 = committee report, no floor action; 6 = House and Senate cannot reconcile their bills	Summary coding 1 = veto player problems; 2 = internal party dissent
Broad cybersecurity reform	1—The House passed a measure (H.R. 3523) with some support from both Democrats and Republicans. Senate Republicans blocked a Democratic-backed bill in the Senate (S. 3414).	1
Filibuster reform	1—Reid and McConnell made a "gentlemen's agreement" on the filibuster, but it faded throughout the two-year session. Other proposals to reform filibuster rules failed to reach the necessary two-thirds threshold for adoption. Even Democratic senators were split on these proposals, which failed to garner even fifty votes (S. Con. Res. 10 and S. Con. Res. 21).	2
DISCLOSE Act reforms	1—Senate Republicans blocked cloture on the Democrats' DISCLOSE Act (S. 3369), which would have required more groups spending money in elections to disclose their donors.	1
Help women in the workforce (pay equity, family leave, child care, etc.)	1—Cloture on the Democrats' Paycheck Fairness Act (S. 3220) was blocked by Senate Republicans.	1

113th Congress 2013–14 (Republicans)

Deficit reduction (tied to debt limit)	4—After the drama of the 112th Congress, Republicans seemed unwilling and unable to take any action to advance legislation tying deficit reduction measures to a debt-limit increase. The Republican leadership in both chambers ultimately backed a clean debt-limit bill.	2
Replace No Child Left Behind (Elementary and Secondary Education Act reauthorization)	3—House Republicans passed a partisan bill (H.R. 5), Senate Democrats did not advance their ESEA reauthorization bill (S. 1094).	1
Increase energy independence and domestic energy production	3—House Republicans passed several bills rolling back energy regulations (including H.R. 2 and H.R. 2728). The Senate tried to work on a bipartisan measure but failed over concerns of budget offsets.	1
Broad tax overhaul	4—Ways and Means chairman Dave Camp (R-MI) unveiled a tax overhaul (H.R. 1) late in the Congress, but there was not enough time to take any serious action on it.	2

Priority	Outcome 1 = Senate's sixty-vote threshold; 2 = presidential veto; 3 = only one chamber passes; 4 = no formal action; 5 = committee report, no floor action; 6 = House and Senate cannot reconcile their bills	Summary coding 1 = veto player problems; 2 = internal party dissent
Health entitlement reform (Medicare)	4—No action was taken in either chamber to reform entitlement spending.	2
Restrict taxpayer funding for abortions	3—A House bill to prohibit the use of federal funds for abortions passed the Republican-controlled House (H.R. 7) but was not taken up in the Democratic-controlled Senate.	1
113th Congress 2013–14 (Democrats)		
Replace No Child Left Behind (Elementary and Secondary Education Act reauthorization)	3—House Republicans passed a partisan bill (H.R. 5); Senate Democrats did not advance their ESEA reauthorization bill (S. 1094).	1
Pass new gun control legislation	1—Several gun control measures opposed by most Republicans failed sixty-vote thresholds in the Senate (S. 649).	1
Voting and campaign finance reform	4—Democrats never seemed to get started on a reauthorization of the Voting Rights Act or on any campaign finance proposals.	2
Comprehensive immigration reform	3—The Senate passed a bipartisan immigration reform and border security bill (S. 744), but House Republicans declined to take up the bill.	1
Deficit reduction (vague)	4—Both parties discussed deficit reduction plans, but no formal legislative action was taken in either chamber.	2
Increase workers' wages and compensation	1—Republicans blocked cloture on a minimum wage increase in the Senate (S. 1737) and blocked Democratic attempts to force action in the House.	1
Bolster US tech innovation	4—A lot of discussion occurred, but no action was taken on a package of Democratic proposals.	2
114th Congress 2015–16 (Republicans)		
Keystone XL pipeline approval	2—The Republican-controlled House and Senate passed a Keystone XL pipeline approval bill with limited Democratic support (S. 1), but an override vote failed in the Senate after Obama's veto.	1
Repeal and replace the Affordable Care Act	2—House and Senate Republicans used budget reconciliation to send an ACA repeal to Obama's desk with almost no Democratic support (H.R. 3762). It was vetoed, and an override vote in the House fell far short.	1

(*continued*)

Priority	Outcome 1 = Senate's sixty-vote threshold; 2 = presidential veto; 3 = only one chamber passes; 4 = no formal action; 5 = committee report, no floor action; 6 = House and Senate cannot reconcile their bills	Summary coding 1 = veto player problems; 2 = internal party dissent
Broad tax overhaul	4—Ways and Means chair Dave Camp (R-MI) unveiled a tax reform package in late 2014 (Tax Reform Act of 2014), but internal disagreements among Republicans over whether tax reform was possible or a priority, coupled with fierce opposition from Democrats, prevented any further action.	2
Pass an infrastructure and energy bill expanding domestic energy production	6—The House and Senate both advanced omnibus energy security and infrastructure bills (H.R. 8 and S. 2012). Conferees were unable to resolve differences between the more partisan House bill and the more bipartisan Senate bill, with House conferees unwilling to make the concessions necessary to get Democratic votes in the Senate.	2
Approve Trans-Pacific Partnership trade deal	4—After a lot of debate, neither chamber took action to approve the Trans-Pacific Partnership trade deal. Disagreements existed within both parties over whether TPP was the right move.	2
Prohibit federal funding for abortion	1—The House passed H.R. 7 on a party-line vote. Senate Democrats blocked cloture on a similar measure in the Senate (S. 1881).	1
Patent reform	5—House and Senate committees advanced patent reform bills with initial bipartisan support (H.R. 9 and S. 1137). However, the effort halted amid lobbying efforts from industries opposed to the measure and concerns among some Republicans that the overhaul might unwittingly hurt patent holders.	2
115th Congress 2017–18 (Republicans)		
Obamacare repeal and replace	3—The House passed an Obamacare repeal and replace bill (H.R. 1628), but the Senate was unable to clear one, despite the use of budget reconciliation procedures that prohibited filibusters.	2
Domestic spending cuts	3—House passed H.R. 3 rescinding $15 billion in budget authority. But the Senate declined to move forward owing to the opposition of two Republican senators, depriving Senate Republicans of a majority.	2

Priority	Outcome 1 = Senate's sixty-vote threshold; 2 = presidential veto; 3 = only one chamber passes; 4 = no formal action; 5 = committee report, no floor action; 6 = House and Senate cannot reconcile their bills	Summary coding 1 = veto player problems; 2 = internal party dissent
Reform of agency rule making	3—The House passed H.R. 5 reforming the rule-making process, but the Senate declined to advance a companion bill from committee.	2
End taxpayer funding of abortion	3—The House passed H.R. 7 prohibiting qualified health plans under the ACA from covering abortions, but the Senate did not consider a similar measure.	2

Table A.3 Descriptions of majority party priority success cases and coding

Priority	How it succeeded

99th Congress 1985–86 (Republicans)

Reduce the federal budget/cut spending	*Back down*: Republicans had to back down on some of their most controversial proposals, including proposals to increase defense spending and establish COLA reductions for Social Security.

99th Congress 1985–86 (Democrats)

Tax reform/reduce budget deficit	*Seek broad support/Back down*: Democratic leaders on tax reform, particularly Rep. Rostenkowski, and the Reagan White House set out to find a point of compromise on tax reform from the start of the process. Nonetheless, Democrats had to back off from various aspects of the original House bill, including lower overall tax rates for high-income Americans than originally proposed, to secure final passage (H.R. 3838).
Reauthorize the farm bill	*Back down*: Both sides eyed broad changes to farm subsidies, but they settled for a pared-down bill that reauthorized farm programs but did not make the sweeping changes talked about at the start of the Congress.
Reduce unemployment through job training	*Seek broad support*: Democrats proposed an expansion of the popular Job Training Partnership Act to send more money to states for job training programs, winning support on both sides of the aisle.
Pursue arms control with the Soviets	*Back down*: Democrats backed off from the proposals to eliminate or curtail several controversial weapons programs but were able to get reductions in MC missile funding.
Increase child nutrition programs	*Seek broad support*: Democrats started the Congress proposing a much smaller increase to child nutrition programs than they did in the previous Congress but still faced Republican opposition. The increases were eventually attached to the 1987 defense authorization to ease passage (H.R. 7).
Reauthorize the Water Resources Development Act	*Seek broad support*: Democrats backed down from the price tag on the House bill ($20 billion reduced to $16 billion), but there was broad support in Congress for new funding for water projects.
Pass armor-piercing bullet ban	*Seek broad support*: A ban on so-called cop-killer bullets found only limited opposition from the more fervent gun-rights lawmakers and passed both chambers overwhelmingly.
Reauthorize programs under the Coastal Zone Management Act	*Back down*: Democrats had to agree to freeze spending on the Coastal Zone Management programs in order to ease its passage.

100th Congress 1987–88 (Democrats)

Reduce the budget deficit with budget reforms	*Back down*: Democrats aimed to reduce the deficit through a combination of tax increases and cuts to defense spending, but this engendered opposition from Republicans. The final legislation setting spending and revenue limits for 1988 and 1989 resulted from a "budget summit" with President Reagan and did not go as far as Democrats initially wanted.
Reauthorize the Elementary and Secondary Education Act	*Seek broad support*: Democrats successfully drafted and passed a broadly supported, bipartisan ESEA reauthorization.

Priority	How it succeeded
Reauthorize clean water programs	*Seek broad support:* After years of failing to reauthorize the nation's clean water programs, Democrats sought to draft passable legislation, and Reagan's veto was overturned with strong support in both parties (H.R. 1).
Reorganize Farm Credit System and provide aid to farmers	*Seek broad support:* With the nation's farm credit system in crisis, both parties worked toward a solution. Battle lines in the fight centered on two cross-party coalitions. In the end, everyone worked toward a compromise to provide for the most complete reorganization in the seventy-one-year history of the Farm Credit System (H.R. 3030).
Ratify two US-Soviet treaties limiting nuclear weapons (INF treaty and ABM treaty)	*Back down:* The Senate focused on the popular INF treaty, ratifying it with broad bipartisan support, but avoided a potentially more contentious and partisan fight on an ABM treaty.
Reauthorize surface transportation programs	*Steamroll:* Democrats were able to push their surface transportation bill through, getting most of what they wanted with an overall price tag matching that of a bill passing the House in the previous Congress. In the Senate, Reagan's veto of the measure was overridden by two votes, despite personal pressure from Reagan to line up votes against the override (H.R. 2). This was a big win for Democrats and an embarrassment for the president.
Enact legislation to address and fix the country's savings and loan crisis	*Back down:* Congress met its goal on the first bailout, but congressional leadership couldn't spur action a second bailout.
Establish a national policy to deal with the AIDS crisis	*Back down:* Democrats backed down on provisions to provide for confidentiality and protect against discrimination in order to get the bill passed and ensure the president's support.
Reauthorize and reform housing assistance programs	*Back down:* House Democrats originally aimed for over $25 billion in spending on housing assistance programs but settled for closer to $15 billion.
Establish "effective schools" and "even start" programs	*Seek broad support:* The Effective Schools and Even Start Act was broadly supported by both parties and was included as part of a larger omnibus education bill with little controversy.
Address national air transportation problems (e.g., delays, safety, and concerns over mergers) by reauthorizing and revising airline policies	*Back down:* Democrats had to drop consumer protection provisions in order to pass the law.
Take action on pay equity, reducing discrimination and inequities in both pay and federal benefits (including Social Security)	*Back down:* The final bill was enacted after compromises over provisions to reduce welfare dependency and mandate welfare coverage for poor two-parent families.

(*continued*)

Table A.3 (*continued*)

Priority	How it succeeded
101st Congress 1989–90 (Democrats)	
Pass a new clean air bill	*Seek broad support/Back down*: A clean air bill was an area of agreement between the Bush White House and congressional Democrats, so they worked to develop a compromise proposal from the start. Negotiations over the final bill took almost two years, with both sides giving and taking.
Renew low-income housing assistance and homelessness programs	*Back down*: House Democrats had to back down from a provision in their bill that would have allowed for far more spending on housing and homeless programs and for more new housing construction. The final package looked much more like the compromise Senate measure.
Raise the minimum wage	*Back down*: Bush's veto compelled Democrats to settle for a lower minimum wage, subminimum wages for some workers, and other compromises.
Pass affordable child care legislation	*Logroll with opposition/Back down*: After a long battle, both sides got some of what they wanted and both sides backed down. Democrats preferred federal grants to subsidize child care costs, while the Bush administration preferred tax credits and deductions. The final bill included some of each, with Democrats settling for less overall spending than they hoped and the White House accepting more federal standards than it liked.
Pass congressional ethics reform, including honorarium ban	*Back down*: Proponents of ethics reform had to settle for an ethics reform package that accomplished less than the lofty goals of the House task force.
Budget deficit reduction	*Back down*: Facing automatic sequester from Gramm-Rudman kicking in, both sides were motivated to make a deal on deficit reduction. House Democrats passed a "soak the rich" bill on a party-line vote.
Combat drugs on streets and in schools/fully fund existing antidrug programs	*Back down*: Democrats had an ambitious antidrug agenda and succeeded in enacting a lot of it, including increased funding for antidrug programs and the establishment of new antidrug education programs. However, other efforts, including attempts to establish new prevention and treatment programs, were dropped in bicameral negotiations.
Pass legislation requiring Congress to be notified of any covert CIA action within forty-eight hours of its being planned	*Back down*: Democrats wanted legislation requiring the president to inform Congress about any CIA covert operations within forty-eight hours of its being planned but settled for an informal deal in which the Bush administration promised to keep Congress apprised.
Establish a program of voluntary national service	*Back down/Logroll with opposition*: Efforts to establish a program of voluntary national service required both compromise and logrolling to get passed. Democrats had to settle for less than half the cost of the program initially proposed, and the Bush administration's prioritized "Points of Light" foundation had to be included to get the White House on board.
Improve the quality of US health care	*Back down*: Democrats set out to dramatically expand Medicaid but settled for modest increases in the program's funding.

Table A.3 (*continued*)

Priority	How it succeeded
Increase investment in early childhood education	*Steamroll*: Democrats pushed through dramatic increases in Head Start funding, which Bush signed despite his reservations.
Restrict foreign ownership/ acquisitions	*Back down*: Without enough support, congressional Democrats could not move forward with a bill restricting foreign ownership of US companies, and they settled for less ambitious legislation.
Expand vocational and applied tech educational programs	*Seek broad support*: Vocational education programs had broad support in both parties, and a reauthorization and expansion passed easily.

102nd Congress 1991–92 (Democrats)

Priority	How it succeeded
Provide a cost-of-living increase to disabled veterans	*Seek broad support*: Though some lawmakers wanted to attach additional compensation for veterans with cancer caused by Agent Orange, an agreement to consider the proposals separately led to the quick enactment of a COLA increase.
Reform the bank insurance deposit system	*Back down*: House Democrats, working with the Bush administration, twice tried to pass a broad banking overhaul including language permitting interstate branching (H.R. 6). Both attempts failed, with opposition coming from both parties. Negotiators settled for a narrower bill aimed at shoring up the FDIC (S. 543).
Restore antidiscrimination employment laws	*Steamroll*: Republicans dropped their opposition to antidiscrimination legislation in the wake of the Anita Hill controversy. Democrats made only minor concessions, including agreeing to a ceiling on monetary awards for damages.
Reauthorize surface transportation programs	*Logroll with opposition*: Democrats and the Bush White House could both claim victory, each getting something of what they wanted. Democrats got more direct federal money for projects than Bush wanted. Bush got more flexibility for states and incentives for private-sector investment.
Reform the unemployment compensation system	*Back down/Steamroll*: Democrats were able to pressure Bush into accepting a broad unemployment compensation bill. This was a big win for Democrats, but they had to agree to fewer permanent changes to the unemployment compensation system to get Bush's final sign-off.
Expand federal job training programs	*Seek broad support*: Democrats, led by Sen. Kennedy and Sen. Ford, sought to develop a broadly supported bill to amend and improve the Job Training Partnership Act. The final bill was seen as an all-around success, strengthening and clarifying federal regulations, closing loopholes, and targeting aid to those most in need.
Pass energy independence legislation, including energy conservation policies	*Back down*: Both sides set aside debates over more controversial items, including offshore and ANWR drilling, fuel efficiency standards for automobiles, and energy taxes aimed at curbing consumption. The final bill represented areas of agreement between the parties but was seen as a missed opportunity to make bigger strides.
Tax deadline extension for troops in Iraq	*Seek broad support*: Virtually no opposition existed to a popular proposal to extend the tax deadline for troops fighting in Iraq.

(*continued*)

Table A.3 (*continued*)

Priority	How it succeeded
103rd Congress 1993–94 (Democrats)	
Pass legislation guaranteeing family and medical leave	*Seek broad support*: With a Democratic president, the Family Leave Act, which had broad support among Democrats and many Republicans, was easily enacted into law.
Expand national voter registration/Enact Motor Voter	*Steamroll*: Democrats had to back down on only one provision included in previous iterations of the bill (which would have required registration forms to be available in unemployment offices). Otherwise, with a Democratic president, Motor Voter sailed to passage with limited Republican support.
NIH reauthorization	*Seek broad support*: The Democrats' NIH reauthorization proposal was broadly supported (minus a few provisions drawing opposition from House Republicans). With a Democratic president it was easily enacted.
Reduce the federal deficit	*Back down*: Democrats had to negotiate entirely among factions within their own party. Liberals had to agree to cuts to Medicare, and some conservative Democrats were unhappy with many of the tax provisions. In the end, everyone got something and gave up something to get the proposal enacted.
Revise and reauthorize the Elementary and Secondary Education Act	*Back down*: Democrats had to settle for a smaller redistribution of education dollars and had to drop proposed mandatory "opportunity to learn" standards in order to gain support among Republicans and conservative Democrats.
Enact legislation combating crime, drugs, and violence	*Steamroll/Back down*: Democrats pushed through an omnibus crime bill over the opposition of the Republican leadership. The final bill looked a lot like the initial proposal, but Democrats had to make some important concessions including reducing the overall price tag of the bill and adjusting several provisions. Nonetheless, they never gave up much to the Republicans along the way.
Reauthorize child nutrition and school lunch programs	*Seek broad support*: Reauthorization of child nutrition programs was uncontroversial.
104th Congress 1995–96 (Republicans)	
Establish a line-item veto	*Seek broad support*: The line-item veto was popular among Republicans and enough Democrats (including Clinton) to pass easily in both chambers.
Pass congressional rules reforms and reorganization	*Seek broad support/Back down*: Most of the reforms proposed by House Republicans were popular in both parties.
Pass tough on crime legislation	*Seek broad support/Back down*: House Republicans passed six different crime proposals. Those that made it into law either were broadly popular in both parties or were watered down before final enactment.
Unfunded mandates reform	*Seek broad support*: Unfunded mandates reform found broad support in both parties. A few minor details required negotiations, but this was one of the first Contract with America planks enacted into law.

Priority	How it succeeded
Welfare reform	*Back down*: After Clinton twice vetoed welfare reform packages that had little Democratic support, Republicans narrowed the scope of reform, including removing language to reform Medicaid, in order to gain some Democratic support and a signature from Clinton.
Expand NATO/Reduce US payments to UN and involvement in UN peacekeeping	*Back down*: Republicans originally wanted to require NATO to take in several Soviet bloc counties and reduce US payments to and involvement in UN activities. However, they had to settle for watered-down language promoting the inclusion of Soviet bloc counties, and they were unable to alter US involvement in the UN.
Raise the Social Security senior citizens earnings limits	*Seek broad support*: Raising the Social Security earnings limit was a popular proposal in both parties.
Securities litigation reform	*Seek broad support*: The proposal was popular among Republicans and many Democrats and passed easily.
Enact broad spending cuts	*Back down*: Republicans had to settle for much smaller spending cuts than they had promoted during the 1994 campaign, securing about $22 billion in cuts for FY 1996 (and even less for FY 1997) compared with initial proposals of over $100 billion in cuts.
Expand and speed up completion of missile defense system	*Back down*: House Republicans included an ambitious missile defense proposal in H.R. 7 but could not move forward with it in the Senate. Ultimately they were only able to secure some increases in funding for antimissile defense, and Clinton's deployment plan remained untouched.

105th Congress 1997–98 (Republicans)

Priority	How it succeeded
Enact tax cuts	*Back down*: Republicans backed down on their demands for much larger tax cuts in seeking a compromise with the Clinton White House.
Deficit reduction/ balanced budget	*Logroll with opposition*: Republicans had to agree to include several Democratic Party priorities to get this passed, including a new children's health initiative costing $20 billion, child tax credit provisions that matched the Clinton administration's goals, a restoration of some welfare benefits, and more.
Enact education reform including school aid and school choice	*Back down*: Republicans backed off their more controversial proposals on education savings accounts and school choice to pass some bipartisan education proposals.
Working Families Flexibility/comp time and flex time for working families	*Back down*: Republicans backed down on some of the core provisions of the Working Families Flexibility Act and passed a child tax credit.
Surface transportation reauthorization	*Back down*: Negotiations between Republican leadership and Transportation Committee Republicans resulting in both sides' compromising and producing TEA-21.
Expand and speed up completion of a national missile defense system	*Back down*: Republicans were able to secure billions in funding for a national missile defense system but couldn't get the Clinton White House to accept an ambitious enough plan to implement such a system.

(*continued*)

Table A.3 (*continued*)

Priority	How it succeeded
Individuals with Disabilities Education Act reauthorization	*Seek broad support*: Republicans sought to produce a bipartisan IDEA reauthorization after failing to pass a more partisan proposal in the previous Congress.
Streamline child adoption processes	*Seek broad support*: Proponents sought to produce a bipartisan proposal on child adoption and were successful.
Public housing reform	*Back down*: House Republicans backed off from their proposal to repeal the Housing Act and agreed to a more modest proposal advanced in the Senate to replace public housing programs with block grants.
Higher Education reauthorization and reform	*Seek broad support*: Republicans sought to produce a bipartisan Higher Education reauthorization.
Pass the Border Smog Reduction Act, prohibiting foreign vehicles from repeatedly crossing the border	*Seek broad support*: The Border Smog Reduction Act was popular with both parties.

106th Congress 1999–2000 (Republicans)

Complete Clinton impeachment proceedings	*Steamroll*: Republicans pushed the impeachment proceedings through to their completion, though they didn't get their preferred outcome.
Support faith-based charities	*Logroll with opposition*: The charitable choice provisions Republicans secured were part of a broader logroll with Democrats to pass an omnibus antipoverty measure at the end of the 106th Congress.
Repeal Social Security earnings test	*Seek broad support*: A proposal to eliminate the Social Security earnings test was popular with both Democrats and Republicans.
Financial services reforms and reauthorization	*Back down*: Republicans had to back down on some of their more conservative proposals regarding financial services reform to pass Gramm-Leach-Bliley.
Increase spending to fight the drug trade	*Logroll with opposition*: Republicans we able to get new funds to fight the drug trade included as part of a broader supplemental spending deal with Democrats.

107th Congress 2001–2 (Republicans)

Revise and reauthorize the Elementary and Secondary Education Act	*Back down*: Both Republicans and Democrats had to back down on some of their preferred outcomes. Democrats got less money than they aimed for but more than Republicans proposed. Republicans got more testing tied to funding but did not get block grants or private school vouchers.
Enact broad tax cuts	*Back down*: Republicans had to back down on some of their proposals to gain Democratic votes, including tilting the cuts more toward the lower end of the income spectrum and agreeing to sunsets for most of the package.
Expand and speed up completion of missile defense system	*Steamroll*: After 9/11 Democrats couldn't fight against national security proposals.
Increase military funding	*Steamroll*: After 9/11 Democrats couldn't fight against national security proposals.

Table A.3 (*continued*)

Priority	How it succeeded
Pass the Railroad Retirement and Survivors' Improvement Act of 2001	*Seek broad support*: Republicans' proposal to reform railroad retirement policies was popular in both parties.

107th Congress 2001–2 (Democrats)

Broad tax reform	*Back down*: Republicans had to back down on some of their proposals to gain Democratic votes, including tilting the cuts more toward the lower end of the income spectrum and agreeing to sunsets for most of the package. Democrats remained unhappy with the size and scope of the package.
Revise and reauthorize the Elementary and Secondary Education Act	*Back down*: Both Republicans and Democrats had to back down on some of their preferred outcomes. Democrats got less money than they aimed for but more than Republicans proposed. Republicans got more testing tied to funding but did not get block grants or private school vouchers.

108th Congress 2003–4 (Republicans)

Establish Medicare prescription drug coverage	*Steamroll*: Republican leaders had to negotiate with conservatives to keep them on board, adding Health Savings Accounts to the bill, but were able to push Medicare Part D through with limited Democratic support.
Pass Bush tax cuts part 2/tax reform	*Back down*: Republicans had to back down on the original size of the proposal and find a way to coalesce support between conservatives who wanted a big cut and moderates concerned about the deficit.
Expand war on terror/ provide war spending	*Steamroll*: With the 2004 elections looming, Democrats found it hard to opposed war funding.
Regulatory and tax relief for businesses	*Seek broad support*: Senate Republicans worked to build a bipartisan bill.
Enact unemployment benefits extension	*Seek broad support*: With the president in support, passage of an extension was uncontroversial.
Homeland security amendments	*Seek broad support*: Both parties agreed to uncontroversial proposals to provide lots of money to DHS while avoiding more dicey debates over how best to oversee and alter the new department
Promote US trade and exports (two cases)	*Seek broad support*: The trade agreements were not highly controversial, even though they were opposed by a good number of Democrats.
Intelligence reform and counterterrorism/ enact 9/11 Commission recommendations	*Seek broad support*: Recommendations from the 9/11 Commission found broad support on Capitol Hill.
Pass the partial-birth abortion ban	*Steamroll*: Few concessions were made along the way to passing this bill. Just enough Democratic support was found to ensure passage.

(*continued*)

Table A.3 (*continued*)

Priority	How it succeeded
109th Congress 2005–6 (Republicans)	
Pass a domestic energy plan to reduce energy costs and increase oil and gas drilling	*Back down*: Republicans had to drop their plan to open up ANWR for oil drilling in the face of Democratic opposition.
Enact a tax overhaul and make Bush tax cuts permanent	*Back down*: Republican leaders had to scale back their plans for the Bush tax cuts owing to disagreements between moderates and conservatives about extending many of the cuts and paying for the extensions.
Reauthorize surface transportation programs	*Seek broad support*: Republicans began the process seeking to a build a surface transportation bill that could garner broad support.
Pass class-action lawsuit and tort reform	*Back down*: Republicans made some limited concessions to gain the support of enough Senate Democrats to push the proposal across the finish line.
PATRIOT Act partial reauthorization	*Back down*: Republicans had to agree to several compromises, most notably imposing sunsets on several provisions, to get Democratic support for passage in the Senate.
Continue Iraq and Afghanistan war spending	*Steamroll*: Democrats couldn't object to continued funding for the troops in Iraq and Afghanistan.
Pass workforce training and related education legislation	*Seek broad support*: A proposal to renew vocational and tech education programs was popular in both parties.
Enact pension reform	*Seek broad support/Back down*: Republicans largely sought to make a proposal that could garner bipartisan support in the face of a looming pension crisis, garnering the support of some unions (notably the UAW). Nevertheless, Democrats forced some concessions in the Senate and Republicans had to give up on their plan to couple the pension bill with various tax measures.
Reauthorize the Voting Rights Act	*Seek broad support*: A bill to renew the VRA was uncontroversial in both parties.
110th Congress 2007–8 (Democrats)	
Student loan interest rate reduction	*Seek broad support*: Democrats proposed a popular policy on student loan interest rates that many Republicans supported or felt compelled to support.
Repeal oil industry tax breaks and bolster renewable energy	*Back down*: Democrats backed down on proposals to create renewable energy standards and proposals to reduce tax incentives for oil and gas and shift them to renewable energy sources.
Pass congressional ethics/lobbying reform	*Seek broad support/Back down*: Most of the reform proposals on lobbying were popular and had broad support in both parties. Democratic leaders had to acquiesce to the demands of some conservatives on earmark reform to get the final package through.
Pass a minimum wage increase coupled with small-business tax breaks	*Logroll with opposition*: Democrats had to give Republicans larger small-business tax breaks to get their minimum wage bill through.

Table A.3 *(continued)*

Priority	How it succeeded
Enact 9/11 Commission recommendations alongside port security funding increase	*Back down*: Democrats had to give in to Republican demands on several fronts, including how DHS grants would be distributed and the nature of labor rights for TSA agents to get the bill across the finish line.
Pass PAYGO	*Steamroll*: Without needing a presidential signature, Democrats were able to push through new PAYGO rules with little Republican support.
Rebuild and modernize the military	*Seek broad support*: Democrats primarily proposed popular policies to increase pay and benefits to soldiers and veterans. Some concessions had to be made to the Bush White House before passage.
Enact FISA reforms	*Back down*: Democrats largely had to back down on their goals of expanding civil liberties protections and rolling back immunity for telecommunications companies that cooperated with the Bush administration.

111th Congress 2009–10 (Democrats)

Pass an economic stimulus package	*Back down*: Democrats backed down on the size and scope of the stimulus proposal in order to get enough Republican votes to pass it in the Senate.
Enact comprehensive health care reform	*Steamroll*: Democratic leaders and the Obama White House had to back down on proposals for a public option and spending on abortion services to keep Democrats united and pass the ACA. However, the bill got Democrats a once-in-a-generation victory on health care reform.
Broad financial sector reform and mortgage relief (Dodd-Frank)	*Steamroll*: Democrats got most of what they set out to get with Dodd-Frank, and they pushed it through despite strong Republican opposition.
SCHIP reauthorization	*Seek broad support*: With a new Democratic president, Democrats could propose and get what they wanted on SCHIP.
Address college costs and affordability	*Back down*: Democrats had to scale back funding for community colleges after a CBO score downgraded the expected savings in other provisions of the bill meant to free up revenues.
Gender pay equity legislation	*Seek broad support/Back down*: The Lilly Ledbetter Fair Pay Act was a popular proposal that could sail through with a Democratic president ready to sign. However, Democrats had to give in on broader legislation making it easier for women to allege discrimination in the workplace.

112th Congress 2011–12 (Republicans)

Cut federal spending and preserve Bush-era tax cuts (for deficit reduction)	*Back down/Logroll with opposition*: Throughout the two years, Republicans had to give in to Democratic demands on defense spending cuts and eliminates' some Bush tax cuts to get some of what they wanted in cuts to domestic nondefense spending and an extension of the Bush tax cuts for most Americans.
Reauthorize surface transportation programs/reform the Highway Trust Fund	*Back down*: Republicans had to back down on more controversial proposals in the partisan House bill, including their plans to increase revenues through new oil and gas leases and an increase in federal employees' contributions to their pensions.

(continued)

Table A.3 (*continued*)

Priority	How it succeeded
Broad tax overhaul	*Back down*: Republicans backed down from their ambitious proposals to reform the tax code (primarily to expand the tax base) but preserved most of the Bush tax cuts.
Congressional process reforms	*Back down*: Without support from Democrats, Republicans had to back off from their more ambitious bicameral budget process reforms.

112th Congress 2011–12 (Democrats)

End Bush-era tax cuts for rich and preserve federal spending	*Back down/Logroll with opposition*: The fiscal cliff deal enabled Democrats to win a victory rolling back the Bush tax cuts for the richest Americans, but they had to give in to Republican demands on discretionary spending cuts.
Reauthorize surface transportation programs/reform the Highway Trust Fund	*Back down/Seek broad support*: Senate Democrats sought to propose a modest, bipartisan bill from the start. However, they had to back down on the length of their proposal to get it passed. Democrats had primarily sought a long-term extension.

113th Congress 2013–14 (Democrats)

Reauthorize the Violence against Women Act	*Steamroll*: Democrats' proposal to reauthorize VAWA wasn't something Republicans could oppose politically. Democrats got everything they wanted.
Reauthorize the farm bill	*Seek broad support/Back down*: Democrats sought to build a bipartisan package in the Senate, moving closer to Republican positions on new farm program funding and embracing bigger cuts to SNAP than they had previously been willing to accept (~$8 billion in cuts—though far less than the $20–40 billion proposed by House Republicans).
Pass Hurricane Sandy relief and aid	*Back down*: Democrats had to agree to a smaller package than they initially proposed to please House conservatives and gain passage.
Reauthorize surface transportation programs	*Back down*: Everyone backed down as Congress passed only a short-term extension of the highway bill.
Expand veterans' benefits	*Back down*: Democrats were able to secure only increases in health care spending for veterans and couldn't make any progress on other veterans' benefits.
Climate change/ renewable energy legislation	*Back down/seek broad support*: Democrats couldn't get most of what they wanted, but Republicans agreed to an extension of existing tax breaks on renewable energy.

114th Congress 2015–16 (Republicans)

Replace No Child Left Behind (Elementary and Secondary Education Act reauthorization)	*Back down*: Republicans had to back down on more controversial proposals in the partisan House bill.
Expand federal health care research policies and streamline drug approval (21st Century Cures Act)	*Logroll with opposition*: The CURES Act got over the finish line by logrolling competing Democratic and Republican priorities on health care. Democrats got increased HHS funding for various programs and research, Republicans got streamlined FDA drug approval processes.

Table A.3 (*continued*)

Priority	How it succeeded
Permanent Medicare sustainable growth rate (SGR) repeal	*Seek broad support/Logroll with opposition*: Democratic and Republican negotiators found a policy fix for the Medicare SGR but had to add policy sweeteners to please liberals and health care providers.
Pass a veterans' job bill	*Seek broad support*: Republicans enacted a small Obamacare change that exempted veteran employees from certain ACA requirements.
Pass a veterans' job bill	*Seek broad support*: The "Hire More Heroes Act," which passed as part of P.L. 114-41, was a broadly supported measure exempting veteran-employees from certain ACA requirements.

115th Congress 2017–18 (Republicans)

Priority	How it succeeded
Tax cuts/tax reform	*Steamroll*: Using budget reconciliation, House and Senate Republicans were able to push their signature achievement, the Tax Cuts and Jobs Act (TCJA), into law without a single Democratic vote.
FAA reauthorization	*Back down*: House Republicans had to back off from their controversial proposal to privatize air traffic control, and Congress passed a broadly bipartisan five-year FAA reauthorization.
Opioid crisis response	*Seek broad support*: Both parties wanted to take action on opioids, and the final bill was an omnibus combining numerous measures sponsored by members of both parties.
Water resources development	*Seek broad support*: Republicans sought to pass a bipartisan water resources development reauthorization as part of their broad efforts on "infrastructure." The proposal passed with broad support in both chambers.
Rollback of financial regulations (Dodd/Frank)	*Back down*: Republicans sought broad rollbacks of the 2010 Dodd-Frank reforms, including the House Republicans' far-reaching H.R. 10, but they settled for narrow legislation exempting community and regional banks from more stringent regulatory oversight.
Farm bill	*Back down/Seek broad support*: Senate Republicans sought a broadly bipartisan bill, while House Republicans initially passed a partisan bill by a narrow margin. In the end, House Republicans had to back down on all their controversial provisions, including changes to the Food Stamp program.
Obama administration rules rollback	*Steamroll*: Under the Congressional Review Act, Republicans were able to roll back numerous Obama-era regulations on party-line votes.

Additional Quantitative Analyses

This appendix supplies additional analyses referred to in chapters 2, 4, and 5. Figure B.1 replicates the analysis in figure 2.5 using only a subset of agenda items identified in more than one of our sources. Figure B.2 replicates the analysis in figure 2.6 using only this subset as well. Table B.1 shows the multivariate analyses of pathways of success referred to in chapter 4. Table B.2 replicates the regression models presented in table 5.1, but with each of the separate indicators of regular order violations included instead of the indexes. Table B.3 is a similar replication for the regression models presented in table 5.2.

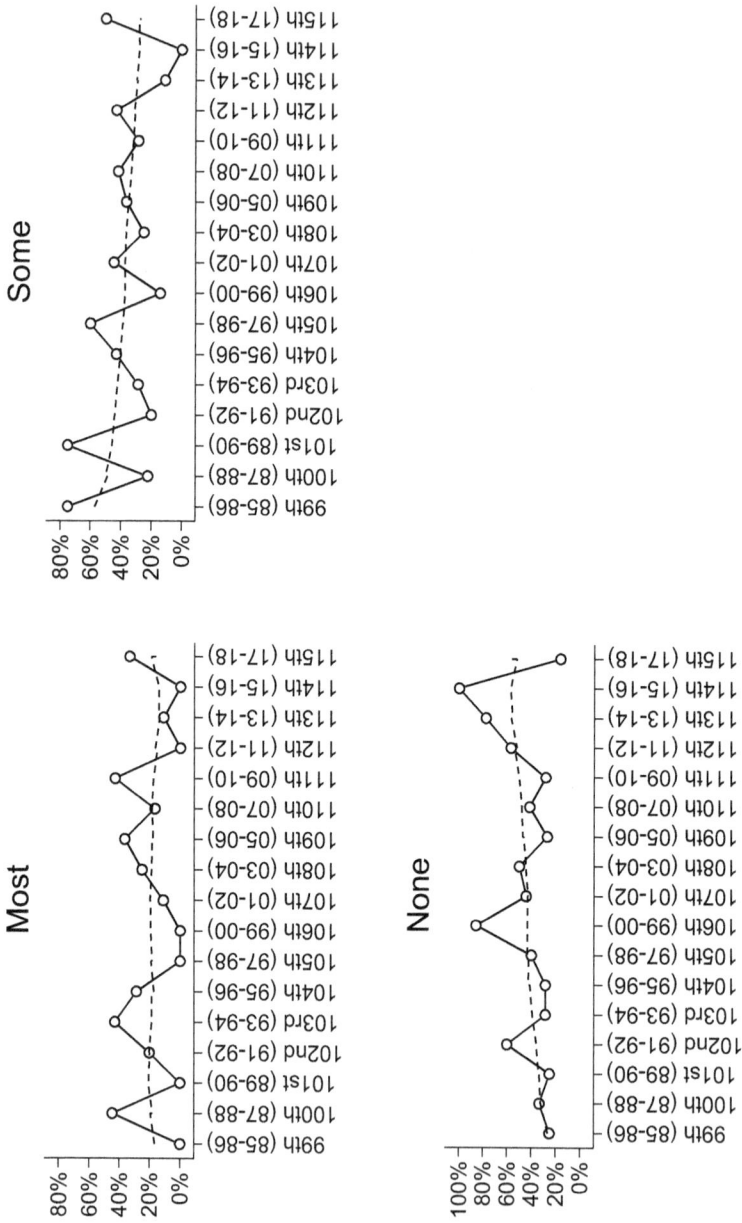

Figure B.1. Legislative outcomes of majority party agenda items among items identified in more than one source
Note: The 99th, 107th, 112th, and 113th Congresses featured split party control of the House and
Senate. The combined agenda items of both parties are included in these tallies.

With support of minority party in House or Senate

Over opposition of minority party in both chambers

With support of minority party leaders in House or Senate

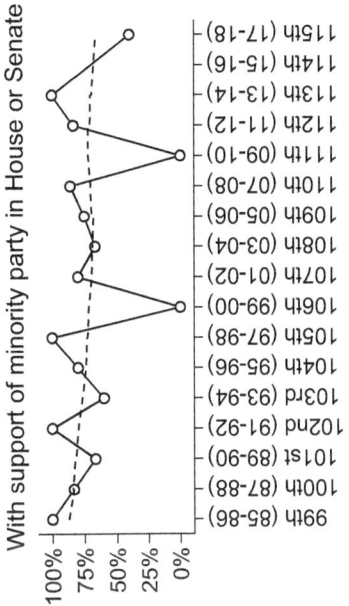

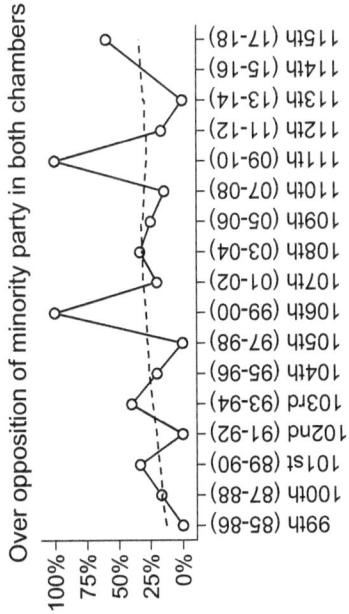

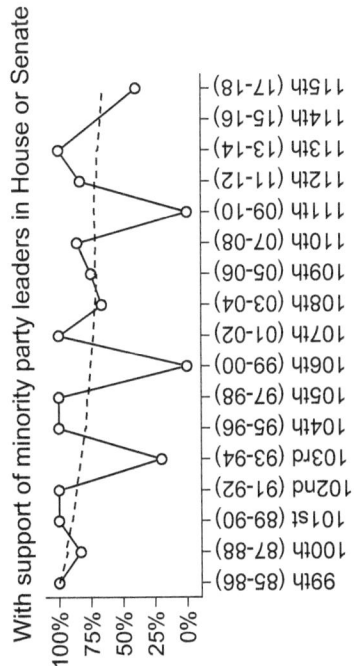

Figure B.2. How majority parties succeed on their agendas among items identified in more than one source

Note: The 99th, 107th, 112th, and 113th Congresses featured split party control of the House and Senate. The combined agenda items of both parties are included in these tallies. The 114th Congress did not feature any agenda successes among this subset of items.

Table B.1 Predicting pathways of success on majority party priority agenda items, 99th–115th Congresses

	Seek broad support		Back down		Bipartisan logroll		Steamroll	
	(1)	(2)	(3)	(4)	(5)	(6)	(7)	(8)
House party median difference	0.064		3.277		7.985		-1.573	
	(2.573)		(4.107)		(5.872)		(4.036)	
House majority party unity	-18.060		-20.770		-33.890		35.460	
	(21.650)		(24.510)		(61.660)		(22.320)	
House majority party seats	-0.014		0.011		-0.002		0.021	
	(0.015)		(0.018)		(0.042)		(0.021)	
Senate party median difference		-1.329		1.187		11.030		0.107
		(2.011)		(2.721)		(10.380)		(3.799)
Senate majority party unity		-15.57**		17.40*		6.914		15.130
		(5.003)		(6.960)		(16.570)		(9.980)
Senate majority party seats		0.000		0.050		0.148		-0.074
		(0.059)		(0.073)		(0.184)		(0.099)
First Congress of a presidency	-0.433	-0.594**	0.721	0.855*	-1.109	-1.347	-0.263	0.039
	(0.294)	(0.226)	(0.386)	(0.369)	(0.963)	(1.468)	(0.351)	(0.511)
Divided government	-0.648**	-0.468**	0.902*	0.735*	a	a	-1.296**	-1.581**
	(0.238)	(0.163)	(0.438)	(0.345)			(0.354)	(0.489)
Divided chambers	-0.002	-0.192	0.302	0.817	-0.211	0.194	0.561	0.441
	(0.624)	(0.332)	(0.687)	(0.539)	(0.896)	(0.778)	(0.859)	(0.747)
Constant	18.850	14.59**	11.510	-19.56*	21.120	-23.530	-34.980	-10.220
	(20.760)	(4.564)	(22.450)	(8.298)	(59.4)	(13.7)	(20.290)	(8.610)
N	138	138	138	138	138	138	138	138

Note: Results are logistic regression analyses with robust standard errors correcting for clustering by Congress. *p < .05; **p < .01.
a Divided government was dropped from these analyses because bipartisan logrolls were never used during divided government.

Table B.2 Predicting levels of partisanship on passage votes in the House, 1987–2016

	Initial passage			Final passage		
	(1) % minority party	(2) 50% party vote	(3) 90% party vote	(4) % minority party	(5) 50% party vote	(6) 90% party vote
Bill-level variables						
No House committee	0.064	−0.555	−0.456	0.010	−0.428	0.110
hearings	(0.038)	(0.313)	(0.529)	(0.034)	(0.389)	(0.934)
No House committee	0.005	0.703*	0.618	0.018	0.874*	−0.233
report	(0.045)	(0.356)	(0.556)	(0.039)	(0.429)	(1.106)
Closed rule	−0.215**	1.286**	0.709	−0.245**	1.575**	1.309
	(0.039)	(0.295)	(0.434)	(0.033)	(0.315)	(0.674)
House layover less than	0.040	−0.268	0.413	−0.006	−0.133	0.860
seventy-two hours	(0.028)	(0.227)	(0.380)	(0.024)	(0.254)	(0.665)
House late-stage	−0.146**	0.799**	0.676*	−0.041	0.180	0.114
adjustment	(0.029)	(0.220)	(0.345)	(0.024)	(0.255)	(0.608)
No Senate committee				−0.044	0.356	0.362
hearings				(0.033)	(0.358)	(0.863)
No Senate committee				0.038	−0.501	−0.302
report				(0.033)	(0.372)	(0.916)
Filled amendment tree				−0.066	0.585	−0.368
				(0.044)	(0.420)	(0.882)
Cloture invoked				0.005	0.194	0.046
				(0.031)	(0.311)	(0.677)
Senate late-stage				−0.032	0.071	1.013
adjustment				(0.029)	(0.300)	(0.633)
No conference report				0.123**	−0.635*	−0.724
				(0.029)	(0.307)	(0.762)
Appropriations bill	−0.108**	0.324	0.419	0.042	−0.536	−0.773
	(0.030)	(0.241)	(0.379)	(0.027)	(0.286)	(0.750)
Constant	0.771**	−1.345**	−3.492**	0.773**	−1.357**	−5.977**
	(0.036)	(0.262)	(0.383)	(0.040)	(0.326)	(1.383)
Random-effects parameters						
Congress	0.008	0.238	0.167	0.013	0.412	4.312
	(0.004)	(0.140)	(0.249)	(0.005)	(0.220)	(4.219)
Policy issue	0.005	0.296	0.283	0.002	0.241	0.640
	(0.003)	(0.184)	(0.282)	(0.001)	(0.180)	(0.865)
N	621	621	621	621	621	621

Note: Columns 1 and 4 are multilevel mixed-effects linear regressions; columns 2, 3, 5, and 6 are multilevel mixed-effects logistic regressions. $*p < .05$; $**p < .01$.

Table B.3 Predicting levels of partisanship on passage votes in the Senate, 1987–2016

	Initial passage			Final passage		
	(1) % minority party	(2) 50% party vote	(3) 90% party vote	(4) % minority party	(5) 50% party vote	(6) 90% party vote
Bill-level variables						
No House committee				0.043	−0.460	0.933
hearings				(0.028)	(0.534)	(1.471)
No House committee				−0.061	1.050	0.577
report				(0.032)	(0.576)	(1.821)
Closed rule				−0.091**	1.390**	0.872
				(0.027)	(0.383)	(1.105)
House layover less than				0.012	−0.344	−1.149
seventy-two hours				(0.020)	(0.344)	(1.154)
House late-stage				−0.039	0.127	−0.484
adjustment				(0.020)	(0.332)	(0.917)
No Senate committee	−0.014	0.146	1.414	0.000	−0.329	1.135
hearings	(0.026)	(0.405)	(0.960)	(0.027)	(0.494)	(1.353)
No Senate committee	−0.015	0.595	−0.328	−0.028	0.564	−0.225
report	(0.026)	(0.405)	(0.904)	(0.028)	(0.501)	(1.511)
Filled amendment tree	−0.029	0.267	0.105	−0.040	0.047	−0.227
	(0.037)	(0.458)	(0.937)	(0.036)	(0.521)	(1.310)
Cloture invoked	−0.130**	1.397**	1.047	−0.067**	0.769*	0.984
	(0.026)	(0.347)	(0.758)	(0.026)	(0.383)	(0.984)
Senate late-stage	−0.001	0.030	0.137	0.019	−0.072	0.492
adjustment	(0.024)	(0.350)	(0.700)	(0.024)	(0.382)	(0.929)
No conference report				0.065**	−0.484	−2.699
				(0.024)	(0.408)	(1.385)
Appropriations bill	−0.006	−0.385	−0.753	0.017	−0.430	−2.230
	(0.022)	(0.358)	(0.971)	(0.022)	(0.381)	(1.494)
Constant	0.889**	−2.874**	−6.547**	0.860**	−2.730**	−7.862**
	(0.031)	(0.429)	(1.347)	(0.034)	(0.503)	(2.955)
Random-effects parameters						
Congress	0.007	0.646	3.064	0.009	1.109	12.889
	(0.003)	(0.380)	(2.946)	(0.004)	(0.663)	(18.208)
Policy issue	0.004	0.835	2.010	0.002	0.646	4.164
	(0.002)	(0.505)	(1.812)	(0.001)	(0.499)	(4.157)
N	621	621	621	621	621	621

Note: Columns 1 and 4 are multilevel mixed-effects linear regressions; columns 2, 3, 5, and 6 are multilevel mixed-effects logistic regressions. $*p < .05$; $**p < .01$.

APPENDIX C

Notes on the Interviews

Thirty elite interviews with long-serving members of Congress and congressional staffers were conducted for this book. Each of the members we interviewed had served at least thirty years in the House or Senate and had risen to a position of prominence. The staffers we interviewed varied more in their tenures on Capitol Hill. Some had served in various capacities in the House or Senate for nearly forty years, while others had closer to ten years of service within Congress. Some had served in both chambers, some in just one. Some had also served in the executive branch or the White House, and others had also been lobbyists. Generally these individuals could be described as having worked at a high level in Washington politics and policy-making *for decades* and thus as able to provide us with broad, long-term perspectives on congressional lawmaking, including major and notable cases of lawmaking, and to discuss how things had, and had not, changed.

Each of these staffers had held a position of importance when in Congress—staff directors, legislative directors, chiefs of staff, policy directors, and so on—with some holding multiple important positions during their careers. Most had served representatives or senators who themselves at some point held party leadership positions or top positions on congressional committees. A few spent most of their careers with representatives or senators who never rose (or had not yet risen) to key positions of leadership in their party or on a committee. But overall these were congressional staffers of note, influence, and importance.

Table C.1 provides a brief overview of some of the characteristics of the interviewees. Half were Democrats and half were Republicans, providing a balanced look at the politics of congressional lawmaking. Most had experience working in the House of Representatives (83 percent), while a smaller but still substantial percentage (27 percent) had experience in the Senate.

Table C.1. The interviewees

By party	
Democrats	50%
Republicans	50%
By chamber	
House service	83%
Senate service	27%
N	30

We gained access to these individuals using a snowball, or cluster, sampling approach (Esterberg 2002, 93–94). Starting with a small set of individuals with whom we had existing contacts, we conducted initial interviews and asked them to refer us to others who might be willing to sit for an interview. With these referrals we were able to conduct interviews with a more diverse set of people, letting us gain the perspectives of individuals in Washington who were well outside our individual networks. We approached each interviewee by email, but the specific language we used varied in each case. Generally we identified who had suggested them, provided a brief overview of the research project, and explained that the interview would be "not for attribution," or anonymous. The process of obtaining and conducting the interviews was approved by the Institutional Review Boards at both the University of Maryland and the University of Utah.

The interviews typically lasted thirty minutes to an hour, with most lasting forty-five minutes or more and some well over an hour. The interviews were relatively unstructured. Each interviewee was asked similar questions about factors important in congressional lawmaking, the strategies congressional actors employ, the processes used, how things had and had not changed during their tenures, and so on. Most interviewees were asked about specific cases of lawmaking, but how specific or abstract they were depended on the person. An unstructured interview process gives researchers the ability to uncover important information and patterns that they might not have thought to explore. Indeed, our interviews were often exploratory, as we sought to uncover how successful lawmaking happens in Congress, how it fails, and how congressional actors approach these tasks.

The interviews and the evidence uncovered through them are of fundamental importance to this study. Crucial to understanding lawmaking in Congress is understanding the motivations of the key actors. The interviews allowed us to explore, in their own words, how lawmakers and staff approach lawmaking in a polarized era, which in turn provided us with irreplaceable insight into majority party capacity in Congress, how congressional lawmaking remains fundamentally unchanged, and more. Without this qualitative component, this study could not have been done.

NOTES

CHAPTER ONE

1. Quoted in Ben Weyl, "Ryan Plans to Steamroll Democrats with Budget Tool," *Politico*, October 6, 2016.

2. "Full Text: Speaker Ryan's Opening Day Address to the House," January 3, 2017, https://web.archive.org/web/20170104142140/http://www.speaker.gov/press-release /speaker-ryans-remarks-house-representatives-0.

3. These metrics show average party loyalty for representatives and senators on votes on which at least half of Democrats opposed at least half of Republicans.

4. Restrictive special rules are understood here as any that limit amending opportunities on the floor of the House, while closed rules are understood as those that bar all amending activity on a bill.

5. Specifically, Cox and McCubbins (2005, 7n6) write, "a 'favorable record' may include both positive achievements (enacting new laws) and negative achievements (protecting old laws)."

6. David Davenport, "A Growing Cancer on Congress: The Curse of Party-Line Voting," *Forbes*, December 13, 2017.

7. Ibid.

8. Nash Jenkins and Maya Rhodan, "The Republican Tax Bill Proves That Bipartisanship Is Dead," *Time*, December 20, 2017.

9. Domenico Montanaro, "McCain's Death Marks the Near-Extinction of Bipartisanship," National Public Radio, August 30, 2018.

10. Matt Ford, "Someone Please Tell Joe Biden That Bipartisanship Is Dead," *New Republic*, June 12, 2019, https://newrepublic.com/article/154183/someone-please-tell-joe -biden-bipartisanship-dead.

11. Karen Tumulty, "Something Rare and Wondrous Is Happening in Congress," *Washington Post*, November 28, 2018.

12. Julie Rovner and Shefall Luthra, "Bipartisan Senate Budget Deal Boosts Health Programs," *Washington Post*, February 7, 2018.

13. For a set of recent examples, see Carl Hulse, "Bewildered by That Rarest of Sightings in Washington: Bipartisanship," *New York Times*, September 15, 2017; Abby Goodnough, "In Rare Bipartisan Accord, House and Senate Reach Compromise on Opioid Bill," *New York Times*, September 26, 2018; Ryan Tracy and Andrew Ackerman, "How Congress Rolled Back Banking Rules in a Rare Bipartisan Deal," *Wall Street Journal*, May 23, 2018.

14. Quoted in "Lexington: Dicing with Debt and the Future," *Economist*, July 16, 2011, 36.

15. Tom Kenworthy, "Hill Democrats Draft Nonlethal Contra Aid," *Washington Post*, February 24, 1988, A1.

16. For recent reviews, see Barber and McCarty (2015) and Lee (2015).

17. For example, House Republicans in the 104th Congress were able to pass a number of partisan spending bills out of the House, but most of these partisan achievements were stripped from spending packages before President Clinton's vetoes in late 1995 or were dropped from the final spending deal enacted in April 1996. Similarly, when Rohde (1991, 105–18) focuses on House Democrats' efforts to pass a partisan platform in 1987, he finds that the Democrats were initially successful, but of the six agenda items he analyzes closely, four ultimately won bipartisan support in one or both chambers (the Water Quality Act [Pub. L. 100-4], the Highway bill [Pub. L. 100-17], the defense authorization bill [Pub. L. 100-180], and the Family Support Act [Pub. L. 100-485]). The remaining two—the budget resolution and a budget reconciliation package—were both considered under special rules that allowed for more majoritarian lawmaking.

18. We select 1973 as a starting point because it represents the twentieth century's lowest point for party conflict and cohesion in Congress. Mayhew's landmark laws data are obtained here: http://campuspress.yale.edu/davidmayhew/datasets-divided-we -govern/. The data include information on the final roll call taken in each chamber on each law. We verified these roll-call totals and added in missing data on party splits on each vote.

19. CQ Newsmaker Transcripts, "House Speaker Boehner Participates in a Discussion at the Newseum," Washington Ideas Forum, October 6, 2011.

20. The 2018 budget agreement (H.R. 1892) passed the House 240–186 (D 73–119; R 167–67) and the Senate 71–28 (D 36–11; R 34–16). The FY 2018 omnibus appropriations (H.R. 1625) passed the House 256–167 (D 111–77; R 145–90) and the Senate 65–32 (D 39–8; R 25–23).

CHAPTER TWO

1. Quoted in Carl Hulse and Robert Pear, "Departing Lawmakers Bemoan the Decline of Compromise," *New York Times*, January 2, 2015, A11.

2. Quoted in Claudia Dreifus, "Exit Reasonable Right," *New York Times Book Review*, June 2, 1996, 26.

3. Pub. L. 111-148.

4. Pub. L. 115-97.

5. We use Congressional Bills Project data on each House bill for these analyses (E. Scott Adler and John Wilkerson, Congressional Bills Project [1973–2018], NSF 00880066 and 00880061).

6. For these analyses we use a unique dataset of measures receiving passage votes in the Senate. Because the Senate often takes initial votes on House-passed measures (whereas the House infrequently takes initial votes on Senate-passed bills), it was important to build a separate dataset for the Senate.

7. Initial passage votes should exhibit more partisanship than we might find by looking at the final votes in each chamber before a bill is enrolled. A bill might pass the House or Senate by a close party-line vote but need to broaden its appeal to get through the other chamber. It is quite common for conference reports, for instance, to earn more votes than earlier versions of a bill.

8. Mayhew's landmark laws data are obtained here: http://campuspress.yale.edu/david mayhew/datasets-divided-we-govern/. The data often include information on the final roll call taken in each chamber on each law. We verified these roll-call totals, added in missing roll calls, and added in missing data on party splits on each vote.

9. In the House, these speeches immediately follow the vote to elect the Speaker of the House. In the Senate, they take place at some point during the first few days of the new Congress but are easily identifiable, usually with a speech title indicating that the majority leader will be discussing the agenda for the new Congress.

10. In each Congress, the first several bill slots (typically H.R. 1–10 in the House and S. 1–5 in the Senate, though it varies) are reserved for the majority leadership and are typically filled with priority bills. See Curry (2015, 93–94) for more on the use of this metric.

11. There is no trend toward majority parties' setting forth either more or fewer agenda items per Congress.

12. That our approach to measuring majority party priorities does not work before 1985 may also suggest that congressional majority parties did not consistently set forth clear programmatic agendas in earlier years. The seemingly permanent Democratic majority party of the twentieth century may have functioned to some extent as a catchall party or party of state (Mayhew 1974, 103).

13. It was not unusual for priority items to fail to receive floor votes in House or Senate (see chapter 3). Often committees would report bills that never advanced to floor consideration, and on some proposals no formal legislative action was taken at all.

14. For these purposes we recorded the votes of the Speaker, majority leader, majority whip, minority leader, and minority whip in the House and the majority leader, majority whip, minority leader, and minority whip in the Senate.

15. In some Congresses, majority party agenda items make up a larger share of landmark laws (maximum is 56 percent), and in other Congresses they constitute a smaller share (minimum is 17 percent). But majority party agenda successes do not constitute a clearly increasing or decreasing share of Mayhew's landmark laws over the period.

16. More than half (58 percent) of majority party agenda successes were landmark enactments according to Mayhew through the 115th Congress.

17. Under unified government, on average 80 percent of the House minority party supports enacted legislation, compared with 82 percent under divided government. This difference is statistically significant ($t = -1.702$; $p = .044$) but not substantively significant. Under unified government, on average 72 percent of the Senate minority party supports enacted legislation, compared with 83 percent under divided government. Again, this is a statistically significant difference ($t = -7.186$; $p < .001$), but it shows high levels of minority party support under both unified and divided government.

18. A time counter takes a slightly negative but not significant ($b = -0.006$; $p = .236$) coefficient for landmark laws.

19. As Jenkins and Monroe (2016) demonstrate, party rolls are just one way to assess party influence and party support in a legislature. This is why we present rolls alongside other measures of minority party support. Nevertheless, rolls continue to be a common metric employed by legislative scholars (see, e.g., Anzia and Jackman 2012; Carson, Monroe, and Robinson 2011).

20. Notably, this nontrend stands in contrast to significant increases in minority party rolls found when looking at *all* House roll-call votes as party strength and polarization increase (see, e.g., Cox and McCubbins 2005, 201–19).

21. A time counter takes a negative but not statistically significant coefficient ($b = -0.002$; $p = .406$) for all laws and a positive but not significant coefficient ($b = 0.005$; $p = .498$) for landmark laws.

22. Under unified government, the House minority party is rolled on 19 percent of new laws as opposed to 16 percent under divided government ($p = .53$). Under unified government, the Senate minority party is rolled on 26 percent of new laws as opposed to 12 percent under divided government ($p = .05$).

23. A time counter takes a positive but not significant ($b = 0.007$; $p = .073$) coefficient for all laws.

24. The overtime trend in Senate minority rolls on landmark laws is not statistically significant ($b = 0.002$; $p = .823$).

25. In recent years, senators sometimes agree via a unanimous consent agreement (UCA) to set the vote threshold for final passage to sixty votes. This is often done to limit the number of votes that need to be taken on the Senate floor. Since sixty votes would be needed for cloture to end debate on a bill, senators sometimes agree to forgo cloture votes and simply require that sixty senators support the bill for it to pass.

26. A time counter has a negative but not significant impact ($b = -0.004$; $p = .167$) for all laws.

27. A time counter has a negative but not significant impact ($b = 0.008$; $p = .170$) for landmark laws.

28. A time counter has a positive and significant impact ($b = 0.028$; $p = .003$) for landmark laws.

29. The Policy Agendas Project codes all legislation as addressing one of twenty major issue areas. More detail on the Policy Agendas Project data can be found at https://www.comparativeagendas.net/us.

30. The results of these analyses can be found in the supplemental materials to Curry and Lee (2019a).

31. Note that majority party agenda items differ substantially from presidential agendas under divided government and are not identical to presidential agendas even in unified government.

32. This high recent rate of failure aligns with research finding that increased partisanship and party conflict yielded higher rates of gridlock (e.g., Binder 2003, 2014).

33. A test of difference of means yields $t = -0.93$ ($p = .18$), $n = 265$.

34. A test of difference of means yields $t = 3.52$ ($p < .001$), $n = 265$.

35. A test of differences of means yields $t = -2.00$ ($p = .02$), $n = 265$.

36. Pub. L. 111-203.

37. Pub. L. 108-27.

38. Pub. L. 109-2.

39. Pub. L. 103-3.

40. Pub. L. 103-31.

41. Pub. L. 111-3.

42. Pub. L. 105-33.

43. Pub. L. 103-322.

44. Pub. L. 108-173.

45. See, for example, Michelle Alexander, "Why Hillary Clinton Doesn't Deserve the Black Vote," Nation, February 10, 2016, https://www.thenation.com/article/hillary-clinton-does-not-deserve-black-peoples-votes/.

46. Peter Baker, "Bill Clinton Disavows His Crime Law as Jailing Too Many for Too Long," New York Times, July 15, 2015, A16.

47. Edwin Feulner and Alison Acosta Fraser, "A Line in the Sand for Fiscally Responsible Lawmakers," *Heritage Foundation*, October 6, 2005, https://www.heritage.org/budget-and-spending/report/line-the-sand-fiscally-responsible-lawmakers.

48. Henry J. Kaiser Family Foundation, "Medicare Part D in 2018: The Latest on Enrollment, Premiums, and Cost Sharing," May 17, 2018, https://www.kff.org/medicare/issue-brief/medicare-part-d-in-2018-the-latest-on-enrollment-premiums-and-cost-sharing/.

49. Juliette Cubanski and Tricia Neuman, "The Facts on Medicare Spending and Financing," Henry J. Kaiser Family Foundation, June 22, 2018, updated August 20, 2019, https://www.kff.org/medicare/issue-brief/the-facts-on-medicare-spending-and-financing/.

50. Pub. L. 99-514.

51. Pub. L. 101-549.

52. Pub. L. 104-193.

53. Pub. L. 105-33.

54. Pub. L. 106-102.

55. Pub. L. 107-110.

56. Pub. L. 112-240.

57. Pub. L. 114-255.

58. A time counter has a positive but not statistically significant impact (b = 0.018; p = .286).

59. Staffer, November 5, 2018 (1). Parenthetical numbers next to the dates of interviews delineate separate interviews that took place on the same day.

60. Member, July 27, 2017.

61. Ibid.

62. Staffer, October 30, 2018.

63. Staffer, November 5, 2018 (1).

64. Staffer, December 4, 2017 (2).

65. Staffer, October 10, 2017 (2).

66. Staffer, October 11, 2017 (1).

67. Staffer, November 5, 2018 (2).

68. Staffer, October 30, 2018.

69. Ibid.

70. Staffer, November 6, 2018 (3).

71. Staffer, November 6, 2018 (2).

72. Member, July 27, 2016.

73. Staffer, September 18, 2017.

74. Staffer, November 6, 2018 (4).

75. Staffer, October 9, 2017.

76. Staffer, November 6, 2018 (4).

77. Staffer, October 10, 2017.

78. Staffer, November 5, 2018 (1).

79. Ibid.

80. Staffer, November 6, 2018 (4).

81. Staffer, November 5, 2018 (1).

82. Staffer, October 9, 2017.

83. Ibid.

84. Ibid.

85. Staffer, November 5, 2018 (2).

86. Staffer, October 9, 2017.

87. Staffer, July 14, 2016.

88. Staffer, October 11, 2017.
89. Ibid.
90. Staffer, November 5, 2018 (2).
91. Staffer, December 4, 2017 (4).
92. Staffer, December 4, 2017 (3).
93. Staffer, October 11, 2017 (3).
94. Staffer, October 30, 2018.
95. Staffer, November 5, 2018 (2).
96. Pub. L. 114-255, chapter 2.

CHAPTER THREE

1. Lindsey Graham (@LindseyGrahamSC), Twitter Post, December 21, 2017, 12:34 p.m. Accessed at https://twitter.com/lindseygrahamsc/status/943942815905665025?lang=en.
2. From 1985 to 2019, the Senate majority party held sixty votes for only roughly five months. Democrats controlled sixty Senate seats from July 7, 2009, to August 25, 2009, and from September 25, 2009, to February 4, 2010.
3. A time counter takes a positive, statistically significant coefficient across the sixteen Congresses in the study ($b = 0.3$; $p < .001$).
4. For this difference of means, $t = -0.67$; $p = .251$.
5. Drawing on coverage in CQ *Magazine* and CQ *Almanac*, two research assistants worked separately to code each case. In a large majority there was no ambiguity about where and how bills failed. On the roughly one-quarter of bills on which coders initially came to different conclusions, further research was conducted and the cases were discussed together as a group to reach a final coding decision. Descriptions of the cases along with their coding are provided in appendix A.
6. We do not find any cases in our period where a majority party agenda item failed because of a veto or veto threat under unified government. Note that a bill can be classed as failing because of a presidential veto even when a veto is not formally issued, if it is clear from the reporting that the majority party gave up pressing forward on a bill because it did not expect to overcome a veto.
7. We cannot be certain that our data on this point are comprehensive, given the thinness of news coverage of policy initiatives that do not progress in the legislative process. There may be some additional cases beyond what we code here where majority parties did not pursue an agenda item because of a sense of futility due to expected future veto players. On the other hand, majority party leaders also have a motive to downplay intraparty divisions so as to blame the opposing party veto players for failure to move forward on an agenda item.
8. Brian Faler, Rachel Bade, Kelsey Snell, and Lauren French, "How the GOP Lost Its Nerve on Tax Reform," *Politico*, December 5, 2013, https://www.politico.com/story/2013/12/tax-code-gop-leaders-100693.
9. Erica Werner, "Senate Rejects Billions in Trump Spending Cuts as Two Republicans Vote No," *Washington Post*, June 20, 2018, https://www.washingtonpost.com/business/economy/senate-rejects-billions-in-trump-spending-cuts-as-two-republicans-vote-no/2018/06/20/1a44df9a-74aa-11e8-b4b7-308400242c2e_story.html?utm_term=.89eeba721e6a.
10. Allan Freedman, "Dole Gambles on Legislation to Protect Property Rights," CQ *Magazine*, May 4, 1996, 1215–16.

11. "2004 Legislative Summary: Estate Tax Repeal Extension," *CQ Weekly*, December 4, 2004, 2870.

12. Shawn Zeller, "Small Inventors Fear Giants Behind Patent Bill," *CQ Weekly*, June 1, 2015, 31–35.

13. "Congress Stymied on Education Law," in *CQ Almanac 2011*, 67th ed., ed. Jan Austin (Washington, DC: CQ-Roll Call Group, 2012), 8-6-8-7, http://library.cqpress.com/cqalmanac/cqal-1390-77518-2462230.

14. Note that in both circumstances (veto and sixty-vote threshold), most cases are coded as being blocked by opposition-party veto players. Generally this indeterminacy does not affect our coding of the overall incidence of agenda death-by-opposing party veto player.

15. Unreconciled bicameral agreement is a greater problem when House and Senate are controlled by the same party because the House and Senate are more likely to pass legislation dealing with a common party priority in such Congresses. In Congresses where House and Senate are controlled by different parties, by contrast, the second chamber is less likely to act at all on the first chamber's partisan priorities.

16. Chuck Alston, "Showdown on Spending Limits Moves toward White House," *CQ Weekly*, August 4, 1990, 2478–83.

17. "Energy: A Jolt Likely for Power Grid," *CQ Weekly*, January 4, 2016, http://library.cqpress.com/cqweekly/weeklyreport114-000004810686.

18. Note, furthermore, that party agendas are not longer in unified government. In unified government, the average number of majority party agenda items is fourteen, compared with sixteen in divided government ($t = 1.4$; $p = .18$).

19. This different is not statistically significant ($t = 0.925$; $p = .178$).

20. This difference is not statistically significant ($t = -2.324$; $p = .011$).

21. This difference is statistically significant ($t = -2.441$; $p = .008$).

22. In Congresses with divided party control of House and Senate, only 2 percent of agenda items failed because the leadership did not schedule a committee-reported bill for floor consideration. In other Congresses these patterns characterize 16 percent of agenda failures, a statistically significant difference ($t = 2.058$; $p = .021$).

23. On average, committee inaction accounts for 26 percent of agenda failures in divided government and for 23 percent of agenda failures in unified government ($t = -0.483$; $p = .315$).

24. $t = -1.754$; $p = .041$.

25. $t = -1.377$; $p = .085$.

26. $t = 1.754$; $p = .041$.

27. $t = -1.377$; $p = .085$.

28. This difference is not statistically significant ($t = -0.29$; $p = .386$).

29. This difference is not statistically significant ($t = 0.29$; $p = .386$).

30. We do not count in this list the 107th Congress, which had unified government for only four months, from January 20, 2001, to May 24, 2001.

31. "Alternative Health-Care Proposals," in *CQ Almanac 1993*, 49th ed. (Washington, DC: Congressional Quarterly, 1994), 344–45, http://library.cqpress.com/cqalmanac/cqal93-1105867.

32. "House Energy and Commerce: Panel Finds Consensus Unattainable," in *CQ Almanac 1994*, 50th ed. (Washington, DC: Congressional Quarterly, 1995), 335–36, http://library.cqpress.com/cqalmanac/cqal94-1103590.

33. Douglas Jehl, "Mitchell Rejects President's Offer of Seat on Court," *New York Times*, April 13, 1994, A1.

34. "Clinton's Health Care Plan Laid to Rest," in *CQ Almanac 1994*, 50th ed. (Washington, DC: Congressional Quarterly, 1995), 319–55, http://library.cqpress.com/cqalmanac/cqal94-1103561.

35. Alan K. Ota, "Bush Stands Behind Tax Cuts," *CQ Weekly*, January 24, 2004, 200, http://library.cqpress.com/cqweekly/weeklyreport108-000000978291.

36. See the American Jobs Creation Act of 2004 (Pub. L. 108-357), which passed the Senate (69–17) and House (280–141).

37. Alan K. Ota, "Bush Stands Behind Tax Cuts," *CQ Weekly*, January 24, 2004, 201.

38. Alex Wayne, "GOP of Three Minds on Next Social Security Step," *CQ Weekly*, October 31, 2005, 2896.

39. Adriel Bettelheim and Alex Wayne, "Dependable Bush Supporters Hang Back on Social Security," *CQ Weekly*, January 17, 2005, 112–14.

40. "Bush Boosts His Success Rate Even While Retreating on Key Issues," in *CQ Almanac 2005*, 61st ed. (Washington, DC: Congressional Quarterly, 2006), B-3–B-8. http://library.cqpress.com/cqalmanac/cqal05-766-20088-1041720.

41. Alex Wayne, "2005 Legislative Summary: Social Security Overhaul," *CQ Weekly*, January 2, 2006, 50, http://library.cqpress.com/cqweekly/weeklyreport109-000002022076.

42. Quoted in John M. Broder, "Geography Is Dividing Democrats over Energy," *New York Times*, January 27, 2009, A1.

43. The American Clean Energy and Security Act of 2009 (H.R. 2443) passed the House by a vote of 219–212 (D 211–44; R 8–168). The forty-four Democrats voting no were largely from rural and conservative districts. Without the eight Republican votes, the bill would have failed, 211–220.

44. Alan K. Ota, "Democrats Looking for a Few Green Republicans," *CQ Weekly*, July 13, 2009, 1618.

45. Coral Davenport, "Compromises Could Doom Senate Energy Bill," *CQ Weekly*, June 15, 2009, 1389, http://library.cqpress.com/cqweekly/weeklyreport111-000003143181.

46. The Democrats' "new strategy" proposal that garnered the most votes was an amendment by Rep. Jim McGovern (D-MA) requiring that the president send Congress a new intelligence estimate on Afghanistan and a plan for redeploying US troops. It was rejected 162–260 (House roll-call vote 433, July 1, 2010).

47. See House roll-call vote 430 (July 1, 2010) on the amendment by Appropriations chair David R. Obey (D-WI) to add $22.8 billion for schools and other domestic priorities.

48. "Funding for Afghanistan, Iraq Wars," in *CQ Almanac 2010*, 66th ed., ed. Jan Austin (Washington, DC: CQ-Roll Call Group, 2011), 2-15–2-16, http://library.cqpress.com/cqalmanac/cqal10-1278-70356-2371484.

49. David Rogers, "Inouye Balks at War Funding Fix," *Politico*, November 10, 2009.

50. Jennifer Steinhauer, "Republicans in Congress Plan Swift Action on Ambitious Agenda with Trump," *New York Times*, November 9, 2016, P14.

51. S. Con. Res. 3, passed on January 13, 2017.

52. Heritage Action, "'No' on American Health Care Act (H.R. 1628)," March 23, 2017, http://heritageaction.com/key-votes/no-american-health-care-act-h-r-1628/.

53. H.R. 1628, American Health Care Act of 2017.

54. House roll-call vote 256, May 4, 2017.

55. S. Amdt. 667 to S. Amdt. 267, July 28, 2017.

56. These twenty-one failures are, for Democrats, to revise federal housing programs in the 99th Congress (enacted in the 100th); to reauthorize federal water quality programs in the 99th Congress (enacted in the 100th); to amend the Clean Air Act in the

100th Congress (enacted in the 101st); to extend federal child care programs in the 100th Congress (enacted in the 101st); to pass family and medical leave in the 102nd Congress (enacted in the 103rd); to enact health care reform in the 110th (enacted in the 111th). For Republicans they are to pass tax cuts in the 104th Congress (enacted in the 105th); to pass an overhaul of financial services regulations in the 105th Congress (enacted in the 106th); to pass a partial birth abortion ban in the 105th and 106th Congresses (enacted in the 108th); to pass a Medicare overhaul in the 106th and 107th Congresses (enacted in the 108th); to pass a K-12 education overhaul in the 106th Congress (enacted in the 107th); to expand antimissile defense programs in the 106th Congress (enacted in the 107th); to cut taxes in the 106th Congress (enacted in the 107th); to pass a domestic energy plan in the 107th Congress (enacted in the 108th and 109th); to pass class action lawsuit reform in the 108th Congress (enacted in the 109th); to extend some of the Bush tax cuts in the 108th Congress (enacted in the 109th); to replace No Child Left Behind in the 113th Congress (enacted in the 114th); and to reform the tax code in the 113th and 114th Congresses (enacted in the 115th).

57. Staffer, August 6, 2016.
58. Staffer, December 4, 2017.
59. Staffer, October 11, 2017 (2).
60. Ibid.
61. Staffer, July 14, 2016.
62. Staffer, December 5, 2017.
63. Staffer, November 6, 2018 (3).
64. Staffer, October 10, 2017 (1).
65. Staffer, December 5, 2017.
66. Staffer, December 4, 2017 (4).
67. Staffer, December 4, 2017 (1).
68. Staffer, December 4, 2017 (1)
69. Ibid.
70. Staffer, December 4, 2017 (2).
71. Staffer, December 4, 2017 (3).
72. Staffer, December 6, 2017 (2).
73. Ibid.
74. Member, July 27, 2016.
75. Staffer, December 4, 2017 (2).
76. Ibid.
77. Staffer, November 6, 2018 (4).
78. Staffer, October 17, 2016.
79. Staffer, August 5, 2016.
80. Member, July 28, 2016.
81. Because there are no trends over time to show, the figure does not display the frequency with which majorities fail because of the inaction of the second chamber for reasons other than the Senate's sixty-vote threshold (#3 in the failure coding). The incidence with which parties fail because the House and Senate cannot reconcile their bills (#6 in our coding scheme) is also not shown both because there is little change and because it is a very infrequent type of majority party failure.
82. A time counter takes a negative, but not statistically significant, coefficient (−0.001; $p = .819$) in a simple regression analysis of the share of majority party failures blocked by the Senate filibuster.

83. A simple regression model of the percentage of agenda items that fail by presidential veto in each Congress studied (n = 17) including just a time counter variable and a divided government variable returns a statistically insignificant time-counter coefficient (–0.004; p = .613).

84. A time counter takes a positive, but not statistically significant coefficient (0.008; p = .361) in a simple regression analysis of the share of failed majority party agenda items that did not advance in committee.

85. A time counter takes a negative, but not statistically significant coefficient (–0.009; p = .184) in a simple regression analysis of the share of failed majority party agenda items that involved committee-reported bills not being scheduled for floor action.

86. A time counter takes a negative, but not statistically significant coefficient (–0.005; p = .658) in a regression analysis of the share of failed agenda items blocked by veto players. Adding in a control for divided government does not change the results.

87. Quoted in Joel Achenbach, "The Proud Compromisers: Senators Relish Their Role as the Upper Body," *Washington Post*, January 9, 1999, A11.

88. Staffer, December 4, 2017 (2).

89. Press release, "Full Text: Speaker Ryan's Farewell Address," December 19, 2018, https://web.archive.org/web/20181219233524/https://www.speaker.gov/press-release/full-text-speaker-ryans-farewell-address.

90. Robinson Meyer, "Democrats Are Shockingly Unprepared to Fight Climate Change," *Atlantic*, November 15, 2017, https://www.theatlantic.com/science/archive/2017/11/there-is-no-democratic-plan-to-fight-climate-change/543981/.

91. Damian Paletta, "McConnell Calls Deficit 'Very Disturbing,' Blames Federal Spending, Dismisses Criticism of Tax Cut," *Washington Post*, October 16, 2018, https://www.washingtonpost.com/business/economy/mcconnell-calls-deficit-very-disturbing-blames-federal-spending-dismisses-criticism-of-tax-cut/2018/10/16/a5b93da0-d15c-11e8-8c22-fa2ef74bd6d6_story.html?utm_term=.fff0413e3431.

92. According to *CQ Magazine*, Republican cohesion on party-unity votes in 2017 was 92 percent in the House (second highest recorded since 1945) and 97 percent in the Senate (highest on record since 1945).

CHAPTER FOUR

1. Quoted in Martin Tolchin, "What Becomes of Those Ideals, or Those Idealists," *New York Times*, August 7, 1984, B6.

2. Quoted in Rep. Jim Himes (D-CT), "Compromise," *Congressional Record* 159, pt. 131, September 28, 2013, H5928.

3. H.R. 1 (111th Congress) initially passed the House 244–177 without any Republican yea votes (roll-call vote 46), and the conference report passed 246–183 (roll-call vote 70), similarly without any Republicans in support.

4. The cloture vote of importance was on the Collins-Nelson amendment to the bill (S. Amdt. 570 to H.R. 1), which was invoked 61–36 (roll-call vote 59, 111th Congress).

5. The trends over time for "most" (b = –0.007; p = .308) and "some" (b = –0.009; p = .102) successes are both not statistically significant.

6. t = 0.672; p = .251.

7. t = –0.787; p = .216.

8. t = 1.389; p = .083.

9. t = 0.858; p = .196.

10. t = 2.173; p = .015.

11. t = 3.401; p = .0004.

12. Bivariate regressions with a time counter report the following coefficients and p-statistics: For bipartisan logrolls, $b = 0.008$; $p = .305$. For seek broad support, $b = -0.001$; $p = .921$. For back down, $b = -0.001$; $p = .935$. For steamroll, $b = 0.005$; $p = .473$.

13. Also sometimes referred to as "A New Direction for America."

14. Staffer, December 4, 2017 (3).

15. Staffer, December 5, 2017.

16. Staffer, October 11, 2017 (3).

17. These differences are not statistically significant. For unified vs. divided chambers, $t = 0.67$; $p = .251$. For unified vs. divided government, $t = 1.288$; $p = .100$.

18. For divided vs. unified government, $t = -2.27$; $p = .013$. For divided vs. unified chambers, $t = -2.14$; $p = .017$.

19. Staffer, December 4, 2017 (3).

20. Staffer, December 4, 2017 (3).

21. Staffer, October 9, 2017.

22. Staffer, December 5, 2017.

23. Staffer, October 11, 2017 (3).

24. Staffer, September 9, 2016.

25. Staffer, September 9, 2016.

26. Staffer, December 4, 2017 (2).

27. The difference in likelihood of a steamroll is statistically significant between unified and divided government ($b = -1.311$; $p = .017$) but not between unified and divided chambers ($b = -0.208$; $p = .760$).

28. $t = 1.852$; $p = .033$.

29. For *seek broad support*, $t = 5.65$; $p < .001$. For *back down*, $t = -13.494$; $p < .001$. For *steamroll*, $t = 5.165$; $p < .001$. For *logroll*, $t = -2.194$; $p = .015$.

30. There are no data points for the 112th and 114th Congresses, since there were no "most" victories in those years.

31. Time trends are not significant for seeking broad support ($b = -0.435$; $p = .305$) and steamrolling ($b = 0.068$; $p = .552$).

32. $b = -0.045$; $p = .834$.

33. $b = 0.246$; $p = .074$.

34. Jonathan Glater, "New York to Take Legal Action over Steering of Students to Lender," *New York Times*, March 23, 2007, A12.

35. Jonathan Glater, "Education Dept. Is Urged to Explain Loan Subsidy," *New York Times*, March 8, 2007, A15.

36. "Democrats Succeed in Revamping Federal Student Loan Programs," in *CQ Almanac 2007*, 63rd ed., ed. Jan Austin (Washington, DC: Congressional Quarterly, 2008), 8-3–8-5.

37. H.R. 5 passed the House 356–71.

38. Libby George, "Student Loan Bill Draws Veto Threat," *CQ Weekly*, July 16, 2007, 2119.

39. Ibid.

40. Libby George, "Fall Agenda: Student Loan Interest Rates," *CQ Weekly*, September 3, 2007, 2546.

41. H.R. 2164 (102nd Congress) passed the House 312–97. This bill would have established an "expedited rescissions" process, similar to one considered in 1995, that would allow the president to send a list of rescissions from appropriations bills to Congress for quick consideration in both chambers. This was considered a compromise line-item measure and showed how broad support was in Congress in the early 1990s for some sort of budget-cutting mechanism like a line-item veto.

42. "Small Step toward Line-Item Veto," in *CQ Almanac 1992*, 48th ed. (Washington, DC: Congressional Quarterly, 1993), 114–15.

43. H.R. 2 passed the House 294–134.

44. Andrew Taylor, "Line-Item Veto Compromise Easily Passes Senate," *CQ Weekly*, March 25, 1995, 854–56.

45. S. 4 passed the Senate on March 23, 1995.

46. H.R. 391 provided for the enactment of the Senior Citizens' Right to Work Act of 1996, the Line Item Veto Act, and the Small Business Growth and Fairness Act of 1996.

47. "Law Restricts Unfunded Mandates," in *CQ Almanac 1995*, 51st ed. (Washington, DC: Congressional Quarterly, 1996), 3-15–3-20.

48. David Hosansky, "GOVERNMENT OPERATIONS: Mandate Bill Is More Moderate Than Proposal in 'Contract,'" *CQ Weekly*, January 7, 1995, 40.

49. H.R. 5 passed the House 360–74 with 130 Democrats (64 percent) voting for passage. S. 1 passed the Senate 86–10 with 35 Democrats (78 percent) in favor of passage.

50. David Hosansky, "House Passes 'Contract' Priority to Curb Mandates on States," *CQ Weekly*, February 4, 1995, 361–63.

51. Isaiah J. Poole, "'Get It Done' Will Be Mantra for Next Try at Highway Bill," *CQ Weekly*, January 10, 2005, 82–84.

52. Isaiah J. Poole, "Surface Transportation Legislation Begins Anew in House and Senate," *CQ Weekly*, February 7, 2005, 312.

53. Isaiah J. Poole, "No Exit This Time for Highway Bill," *CQ Weekly*, March 14, 2005, 654–55.

54. Kathryn A. Wolfe, "Highway Bill Caught by the Calendar," *CQ Weekly*, May 23, 2005, 1374–75.

55. Siobhan Hughes, "Veto Threat Lengthens Odds against Senate Pension Bill," *CQ Weekly*, January 24, 2004, 216–17.

56. Michael R. Crittenden, "Pension Overhaul Initiative Aims to Address Worries over Retirement Insecurity," *CQ Weekly*, January 17, 2005, 117.

57. Michael R. Crittenden, "Fall Agenda: Pension System Overhaul," *CQ Weekly*, September 5, 2005, 2318.

58. H.R. 2830 passed the House 294–132.

59. S. 1783.

60. Two of the nineteen total steamrolls were majority party victories classified as "some" victories. Therefore, in this section of the chapter we refer to the seventeen steamrolls that were "most" victories.

61. Daniel J. Parks, "Fall Clash over Spending Priorities Could Set Course for Rest of 107th," *CQ Weekly*, July 28, 2001, 1839–41.

62. Pat Towell, "Specter of Force Reductions Roils Defense Bill Debate," *CQ Weekly*, August 11, 2001, 1987–90.

63. The conference report on H.R. 4546 (Pub. L. 107-314) passed both chambers by a voice vote.

64. The missile defense system funding (Pub. L. 107-107) passed as part of S. 1438.

65. Developing and funding an expanded missile defense system was a Republican priority in the 104th, 105th, and 106th Congresses, but Republicans were never able to secure more than small funding increases for the project. Increases in military spending generally were part of Republican Party doctrine in the 1980s and 1990s, with Democrats advocating reductions in Department of Defense spending, especially after the end of the Cold War.

66. See Pub. L. 108-106 and Pub. L. 109-13.

67. "Domestic-Violence Law Is Renewed," in *CQ Almanac 2013*, 69th ed. (Washington, DC: CQ-Roll Call Group, 2014), 9-11–9-12.

68. Lauren Smith, "2012 Legislative Summary: Violence against Women Act," *CQ Weekly*, January 14, 2013, 96.

69. S. 47 passed 78–22, with twenty-three Republican senators in support (a majority of the party).

70. Jonathan Weisman, "Violence Act Returns in Test of Republicans' Appeal to Women," *New York Times*, February 4, 2013.

71. Linda Greenhouse, "Court, 5–4, Affirms a Right to Reopen Bias Settlements," *New York Times*, June 13, 1989.

72. Senate Document 101-35, "Message from the President of the United States Returning without My Approval S. 2104, the Civil Rights Act of 1990," October 22, 1990.

73. Just thirty-four Republicans supported the bill on final passage in the House, and nine did so in the Senate.

74. Both quotations from "Compromise Civil Rights Bill Passed," in *CQ Almanac 1991*, 47th ed. (Washington, DC: Congressional Quarterly, 1992), 251–61.

75. Joan Biskupic, "Senate Passes Sweeping Measure to Overturn Court Rulings," *CQ Weekly*, November 2, 1991, 3200–3204.

76. These nine steamroll cases mostly overlap with the twelve partisan victories identified in chapter 2. There are four partisan victories among the twelve in chapter 2 not included among these nine partisan steamrolls: the SCHIP reauthorization (Democrats, 111th Congress), which is coded as the majority seeking broad support; the effort at class action lawsuit and tort reform (Republicans, 109th Congress), which is coded as backing down; the second round of the Bush tax cuts (Republicans, 108th Congress), which is coded as the majority backing down; and the Family and Medical Leave Act (Democrats, 103rd Congress), which is coded as the majority seeking broad support. In addition, there is one case among these nine steamrolls not included among the twelve partisan victories identified in chapter 2: the Clinton impeachment. This curious case in which the Republicans made it a priority to "complete" the impeachment proceedings in the Senate during the 106th Congress represents a case of steamrolling (Republicans pushed forward without any Democratic support), but one in which the GOP got only *some* of what it wanted. Indeed, the House impeached Clinton, and the proceedings were wrapped up in the Senate during the 106th Congress, but the Republicans did not get everything they wanted: Clinton was acquitted by the Senate mostly along partisan lines.

77. "Congress Stymied on Education Law," in *CQ Almanac 2011*, 67th ed., ed. Jan Austin (Washington, DC: CQ-Roll Call Group, 2012), 8-6–8-7, http://library.cqpress.com /cqalmanac/cqal-1390-77518-2462230.

78. "Frustrated with 'No Child Left Behind,' Congress Takes a New Path on Schools," in *CQ Almanac 2015*, 71st ed. (Washington, DC: CQ-Roll Call Group, 2016), 8-11–8-15.

79. Melissa Attias and Carolyn Phenicie, "Lamar Alexander Plans to Take Senators to School," *CQ Weekly*, February 9, 2015, 14–15.

80. "Anatomy of a Vote: Education Overhaul Is Latest Bipartisan Deal," *CQ Weekly*, December 14, 2015.

81. Catherine Boudreau and Helena Bottemiller Evich, "Farm Bill Compromise Primed for Passage," *Politico*, December 11, 2018.

82. Ibid.

83. Quoted in Ryan McCrimmon, "Farm Bill Hits House Floor Today," *Politico: Morning Agriculture*, December 12, 2018.

84. James Risen and Eric Lichtblau, "Bush Lets U.S. Spy on Callers without Courts," *New York Times*, December 15, 2005.

85. Ellen Nakashima, "Democrats to Offer New Surveillance Rules," *Washington Post*, October 7, 2007.

86. James Risen, "Panel Drops Immunity from Eavesdropping Bill," *New York Times*, November 16, 2007.

87. During Senate consideration of its FISA measure, a Democratic substitute sponsored by Harry Reid (D-NV) failed 36–60.

88. Tim Starks, "Revised FISA Bill Sneaks through House," *CQ Weekly*, March 17, 2008, 725.

89. "Bush Prevails on FISA Overhaul," in *CQ Almanac 2008*, 64th ed., ed. Jan Austin (Washington, DC: Congressional Quarterly, 2009), 6-12–6-16.

90. David G. Savage, "U.S. Supreme Court Ends Suit against Telecom Firms for Aiding NSA," *Los Angeles Times*, October 9, 2012.

91. Amie Parnes and Bernie Becker, "Obama Picks Election-Year Tax Fight with $250,000 Ceiling for Lower Rate," *The Hill*, July 10, 2012.

92. "Last-Minute Deal Averts Fiscal Cliff, Punts Big Issues to New Congress," in *CQ Almanac 2012*, 68th ed., (Washington, DC: CQ-Roll Call Group, 2013), 7-3–7-7.

93. "After 60 Years, Most Control Sent to States," in *CQ Almanac 1996*, 52nd ed. (Washington, DC: Congressional Quarterly, 1997), 6-3–6-24.

94. Clinton vetoed H.R. 4 as well as H.R. 2491, a broader budget reconciliation measure that included many of the Republicans' welfare provisions.

95. "SOCIAL POLICY: Welfare," *CQ Weekly*, November 2, 1996, 3148–49.

96. Lily Rothman, "Why Clinton Signed the Welfare Reform Bill, as Explained in 1996," *Time*, August 19, 2016, https://time.com/4446348/welfare-reform-20-years/.

97. John F. Harris and Dan Balz, "Delicate Moves Led to Tax Cut," *New York Times*, May 27, 2001.

98. "Landmark Education Bill Signed," in *CQ Almanac 2001*, 57th ed. (Washington, DC: Congressional Quarterly, 2002), 8-3–8-8.

99. "Major Overhaul Enacted of Rules Governing the Financial Services Industry," in *CQ Almanac 1999*, 55th ed. (Washington, DC: Congressional Quarterly, 2000), 5-3–5-31.

100. "Congress Completes 'Cures' Bill to Speed Up Drug Approval Process," in *CQ Almanac 2016*, 72nd ed., (Washington, DC: CQ-Roll Call Group, 2017), 8-3–8-5.

101. The final votes were 392–26 in the House and 94–5 in the Senate.

CHAPTER FIVE

1. Justin Amash, "House GOP's 'Govern by Crisis' Model Is Broken," CNN.com, October 4, 2015.

2. Quoted in staff editorial, "'The Problem Is the Problem,'" *Washington Post*, July 18, 1984.

3. See, for example, former representatives Cliff Stearns (R-FL) and Martin Frost (D-TX), "Congress Must Listen to John McCain," *The Hill*, July 28, 2017; Thomas Kaplan and Robert Pear, "Secrecy Surrounding Senate Health Bill Raises Alarms in Both Parties," *New York Times*, June 15, 2017.

4. A few important exceptions exist. Sinclair (2016) presents unorthodox processes as tools used to adapt to challenging legislative circumstances; and Wallner (2013, 67) notes that unorthodox processes "create the conditions necessary for bipartisan cooperation at the leadership level."

5. H.R. 1, 112th Congress.

6. Specifically, H.R. 92 (112th Congress) allowed members to offer amendments to H.R. 1 as long as they had those amendments printed in the *Congressional Record* the day before, which was not a particularly burdensome requirement.

7. H.R. 1 began being read for amendments about 2:00 p.m. on February 15 and passed the House about 4:40 a.m. on February 19.

8. No Democrats voted for final passage of the bill.

9. H.R. 5055, 114th Congress.

10. Lindsey McPherson, "In Reversal, House Backs LGBT Anti-discrimination Measure," *Roll Call*, May 25, 2016.

11. Lindsey McPherson, "House Rejects Spending Bill after Gay Rights Measure Added," *Roll Call*, May 26, 2016.

12. The Affordable Care Act was the subject of over thirty congressional hearings during the 111th Congress and was marked up by three House committees and one Senate committee. In general, the development of the ACA followed a very traditional process, with unorthodox tactics used only later as congressional Democrats pushed for final passage in the House and Senate.

13. Dodd-Frank was the subject of over eighty congressional hearings during the 111th Congress and was marked up by committees in both the House and the Senate.

14. See, e.g., H.R. 1625 and H.R. 244 (115th Congress), and H.R. 2029 (114th Congress).

15. See H.R. 8 (112th Congress).

16. *CQ Magazine* discontinued its regular listing of important legislation to watch during the 114th Congress, so for those years (2015–16) we searched articles in *CQ Magazine* for mentions of new laws enacted by Congress by their bill numbers (e.g., H.R. 123). Any law receiving mention in *CQ Magazine*'s coverage was included in our data. This effort yielded a number of laws for the 114th Congress similar to that identified for the other Congresses.

17. A list of these laws and further details about the data are found in the supplemental online appendix to Curry and Lee (2020).

18. The indicators we employ are not an exhaustive list of unorthodox processes. For instance, Sinclair (2016) also identifies omnibus legislating and "summits" as unorthodox tactics. However, omnibus legislation and summits are not easily defined, identified, or measured. Moreover, our "late stage adjustments" measures would likely capture much omnibus legislating and most of the outcomes of summits.

19. Because arguments about regular order and partisanship focus on the ability/inability of different procedures to build bipartisan support for a proposal, our measure is designed to capture the amount of partisan disagreement on the legislation when it passed the House and Senate.

20. For each measure, we coded votes to pass each bill by unanimous consent and by voice vote as if they were the same as unanimous roll-call votes. We replicated each test removing voice votes from the analyses, but the results were the same.

21. We used the Congressional Bills Project's coding of each new law's issue area (one of twenty issue areas) from the Policy Agendas Project codebook. Congressional Bills Project data and codebooks can be accessed at http://www.congressionalbills.org/.

22. Note that, across the analyses in table 5.1 and table 5.2, multicollinearity is not an issue. The unorthodox development and management indexes are not highly correlated ($r = 0.37$ in the House; $r = 0.19$ in the Senate; $r = 0.51$ for the final passage models with both chambers).

23. To assess the robustness of our findings we ran several other analyses. Among the most notable are IRT (item response theory) models that allow the different

indicators to be weighted dynamically, "uncovering" the latent unorthodoxy of the bill development and management processes for each law, and models separating years before and after 2001 and assessing any change over time. Our findings hold across these and other specifications, all found in the supplemental online appendix to Curry and Lee (2020).

24. Pub. L. 114-10.
25. Staffer, December 4, 2017 (1).
26. Staffer, October 11, 2017 (1).
27. Staffer, November 6, 2018 (1).
28. Ibid.
29. Staffer, December 5, 2017.
30. Staffer, December 6, 2018 (2).
31. Ibid.
32. Staffer, October 11, 2017 (1).
33. Staffer, September 9, 2016.
34. Staffer, August 5, 2016.
35. Staffer, October 11, 2017 (1).
36. Staffer, December 4, 2017 (4).
37. Staffer, August 2, 2016.
38. Staffer, December 4, 2017 (1).
39. Staffer, September 9, 2016.
40. Staffer, October 17, 2016.
41. Staffer, November 6, 2018 (1).
42. Member, July 28, 2016.
43. Staffer, November 6, 2018 (3).
44. Staffer, October 17, 2016.
45. Staffer, December 6, 2017 (2).
46. Staffer, September 9, 2016.
47. Staffer, August 2, 2016.
48. Staffer, August 24, 2016.
49. Staffer, October 10, 2017 (2).
50. Staffer, December 4, 2017 (4).
51. Staffer, October 11, 2017 (1).
52. Staffer, December 6, 2018 (2).
53. Ibid.
54. Staffer, December 5, 2017.
55. Staffer, December 4, 2017 (3).
56. Staffer, November 6, 2018 (4).
57. Staffer, October 10, 2017 (1).
58. Staffer, October 9, 2017.
59. Staffer, September 9, 2016.
60. Staffer, August 24, 2016.
61. Ibid.
62. Staffer, September 9, 2016.
63. Staffer, September 9, 2016.
64. Staffer, August 2, 2016.
65. Staffer, October 9, 2017.
66. Staffer, August 2, 2016.
67. Staffer, September 9, 2016.

68. Staffer, August 24, 2016.
69. Staffer, September 9, 2016.
70. Staffer, August 24, 2016.
71. Staffer, October 11, 2017 (3).
72. Staffer, November 6, 2018 (4).
73. Staffer, November 6, 2018 (2).
74. Staffer, August 24, 2016.
75. Staffer, November 6, 2018 (4).
76. Staffer, December 5, 2017.
77. The legislation passed the House 392–37 and the Senate 92–8.
78. Specifically, Congress passed seventeen doc fixes from 2002 to 2014.
79. Staffer, August 24, 2016.
80. Staffer, July 29, 2016.
81. Staffer, August 2, 2016.
82. Ibid.
83. Ibid.
84. Ibid.
85. Staffer, July 29, 2016.
86. Staffer, August 24, 2016.
87. Ibid.
88. Staffer, August 2, 2016.
89. Staffer, August 24, 2016.
90. Staffer, October 11, 2017 (3).
91. Staffer, August 2, 2016.
92. Ibid.
93. Staffer, July 29, 2016.
94. Staffer, August 2, 2016.
95. Ibid.
96. Member, June 26, 2016.
97. Staffer, September 18, 2017.

CHAPTER SIX

1. Doyle McManus, "What Compromise Looks Like," *Los Angeles Times*, December 14, 2014.
2. C. Vann Woodward, "The Great Civil Rights Debate," *Commentary*, October 1, 1957.
3. Articles published in the *New York Times* and *Washington Post* furnish suitable data for identifying legislators' public reactions to legislative action for several reasons. These two periodicals have provided consistent coverage of congressional action over the period studied. While political actors can also issue press releases, it is primarily through the media that their statements are communicated to the public. Despite a changing media environment, the *Times* and the *Post* are still predominant forces in news coverage. Although print readership has declined with the rise of the internet, digital newspaper readership has grown in recent years (see, e.g., Jeffrey Gottfried and Elisa Shearer, "Americans' Online News Use Is Closing in on TV News Use," Pewresearch.org, September 7, 2017), and both are still considered major news outlets. And while different media sources may provide different styles of coverage than the *Times* and *Post*, if the way members and policy advocates describe policy outcomes has changed, we should expect to observe these changes in the coverage in the *Times* and *Post* as well.

4. These unassigned quotations, were sometimes taken from the text of the legislation, represent basic statements of fact (e.g., "Now on to conference!"), or quote a member of Congress or other actor simply describing what went on (e.g., "The Speaker told us we would vote on this by noon").

5. Our focus is on media portrayals of successful legislative action rather than coverage of inaction or gridlock. Indeed, coverage of gridlock in Congress can also affect public perceptions of Congress as an institution or create an impression of severe partisan infighting on Capitol Hill. However, here we are interested in finding out whether descriptions of *successful* legislative action create an identifiable impression about bills and laws passed by Congress.

6. Martin Tolchin, "House Approves Budget Plan Supported by Reagan, 270–154; Democrats Split on Key Vote/President 'Grateful,'" *New York Times*, March 8, 1981.

7. Martin Tolchin, "Senate Approves Rights Panel Bill," *New York Times*, November 15, 1983.

8. Anne Swardson, "Senate Approves Tax Revision, 74–23," *Washington Post*, September 28, 1986.

9. Carolyn Y. Johnson, "House Passes Bill Expediting Therapies," *Washington Post*, December 1, 2016.

10. Lyndsey Layton, "Senate Overwhelmingly Passes New National Education Legislation," *Washington Post*, December 9, 2015.

11. "House Approves Bill to Match Recipients with Organ Donors," *New York Times*, June 22, 1984.

12. Carl Hulse, "Senate Approves Tobacco Buyout and New Curbs," *New York Times*, July 16, 2004.

13. David Binder, "Senate Approves a 200-Mile Limit on Fishing Rights," *New York Times*, January 29, 1976.

14. Mary Russell, "House Approves Authority to Regulate Ocean Mining," *Washington Post*, July 27, 1978.

15. Martin Tolchin, "House Approves Budget Plan Supported by Reagan, 270–154; Democrats Split on Key Vote/President 'Grateful,'" *New York Times*, March 8, 1981.

16. Paul Taylor, "Senate Approves B1 Funds, Giving Reagan 2nd Victory," *Washington Post*, December 4, 1981.

17. Katharine Q. Seelye, "The Crime Bill: Overview; House Approves Crime Bill after Days of Bargaining, Giving Victory to Clinton," *New York Times*, August 22, 1994.

18. Ed O'Keefe, "House Passes Farm Bill without Food Stamp Funds," *Washington Post*, July 12, 2013.

19. Lori Montgomery and Rosalind S. Helderman, "Congress Approves 'Fiscal Cliff' Measure," *Washington Post*, January 2, 2013.

20. Paul Kane and Lori Montgomery, "House Passes Debt-Limit Measure," *Washington Post*, August 2, 2011.

21. Lori Montgomery, "Congress Approves Obama's $3.4 Trillion Spending Blueprint," *Washington Post*, April 30, 2009.

22. "Congress Approves Magna Carta Trip," *Washington Post*, April 6, 1976.

23. Michael Abramowitz and Tom Kenworthy, "House Yields to Bush on Some Abortion Funds; Congress Passes D.C. Bill Despite Veto Threat," *Washington Post*, November 16, 1989.

24. Ed O'Keefe, "House Passes Farm Bill without Food Stamp Funds," *Washington Post*, July 12, 2013.

25. William H. Jones, "House Passes Rail Aid," *Washington Post*, February 20, 1975.

26. Karen W. Arenson, "Congress Approves Bill to Raise $98.3 Billion in Taxes," *New York Times*, August 20, 1982.
27. David Shribman, "House Approves a Plan for Rescue of Social Security," *New York Times*, March 10, 1983.
28. Kathleen Day, "Senate Passes Banking Bill, Paving Way for Overhaul; House Backers Trying to Push Through Similar Measure," *Washington Post*, March 31, 1988.
29. Katharine Q. Seelye, "The Crime Bill: Overview; House Approves Crime Bill after Days of Bargaining, Giving Victory to Clinton," *New York Times*, August 22, 1994.
30. Barbara Vobejda, "Senate Passes Welfare Overhaul; President Indicates His Support," *Washington Post*, September 20, 1995.
31. Both quotations are from Helen Dewar, "Senate Approves Tobacco Legislation; Regulation Is Paired with Farmer Buyout," *Washington Post*, July 16, 2004.
32. Paul Kane and Philip Rucker, "Congress Approves Budget Deal, Prepares for Debate over Debt Ceiling," *Washington Post*, April 15, 2011.
33. David M. Herszenhorn, "House Approves Budget, Providing 'Clean' Exit That Boehner Sought," *New York Times*, October 29, 2015.
34. Jennifer Steinhauer and Robert Pear, "Sweeping Health Measure, Backed by Obama, Passes Senate," *New York Times*, December 8, 2016.
35. Spencer Rich, "House Approves a Version of Carter Welfare Plan," *Washington Post*, November 8, 1979.
36. Steven V. Roberts, "House Approves Funds on Fuel Aid and Jobless," *New York Times*, February 10, 1982.
37. "Senate Passes Measure for a U.S. Death Penalty," *Washington Post*, February 23, 1984.
38. Helen Dewar, "Senate Approves School Aid Revision; GOP Prayer-Related Filibuster against Clinton-Backed Bill Defeated," *Washington Post*, October 6, 1994.
39. Jonathan Wiesman, "House Passes Money Bill and Budget Blueprint," *New York Times*, March 21, 2013.
40. Ashley Parker, "House Passes Military Bill after Fight on Budget Cuts," *New York Times*, May 15, 2015.
41. Edward Walsh, "House Passes Superfund Bill; Senate Urges Reagan to Sign," *Washington Post*, October 8, 1986.
42. Richard L. Berke, "Senate Passes Rights Bill, but Vote Is Not Enough to Override Veto," *New York Times*, October 17, 1990.
43. Jerry Gray, "Senate Approves a Big Budget Bill, Beating Deadline," *New York Times*, October 1, 1996.
44. Coral Davenport, "House Passes Keystone Bill Despite Obama's Opposition," *New York Times*, February 11, 2015.
45. $b = 0.003$; $p = .135$; $b = -0.002$; $p = .407$, respectively.
46. $b = -0.0007$; $p = .630$.
47. $b = 0.001$; $p = .491$ for positive credit claiming; $b = -0.002$; $p = .423$ for blaming for losing.
48. $b = -0.001$; $p = .430$ for mixed credit claiming; $b = 0.001$; $p = .471$ for blaming despite winning.
49. A time counter is positive and significant for positive quotations ($b = 0.007$; $p = .009$) and negative quotations ($b = -0.006$; $p = .025$) among majority party lawmakers.
50. A time counter has no statistically significant effect after 1980 for either positive quotations ($b = 0.006$; $p = .080$) or negative quotations ($b = -0.005$; $p = .189$) among majority party lawmakers.

51. A time counter has no statistically significant effect for the proportion of negative quotations ($b = 0.003$; $p = .374$) among minority party lawmakers.
52. A time counter has no statistically significant effect for the proportion of positive credit-claiming quotations ($b = 0.005$; $p = .086$) among majority party lawmakers.
53. A time counter has a negative and significant effect for the proportion of "blaming for losing" quotations ($b = -0.007$; $p = .008$) among majority party lawmakers.
54. A time counter has no statistically significant effect after 1980 for "blaming for losing" quotations ($b = -0.005$; $p = .091$) among majority party lawmakers.
55. A simple logistic regression predicting the likelihood that a quotation is positive shows that dummy variables for party leaders and committee leaders have positive and statistically significant effects.

CHAPTER SEVEN

1. David Shribman, "The Culprits behind Today's Polarized Politics," *Pittsburgh Post-Gazette*, November 19, 2011. Accessed at https://www.post-gazette.com/opinion/david-shribman/2011/11/20/The-culprits-behind-today-s-polarized-politics/stories/201111200293.
2. As Wickham-Jones (2018) covers extensively, the committee's report had many critics on its initial publication and was in many ways a punching bag for political scientists for some time afterward. But today it has come to represent an important school of thought about a party-led system of democratic governance in the United States, with party responsibility at its core.
3. Gary Andres, "'Over-promising and Under-delivering' in Washington and How to Fix It," *The Hill*, May 19, 2017, https://thehill.com/blogs/congress-blog/politics/334292-over-promising-and-under-delivering-in-washington-and-how-to-fix.
4. Trudy Lieberman, "Wrong Prescription? The Failed Promise of the Affordable Care Act," *Harper's*, July 2015, https://harpers.org/archive/2015/07/wrong-prescription/?single=1.
5. Danielle Kurtzleben, "2018 Is the Year Democrats Got Comfortable Talking Health Care Again," National Public Radio, October 25, 2018, https://www.npr.org/2018/10/25/660281890/2018-is-the-year-democrats-got-comfortable-talking-health-care-again.
6. Erica Werner and Damien Paletta, "GOP Campaigns Ditch Tax Law and Focus on Immigration, Crime Ahead of Midterm Elections," *Washington Post*, October 26, 2018, https://www.washingtonpost.com/business/economy/gop-campaigns-ditch-tax-law-and-go-negative-as-midterm-election-approaches/2018/09/26/aa51e8ca-c041-11e8-be77-516336a26305_story.html?utm_term=.0e8a37f4d9a2.
7. Brian Faler, "Trump Wants New Middle-Class Tax Cut 'of about 10 Percent,'" *Politico*, October 22, 2018, https://www.politico.com/story/2018/10/22/trump-middle-class-tax-cut-924446.
8. See, for example, Matt Ford, "Someone Please Tell Joe Biden That Bipartisanship Is Dead," *New Republic*, June 12, 2019, https://newrepublic.com/article/154183/someone-please-tell-joe-biden-bipartisanship-dead; Harold Meyerson, "Biden's Bipartisan Illusions," *American Prospect*, May 7, 2019, https://prospect.org/article/bidens-bipartisan-illusions; Helaine Olen, "What Biden Really Means When He Talks about Bipartisanship," *Washington Post*, June 12, 2019, https://www.washingtonpost.com/opinions/2019/06/12/what-joe-biden-really-means-when-he-talks-about-bipartisanship/?utm_term=.5a6640bb1a02.

9. Eric Bradner and Dan Merica, "Biden Slams Critics of Working with GOP: 'Why Don't You All Go Home Then, Man?,'" CNN Politics, June 17, 2019, https://www.cnn .com/2019/06/17/politics/joe-biden-dismisses-2020-critics-of-bipartisan-approach /index.html.
10. We are grateful to Jenny Mansbridge for suggesting the term.
11. Staffer, September 9, 2016.
12. Staffer, November 6, 2018 (4).
13. Staffer, November 6, 2018 (2).
14. Staffer, October 17, 2016.
15. Staffer, November 6, 2018 (3).
16. STEW (@StewSays), Twitter Post, December 11, 2018, 1:59 p.m. Accessed at https:// twitter.com/StewSays/status/1072611773298171904.
17. Mike Ricci (@riccimike), Twitter Post, December 18, 2018, 6:02 p.m. Accessed at https://twitter.com/riccimike/status/1075209778731864064.

REFERENCES

Abramowitz, Alan I., Brad Alexander, and Matthew Gunning. 2006. "Incumbency, Redistricting, and the Decline of Competition in U.S. House Elections." *Journal of Politics* 68 (1): 75–88.

Adler, E. Scott, and John D. Wilkerson. 2012. *Congress and the Politics of Problem Solving.* New York: Cambridge University Press.

Aldrich, John H., and David W. Rohde. 2000a. "The Consequences of Party Organization in the House: The Role of the Majority and Minority Parties in Conditional Party Government." In *Polarized Politics: Congress and the President in a Partisan Era*, edited by Jon R. Bond and Richard Fleisher, 31–72. Washington, DC: CQ Press.

———. 2000b. "The Republican Revolution and the House Appropriations Committee." *Journal of Politics* 62 (1): 1–33.

American Political Science Association, Committee on Political Parties. 1950. "Towards a More Responsible Two-Party System." Supplement, *American Political Science Review* 44 (3): 1–99.

Anzia, Sarah F., and Molly C. Jackman. 2012. "Legislative Organization and the Second Face of Power: Evidence from U.S. State Legislatures." *Journal of Politics* 75 (1): 210–24.

Arnold, R. Douglas. 1990. *The Logic of Congressional Action.* New Haven, CT: Yale University Press.

Atkinson, Mary Layton. 2017. *Combative Politics: The Media and Public Perceptions of Lawmaking.* Chicago: University of Chicago Press.

Barber, Michael J., and Nolan McCarty. 2015. "Causes and Consequences of Polarization." In *Solutions to Political Polarization in America*, ed. Nathaniel Persily, 15–58. New York: Cambridge University Press.

Bekafigo, Marija Anna. 2014. "How Is Leadership Exercised in the US House? Party Leaders' and Committee Chairs' 'Actions.'" *Social Science History* 38 (3–4): 291–310.

Bendix, William. 2016a. "Bypassing Congressional Committees: Parties, Panel Rosters, and Deliberative Processes." *Legislative Studies Quarterly* 41 (3): 687–714.

———. 2016b. "Neglect, Inattention, and Legislative Deficiencies: The Consequences of One-Party Deliberations in the U.S. House." *Congress and the Presidency* 43 (1): 82–102.

Bennett, W. Lance. 2012. *News: The Politics of Illusion.* New York: Longman.

Biggs, Jeffrey R., and Thomas S. Foley. 1999. *Honor in the House: Speaker Tom Foley.* Pullman: Washington State University Press.

Binder, Sarah A. 1996. *Minority Rights, Majority Rule: Partisanship and the Development of Congress.* New York: Cambridge University Press.

———. 2003. *Stalemate: Causes and Consequences of Legislative Gridlock.* Washington, DC: Brookings Institution Press.

———. 2014. "Polarized We Govern?" Center for Effective Public Management, Brookings Institution. https://www.brookings.edu/wp-content/uploads/2016/06/Brookings CEPM_Polarized_figReplacedTextRevTableRev.pdf.

———. 2015. "The Dysfunctional Congress." *Annual Review of Political Science* 18:85–101.

Binder, Sarah A., and Steven S. Smith. 2001. *Politics or Principle? Filibustering in the United States Senate.* Washington, DC: Brookings Institution Press.

Bolling, Richard. 1965. *House Out of Order.* New York: E. P. Dutton.

———. 1968. *Power in the House: A History of the Leadership of the House of Representatives.* New York: E. P. Dutton.

Bond, Jon R., and Richard Fleisher. 1990. *The President in the Legislative Arena.* Chicago: University of Chicago Press.

Brady, David W., and Charles S. Bullock III. 1980. "Is There a Conservative Coalition in the House?" *Journal of Politics* 42 (May): 549–59.

Brady, David W., Joseph Cooper, and Patricia A. Hurley. 1979. "The Decline of Party in the U.S. House of Representatives, 1887–1968." *Legislative Studies Quarterly* 4 (3): 381–407.

Brookings Institution. 2019. *Vital Statistics on Congress.* March 4. https://www.brookings .edu/multi-chapter-report/vital-statistics-on-congress/.

Bryce, James. 1888. *The American Commonwealth.* New York: Macmillan.

Burns, James MacGregor. 1963. *The Deadlock of Democracy.* Englewood Cliffs, NJ: Prentice-Hall.

Butler, Daniel M., and Eleanor Neff Powell. 2014. "Understanding the Party Brand: Experimental Evidence on the Role of Valence." *Journal of Politics* 76 (2): 492–505.

Cameron, Charles M. 2000. *Veto Bargaining: Presidents and the Politics of Negative Power.* New York: Cambridge University Press.

Canes-Wrone, Brandice. 2006. *Who Leads Whom? Presidents, Policy, and the Public.* Chicago: University of Chicago Press.

Canes-Wrone, Brandice, David W. Brady, and John F. Cogan. 2002. "Out of Step, out of Office: Electoral Accountability and House Members' Voting." *American Political Science Review* 96 (1): 127–40.

Canes-Wrone, Brandice, and Scott de Marchi. 2002. "Presidential Approval and Legislative Success." *Journal of Politics* 64 (2): 491–509.

Carey, John M. 2007. "Competing Principals, Political Institutions, and Party Unity in Legislative Voting." *American Journal of Political Science* 51:92–107.

Carrubba, Clifford, and Matthew Gabel. 2008. "Legislative Voting Behavior, Seen and Unseen: A Theory of Roll-Call Vote Selection." *Legislative Studies Quarterly* 33 (4): 543–72.

Carson, Jamie L., Gregory Koger, Matthew J. Lebo, and Everett Young. 2010. "The Electoral Costs of Party Loyalty in Congress." *American Journal of Political Science* 54 (3): 598–616.

Carson, Jamie L., Nathan W. Monroe, and Gregory Robinson. 2011. "Unpacking Agenda Control in Congress: Individual Roll Rates and the Republican Revolution." *Political Research Quarterly* 64 (1): 17–30.

Chaisty, Paul, Nic Cheeseman, and Timothy Power. 2014. "Rethinking the 'Presidentialism Debate': Conceptualizing Coalitional Politics in Cross-Regional Perspective." *Democratization* 21 (1): 72–94.

Cheibub, José Antonio, Adam Przeworski, and Sebastian M. Saiegh. 2004. "Government Coalitions and Legislative Success under Presidentialism and Parliamentarism." *British Journal of Political Science* 34 (4): 565–87.

Clinton, Joshua D., and John Lapinski. 2008. "Laws and Roll Calls in the U.S. Congress, 1891–1994." *Legislative Studies Quarterly* 33 (4): 511–41.

Cooper, Joseph, and David W. Brady. 1981. "Institutional Context and Leadership Style: The House from Cannon to Rayburn." *American Political Science Review* 75 (2): 411–25.

Cox, Gary W., and Mathew D. McCubbins. 2005. *Setting the Agenda: Responsible Party Government in the U.S. House of Representatives.* New York: Cambridge University Press.

"CQ Vote Studies: Party Unity." 2018. *CQ Magazine,* February 12. http://library.cqpress.com/cqweekly/weeklyreport115-000005263236.

"CQ Vote Studies: Party Unity." 2019. *CQ Magazine,* February 25. http://library.cqpress.com/cqweekly/weeklyreport116-000005468029.

Crespin, Michael H., and Anthony J. Madonna. 2016. "New Directions in Legislative Research: Lessons from Inside Congress." *PS: Political Science and Politics* 49 (3): 473–77.

Curry, James M. 2015. *Legislating in the Dark: Information and Power in the House of Representatives.* Chicago: University of Chicago Press.

———. 2019. "Congressional Processes and Public Approval of New Laws." *Political Research Quarterly* 72 (3): 878–93.

Curry, James M., and Frances E. Lee. 2019a. "Non-party Government: Bipartisan Lawmaking and Party Power in Congress," *Perspectives on Politics* 17 (1): 47–65.

———. 2019b. "Congress at Work: Legislative Capacity and Entrepreneurship in the Contemporary Congress." In *Can America Govern Itself?,* edited by Frances E. Lee and Nolan McCarty, 181–219. New York: Cambridge University Press.

———. 2020. "What Is Regular Order Worth? Partisan Lawmaking and Congressional Processes." *Journal of Politics* 82 (2): 627–41.

Davis, Christopher M. 2017. "Instances in Which Opportunities for Floor Amendment Were Limited by the Senate Majority Leader or His Designee Filling or Partially Filling the Amendment Tree: 1985–2017." Congressional Research Service Memorandum, June 9.

Den Hartog, Chris, and Nathan W. Monroe. 2011. *Agenda Setting in the U.S. Senate: Costly Consideration and Majority Party Advantage.* New York: Cambridge University Press.

Donnelly, Christopher P. 2019. "Yea or Nay: Do Legislators Benefit from Voting against Their Party?" *Legislative Studies Quarterly* 44 (3): 421–53.

Drutman, Lee. 2016. "Political Dynamism: A New Approach to Making Government Work Again." *New America,* February. https://www.newamerica.org/new-america/policy-papers/political-dynamism/.

Edwards, George C., III. 1990. *At the Margins: Presidential Leadership of Congress.* New Haven, CT: Yale University Press.

Egar, William T. 2016. "Tarnishing Opponents, Polarizing Congress: The House Minority Party and the Construction of the Roll-Call Record." *Legislative Studies Quarterly* 41 (4): 935–64.

Esterberg, Kristin G. 2002. *Qualitative Methods in Social Research.* Boston: McGraw-Hill.

Evans, C. Lawrence. 2001. "Committees, Leaders, and Message Politics." In *Congress Reconsidered,* 7th ed., edited by Lawrence C. Dodd and Bruce I. Oppenheimer, 217–43. Washington, DC: CQ Press.

———. 2018. *The Whips: Building Party Coalitions in Congress.* Ann Arbor: University of Michigan Press.

Evans, C. Lawrence, and Walter J. Oleszek. 2002. "Message Politics and Senate Procedure." In *The Contentious Senate: Partisanship, Ideology, and the Myth of Cool Judgment,* edited by Colton C. Campbell and Nicol C. Rae, 107–30. New York: Rowman and Littlefield.

Fenno, Richard F. 1962. "The House Appropriations Committee as a Political System: The Problem of Integration." *American Political Science Review* 56 (2): 310–24.

———. 1966. *The Power of the Purse: Appropriations Politics in Congress*. Boston: Little, Brown.

———. 1978. *Homestyle: House Members in Their Districts*. Boston: Little, Brown.

Finocchiaro, Charles J., and David W. Rohde. 2008. "War for the Floor: Partisan Theory and Agenda Control in the U.S. House of Representatives." *Legislative Studies Quarterly* 33 (1): 35–61.

Fiorina, Morris P. 1980. "The Decline of Collective Responsibility in American Politics." *Daedalus* 109 (Summer): 25–45.

———. 2017. *Unstable Majorities: Polarization, Party Sorting, and Political Stalemate*. Stanford, CA: Hoover Institution Press.

Fitzgerald, Mary. 2005. "Greater Convenience but Not Greater Turnout: The Impact of Alternative Voting Methods on Electoral Participation in the United States." *American Politics Research* 33 (6): 842–67.

Gailmard, Sean, and Jeffrey A. Jenkins. 2007. "Negative Agenda Control in the Senate and House: Fingerprints of Majority Party Power." *Journal of Politics* 69 (3): 689–700.

Gelman, Jeremy. 2017. "Rewarding Dysfunction: Interest Groups and Intended Legislative Failure." *Legislative Studies Quarterly* 42 (4): 661–92.

Gilligan, Thomas W., and Keith Krehbiel. 1990. "Organization of Informative Committees by a Rational Legislature." *American Journal of Political Science* 34 (2): 531–64.

Gingrich, Newt. 1994. "The Capitol Steps Contract and Cynicism in Washington, DC." *Congressional Record*, September 22, H9526–H9527.

Green, Matthew N. 2015. *Underdog Politics: The Minority Party in the U.S. House of Representatives*. New Haven, CT: Yale University Press.

Grimmer, Justin. 2013. *Representational Style in Congress: What Legislators Say and Why It Matters*. New York: Cambridge University Press.

Groeling, Tim. 2010. *When Politicians Attack: Party Cohesion in the Media*. New York: Cambridge University Press.

Groseclose, Tim, and Nolan McCarty. 2001. "The Politics of Blame: Bargaining before an Audience." *American Journal of Political Science* 45 (1): 100–119.

Hanson, Peter. 2014. *Too Weak to Govern: Majority Party Power and Appropriations in the U.S. Senate*. New York: Cambridge University Press.

Harbridge, Laurel. 2015. *Is Bipartisanship Dead? Policy Agreement and Agenda-Setting in the House of Representatives*. New York: Cambridge University Press.

Harbridge, Laurel, and Neil Malhotra. 2011. "Electoral Incentives and Partisan Conflict in Congress: Evidence from Survey Experiments." *American Journal of Political Science* 55 (3): 494–510.

Harris, Douglas B. 2013. "Let's Play Hardball: Congressional Partisanship in the Television Era." In *Politics to the Extreme: American Political Institutions in the Twenty-First Century*, edited by Scott A. Frisch and Sean Q. Kelly, 93–115. New York: Palgrave Macmillan.

Hess, Douglas R., Michael J. Hanmer, and David W. Nickerson. 2016. "Encouraging Local Compliance with Federal Civil Rights Laws: Field Experiments with the National Voter Registration Act." *Public Administration Review* 76 (1): 165–74.

Hetherington, Marc J. 2001. "Resurgent Mass Partisanship: The Role of Elite Polarization." *American Political Science Review* 95 (3): 619–31.

Hofstadter, Richard. 1948. *The American Political Tradition and the Men Who Made It*. New York: Knopf.

Howard, Nicholas O., and Mark E. Owens. 2019. "Circumventing Legislative Committees: The US Senate." *Legislative Studies Quarterly*. https://doi.org/10.1111/lsq.12269.

Jacobson, Gary C. 2017. "Partisanship, Money, and Competition: Elections and the Transformation of Congress since the 1970s." In *Congress Reconsidered*, 11th ed., edited by Lawrence C. Dodd and Bruce I. Oppenheimer, 117–44. Washington, DC: CQ Press.

Jenkins, Jeffrey A., and Nathan W. Monroe. 2016. "On Measuring Legislative Agenda-Setting Power." *American Journal of Political Science* 60 (1): 158–74.

Johnson, Haynes, and David S. Broder. 1996. *The System: The American Way of Politics at the Breaking Point*. Boston: Little, Brown.

Jones, David R. 2013. "Do Major Policy Enactments Affect Public Evaluations of Congress? The Case of Health Care Reform." *Legislative Studies Quarterly* 38 (2): 185–204.

Kiewiet, D. Roderick, and Mathew D. McCubbins. 1991. *The Logic of Delegation: Congressional Parties and the Appropriations Process*. Chicago: University of Chicago Press.

Koger, Gregory. 2010. *Filibustering: A Political History of Obstruction in the House and Senate*. Chicago: University of Chicago Press.

Koger, Gregory, and Matthew J. Lebo. 2017. *Strategic Party Government: Why Winning Trumps Ideology*. Chicago: University of Chicago Press.

Krehbiel, Keith. 1991. *Information and Legislative Organization*. Ann Arbor: University of Michigan Press.

———. 1998. *Pivotal Politics: A Theory of U.S. Lawmaking*. Chicago: University of Chicago Press.

Lee, Frances E. 2009. *Beyond Ideology: Politics, Principles, and Partisanship in the U.S. Senate*. Chicago: University of Chicago Press.

———. 2015. "How Party Polarization Affects Governance." *Annual Review of Political Science* 18:261–82.

———. 2016. *Insecure Majorities: Congress and the Perpetual Campaign*. Chicago: University of Chicago Press.

———. 2018. "The 115th Congress and Questions of Party Unity in a Polarized Era." *Journal of Politics* 80 (4): 1464–73.

Lewallen, Jonathan, Sean M. Theriault, and Bryan D. Jones. 2016. "Congressional Dysfunction: An Information Processing Perspective." *Regulation and Governance* 10 (2): 179–90.

Mainwaring, Scott, and Matthew S. Shugart. 1997. "Juan Linz, Presidentialism, and Democracy: A Critical Appraisal." *Legislative Studies Quarterly* 29 (4): 449–71.

Mann, Thomas E., and Norman J. Ornstein. 2012. *It's Even Worse Than It Looks: How the American Constitutional System Collided with the New Politics of Extremism*. New York: Basic Books.

Mayhew, David R. 1974. *Congress: The Electoral Connection*. New Haven, CT: Yale University Press.

———. 2005. *Divided We Govern: Party Control, Lawmaking, and Investigations, 1946–2002*. 2nd ed. New Haven, CT: Yale University Press.

———. 2011. *Partisan Balance: Why Political Parties Don't Kill the U.S. Constitutional System*. Princeton, NJ: Princeton University Press.

McCarty, Nolan. 2019. *Polarization: What Everyone Needs to Know*. New York: Oxford University Press.

McCarty, Nolan, Keith T. Poole, and Howard Rosenthal. 2016. *Polarized America: The Dance of Ideology and Unequal Riches*. 2nd ed. Cambridge, MA: MIT Press.

Meinke, Scott R. 2016. *Leadership Organizations in the House of Representatives*. Ann Arbor: University of Michigan Press.

Miller, Clem. 1962. *Member of the House*. Edited by John W. Baker. New York: Charles Scribner's Sons.

Monroe, Nathan W., and Gregory Robinson. 2008. "Do Restrictive Rules Produce Non-median Outcomes? A Theory with Evidence from the 101st–108th Congresses." *Journal of Politics* 70 (1): 217–31.

Mutz, Diana C. 2015. *In-Your-Face Politics: The Consequences of Uncivil Media.* Princeton, NJ: Princeton University Press.

Oberlander, Jonathan. 2012. "The Bush Administration and the Politics of Medicare Reform." In *Building Coalitions, Making Policy: The Politics of the Clinton, Bush, and Obama Presidencies,* edited by Martin A. Levin, Daniel DiSalvo, and Martin M. Shapiro, 150–80. Baltimore: Johns Hopkins University Press.

Patty, John W. 2008. "Equilibrium Party Government." *American Journal of Political Science* 52 (3): 636–55.

Pearson, Kathryn. 2015. *Party Discipline in the U.S. House of Representatives.* Ann Arbor: University of Michigan Press.

Peters, Ronald M., and Cindy Simon Rosenthal. 2010. *Speaker Nancy Pelosi and the New American Politics.* New York: Oxford University Press.

Polsby, Nelson W. 1968. "The Institutionalization of the U.S. House of Representatives." *American Political Science Review* 62 (1): 144–68.

———. 1975. "Legislatures." In *Handbook of Political Science,* edited by Fred I. Greenstein and Nelson W. Polsby, 257–320. New York: Addison-Wesley.

———. 2004. *How Congress Evolves: Social Bases of Institutional Change.* New York: Oxford University Press.

Raile, Eric D., Carlos Pereira, and Timothy J. Power. 2011. "The Executive Toolbox: Building Legislative Support in a Multiparty Presidential Regime." *Political Research Quarterly* 64 (2): 323–34.

Ramirez, Mark D. 2009. "The Dynamics of Partisan Conflict on Congressional Approval." *American Journal of Political Science* 53:681–94.

Reynolds, Molly E. 2017. *Exceptions to the Rule: The Politics of Filibuster Limitations in the U.S. Senate.* Washington, DC: Brookings Institution Press.

Rohde, David W. 1991. *Parties and Leaders in the Postreform House.* Chicago: University of Chicago Press.

Rosenblum, Nancy L. 2008. *On the Side of the Angels: An Appreciation of Parties and Partisanship.* Princeton, NJ: Princeton University Press.

Rosenbluth, Frances McCall, and Ian Shapiro. 2018. *Responsible Parties: Saving Democracy from Itself.* New Haven, CT: Yale University Press.

Rosenfeld, Sam. 2017. *The Polarizers: Postwar Architects of Our Partisan Era.* Chicago: University of Chicago Press.

Ryan, Josh M. 2018. *The Congressional Endgame: Interchamber Bargaining and Compromise.* Chicago: University of Chicago Press.

Rybicki, Elizabeth. 2017. "Availability of Legislative Measures in the House of Representatives (the 'Three-Day Rule')." Congressional Research Service, RS22015.

Samuels, David J., and Matthew S. Shugart. 2010. *Presidents, Parties, and Prime Ministers: How the Separation of Powers Affects Party Organization and Behavior.* New York: Cambridge University Press.

Schaffner, Brian F., and Patrick J. Sellers, eds. 2009. *Winning with Words: The Origins and Impact of Political Framing.* New York: Routledge.

Schattschneider, E. E. 1942. *Party Government: American Government in Action.* New York: Transaction.

———. 1948. *The Struggle for Party Government.* College Park: Program in American Civilization, University of Maryland.

Schickler, Eric. 2001. *Disjointed Pluralism: Institutional Innovation and the Development of the U.S. Congress*. Princeton, NJ: Princeton University Press.

Sellers, Patrick J. 2010. *Cycles of Spin: Strategic Communication in the U.S. Congress*. New York: Cambridge University Press.

Shugart, Matthew S., and John M. Carey. 1992. *Presidents and Assemblies: Constitutional Design and Electoral Dynamics*. New York: Cambridge University Press.

Sinclair, Barbara. 2016. *Unorthodox Lawmaking: New Legislative Processes in the U.S. Congress*. 5th ed. Washington, DC: CQ Press.

Skocpol, Theda. 1996. *Boomerang: Clinton's Health Security Effort and the Turn against Government in U.S. Politics*. New York: Norton.

Smith, Steven S. 1989. *Call to Order: Floor Politics in the House and Senate*. Washington, DC: Brookings Institution Press.

———. 2007. *Party Influence in Congress*. New York: Cambridge University Press.

———. 2014. *The Senate Syndrome: The Evolution of Procedural Warfare in the Modern US Senate*. Norman: University of Oklahoma Press.

Stid, Daniel D. 1994. "Woodrow Wilson and the Problem of Party Government." *Polity* 26 (4): 553–78.

Sundquist, James L. 1968. *Politics and Policy: The Eisenhower, Kennedy and Johnson Years*. Washington, DC: Brookings Institution Press.

Taylor, Andrew J. 2013. *Congress: A Performance Appraisal*. New York: Routledge.

Theriault, Sean M. 2008. *Party Polarization in Congress*. New York: Cambridge University Press.

Thorning, Michael. 2019. "Healthy Congress Index: 115th Congress Functioned Poorly, Derelict in Basic Duties." January 31. https://bipartisanpolicy.org/blog/115th-congress -functioned-poorly-derelict-in-basic-duties/.

Tiefer, Charles. 2016. *The Polarized Congress: The Post-traditional Procedure of Its Current Struggles*. Lanham, MD: University Press of America.

Wallner, James I. 2013. *The Death of Deliberation: Partisanship and Polarization in the United States Senate*. New York: Lexington Books.

Warren, Mark E., and Jane Mansbridge. 2015. "Deliberative Negotiation." In *Political Negotiation: A Handbook*, edited by Jane Mansbridge and Cathie Jo Martin, 141–98. Washington, DC: Brookings Institution Press.

Wawro, Gregory J. 2011. "The Supermajority Senate." In *The Oxford Handbook of the American Congress*, edited by Eric Schickler and Frances E. Lee, 426–50. New York: Oxford University Press.

Wawro, Gregory J., and Eric Schickler. 2006. *Filibuster: Obstruction and Lawmaking in the U.S. Senate*. Princeton, NJ: Princeton University Press.

Wickham-Jones, Mark. 2018. *Whatever Happened to Party Government?* Ann Arbor: University of Michigan Press.

Wilson, Woodrow. 1885. *Congressional Government: A Study in American Politics*. Boston: Houghton Mifflin.

———. 1908. *Constitutional Government of the United States*. New York: Columbia University Press.

Woon, Jonathan, and Jeremy C. Pope. 2008. "Made in Congress? Testing the Electoral Implications of Party Ideological Brand Names." *Journal of Politics* 70 (3): 823–36.

Young, Garry, and Vicky Wilkins. 2007. "Vote Switchers and Party Influence in the U.S. House." *Legislative Studies Quarterly* 32 (1): 59–77.

Zelizer, Julian E. 2004. *On Capitol Hill: The Struggle to Reform Congress and Its Consequences, 1948–2000*. New York: Cambridge University Press.

www.ingramcontent.com/pod-product-compliance
Lightning Source LLC
Chambersburg PA
CBHW060027030426
42334CB00019B/2206